THE WORLD'S CLASSICS

524

Five Plays
by
BEN JONSON

Oxford University Press, Ely House, London W.1

GLASGOW   NEW YORK   TORONTO   MELBOURNE   WELLINGTON
CAPE TOWN   SALISBURY   IBADAN   NAIROBI   DAR ES SALAAM   LUSAKA   ADDIS ABABA
BOMBAY   CALCUTTA   MADRAS   KARACHI   LAHORE   DACCA
KUALA LUMPUR   SINGAPORE   HONG KONG   TOKYO

Five Plays
by
BEN JONSON

LONDON
OXFORD UNIVERSITY PRESS

BEN JONSON

Born, ? Westminster, ? 1573
Died, London, 6 August 1637

This volume of plays by Jonson was first published in
The World's Classics *in 1953 and reprinted in 1956,*
1959, 1960, 1962, 1964, 1966, and 1970

PRINTED IN GREAT BRITAIN

CONTENTS

EVERY MAN IN
HIS HUMOUR

Euery

MAN IN
HIS
HVMOVR.

A Comœdie.

Acted in the yeere 1598. By the then
Lord Chamberlaine his
Seruants.

The Author B. I.

IUVEN.

Haud tamen inuideas vati, quem pulpita pascunt.

LONDON,
Printed by WILLIAM STANSBY.

M. DC. XVI.

Euery

MAN IN
Lord Chamberlaine his
Seruants.

The Author B. I.

M. DC. XVI.

TO THE MOST
LEARNED, AND
MY HONOUR'D
FRIEND.
Mr. Cambden, CLARENTIAUX.

SIR,

THERE are, no doubt, a supercilious race in the world who will esteem all office, done you in this kind, an injury; so solemn a vice it is with them to use the authority of their ignorance to the crying down of Poetry or the Professors: But my gratitude must not leave to correct their error, since I am none of those that can suffer the benefits conferr'd upon my youth to perish with my age. It is a frail memory that remembers but present things: And, had the favour of the times so conspir'd with my disposition, as it could have brought forth other, or better, you had had the same proportion, and number of the fruits, the first. Now, I pray you to accept this, such, wherein neither the confession of my manners shall make you blush nor of my studies repent you to have been the instructer: And, for the profession of my thankfulness, I am sure it will, with good men, find either praise, or excuse.

Your true lover

BEN. JONSON.

The Persons of the Play

KNOWELL, *an old gentleman.*
EDWARD KNOWELL, *his son.*
BRAINWORM, *the Father's man.*
MR. STEPHEN, *a country gull.*
DOWNRIGHT, *a plain squire.*
WELLBRED, *his half-brother.*
JUSTICE CLEMENT, *an old merry magistrate.*
ROGER FORMAL, *his clerk.*

KITELY, *a merchant.*
DAME KITELY, *his wife.*
MRS. BRIDGET, *his sister.*
MR. MATTHEW, *the town gull.*
CASH, *Kitely's man.*
COB, *a water-bearer.*
TIB, *his wife.*
CAPTAIN BOBADIL, *a Pauls-man.*

THE SCENE
LONDON

EVERY MAN IN
HIS HUMOUR

PROLOGUE

THOUGH need make many Poets, and some such
As art and nature have not better'd much;
Yet ours, for want, hath not so loved the stage
As he dare serve th' ill customs of the age:
Or purchase your delight at such a rate
As, for it, he himself must justly hate.
To make a child, now swaddled, to proceed
Man, and then shoot up, in one beard, and weed,
Past threescore years: or, with three rusty swords,
And help of some few foot-and-half-foot words,
Fight over York and Lancaster's long wars:
And in the tiring-house bring wounds to scars.
He rather prays, you will be pleas'd to see
One such, to-day, as other plays should be.
Where neither Chorus wafts you o'er the seas;
Nor creaking throne comes down, the boys to please;
Nor nimble squib is seen, to make afear'd
The gentlewomen; nor roll'd bullet heard
To say, it thunders; nor tempestuous drum
Rumbles, to tell you when the storm doth come;
But deeds, and language, such as men do use:
And persons, such as Comedy would choose
When she would show an image of the times,
And sport with human follies, not with crimes.
Except we make 'em such by loving still
Our popular errors, when we know they're ill.
I mean such errors, as you'll all confess
By laughing at them, they deserve no less:
Which when you heartily do, there's hope left, then,
You, that have so grac'd monsters, may like men.

ACT I. SCENE I

A street.

Enter Knowell, *at the door of his house.*

Kno. A goodly day toward! and a fresh morning!
Brainworm.

Enter Brainworm.

Call up your young master: bid him rise, sir.
Tell him, I have some business to employ him.
    Bra. I will, sir, presently.
    Kno.   But hear you, sirrah,
If he be at his book, disturb him not.
    Bra.   Well, sir.   [*Exit.*
    Kno. How happy, yet, should I esteem myself
Could I (by any practice) wean the boy
From one vain course of study he affects.
He is a scholar, if a man may trust
The liberal voice of fame, in her report
Of good account, in both our universities,
Either of which hath favour'd him with graces:
But their indulgence must not spring in me
A fond opinion that he cannot err.
Myself was once a student; and, indeed,
Fed with the self-same humour he is now,
Dreaming on nought but idle poetry,
That fruitless and unprofitable art,
Good unto none, but least to the professors,
Which, then, I thought the mistress of all knowledge:
But since, time, and the truth have wak'd my judgement,
And reason taught me better to distinguish
The vain from th' useful learnings.

Enter Mr. Stephen.

                                   Cousin Stephen!
What news with you, that you are here so early?
    Ste. Nothing, but e'en come to see how you do, uncle.
    Kno. That's kindly done; you are welcome, coz.

Ste. Aye, I know that, sir, I would not ha' come else.
How does my cousin Edward, uncle?

Kno. O, well, coz, go in and see: I doubt he be scarce
stirring yet.

Ste. Uncle, afore I go in, can you tell me an' he have
e'er a book of the sciences of hawking and hunting? I
would fain borrow it.

Kno. Why, I hope you will not a-hawking now, will
you?

Ste. No wusse; but I'll practise against next year, uncle:
I have bought me a hawk, and a hood, and bells, and all;
I lack nothing but a book to keep it by.

Kno. O, most ridiculous.

Ste. Nay, look you now, you are angry, uncle: why, you
know, an a man have not skill in the hawking and hunting-
languages nowadays, I'll not give a rush for him. They are
more studied than the Greek or the Latin. He is for no
gallant's company without 'em. And by gad's lid I scorn it,
aye, so I do, to be a consort for every hum-drum, hang 'em
scroyles, there's nothing in 'em, i' the world. What do you
talk on it? Because I dwell at Hogsden, I shall keep com-
pany with none but the archers of Finsbury? Or the
citizens, that come a-ducking to Islington ponds? A fine
jest, i' faith! 'Slid, a gentleman must show himself like a
gentleman. Uncle, I pray you be not angry, I know what
I have to do, I trow; I am no novice.

Kno. You are a prodigal absurd coxcomb: Go to.
Nay, never look as me, it's I that speak.
Tak't as you will, sir, I'll not flatter you.
Ha' you not yet found means enough to waste
That which your friends have left you, but you must
Go cast away your money on a kite,
And know not how to keep it when you ha' done?
O it's comely! this will make you a gentleman!
Well cousin, well! I see you are e'en past hope
Of all reclaim. Aye, so, now you are told of it,
You look another way.

Ste.   What would you ha' me do?

Kno. What would I have you do? I'll tell you, kinsman,

Learn to be wise, and practise how to thrive,
That would I have you do: and not to spend
Your coin on every bauble that you fancy,
Or every foolish brain that humours you.
I would not have you to invade each place,
Nor thrust yourself on all societies,
Till men's affections, or your own desert,
Should worthily invite you to your rank.
He that is so respectless in his courses,
Oft sells his reputation at cheap market.
Nor would I, you should melt away yourself
In flashing bravery, lest while you affect
To make a blaze of gentry to the world,
A little puff of scorn extinguish it,
And you be left, like an unsavoury snuff,
Whose property is only to offend.
I'd ha' you sober, and contain yourself;
Not, that your sail be bigger than your boat:
But moderate your expenses now, at first,
As you may keep the same proportion still.
Nor stand so much on your gentility,
Which is an airy and mere borrow'd thing
From dead men's dust and bones: and none of yours
Except you make, or hold it. Who comes here?

Enter a Servant.

Serv. Save you, gentlemen.

Ste. Nay, we do not stand much on our gentility, friend;
yet you are welcome, and I assure you mine uncle here is
a man of a thousand a year, Middlesex land: he has but one
son in all the world; I am his next heir (at the common law),
master Stephen, as simple as I stand here, if my cousin die
(as there's hope he will). I have a pretty living o' mine own
too, beside, hard-by here.

Serv. In good time, sir.

Ste. 'In good time, sir?' why! and in very good time, sir.
You do not flout, friend, do you?

Serv. Not I, sir.

Ste. Not you, sir? you were not best, sir; an' you should,

here be them can perceive it, and that quickly too: go to.
And they can give it again soundly too, an' need be.

Serv. Why, sir, let this satisfy you: good faith, I had no
such intent.

Ste. Sir, an' I thought you had, I would talk with you,
and that presently.

Serv. Good master Stephen, so you may, sir, at your
pleasure.

Ste. And so I would, sir, good my saucy companion! an'
you were out o' mine uncle's ground, I can tell you; though
I do not stand upon my gentility neither, in 't.

Kno. Cousin! cousin! will this ne'er be left?

Ste. Whorson base fellow! a mechanical serving-man!
By this cudgel, and 't were not for shame, I would——

Kno. What would you do, you peremptory gull?
If you can not be quiet, get you hence.
You see, the honest man demeans himself
Modestly to'ards you, giving no reply
To your unseason'd, quarrelling, rude fashion:
And still you huff it, with a kind of carriage,
As void of wit, as of humanity.
Go, get you in; 'fore heaven, I am asham'd
Thou hast a kinsman's interest in me.   [*Exit* Mr. Stephen.

Serv. I pray you, sir. Is this master Knowell's house?

Kno. Yes, marry is it, sir.

Serv. I should enquire for a gentleman, here, one master
Edward Knowell: do you know any such, sir, I pray
you?

Kno. I should forget myself else, sir.

Serv. Are you the gentleman? cry you mercy, sir: I was
requir'd by a gentleman i' the city, as I rode out at this end
o' the town, to deliver you this letter, sir.

Kno. To me, sir! What do you mean? pray you remem-
ber your court'sie.

To his most selected friend, master Edward Knowell.
What might the gentleman's name be, sir, that sent it? nay,
pray you be cover'd.

Serv. One master Wellbred, sir.

Kno. Master Wellbred! A young gentleman, is he not?

11

Serv. The same, sir; master Kitely married his sister: the rich merchant i' the Old Jewry.

Kno. You say very true. Brainworm!

Enter Brainworm

Bra. Sir.

Kno. Make this honest friend drink here: pray you go in.   [*Exeunt* Brainworm *and* Servant.

This letter is directed to my son:
Yet, I am Edward Knowell too, and may
With the safe conscience of good manners, use
The fellow's error to my satisfaction.
Well, I will break it ope (old men are curious)
Be it but for the style's sake, and the phrase,
To see, if both do answer my son's praises,
Who is, almost, grown the idolator
Of this young Wellbred: what have we here? what's this?

 Why, Ned, I beseech thee; hast thou forsworn all thy friends i' the Old Jewry? or dost thou think us all Jews that inhabit there, yet? If thou dost, come over, and but see our frippery: change an old shirt for a whole smock with us. Do not conceive that antipathy between us, and Hogsden, as was between Jews and hogs-flesh. Leave thy vigilant father alone, to number over his green apricots, evening and morning, o' the north-west wall: An' I had been his son, I had sav'd him the labour long since, if, taking in all the young wenches that pass by, at the back door, and coddling every kernel of the fruit for 'em, would ha' serv'd. But, prithee come over to me, quickly, this morning: I have such a present for thee (our Turkey company never sent the like to the Grand-Signior). One is a rhymer, sir, o' your own batch, your own leaven; but doth think himself Poet-major o' the town: willing to be shown, and worthy to be seen. The other—I will not venture his description with you, till you come, because I would ha' you make hither with an appetite. If the worst of 'em be not worth your journey, draw your bill of charges, as unconscionable as any Guildhall verdict will give it you, and you shall be allow'd your viaticum.

         From the Windmill.

From the bordello it might come as well;
The Spittle; or Pict-hatch. Is this the man
My son hath sung so, for the happiest wit,
The choicest brain, the times have sent us forth?
I know not what he may be in the arts;
Nor what in schools: but surely, for his manners,
I judge him a profane and dissolute wretch:
Worse by possession of such great good gifts,
Being the master of so loose a spirit,
Why, what unhallow'd ruffian would have writ
In such a scurrilous manner to a friend!
Why should he think, I tell my apricots?
Or play th' Hesperian dragon with my fruit
To watch it? Well, my son, I had thought
Y' had had more judgement, t' have made election
Of your companions, than t' have ta'en on trust
Such petulant, jeering gamesters, that can spare
No argument or subject from their jest.
But I perceive affection makes a fool
Of any man, too much the father. Brainworm!

Re-enter Brainworm.

Bra. Sir.
Kno. Is the fellow gone that brought this letter?
Bra. Yes, sir, a pretty while since.
Kno. And where's your young master?
Bra. In his chamber, sir.
Kno. He spake not with the fellow, did he?
Bra. No, sir, he saw him not.
Kno. Take you this letter, and deliver it my son,
But with no notice that I have open'd it, on your life.
Bra. O lord, sir, that were a jest, indeed! [*Exit.*
Kno. I am resolv'd I will not stop his journey;
Nor practise any violent means to stay
The unbridled course of youth in him: for that,
Restrain'd, grows more impatient; and, in kind,
Like to the eager but the generous grey-hound,
Who, ne'er so little from his game withheld,
Turns head, and leaps up at his holder's throat.

There is a way of winning, more by love,
And urging of the modesty, than fear:
Force works on servile natures, not the free.
He that's compell'd to goodness may be good,
But 'tis but for that fit: where others drawn
By softness and example get a habit.
Then, if they stray, but warn 'em: and, the same
They should for virtue have done, they'll do for shame.

[*Exit.*

ACT I. SCENE II

A room in Knowell's *house.*

Enter Ed. Knowell, *with a letter, followed by* Brainworm.

E. Kn. Did he open it, sayest thou?

Bra. Yes, o' my word, sir, and read the contents.

E. Kn. That scarce contents me. What countenance, prithee, made he, i' the reading of it? was he angry, or pleas'd?

Bra. Nay, sir, I saw him not read it, nor open it, I assure your worship.

E. Kn. No? how know'st thou, then, that he did either?

Bra. Marry, sir, because he charg'd me, on my life, to tell nobody that he open'd it: which, unless he had done, he would never fear to have it reveal'd.

E. Kn. That's true: well, I thank thee, Brainworm.

Enter Mr. Stephen.

Ste. O, Brainworm, did'st thou not see a fellow here in a what-sha'-call-him doublet! he brought mine uncle a letter e'en now.

Bra. Yes, master Stephen, what of him?

Ste. O, I ha' such a mind to beat him—Where is he? canst thou tell?

Bra. Faith, he is not of that mind: he is gone, master Stephen.

Ste. Gone? which way? when went he? how long since?

Bra. He is rid hence. He took horse at the street door.

Ste. And I stayed i' the fields! whorson scanderbag rogue! O that I had but a horse to fetch him back again.

Bra. Why, you may ha' my master's gelding, to save your longing, sir.

Ste. But I ha' no boots, that's the spite on 't.

Bra. Why, a fine wisp of hay, roll'd hard, master Stephen.

Ste. No, 'faith, it's no boot to follow him, now: let him e'en go, and hang. 'Pray thee, help to truss me a little. He does so vex me——

Bra. You'll be worse vex'd when you are truss'd, master Stephen. Best keep unbrac'd; and walk yourself till you be cold: your choler may founder you else.

Ste. By my faith, and so I will now thou tell'st me on't: How dost thou like my leg, Brainworm?

Bra. A very good leg, master Stephen! but the woollen stocking does not commend it so well.

Ste. Foh, the stockings be good enough, now summer is coming on, for the dust: I'll have a pair of silk, again' winter, that I go to dwell i' the town. I think my leg would show in a silk-hose.

Bra. Believe me, master Stephen, rarely well.

Ste. In sadness, I think it would: I have a reasonable good leg.

Bra. You have an excellent good leg, master Stephen, but I cannot stay to praise it longer now, and I am very sorry for 't.

Ste. Another time will serve, Brainworm. Gramercy for this.   [*Exit* Brainworm.

E. Kn. Ha, ha, ha!

                              [Ed. Knowell *laughs, having read the letter.*

Ste. 'Slid, I hope he laughs not at me; an' he do——

E. Kn. Here was a letter, indeed, to be intercepted by a man's father, and do him good with him! He cannot but think most virtuously both of me and the sender, sure— that make the careful costermonger of him in our *familiar Epistles.* Well, if he read this with patience, I'll be gelt, and troll ballads for Mr. John Trundle, yonder, the rest of my mortality. It is true, and likely, my father may have as much patience as another man; for he takes much physic and oft taking physic makes a man very patient. But would your packet, master Wellbred, had arriv'd at him in such a minute of his patience; then, we had known the end of it, which now is doubtful, and threatens——What! my wise cousin! Nay, then, I'll furnish our feast with one gull more to'ard the mess. He writes to me of a brace, and here's one, that's three: O, for a fourth; Fortune, if ever thou'lt use thine eyes, I entreat thee——

Ste. O, now I see who he laughed at. He laughed at somebody in that letter. By this good light, an he had laugh'd at me——

E. Kn. How now, cousin Stephen, melancholy?

Ste. Yes, a little. I thought you had laugh'd at me, cousin.

E. Kn. Why, what an' I had, coz, what would you ha' done?

Ste. By this light, I would ha' told mine uncle.

E. Kn. Nay, if you would ha' told your uncle, I did laugh at you, coz.

Ste. Did you, indeed?

E. Kn. Yes, indeed.

Ste. Why, then——

E. Kn. What then?

Ste. I am satisfied, it is sufficient.

E. Kn. Why, be so, gentle coz. And I pray you let me entreat a courtesy of you. I am sent for, this morning, by a friend i' the Old Jewry to come to him; it's but crossing over the fields to Moorgate: Will you bear me company? I protest, it is not to draw you into bond, or any plot against the state, coz.

Ste. Sir, that's all one and 't were: you shall command me twice so far as Moorgate to do you good in such a matter. Do you think I would leave you? I protest——

E. Kn. No, no, you shall not protest, coz.

Ste. By my fackins, but I will, by your leave; I'll protest more to my friend than I'll speak of, at this time.

E. Kn. You speak very well, coz.

Ste. Nay, not so neither, you shall pardon me: but I speak to serve my turn.

E. Kn. Your turn, coz? Do you know what you say? A gentleman of your sort, parts, carriage, and estimation, to talk o' your turn i' this company and to me, alone, like a tankard-bearer at a conduit! Fie. A wight that, hitherto, his every step hath left the stamp of a great foot behind him, as every word the savour of a strong spirit! and he! this man! so grac'd, gilded, or (to use a more fit metaphor) so tin-foil'd by nature, as not ten housewives' pewter (again' a good time) shows more bright to the world than he! and he (as I said last, so I say again, and still shall say it) this man! to conceal such real ornaments as these, and shadow their glory, as a milliner's wife does her wrought stomacher, with a smoky lawn, or a black cypress? O coz! It cannot be answer'd, go not about it. Drake's old ship, at Deptford, may sooner circle the world again. Come, wrong not the quality of your desert with looking downward, coz; but hold up your head, so: and let the idea of what you are be portray'd i' your face, that men may read i' your phisnomy, *Here, within this place, is to be seen the true, rare, and accomplish'd monster, or miracle of nature*, which is all one. What think you of this, coz?

Ste. Why, I do think of it; and I will be more proud, and melancholy, and gentlemanlike than I have been, I'll ensure you.

E. Kn. Why, that's resolute, master Stephen! Now, if I can but hold him up to his height, as it is happily begun, it will do well for a suburb-humour: we may hap have a match with the city, and play him for forty pound. Come, coz.

Ste. I'll follow you.

E. Kn. Follow me? you must go before.

Ste. Nay, an' I must, I will. Pray you, show me, good cousin.   [*Exeunt.*

17

ACT I. SCENE III

The lane before Cob's *house.*

Enter Mr. Matthew.

Mat. I think this be the house: what, ho!

Enter Cob.

Cob. Who's there? O, master Matthew! gi' your worship good morrow.

Mat. What! Cob! how do'st thou, good Cob? do'st thou inhabit here, Cob?

Cob. Aye, sir, I and my lineage ha' kept a poor house here, in our days.

Mat. Thy lineage, Monsieur Cob? what lineage? what lineage?

Cob. Why sir, an ancient lineage, and a princely. Mine ance'try came from a king's belly, no worse man: and yet no man neither (by your worship's leave, I did lie in that) but Herring the king of fish (from his belly, I proceed) one o' the monarchs o' the world, I assure you. The first red herring, that was broil'd in Adam and Eve's kitchen, do I fetch my pedigree from, by the Harrots' books. His Cob was my great-great-mighty-great grandfather.

Mat. Why mighty? why mighty? I pray thee.

Cob. O, it was a mighty while ago, sir, and a mighty great Cob.

Mat. How know'st thou that?

Cob. How know I? why, I smell his ghost, ever and anon.

Mat. Smell a ghost? O unsavoury jest! and the ghost of a herring, Cob!

Cob. Aye, sir, with favour of your worship's nose, Mr. Matthew, why not the ghost of a herring-cob, as well as the ghost of rasher-bacon?

Mat. Roger Bacon, thou wouldst say?

Cob. I say rasher-bacon. They were both broil'd o' the coals and a man may smell broil'd meat, I hope? you are a scholar, upsolve me that, now.

Mat. O raw ignorance! Cob, canst thou show me of a gentleman, one Captain Bobadil, where his lodging is?

Cob. Oh, my guest, sir! you mean.

Mat. Thy guest! Alas! ha, ha!

Cob. Why do you laugh, sir? Do you not mean Captain Bobadil?

Mat. Cob, 'pray thee, advise thyself well: do not wrong the gentleman, and thyself too. I dare be sworn, he scorns thy house: he! He lodge in such a base, obscure place, as thy house! Tut, I know his disposition so well, he would not lie in thy bed, if tho'uldst gi' it him.

Cob. I will not give it him though, sir. Mass, I thought somewhat was in't, we could not get him to bed all night! Well, sir, though he lie not o' my bed, he lies o' my bench: an't please you to go up, sir, you shall find him with two cushions under his head, and his cloak wrapt about him, as though he had neither won nor lost, and yet (I warrant) he ne'er cast better in his life than he has done to-night.

Mat. Why? was he drunk?

Cob. Drunk, sir? you hear not me say so. Perhaps he swallow'd a tavern token, or some such device, sir: I have nothing to do withal. I deal with water and not with wine. It's six o'clock: I should ha' carried two turns, by this. What ho? my stopple? come.

Enter Tib.

Mat. Lie in a water-bearer's house! A gentleman of his havings! Well, I'll tell him my mind.

Cob. What, Tib, show this gentleman up to the Captain.

[*Exeunt* Tib *and* Mr. Matthew.

O, an my house were the Brazen-head now! faith, it would e'en speak, *Mo fools yet.* You should ha' some now would take this Mr. Matthew to be a gentleman, at the least. His father's an honest man, a worshipful fishmonger, and so forth; and now does he creep and wriggle into acquaintance with all the brave gallants about the town, such as my guest is: (O, my guest is a fine man) and they flout him invincibly. He useth every day to a merchant's house (where I serve water), one master Kitely's, i' the Old

19

Jewry; and here's the jest, he is in love with my master's sister, mistress Bridget, and calls her mistress: and there he will sit you a whole afternoon sometimes, reading o' these same abominable, vile (a pox on 'em, I cannot abide them) rascally verses, poyetry, poyetry, and speaking of interludes, 'twill make a man burst to hear him. And the wenches, they do so jeer, and ti-he at him—well, should they do so much to me, I'd forswear them all, by the foot of Pharaoh. There's an oath! How many water-bearers shall you hear swear such an oath? O, I have a guest (he teaches me) he does swear the legiblest of any man christen'd: By St. George, the foot of Pharaoh, the body of me, as I am a gentleman and a soldier: such dainty oaths! and withal, he does take this same filthy roguish tobacco, the finest, and cleanliest! it would do a man good to see the fume come forth at 's tunnels! Well, he owes me forty shillings (my wife lent him out of her purse, by sixpence a time) besides his lodging: I would I had it. I shall ha' it, he says, the next action. Helter-skelter, hang sorrow, care'll kill a cat, uptails all, and a louse for the hangman. [*Exit.*

ACT I. SCENE IV

A room in Cob's *house.*

Bobadil *is discovered lying on his bench.*

Bob. Hostess, hostess.

Enter Tib.

Tib. What say you, sir?

Bob. A cup o' thy small beer, sweet hostess.

Tib. Sir, there's a gentleman, below, would speak with you.

Bob. A gentleman! 'ods so, I am not within.

Tib. My husband told him you were, sir.

Bob. What a plague—what meant he?

Mat. Captain Bobadil?

Bob. Who's there? (take away the basin, good hostess.) Come up, sir.

Tib. He would desire you to come up, sir. You come into a cleanly house, here.

Enter Matthew.

Mat. 'Save you, sir. 'Save you, Captain.

Bob. Gentle master Matthew! Is it you, sir? Please you sit down.

Mat. Thank you, good Captain, you may see I am somewhat audacious.

Bob. Not so, sir. I was requested to supper, last night, by a sort of gallants, where you were wish'd for, and drunk to, I assure you.

Mat. Vouchsafe me by whom, good Captain.

Bob. Marry, by young Wellbred, and others. Why, hostess, a stool here for this gentleman.

Mat. No haste, sir, 'tis very well. [*Exit* Tib.

Bob. Body of me! It was so late ere we parted last night, I can scarce open my eyes; I was but new risen, as you came: how passes the day abroad, sir? you can tell.

Mat. 'Faith, some half hour to seven: now, trust me, you have an exceeding fine lodging here, very neat, and private!

Bob. Aye, sir: sit down, I pray you. Master Matthew, in any case, possess no gentlemen of our acquaintance with notice of my lodging.

Mat. Who? I, sir? no.

Bob. Not that I need to care who knows it, for the cabin is convenient, but in regard I would not be too popular, and generally visited, as some are.

Mat. True, Captain, I conceive you.

Bob. For, do you see, sir, by the heart of valour in me, (except it be to some peculiar and choice spirits, to whom I am extraordinarily engag'd, as yourself, or so) I could not extend thus far.

Mat. O Lord, sir, I resolve so.

Bob. I confess I love a cleanly and quiet privacy, above all the tumult and roar of fortune. What new book ha' you there? What! *Go by, Hieronymo!*

Mat. Aye, did you ever see it acted? is't not well penn'd?

Bob. Well penn'd? I would fain see all the poets of these times pen such another play as that was! they'll prate and swagger, and keep a stir of art and devices, when (as I am a gentleman) read 'em, they are the most shallow, pitiful, barren fellows that live upon the face of the earth again!

Mat. Indeed, here are a number of fine speeches in this book! *O eyes, no eyes, but fountains fraught with tears!* There's a conceit! fountains fraught with tears! *O life, no life, but lively form of death!* Another! *O world, no world, but mass of public wrongs!* A third! *Confus'd and fill'd with murder, and misdeeds!* A fourth! O, the Muses! Is't not excellent? Is't not simply the best that ever you heard, Captain? Ha? How do you like it?

Bob. 'Tis good.

Mat. *To thee, the purest object to my sense,*
The most refined essence heaven covers,
Send I these lines, wherein I do commence
The happy state of turtle-billing lovers.
If they prove rough, unpolish'd, harsh, and rude,
Haste made the waste. Thus, mildly, I conclude.

[*Bobadil is making him ready all this while.*

Bob. Nay, proceed, proceed. Where's this?

Mat. This, sir? a toy o' mine own, in my nonage: the infancy of my Muses! But when will you come and see my study? good faith, I can show you some very good things I have done of late—That boot becomes your leg passing well, Captain, methinks!

Bob. So, so, it's the fashion gentlemen now use.

Mat. Troth, Captain, an' now you speak o' the fashion, master Wellbred's elder brother and I are fall'n out exceedingly: this other day, I happen'd to enter into some discourse of a hanger, which I assure you, both for fashion, and workmanship, was most peremptory-beautiful and gentlemanlike! Yet, he condemn'd and cried it down for the most pied and ridiculous that ever he saw.

Bob. Squire Downright? the half-brother? was't not?

Mat. Aye, sir, he.

Bob. Hang him, rook, he! why, he has no more judge-

ment than a malt-horse. By St. George, I wonder you'd
lose a thought upon such an animal: the most peremptory
absurd clown of Christendom this day, he is holden. I pro-
test to you, as I am a gentleman and a soldier, I ne'er
chang'd words with his like. By his discourse he should eat
nothing but hay. He was born for the manger, pannier, or
pack-saddle! He has not so much as a good phrase in his
belly, but all old iron, and rusty proverbs! a good com-
modity for some smith to make hobnails of.

Mat. Aye, and he thinks to carry it away with his man-
hood still, where he comes. He brags he will gi' me the bas-
tinado, as I hear.

Bob. How! He the bastinado! how came he by that
word, trow?

Mat. Nay, indeed, he said cudgel me; I term'd it so, for
my more grace.

Bob. That may be, for I was sure it was none of his
word. But when? when said he so?

Mat. 'Faith, yesterday, they say: a young gallant, a friend
of mine, told me so.

Bob. By the foot of Pharaoh, and 't were my case now,
I should send him a chartel presently. The bastinado! A
most proper and sufficient dependence, warranted by the
great Caranza. Come hither. You shall chartel him. I'll show
you a trick or two you shall kill him with at pleasure: the
first *stoccata* if you will, by this air.

Mat. Indeed, you have absolute knowledge i' the mys-
tery, I have heard, sir.

Bob. Of whom? Of whom ha' you heard it, I beseech
you?

Mat. Troth, I have heard it spoken of divers, that you
have very rare, and un-in-one-breath-utter-able skill, sir.

Bob. By heaven, no, not I; no skill i' the earth: some
small rudiments i' the science, as to know my time, dis-
tance, or so. I have profest it more for noblemen, and
gentlemen's use, than mine own practice, I assure you.

Enter Tib.

Hostess, accommodate us with another bedstaff here,

quickly. Lend us another bedstaff. The woman does not understand the words of action. Look you, sir. Exalt not your point above this state, at any hand, and let your poinard maintain your defence, thus: (give it the gentleman, and leave us.) [*Exit* Tib.] So, sir. Come on: O, twine your body more about, that you may fall to a more sweet comely gentlemanlike guard. So, indifferent. Hollow your body more, sir, thus. Now, stand fast o' your left leg, note your distance, keep your due proportion of time—Oh, you disorder your point, most irregularly!

Mat. How is the bearing of it, now, sir?

Bob. O, out of measure ill! A well-experienc'd hand would pass upon you, at pleasure.

Mat. How mean you, sir, pass upon me?

Bob. Why, thus sir—make a thrust at me—come in upon the answer, control your point, and make a full career at the body. The best-practis'd gallants of the time name it the *passada*: a most desperate thrust, believe it!

Mat. Well, come, sir.

Bob. Why, you do not manage your weapon with any facility or grace to invite me: I have no spirit to play with you. Your dearth of judgement renders you tedious.

Mat. But one *venue*, sir.

Bob. Venue! Fie. Most gross denomination, as ever I heard! O, the *stoccata*, while you live, sir. Note that. Come, put on your cloak, and we'll to some private place, where you are acquainted, some tavern, or so—and have a bit— I'll send for one of these fencers, and he shall breath you by my direction; and then I will teach you your trick. You shall kill him with it at the first, if you please. Why, I will learn you, by the true judgement of the eye, hand, and foot, to control any enemy's point i' the world. Should your adversary confront you with a pistol, 'twere nothing, by this hand; you should, by the same rule, control his bullet in a line: except it were hail-shot, and spread. What money ha' you about you, Mr. Matthew?

Mat. 'Faith, I ha' not past a two shillings, or so.

Bob. 'Tis somewhat with the least: but, come. We will have a bunch of radish, and salt, to taste our wine; and a pipe of tobacco, to close the orifice of the stomach: and then, we'll call upon young Wellbred. Perhaps we shall meet the Coridon, his brother, there: and put him to the question.

ACT II. SCENE I

A Hall in Kitely's *house.*

Enter Kitely, Cash, *and* Downright.

Kit. Thomas, come hither.
There lies a note, within upon my desk;
Here, take my key: It is no matter, neither.
Where is the boy?

Cas.　　　　Within, sir, i' the warehouse.

Kit. Let him tell over, straight, that Spanish gold,
And weigh it, with th' pieces of eight. Do you
See the delivery of those silver stuffs
To Mr. Lucar. Tell him, if he will,
He shall ha' the grograns, at the rate I told him,
And I will meet him, on the Exchange, anon.

Cas. Good, sir.　　　　　　　　*[Exit* Cash.

Kit.　　　　Do you see that fellow, brother Down-
right?

Dow. Aye, what of him?

Kit.　　　　He is a jewel, brother.
I took him of a child, up, at my door,
And christ'ned him, gave him mine own name, Thomas,
Since bred him at the Hospital; where proving
A toward imp, I call'd him home, and taught him
So much, as I have made him my cashier,
And giv'n him, who had none, a surname, Cash:
And find him in his place so full of faith,
That I durst trust my life into his hands.

Dow. So would not I in any bastards, brother,
As, it is like, he is: although I knew
Myself his father. But you said you'd somewhat
To tell me, gentle brother, what is 't? what is 't?

Kit. 'Faith, I am very loath to utter it,

As fearing it may hurt your patience:
But that I know your judgement is of strength,
Against the nearness of affection——

    Dow. What need this circumstance? pray you be direct.

    Kit. I will not say how much I do ascribe
Unto your friendship; nor in what regard
I hold your love: but let my past behaviour,
And usage of your sister, but confirm
How well I've been affected to your——

    Dow. You are too tedious, come to the matter, the matter.

    Kit. Then (without further ceremony), thus.
My brother Wellbred, sir, (I know not how)
Of late, is much declin'd in what he was,
And greatly alter'd in his disposition.
When he came first to lodge here in my house,
Ne'er trust me, if I were not proud of him:
Methought he bare himself in such a fashion,
So full of man, and sweetness in his carriage,
And (what was chief) it show'd not borrow'd in him,
But all he did, became him as his own,
And seem'd as perfect, proper, and possess'd
As breath with life, or colour with the blood.
But, now, his course is so irregular,
So loose, affected, and depriv'd of grace,
And he himself withal so far fall'n off
From that first place, as scarce no note remains
To tell men's judgements where he lately stood.
He's grown a stranger to all due respect,
Forgetful of his friends, and not content
To stale himself in all societies,
He makes my house here common, as a mart,
A theatre, a public receptacle
For giddy humour, and diseased riot;
And here (as in a tavern, or a stews)
He and his wild associates spend their hours,
In repetition of lascivious jests,
Swear, leap, drink, dance, and revel night by night,
Control my servants: and indeed what not?

Dow. 'Sdains, I know not what I should say to him, i' the whole world! He values me at a crack'd three-farthings, for aught I see. It will never out o' the flesh that's bred i' the bone! I have told him enough, one would think, if that would serve: But counsel to him is as good as a shoulder of mutton to a sick horse. Well! he knows what to trust to, for George. Let him spend, and spend, and domineer, till his heart ache; an' he think to be reliev'd by me, when he is got into one o' your city pounds, the Counters, he has the wrong sow by the ear, i' faith: and claps his dish at the wrong man's door. I'll lay my hand o' my halfpenny, ere I part with't to fetch him out, I'll assure him.

Kit. Nay, good brother, let it not trouble you thus.

Dow. S'death, he mads me, I could eat my very spur-leathers for anger! But why are you so tame? Why do you not speak to him, and tell him how he disquiets your house?

Kit. O, there are divers reasons to dissuade, brother.
But would yourself vouchsafe to travail in it
(Though but with plain, and easy circumstance)
It would both come much better to his sense,
And savour less of stomach, or of passion.
You are his elder brother, and that title
Both gives and warrants you authority;
Which (by your presence seconded) must breed
A kind of duty in him, and regard:
Whereas if I should intimate the least,
It would but add contempt to his neglect,
Heap worse on ill, make up a pile of hatred
That, in the rearing, would come tott'ring down,
And, in the ruin, bury all our love.
Nay, more than this, brother, if I should speak
He would be ready from his heat of humour,
And over-flowing of the vapour in him,
To blow the ears of his familiars
With the false breath of telling what disgraces
And low disparagements I had put upon him.
Whilst they, sir, to relieve him in the fable,
Make their loose comments upon every word,

Gesture, or look, I use; mock me all over,
From my flat cap unto my shining shoes:
And, out of their impetuous rioting phant'sies,
Beget some slander, that shall dwell with me.
And what would that be, think you? marry, this;
They would give out (because my wife is fair,
Myself but lately married, and my sister
Here sojourning a virgin in my house)
That I were jealous! nay, as sure as death,
That they would say. And how that I had quarrell'd
My brother purposely, thereby to find
An apt pretext to banish them my house.

   Dow. Mass, perhaps so: They're like enough to do it.

   Kit. Brother, they would, believe it: so should I
(Like one of these penurious quack-salvers)
But set the bills up to mine own disgrace,
And try experiments upon myself:
Lend scorn and envy opportunity
To stab my reputation, and good name——

     Enter Matthew, *struggling with* Bobadil.

   Mat. I will speak to him——

   Bob. Speak to him? away, by the foot of Pharaoh, you shall not, you shall not do him that grace. The time of day to you, Gentleman o' the house. Is Mr. Wellbred stirring?

   Dow. How then? what should he do?

   Bob. Gentleman of the house, it is to you: is he within, sir?

   Kit. He came not to his lodging to-night, sir, I assure you.

   Dow. Why, do you hear? you.

   Bob. The gentleman-citizen hath satisfied me. I'll talk to no scavenger.   [*Exeunt* Matthew *and* Bobadil.

   Dow. How, scavenger? stay, sir, stay?

   Kit. Nay, brother Downright.

   Dow. 'Heart! stand you away, and you love me.

   Kit. You shall not follow him now, I pray you, brother. Good faith, you shall not: I will over-rule you.

   Dow. Ha? scavenger? well, go to, I say little: but, by this good day (God forgive me I should swear) if I put it up so,

say I am the rankest cow that ever pissed. 'Sdains, an' I
swallow this, I'll ne'er draw my sword in the sight of Fleet-
street again, while I live; I'll sit in a barn, with Madge-
howlet, and catch mice first. Scavenger? 'Heart, and I'll
go near to fill that huge tumbrel-slop of yours with some-
what, and I have good luck: your Garagantua breech can-
not carry it away so.

Kit. Oh do not fret yourself thus, never think on't.

Dow. These are my brother's consorts, these! these are
his comrades, his walking mates! he's a gallant, a Cavaliero
too, right hang-man cut! Let me not live, an' I could not
find in my heart to swinge the whole gang of 'em, one after
another, and begin with him first. I am griev'd it should be
said he is my brother, and take these courses. Well as he
brews, so he shall drink, for George, again. Yet he shall
hear on't, and that tightly too, an' I live, i' faith.

Kit. But, brother, let your reprehension, then,
Run in an easy current, not o'er high
Carried with rashness, or devouring choler;
But rather use the soft persuading way,
Whose powers will work more gently, and compose
Th' imperfect thoughts you labour to reclaim:
More winning, than enforcing the consent.

Dow. Aye, Aye, let me alone for that, I warrant you.

[*Bell rings.*

Kit. How now? oh, the bell rings to breakfast.
Brother, I pray you go in, and bear my wife
Company till I come; I'll but give order
For some dispatch of business to my servants——

[*Exit* Downright.

Enter Cob.

Kit. What, Cob? our maids will have you by the back,
I' faith, for coming so late this morning.

Cob. Perhaps so, sir, take heed somebody have not them
by the belly, for walking so late in the evening.

[*He passes by with his tankard.*

Kit. Well, yet my troubled spirit's somewhat eas'd,
Though not repos'd in that security,

29

As I could wish. But I must be content.
Howe'er I set a face on't to the world,
Would I had lost this finger, at a venture,
So Wellbred had ne'er lodg'd within my house.
Why't cannot be, where there is such resort
Of wanton gallants, and young revellers,
That any woman should be honest long.
Is't like that factious beauty will preserve
The public weal of chastity unshaken,
When such strong motives muster, and make head
Against her single peace? no, no. Beware,
When mutual appetite doth meet to treat,
And spirits of one kind, one quality,
Come once to parley in the pride of blood:
It is no slow conspiracy that follows.
Well (to be plain) if I but thought the time
Had answer'd their affections: all the world
Should not persuade me but I were a cuckold.
Marry, I hope, they ha' not got that start:
For opportunity hath baulk'd 'em yet,
And shall do still, while I have eyes and ears
To attend the impositions of my heart.
My presence shall be as an iron bar
'Twixt the conspiring motions of desire:
Yea, every look, or glance, mine eye ejects,
Shall check occasion, as one doth his slave,
When he forgets the limits of prescription.

Enter Dame Kitely *and* Bridget.

Dame. Sister Bridget, pray you fetch down the rose-
water above in the closet. [*Exit* Bridget.] Sweetheart, will
you come in to breakfast?

Kit. An' she have overheard me now?

Dame. I pray thee, good muss, we stay for you.

Kit. By heaven I would not for a thousand angels.

Dame. What ails you, sweetheart? are you not well?
speak, good muss.

Kit. Troth, my head aches extremely, on a sudden.

Dame. Oh, the lord!

Kit. How now? what?

Dame. Alas, how it burns? Muss, keep you warm, good truth, it is this new disease! there's a number are troubled withal! for love's sake, sweetheart, come in, out of the air.

Kit. How simple, and how subtle are her answers.
A new disease, and many troubled with it!
Why, true: she heard me, all the world to nothing.

Dame. I pray thee, good sweetheart, come in; the air will do you harm, in troth.

Kit. The air! she has me i' the wind! sweetheart!
I'll come to you presently: 't will away, I hope.

Dame. Pray heaven it do. [*Exit.*

Kit. A new disease? I know not, new or old,
But it may well be call'd poor mortals' plague:
For, like a pestilence, it doth infect
The houses of the brain. First, it begins
Solely to work upon the phantasy,
Filling her seat with such pestiferous air,
As soon corrupts the judgement; and from thence
Sends like contagion to the memory:
Still each to other giving the infection;
Which, as a subtle vapour, spreads itself,
Confusedly, through every sensive part,
Till not a thought, or motion, in the mind,
Be free from the black poison of suspect.
Ah, but what misery is it, to know this?
Or, knowing it, to want the mind's erection,
In such extremes? Well, I will once more strive,
In spite of this black cloud, myself to be,
And shake the fever off, that thus shakes me. [*Exit.*

ACT II. SCENE II

Moorfields.

Enter Brainworm *disguised.*

Bra. 'Slid, I cannot choose but laugh, to see myself translated thus from a poor creature to a creator; for now must I create an intolerable sort of lies, or my present profession loses the grace: and yet the lie to a man of my coat is as ominous a fruit, as the *Fico.* O sir, it holds for good policy ever, to have that outwardly in vilest estimation, that inwardly is most dear to us. So much for my borrowed shape. Well, the truth is, my old master intends to follow my young, dry-foot, over Moorfields to London, this morning: now I, knowing of this hunting-match, or rather conspiracy, and to insinuate with my young master (for so must we that are blue-waiters, and men of hope and service do, or perhaps we may wear motley at the year's end, and who wears motley, you know) have got me afore, in this disguise, determining here to lie in *ambuscado*, and intercept him in the midway. If I can but get his cloak, his purse, his hat, nay, anything, to cut him off, that is, to stay his journey, *Veni, vidi, vici,* I may say with Captain Caesar. I am made for ever, i' faith. Well, now must I practise to get the true garb of one of these lance-knights, my arm here, and my—young master! and his cousin, Mr. Stephen, as I am true counterfeit man of war, and no soldier!

Enter Ed. Knowell *and* Stephen.

E. Kn. So sir, and how then, coz?

Ste. 'Sfoot, I have lost my purse, I think.

E. Kn. How? lost your purse? where? when had you it?

Ste. I cannot tell, stay.

Bra. 'Slid, I am afeard they will know me, would I could get by them.

E. Kn. What? ha' you it?

Ste. No, I think I was bewitch'd, I——

E. Kn. Nay, do not weep the loss, hang it, let it go.

Ste. Oh, it's here: no, and it had been lost I had not car'd, but for a jet ring mistress Mary sent me.

E. Kn. A jet ring? oh, the posey, the posey?

Ste. Fine, i' faith! 'Though fancy sleep, my love is deep.' Meaning that though I did not fancy her, yet she loved me dearly.

E. Kn. Most excellent!

Ste. And then, I sent her another, and my posey was: *The deeper, the sweeter, I'll be judg'd by St. Peter.*

E. Kn. How, by St. Peter? I do not conceive that!

Ste. Marry, St. Peter, to make up the metre.

E. Kn. Well, there the Saint was your good patron, he help'd you at your need: thank him, thank him.

Bra. [*He is come back.*] I cannot take leave on 'em, so: I will venture, come what will. Gentlemen, please you change a few crowns for a very excellent good blade, here? I am a poor gentleman, a soldier, one that (in the better state of my fortunes) scorn'd so mean a refuge, but now it is the humour of necessity to have it so. You seem to be gentlemen, well affected to martial men, else I should rather die with silence than live with shame: however, vouchsafe to remember it is my want speaks, not myself. This condition agrees not with my spirit——

E. Kn. Where hast thou serv'd?

Bra. May it please you, sir, in all the late wars of Bohemia, Hungaria, Dalmatia, Poland, where not, sir? I have been a poor servitor, by sea and land, at any time this fourteen years, and follow'd the fortunes of the best commanders in Christendom. I was twice shot at the taking of Aleppo, once at the relief of Vienna; I have been at Marseilles, Naples, and the Adriatic gulf, a gentleman-slave in the galleys, thrice, where I was most dangerously shot in the head, through both the thighs, and yet, being thus maim'd, I am void of maintenance, nothing left me but my scars, the noted marks of my resolution.

Ste. How will you sell this rapier, friend?

Bra. Generous sir, I refer it to your own judgement; you are a gentleman, give me what you please.

Ste. True, I am a gentleman, I know that, friend: but what though? I pray you say, what would you ask?

Bra. I assure you, the blade may become the side or thigh of the best prince in Europe.

E. Kn. Aye, with a velvet scabbard, I think.

Ste. Nay, an't be mine, it shall have a velvet scabbard, coz, that's flat: I'd not wear it as 'tis, and you would give me an angel.

Bra. At your worship's pleasure, sir; nay, 'tis a most pure Toledo.

Ste. I had rather it were a Spaniard! but tell me, what shall I give you for it? An' it had a silver hilt——

E. Kn. Come, come, you shall not buy it; hold, there's a shilling, fellow, take thy rapier.

Ste. Why, but I will buy it now, because you say so, and there's another shilling, fellow. I scorn to be out-bidden. What, shall I walk with a cudgel, like Higginbottom? and may have a rapier for money?

E. Kn. You may buy one in the city.

Ste. Tut, I'll buy this i' the field, so I will, I have a mind to't, because 'tis a field rapier. Tell me your lowest price.

E. Kn. You shall not buy it, I say.

Ste. By this money, but I will, though I give more than 'tis worth.

E. Kn. Come away, you are a fool.

Ste. Friend, I am a fool, that's granted: but I'll have it, for that word's sake. Follow me, for your money.

Bra. At your service, sir.   [*Exeunt.*

ACT II. SCENE III

Another part of Moorfields.

Enter Knowell.

Kno. I cannot lose the thought, yet, of this letter,
Sent to my son: nor leave t' admire the change
Of manners, and the breeding of our youth,
Within the kingdom, since myself was one.
When I was young, he liv'd not in the stews
Durst have conceiv'd a scorn, and utter'd it,
On a grey head; age was authority
Against a buffoon: and a man had, then,
A certain reverence paid unto his years,
That had none due unto his life. So much
The sanctity of some prevail'd for others.
But, now, we all are fall'n; youth, from their fear;
And age, from that which bred it, good example.

Nay, would ourselves were not the first, even parents,
That did destroy the hopes in our children:
Or they not learn'd our vices in their cradles,
And suck'd in our ill customs with their milk,
Ere all their teeth be born, or they can speak,
We make their palates cunning! The first words
We form their tongues with are licentious jests!
Can it call, whore? cry bastard? O then, kiss it,
A witty child! Can't swear? The father's darling!
Give it two plums. Nay, rather than't shall learn
No bawdy song, the mother herself will teach it!
But this is in the infancy, the days
Of the long coat: when it puts on the breeches,
It will put off all this. Aye, it is like:
When it is gone into the bone already.
No, no: this dye goes deeper than the coat,
Or shirt, or skin. It stains unto the liver
And heart, in some. And, rather, than it should not,
Note what we fathers do! Look how we live!
What mistresses we keep! at what expense,
In our sons' eyes! where they may handle our gifts,
Hear our lascivious courtships, see our dalliance,
Taste of the same provoking meats with us,
To ruin of our states! Nay, when our own
Portion is fled, to prey on their remainder,
We call them into fellowship of vice!
Bait 'em with the young chamber-maid to seal!
And teach 'em all bad ways to buy affliction!
This is one path! but there are millions more,
In which we spoil our own, with leading them.
Well, I thank heaven, I never yet was he,
That travell'd with my son, before sixteen,
To show him the Venetian courtezans.
Nor read the grammar of cheating I had made,
To my sharp boy at twelve: repeating still
The rule, 'Get money'; still, 'Get money, boy;
No matter by what means; Money will do
More, boy, than my Lord's letter.' Neither have I
Dress'd snails or mushrooms curiously before him,

35

Perfum'd my sauces, and taught him to make 'em;
Preceding still with my grey gluttony
At all the ordinaries: and only fear'd
His palate should degenerate, not his manners.
These are the trade of fathers, now! however,
My son, I hope, hath met within my threshold
None of these household precedents; which are strong
And swift to rape youth to their precipice.
But let the house at home be ne'er so clean—
Swept, or kept sweet from filth; nay, dust and cobwebs:
If he will live abroad with his companions,
In dung and laystalls, it is worth a fear.
Nor is the danger of conversing less
Than all that I have mention'd of example.

Enter Brainworm *disguised as before.*

Bra. My master? nay, faith, have at you: I am flesh'd
now, I have sped so well. Worshipful sir, I beseech you,
respect the estate of a poor soldier, I am asham'd of this
base course of life (God's my comfort) but extremity pro-
vokes me to 't, what remedy?

Kno. I have not for you, now.

Bra. By the faith I bear unto truth, gentleman, it is no
ordinary custom in me, but only to preserve manhood. I
protest to you, a man I have been, a man I may be, by your
sweet bounty.

Kno. 'Pray thee, good friend, be satisfied.

Bra. Good sir, by that hand, you may do the part of a
kind gentleman, in lending a poor soldier the price of two
cans of beer (a matter of small value). The king of heaven
shall pay you, and I shall rest thankful: sweet worship——

Kno. Nay, and you be so importunate——

Bra. Oh, tender sir, need will have his course: I was not
made to this vile use! well, the edge of the enemy could
not have abated me so much [*He weeps*]. It's hard when
a man hath serv'd in his Prince's cause, and be thus—.
Honourable worship, let me derive a small piece of silver
from you, it shall not be given in the course of time, by this
good ground. I was fain to pawn my rapier last night for

36

a poor supper, I had suck'd the hilts long before, I am a
pagan else: sweet honour.

Kno. Believe me, I am taken with some wonder
To think a fellow of thy outward presence
Should (in the frame and fashion of his mind)
Be so degenerate and sordid-base!
Art thou a man? and sham'st thou not to beg?
To practise such a servile kind of life?
Why, were thy education ne'er so mean,
Having thy limbs, a thousand fairer courses
Offer themselves to thy election.
Either the wars might still supply thy wants,
Or service of some virtuous gentleman,
Or honest labour: nay, what can I name,
But would become thee better than to beg?
But men of thy condition feed on sloth,
As doth the beetle on the dung she breeds in,
Not caring how the metal of your minds
Is eaten with the rust of idleness.
Now, afore me, whate'er he be that should
Relieve a person of thy quality,
While thou insist in this loose desperate course,
I would esteem the sin, not thine, but his.

Bra. Faith, sir, I would gladly find some other course,
if so——

Kno. Aye, you'd gladly find it, but you will not seek
it.

Bra. Alas, sir, where should a man seek? in the wars,
there's no ascent by desert in these days; but——and for
service, would it were as soon purchased, as wished for
(the air's my comfort). I know what I would say——

Kno. What's thy name?

Bra. Please you, Fitz-Sword, sir.

Kno. Fitz-Sword?
Say, that a man should entertain thee now,
Would'st thou be honest, humble, just and true?

Bra. Sir, by the place, and honour of a soldier——

Kno. Nay, nay, I like not those affected oaths;
Speak plainly, man: what think'st thou of my words?

Bra. Nothing, sir, but wish my fortunes were as happy as my service should be honest.

Kno. Well, follow me, I'll prove thee, if thy deeds Will carry a proportion to thy words. [*Exit.*

Bra. Yes, sir, straight, I'll but garter my hose. O that my belly were hooped now, for I am ready to burst with laughing! never was bottle or bagpipe fuller. 'Slid, was there ever seen a fox in years to betray himself thus? Now shall I be possess'd of all his counsels: and, by that conduit, my young master. Well, he is resolv'd to prove my honesty; faith, and I am resolv'd to prove his patience: oh, I shall abuse him intolerably. This small piece of service will bring him clean out of love with the soldier for ever. He will never come within the sign of it, the sight of a cassock, or a musket-rest again. He will hate the musters at Mile-end for it, to his dying day. It's no matter, let the world think me a bad counterfeit if I cannot give him the slip at an instant; why, this is better than to have stayed his journey! well, I'll follow him: oh, how I long to be employed.

ACT III. SCENE I

The Old Jewry.

A room in the Windmill Tavern.

Enter Matthew, Wellbred, *and* Bobadil.

Mat. Yes, faith, sir, we were at your lodging to seek you, too.

Wel. Oh, I came not there to-night.

Bob. Your brother delivered us as much.

Wel. Who, my brother Downright?

Bob. He. Mr. Wellbred, I know not in what kind you hold me, but let me say to you this: as sure as honour, I esteem it so much out of the sunshine of reputation, to throw the least beam of regard upon such a——

Wel. Sir, I must hear no ill words of my brother.

Bob. I protest to you, as I have a thing to be saved about me, I never saw any gentlemanlike part——

Wel. Good Captain, 'faces about', to some other discourse.

Bob. With your leave, sir, and there were no more men living upon the face of the earth, I should not fancy him, by St. George.

Mat. Troth, nor I, he is of a rustical cut, I know not how: he doth not carry himself like a gentleman of fashion——

Wel. Oh, Mr. Matthew, that's a grace peculiar but to a few; *quos aequus amavit Jupiter.*

Mat. I understand you, sir.

Young Knowell enters with Stephen.

Wel. No question, you do, or you do not, sir. Ned Knowell! by my soul, welcome; how doest thou sweet spirit, my Genius? 'Slid, I shall love Apollo, and the mad Thespian girls the better, while I live, for this; my dear fury, now I see there's some love in thee! Sirrah, these be the two I writ to thee of. Nay, what a drowsy humour is this, now? why doest thou not speak?

E. Kn. Oh, you are a fine gallant, you sent me a rare letter!

Wel. Why, was't not rare?

E. Kn. Yes, I'll be sworn, I was ne'er guilty of reading the like; match it in all Pliny, or Symmachus' epistles, and I'll have my judgement burn'd in the ear for a rogue: make much of thy vein, for it is inimitable. But I marvel what camel it was that had the carriage of it? For doubtless he was no ordinary beast that brought it!

Wel. Why?

E. Kn. Why, sayest thou? why do'st thou think that any reasonable creature, especially in the morning (the sober time of the day too) could have mista'en my father for me?

Wel. 'Slid, you jest, I hope?

E. Kn. Indeed, the best use we can turn it to is to make a jest on't now: but I'll assure you my father had the full view o' your flourishing style some hour before I saw it.

Wel. What a dull slave was this? But, sirrah, what said he to it, i' faith?

E. Kn. Nay, I know not what he said: but I have a shrewd guess what he thought.

Wel. What? what?

E. Kn. Marry, that thou art some strange dissolute young fellow, and I a grain or two better, for keeping thee company.

Wel. Tut, that thought is like the moon in her last quarter, 'twill change shortly: but, sirrah, I pray thee be acquainted with my two hang-by's, here; thou wilt take exceeding pleasure in 'em, if thou hear'st 'em once go: my wind-instruments. I'll wind 'em up—but what strange piece of silence is this? the sign of the dumb man?

E. Kn. Oh, sir, a kinsman of mine, one that may make your music the fuller, and he please; he has his humour, sir.

Wel. Oh, what is 't? what is 't?

E. Kn. Nay, I'll neither do your judgement nor his folly that wrong, as to prepare your apprehension: I'll leave him to the mercy o' your search; if you can take him, so.

Wel. Well, Captain Bobadil, Mr. Matthew, pray you know this gentleman here, he is a friend of mine, and one that will deserve your affection. I know not your name, sir, [*To* Master Stephen] but I shall be glad of any occasion to render me more familiar to you.

Ste. My name is Mr. Stephen, sir; I am this gentleman's own cousin, sir; his father is mine uncle, sir; I am somewhat melancholy, but you shall command me, sir, in whatsoever is incident to a gentleman.

Bob. [*To* Knowell.] Sir, I must tell you this, I am no general man, but for Mr. Wellbred's sake (you may embrace it at what height of favour you please) I do communicate with you: and conceive you to be a gentleman of some parts; I love few words.

E. Kn. And I fewer, sir. I have scarce enow to thank you.

Mat. [*To* Master Stephen.] But are you indeed, sir, so given to it?

Ste. Aye, truly, sir, I am mightily given to melancholy.

Mat. Oh, it's your only fine humour, sir, your true

melancholy breeds your perfect fine wit, sir: I am melancholy myself divers times, sir, and then do I no more but take pen and paper presently, and overflow you half a score, or a dozen, of sonnets at a sitting.

E. Kn. Sure, he utters them then, by the gross. [*Aside.*

Ste. Truly, sir, and I love such things out of measure.

E. Kn. Aye, faith, better than in measure, I'll undertake.

Mat. Why, I pray you, sir, make use of my study, it's at your service.

Ste. I thank you, sir, I shall be bold, I warrant you; have you a stool there to be melancholy upon?

Mat. That I have, sir, and some papers there of mine own doing, at idle hours, that you'll say there's some sparks of wit in 'em, when you see them.

Wel. Would the sparks would kindle once, and become a fire amongst 'em, I might see self-love burn't for her heresy. [*Aside.*

Ste. Cousin, is it well? am I melancholy enough?

E. Kn. Oh aye, excellent!

Wel. Captain Bobadil, why muse you so?

E. Kn. He is melancholy, too.

Bob. Faith, sir, I was thinking of a most honourable piece of service was perform'd to-morrow, being St. Mark's day: shall be some ten years, now?

E. Kn. In what place, Captain?

Bob. Why, at the beleag'ring of Strigonium, where, in less than two hours, seven hundred resolute gentlemen as any were in Europe, lost their lives upon the breach. I'll tell you, gentlemen, it was the first but the best leaguer that ever I beheld, with these eyes, except the taking in of— what do you call it, last year, by the Genowayes, but that (of all other) was the most fatal and dangerous exploit that ever I was rang'd in, since I first bore arms before the face of the enemy, as I am a gentleman and soldier.

Ste. So, I had as lief as an angel I could swear as well as that gentleman!

E. Kn. Then, you were a servitor at both, it seems! at Strigonium? and what do you call't?

Bob. Oh lord, sir? by St. George, I was the first man that entered the breach: and, had I not effected it with resolution, I had been slain, if I had had a million of lives.

E. Kn. 'Twas pity you had not ten; a cat's, and your own i' faith. But was it possible?   [*Aside.*

Mat. [*Aside to* Stephen.] 'Pray you, mark this discourse, sir.

Ste. So I do.

Bob. I assure you (upon my reputation) 'tis true, and yourself shall confess.

E. Kn. You must bring me to the rack, first.   [*Aside.*

Bob. Observe me judicially, sweet sir, they had planted me three demi-culverins, just in the mouth of the breach; now, sir (as we were to give on), their master gunner (a man of no mean skill and mark, you must think) confronts me with his linstock, ready to give fire; I, spying his intendment, discharg'd my petronel in his bosom, and with these single arms, my poor rapier, ran violently upon the Moors that guarded the ordinance, and put 'em pell-mell to the sword.

Wel. To the sword? to the rapier, Captain?

E. Kn. Oh, it was a good figure observ'd, sir! but did you all this, Captain, without hurting your blade?

Bob. Without any impeach o' the earth: you shall perceive, sir. [*Shows his rapier.*] It is the most fortunate weapon that ever rid on poor gentleman's thigh: shall I tell you, sir? you talk of Morglay, Excalibur, Durindana, or so? tut, I lend no credit to that is fabled of 'em; I know the virtue of mine own, and therefore I dare the boldlier maintain it.

Ste. I marvel whether it be a Toledo or no?

Bob. A most perfect Toledo, I assure you, sir.

Ste. I have a countryman of his, here.

Mat. Pray you, let's see, sir: yes, faith, it is!

Bob. This a Toledo? pish.

Ste. Why do you pish, Captain?

Bob. A Fleming, by heaven, I'll buy them for a guilder a-piece, an' I would have a thousand of them.

E. Kn. How say you, cousin? I told you thus much?

Wel. Where bought you it, Mr. Stephen?

Ste. Of a scurvy rogue soldier (a hundred of lice go with him). He swore it was a Toledo.

Bob. A poor provant rapier, no better.

Mat. Mass, I think it be, indeed! now I look on't better.

E. Kn. Nay, the longer you look on't, the worse. Put it up, put it up.

Ste. Well, I will put it up, but by——(I ha' forgot the Captain's oath, I thought to ha' sworn by it) an' e'er I meet him——

Wel. O, it is past help now, sir, you must have patience.

Ste. Whorson coney-catching rascal! I could eat the very hilts for anger!

E. Kn. A sign of good digestion! you have an ostrich stomach, cousin.

Ste. A stomach? would I had him here, you should see an' I had a stomach.

Wel. It's better as 'tis: come, gentlemen, shall we go?

Enter Brainworm, *disguised as before.*

E. Kn. A miracle, cousin, look here! look here!

Ste. Oh, god's lid, by your leave, do you know me, sir?

Bra. Aye, sir, I know you by sight.

Ste. You sold me a rapier, did you not?

Bra. Yes, marry did I, sir.

Ste. You said it was a Toledo, ha?

Bra. True, I did so.

Ste. But it is none?

Bra. No, sir, I confess it; it is none.

Ste. Do you confess it? gentlemen, bear witness, he has confess'd it. By god's will, and you had not confess'd it——

E. Kn. Oh cousin, forbear, forbear.

Ste. Nay, I have done, cousin.

Wel. Why, you have done like a gentleman, he has confess'd it, what would you more?

Ste. Yet, by his leave, he is a rascal, under his favour, do you see?

E. Kn. Aye, by his leave, he is, and under favour: a pretty piece of civility! Sirrah, how do'st thou like him?

43

Wel. Oh, it's a most precious fool, make much on him: I can compare him to nothing more happily than a drum; for every one may play upon him.

E. Kn. No, no, a child's whistle were far the fitter.

Bra. Sir, shall I entreat a word with you?

E. Kn. With me, sir? you have not another Toledo to sell, ha' you?

Bra. You are conceited, sir; your name is Mr. Knowell, as I take it?

E. Kn. You are i'the right; you mean not to proceed in the catechism, do you?

Bra. No, sir, I am none of that coat.

E. Kn. Of as bare a coat, though; well, say, sir.

Bra. [*Aside to E. Kn.*] 'Faith, sir, I am but servant to the drum extraordinary, and indeed (this smoky varnish being wash'd off, and three or four patches remov'd) I appear your worship's in reversion, after the decease of your good father, Brainworm.

E. Kn. Brainworm! 'Slight, what breath of a conjurer hath blown thee hither in this shape?

Bra. The breath o' your letter, sir, this morning: the same that blew you to the Windmill, and your father after you.

E. Kn. My father?

Bra. Nay, never start; 'tis true he has follow'd you over the fields, by the foot, as you would do a hare i' the snow.

E. Kn. Sirra, Wellbred, what shall we do, sirra? my father is come over, after me.

Wel. Thy father? where is he?

Bra. At Justice Clement's house here, in Colman-street, where he but stays my return; and then——

Wel. Who's this? Brainworm?

Bra. The same, sir.

Wel. Why how, i' the name of wit, com'st thou transmuted thus?

Bra. Faith, a device, a device: nay, for the love of reason, gentlemen, and avoiding the danger, stand not here, withdraw, and I'll tell you all.

Wel. But, art thou sure he will stay thy return?

Bra. Do I live, sir? what a question is that?

Wel. We'll prorogue his expectation then, a little: Brain-worm, thou shalt go with us. Come on, gentlemen, nay, I pray thee, sweet Ned, droop not: 'heart, and our wits be so wretchedly dull, that one old plodding brain can outstrip us all, would we were e'en press'd to make porters of; and serve out the remnant of our days in Thames-street, or at Custom-house quay, in a civil war against the carmen.

Bra. Amen, Amen, Amen, say I.

ACT III. SCENE II

The Old Jewry.

Kitely's *warehouse.*

Enter Kitely *and* Cash.

Kit. What says he, Thomas? Did you speak with him?

Cas. He will expect you, sir, within this half hour.

Kit. Has he the money ready, can you tell?

Cas. Yes, sir, the money was brought in last night.

Kit. O, that's well: fetch me my cloak, my cloak.

[*Exit* Cash.

Stay, let me see, an hour to go and come;
Aye that will be the least: and then 'twill be
An hour, before I can dispatch with him;
Or very near: well, I will say two hours.
Two hours? ha? things, never dreamt of yet,
May be contrived, aye, and effected too,
In two hours' absence: well, I will not go.
Two hours; no, fleering Opportunity,
I will not give your subtlety that scope.
Who will not judge him worthy to be robb'd
That sets his doors wide open to a thief
And shows the felon where his treasure lies?
Again, what earthy spirit but will attempt
To taste the fruit of beauty's golden tree,
When leaden sleep seals up the Dragon's eyes?
I will not go. Business, go by, for once.

No, beauty, no; you are of too good caract,
To be left so, without a guard, or open!
Your lustre too'll enflame, at any distance,
Draw courtship to you, as a jet doth straws,
Put motion in a stone, strike fire from ice,
Nay, make a porter leap you with his burden!
You must be then kept up, close, and well-watch'd,
For, give you opportunity, no quick-sand
Devours or swallows swifter! He that lends
His wife (if she be fair) or time, or place;
Compels her to be false. I will not go.
The dangers are too many. And then, the dressing
Is a most main attractive! Our great heads,
Within the City, never were in safety
Since our little wives wore these little caps: I'll change 'em,
I'll change 'em, straight, in mine. Mine shall no more
Wear three-pil'd acorns, to make my horns ache.
Nor will I go. I am resolv'd for that.

Re-enter Cash *with cloak.*

Carry in my cloak again. Yet, stay. Yet, do too.
I will defer going, on all occasions.

   Cas. Sir. Snare, your scrivener, will be there with th'
bonds.

   Kit. That's true! fool on me! I had clean forgot it,
I must go. What's a clock?

   Cas.   Exchange time, sir.

   Kit. 'Heart, then will Wellbred presently be here, too,
With one or other of his loose consorts.
I am a knave, if I know what to say,
What course to take, or which way to resolve.
My brain (methinks) is like an hour-glass,
Wherein my imaginations run like sands,
Filling up time; but then are turn'd and turn'd:
So that I know not what to stay upon,
And less, to put in act. It shall be so.
Nay, I dare build upon his secrecy,
He knows not to deceive me. Thomas?

   Cas.   Sir.

Kit. Yet now, I have bethought me, too, I will not.
Thomas, is Cob within?

Cas.   I think he be, sir.

Kit. But he'll prate too, there's no speech of him.
No, there were no man o' the earth to Thomas,
If I durst trust him; there is all the doubt.
But, should he have a chink in him, I were gone,
Lost i' my fame for ever: talk for th' Exchange.
The manner he hath stood with, till this present,
Doth promise no such change! what should I fear then?
Well, come what will, I'll tempt my fortune, once.
Thomas—you may deceive me, but I hope—
Your love to me is more——

Cas.   Sir, if a servant's
Duty, with faith, may be call'd love, you are
More than in hope, you are possess'd of it.

Kit. I thank you, heartily, Thomas; gi' me your hand:
With all my heart, good Thomas. I have, Thomas,
A secret to impart unto you—but
When once you have it, I must seal your lips up:
(So far I tell you, Thomas).

Cas.   Sir, for that——

Kit. Nay, hear me out. Think, I esteem you, Thomas,
When I will let you in, thus, to my private.
It is a thing sits nearer to my crest,
Than thou art 'ware of, Thomas. If thou should'st
Reveal it, but——

Cas.   How? I reveal it?

Kit.   Nay,
I do not think thou would'st; but if thou should'st:
'Twere a great weakness.

Cas.   A great treachery.
Give it no other name.

Kit.   Thou wilt not do't, then?

Cas. Sir, if I do, mankind disclaim me ever.

Kit. He will not swear, he has some reservation,
Some conceal'd purpose, and close meaning, sure:
Else (being urg'd so much) how should he choose
But lend an oath to all this protestation?

He's no precisian, that I am certain of.
Nor rigid Roman Catholic. He'll play
At Fayles, and Tick-tack, I have heard him swear.
What should I think of it? urge him again,
And by some other way? I will do so.   [*Aside.*
Well, Thomas, thou hast sworn not to disclose;
Yes, you did swear?

    Cas.   Not yet, sir, but I will,
Please you——

    Kit.   No, Thomas, I dare take thy word.
But; if thou wilt swear, do, as thou think'st good;
I am resolv'd without it; at thy pleasure.

    Cas. By my soul's safety then, sir, I protest
My tongue shall ne'er take knowledge of a word,
Deliver'd me in nature of your trust.

    Kit. It's too much, these ceremonies need not;
I know thy faith to be as firm as rock.
Thomas, come hither, near: we cannot be
Too private in this business. So it is,
(Now he has sworn I dare the safelier venture)   [*Aside.*
I have of late, by divers observations——
(But, whether his oath can bind him, yea, or no;
Being not taken lawfully? ha? say you?
I will ask counsel ere I do proceed:)   [*Aside.*
Thomas, it will be now too long to stay,
I'll spy some fitter time soon, or to-morrow.

    Cas. Sir, at your pleasure.

    Kit.   I will think. And Thomas,
I pray you search the books 'gainst my return,
For the receipts 'twixt me and Traps.

    Cas.   I will, sir.

    Kit. And, hear you, if your mistress's brother, Wellbred,
Chance to bring hither any gentlemen,
Ere I come back; let one straight bring me word.

    Cas. Very well, sir.

    Kit.   To the Exchange; do you hear?
Or here in Colman-street, to Justice Clement's.
Forget it not, nor be not out of the way.

    Cas. I will not, sir.

Kit.   I pray you have a care on't.
Or whether he come, or no, if any other
Stranger, or else, fail not to send me word.

Cas. I shall not, sir.

Kit.   Be't your special business
Now to remember it.

Cas.   Sir, I warrant you.

Kit. But, Thomas, this is not the secret, Thomas,
I told you of.

Cas.   No, sir. I do suppose it.

Kit. Believe me, it is not.

Cas.   Sir, I do believe you.

Kit. By heaven, it is not, that's enough. But, Thomas,
I would not you should utter it, do you see?
To any creature living, yet, I care not.
Well, I must hence. Thomas, conceive thus much:
It was a trial of you, when I meant
So deep a secret to you, I mean not this,
But that I have to tell you; this is nothing, this.
But Thomas, keep this from my wife, I charge you,
Lock'd up in silence, midnight, buried here.
No greater hell, than to be slave to fear.   [*Exit* Kitely.

Cas. Lock'd up in silence, midnight, buried here.
Whence should this flood of passion (trow) take head? ha?
Best dream no longer of this running humour,
For fear I sink! the violence of the stream
Already hath transported me so far,
That I can feel no ground at all! but soft,
Oh, 'tis our water-bearer: somewhat has cross'd him now.

Enter Cob.

Cob. Fasting days? what tell you me of fasting days?
'Slid, would they were all on a light fire for me: They say
the whole world shall be consum'd with fire one day, but
would I had these ember-weeks, and villanous Fridays
burnt in the meantime, and then——

Cas. Why, how now, Cob, what moves thee to this
choler? ha?

Cob. Collar, master Thomas? I scorn your collar, aye,

sir, I am none o' your cart-horse, though I carry, and draw water. An' you offer to ride me, with your collar, or halter either, I may hap show you a jade's trick, sir.

Cas. O, you'll slip your head out of the collar? Why, goodman Cob, you mistake me.

Cob. Nay, I have my rheum and I can be angry as well as another, sir.

Cas. Thy rheum, Cob? thy humour, thy humour? thou mistak'st.

Cob. Humour? mack, I think it be so, indeed: what is that humour? some rare thing, I warrant.

Cas. Marry, I'll tell thee, Cob. It is a gentleman-like monster, bred in the special gallantry of our time, by affectation; and fed by folly.

Cob. How? must it be fed?

Cas. Oh aye, humour is nothing if it be not fed. Didst thou never hear that? it's a common phrase, 'Feed my humour.'

Cob. I'll none on it: Humour, avaunt, I know you not, be gone. Let who will make hungry meals for your monstership, it shall not be I. Feed you, quoth he? 'Slid, I ha' much ado to feed myself; especially on these lean rascally days, too; an't had been any other day but a fasting-day (a plague on them all for me) by this light, one might have done the commonwealth good service, and have drown'd them all i' the flood, two or three hundred thousand years ago. O, I do stomach them hugely! I have a maw now, and't were for Sir Bevis his horse, against 'em.

Cas. I pray thee, good Cob, what makes thee so out of love with fasting days?

Cob. Marry that which will make any man out of love with 'em, I think: their bad conditions, and you will needs know. First, they are of a Flemish breed, I am sure on't, for they raven up more butter than all the days of the week beside; next, they stink of fish and leek-porridge miserably: thirdly, they'll keep a man devoutly hungry all day, and at night send him supperless to bed.

Cas. Indeed, these are faults, Cob.

Cob. Nay, and this were all, 'twere something, but they

are the only known enemies to my generation. A fasting-day no sooner comes but my lineage goes to rack, poor cobs they smoke for it, they are made martyrs o' the gridiron, they melt in passion: and your maids too know this, and yet would have me turn Hannibal [*He pulls out a red herring*] and eat my own fish and blood. My princely coz, fear nothing; I have not the heart to devour you, and I might be made as rich as King Cophetua. O, that I had room for my tears, I could weep salt-water enough now to preserve the lives of ten thousand of my kin. But I may curse none but these filthy Almanacks, for an't were not for them, these days of persecution would ne'er be known. I'll be hang'd, an' some fishmonger's son do not make of 'em; and puts in more fasting days than he should do, because he would utter his father's dried stock-fish and stinking conger.

Cas. 'Slight, peace, thou'lt be beaten like a stock-fish, else: here is Mr. Matthew. Now must I look out for a messenger to my master.   [*Exeunt.*

Enter Wellbred, Ed. Knowell, Brainworm, Bobadil, Matthew, *and* Stephen.

Wel. Beshrew me, but it was an absolute good jest, and exceedingly well carried!

E. Kn. Aye, and our ignorance maintain'd it as well, did it not?

Wel. Yes, faith, but was't possible thou should'st not know him? I forgive Mr. Stephen, for he is stupidity itself!

E. Kn. 'Fore god, not I, and I might have been join'd pattern with one of the seven wise masters, for knowing him. He had so written himself into the habit of one of your poor Infanterie, your decay'd, ruinous, worm-eaten gentlemen of the round: such as have vowed to sit on the 'skirts of the city, let your Provost and his half-dozen of halberdiers do what they can; and have translated begging out of the old hackney pace, to a fine easy amble, and made it run as smooth off the tongue as a shove-groat shilling. Into the likeness of one of these Reformados had he moulded himself so perfectly, observing every trick of their action, as varying the accent, swearing with an emphasis, indeed all, with so special and exquisite a grace, that (hadst thou seen him) thou would'st have sworn he might have been Serjeant-Major, if not Lieutenant-Colonel to the regiment.

Wel. Why, Brainworm, who would have thought thou hadst been such an artificer?

E. Kn. An artificer! An architect! except a man had studied begging all his lifetime, and been a weaver of language from his infancy for the clothing of it! I never saw his rival.

Wel. Where got'st thou this coat, I marvel?

Bra. Of a Houndsditch man, sir. One of the devil's near kinsmen, a broker.

Wel. That cannot be, if the proverb hold; for a crafty knave needs no broker.

Bra. True, sir, but I did need a broker, *Ergo*.

Wel. Well put off! no crafty knave, you'll say.

E. Kn. Tut, he has more of these shifts.

Bra. And yet where I have one, the broker has ten, sir.

Re-enter Cash.

Cas. Francis, Martin, ne'er a one to be found, now? what a spite's this?

Wel. How now, Cash? is my brother Kitely within?

Cas. No sir, my master went forth e'en now: but master Downright is within. Cob! what, Cob? is he gone too?

Wel. Whither went your master, Cash? canst thou tell?

Cas. I know not, to Justice Clement's I think, sir. Cob!
[*Exit.*

E. Kn. Justice Clement, what's he?

Wel. Why, dost thou not know him? he is a city magistrate, a Justice here, an excellent good lawyer, and a great scholar: but the only mad, merry old fellow in Europe! I show'd him you, the other day.

E. Kn. Oh, is that he? I remember him now. Good faith, and he has a very strange presence, methinks; it shows as if he stood out of the rank from other men: I have heard many of his jests i' the university. They say he will commit a man for taking the wall of his horse.

Wel. Aye, or wearing his cloak of one shoulder, or serving of God: anything indeed, if it come in the way of his humour.

Cas. Gasper! Martin! Cob! 'Heart, where should they be, trow? [*Cash comes in and out calling.*

Bob. Master Kitely's man, prithee vouchsafe us the lighting of this match.

Cas. Fire on your match, no time but now to vouchsafe? Francis! Cob! [*Exit.*

Bob. Body of me! here's the remainder of seven pound, since yesterday was seven-night. 'Tis your right Trinidado! did you never take any, master Stephen?

Ste. No truly, sir; but I'll learn to take it now, since you commend it so.

Bob. Sir, believe me (upon my relation) for what I tell you, the world shall not reprove. I have been in the Indies (where this herb grows) where neither myself, nor a dozen gentlemen more (of my knowledge) have received the taste of any other nutriment in the world, for the space of one and twenty weeks, but the fume of this simple only. Therefore it cannot be, but 'tis most divine! Further, take it in the nature, in the true kind so, it makes an antidote, that (had you taken the most deadly poisonous plant in all Italy) it should expel it and clarify you, with as much ease as I speak. And, for your green wound, your Balsamum, and your St. John's wort are all mere gulleries, and trash to it, especially your Trinidado: your Nicotian is good too. I could say what I know of the virtue of it, for the expulsion of rheums, raw humours, crudities, obstructions, with a thousand of this kind; but I profess myself no quack-salver. Only, thus much, by Hercules, I do hold it, and will affirm it (before any Prince in Europe) to be the most sovereign and precious weed that ever the earth tendered to the use of man.

E. Kn. This speech would ha' done decently in a tobacco trader's mouth!

Re-enter Cash *with* Cob.

Cas. At Justice Clement's he is: in the middle of Colman-street.

Cob. O, oh?

Bob. Where's the match I gave thee? Master Kitely's man?

Cas. Would his match, and he, and pipe, and all were at Sancto Domingo! I had forgot it.   [*Exit.*

Cob. By God's me, I marvel what pleasure or felicity they have in taking this roguish tobacco! it's good for nothing but to choke a man and fill him full of smoke and embers: there were four died out of one house, last week, with taking of it, and two more the bell went for, yester-night; one of them (they say) will ne'er 'scape it: he voided a bushel of soot yesterday, upward and downward. By the stocks, an' there were no wiser men than I, I'd have it present whipping, man or woman, that should but deal with a tobacco pipe; why, it will stifle them all in the end, as many as use it; it's little better than rats-bane, or rosaker.

           [*Bobadil* beats him with a cudgel.

All. Oh, good Captain, hold, hold.

Bob. You base cullion, you.

Re-enter Cash.

Cas. Sir, here's your match: come, thou must needs be talking, too, tho'art well enough serv'd.

Cob. Nay, he will not meddle with his match, I warrant you: well, it shall be a dear beating, an' I live.

Bob. Do you prate? Do you murmur?

E. Kn. Nay, good Captain, will you regard the humour of a fool? away, knave.

Wel. Cash, get him away.   [*Exit* Cash *with* Cob.

Bob. A whorson filthy slave, a dung-worm, an excre-ment! Body o' Caesar, but that I scorn to let forth so mean a spirit, I'd ha' stabb'd him into the earth.

Wel. Marry, the law forbid, sir.

Bob. By Pharaoh's foot, I would have done it.

Ste. Oh, he swears admirably! 'By Pharaoh's foot', 'body

of Caesar' I shall never do it, sure, upon mine honour, and by St. George, no, I ha' not the right grace.

Mat. Master Stephen, will you any? By this air, the most divine tobacco, that ever I drunk!

Ste. None, I thank you, sir. O, this gentleman does it rarely too! but nothing like the other. 'By this air', as I am a gentleman: 'by——'   [*Exeunt* Mat. *and* Bob.

Bra. Master, glance, glance! Master Wellbred!

                    [*Master Stephen is practising to the post.*

Ste. As I have somewhat to be saved, I protest——

Wel. You are a fool: it needs no affidavit.

E. Kn. Cousin, will you any tobacco?

Ste. Aye, sir! upon my reputation——

E. Kn. How now, cousin!

Ste. I protest, as I am a gentleman, but no soldier, indeed——

Wel. No, master Stephen? as I remember your name is entered in the artillery garden?

Ste. Aye, sir, that's true: Cousin, may I swear, as I am a soldier, by that?

E. Kn. Oh yes, that you may. It's all you have for your money.

Ste. Then, as I am a gentleman, and a soldier, it is divine tobacco!

Wel. But soft, where's Mr. Matthew? gone?

Bra. No, sir, they went in here.

Wel. O, let's follow them: master Matthew is gone to salute his mistress in verse. We shall ha' the happiness to hear some of his poetry now. He never comes unfurnish'd. Brainworm?

Ste. Brainworm? Where? Is this Brainworm?

E. Kn. Aye, cousin, no words of it, upon your gentility.

Ste. Not I, body of me, by this air, St. George, and the foot of Pharaoh.

Wel. Rare! your cousin's discourse is simply drawn out with oaths.

E. Kn. 'Tis larded with 'em. A kind of French dressing, if you love it.   [*Exeunt.*

ACT III. SCENE III

Colman-street.

A room in Justice Clement's *house.*

Enter Kitely *and* Cob.

Kit. Ha? how many are there, sayest thou?

Cob. Marry sir, your brother, master Wellbred——

Kit. Tut, beside him: what strangers are there, man?

Cob. Strangers? let me see, one, two; master I know not
well, there are so many.

Kit. How? so many?

Cob. Aye, there's some five, or six of them, at the most.

Kit. A swarm, a swarm.
Spite of the devil, how they sting my head.
With forked stings, thus wide, and large! But, Cob
How long hast thou been coming hither, Cob?

Cob. A little while, sir.

Kit. Did'st thou come running?

Cob. No, sir.

Kit. Nay, then I am familiar with thy haste!
Bane to my fortunes: what meant I to marry?
I, that before was rank'd in such content,
My mind at rest too, in so soft a peace,
Being free master of mine own free thoughts,
And now become a slave? What? never sigh,
Be of good cheer, man: for thou art a cuckold,
'Tis done, 'tis done! nay, when such flowing store,
Plenty itself, falls in my wife's lap,
The Cornucopiae will be mine, I know. But, Cob,
What entertainment had they? I am sure
My sister, and my wife, would bid them welcome! ha?

Cob. Like enough, sir, yet I heard not a word of it.

Kit. No: their lips were seal'd with kisses, and the voice,
Drown'd in a flood of joy at their arrival,
Had lost her motion, state, and faculty.
Cob, which of them was't, that first kiss'd my wife,

My sister, I should say? My wife, alas!
I fear not her: ha? who was it, say'st thou?

Cob. By my troth, sir, will you have the truth of it?

Kit. Oh aye, good Cob: I pray thee, heartily.

Cob. Then I am a vagabond, and fitter for Bridewell than your worship's company, if I saw anybody to be kiss'd, unless they would have kiss'd the post, in the middle of the warehouse; for there I left them all, at their tobacco with a pox.

Kit. How? Were they not gone in, then, e'er thou cam'st?

Cob. Oh no, sir.

Kit. Spite of the devil! what do I stay here, then?
Cob, follow me. [*Exit.*

Cob. Nay, soft and fair, I have eggs on the spit; I cannot go yet, sir. Now am I for some five and fifty reasons hammering, hammering revenge: oh, for three or four gallons of vinegar, to sharpen my wits. Revenge: vinegar revenge: vinegar and mustard revenge: nay, and he had not lain in my house, 't would never have griev'd me, but being my guest, one, that I'll be sworn, my wife has lent him her smock off her back, while his one shirt has been at washing; pawn'd her neckerchers for clean bands for him; sold almost all my platters, to buy him tobacco, and he to turn monster of ingratitude, and strike his lawful host! well, I hope to raise up a host of fury for't: here comes Justice Clement.

Enter Justice Clement, Knowell, *and* Formal.

Clem. What's, master Kitely gone? Roger?

For.   Aye, sir.

Clem. 'Heart of me! what made him leave us so abruptly! How now, sirra? what make you here? what would you have, ha?

Cob. An't please your worship, I am a poor neighbour of your worship's——

Clem. A poor neighbour of mine? why, speak, poor neighbour.

Cob. I dwell, sir, at the sign of the water-tankard, hard

by the green lattice: I have paid scot and lot there, any time this eighteen years.

Clem. To the green lattice?

Cob. No, sir, to the parish: marry, I have seldom scap'd scot-free at the lattice.

Clem. O, well! what business has my poor neighbour with me?

Cob. An't like your worship, I am come to crave the peace of your worship.

Clem. Of me, knave? peace of me, knave? did I e'er hurt thee? or threaten thee? or wrong thee? ha?

Cob. No, sir, but your worship's warrant, for one that has wrong'd me, sir: his arms are at too much liberty; I would fain have them bound to a treaty of peace, an' my credit could compass it with your worship.

Clem. Thou goest far enough about for 't, I am sure.

Kno. Why, dost thou go in danger of thy life for him, friend?

Cob. No sir; but I go in danger of my death, every hour, by his means: an' I die, within a twelve-month and a day, I may swear by the law of the land that he kill'd me.

Clem. How? how knave? swear he kill'd thee? and by the law? what pretence? what colour hast thou for that?

Cob. Marry, and't please your worship, both black and blue; colour enough, I warrant you. I have it here, to show your worship.

Clem. What is he that gave you this, sirrah?

Cob. A gentleman and a soldier, he says he is, o' the City here.

Clem. A soldier o' the City? What call you him?

Cob. Captain Bobadil.

Clem. Bobadil? And why did he bob and beat you, sirrah? How began the quarrel betwixt you: ha? speak truly, knave, I advise you.

Cob. Marry, indeed, and please your worship, only because I spake against their vagrant tobacco, as I came by 'em, when they were taking on 't, for nothing else.

Clem. Ha? you speak against tobacco? Formal, his name.

For. What's your name, sirrah?

Cob. Oliver, sir, Oliver Cob, sir.

Clem. Tell Oliver Cob he shall go to the jail, Formal.

For. Oliver Cob, my master, Justice Clement, says, you shall go to the jail.

Cob. O, I beseech your worship, for God's sake, dear master Justice.

Clem. Nay, God's precious: an such drunkards and tankards, as you are, come to dispute of tobacco once; I have done! away with him.

Cob. O, good master Justice, sweet old gentleman.

Kno. Sweet Oliver, would I could do thee any good: Justice Clement, let me entreat you, sir.

Clem. What? a threadbare rascal! a beggar! a slave that never drunk out of better than piss-pot metal in his life! and he to deprave and abuse the virtue of a herb so generally receiv'd in the courts of princes, the chambers of nobles, the bowers of sweet ladies, the cabins of soldiers! Roger, away with him, by God's precious—I say, go to.

Cob. Dear master Justice, let me be beaten again, I have deserv'd it: but not the prison, I beseech you.

Kno. Alas, poor Oliver!

Clem. Roger, make him a warrant; he shall not go, I but fear the knave.

For. Do not stink, sweet Oliver, you shall not go, my master will give you a warrant.

Cob. O, the Lord maintain his worship, his worthy worship.

Clem. Away, dispatch him. [*Exit* Formal *with* Cob. How now, master Knowell! In dumps? In dumps? Come, this becomes not.

Kno. Sir, would I could not feel my cares——

Clem. Your cares are nothing! they are like my cap, soon put on, and as soon put off. What? your son is old enough to govern himself: let him run his course, it's the only way to make him a staid man. If he were an unthrift, a ruffian, a drunkard, or a licentious liver, then you had reason; you had reason to take care: but, being none of these, mirth's my witness, an' I had twice so many cares as you have, I'd drown them all in a cup of sack. Come, come, let's try it: I muse, your parcel of a soldier returns not all this while. *[Exeunt.*

ACT IV. SCENE I

A room in Kitely's *house.*

Enter Downright *and* Dame Kitely.

Dow. Well, sister, I tell you true: and you'll find it so, in the end.

Dame. Alas, brother, what would you have me to do? I cannot help it: you see, my brother brings 'em in here, they are his friends.

Dow. His friends? his friends. 'Slud, they do nothing but haunt him, up and down, like a sort of unlucky spirits, and tempt him to all manner of villany that can be thought of. Well, by this light, a little thing would make me play the devil with some of 'em; and 't were not more for your husband's sake, than anything else, I'd make the house too hot for the best on 'em: they should say and swear hell were broken loose, ere they went hence. But, by God's will, 'tis nobody's fault but yours: for, an' you had done as you might have done, they should have been parboil'd, and bak'd too, every mother's son, ere they should ha' come in, e'er a one of 'em.

Dame. God's my life! did you ever hear the like? what a strange man is this! Could I keep out all them, think you? I should put myself against half a dozen men? should I? Good faith, you'd mad the patient'st body in the world, to hear you talk so, without any sense, or reason!

Enter Bridget, Matthew, *and* Bobadil: *followed by* Wellbred, E. Knowell, Stephen, *and* Brainworm.

Brid. Servant (in troth) you are too prodigal
Of your wit's treasure, thus to pour it forth,
Upon so mean a subject, as my worth.

Mat. You say well, mistress; and I mean, as well.

Dow. Hey-day, here is stuff!

Wel. O, now stand close: pray heaven, she can get him to read: He should do it of his own natural impudence.

Brid. Servant, what is this same, I pray you?

Mat. Marry, an Elegy, an Elegy, an odd toy——

Dow. To mock an ape withal. O, I could sew up his mouth, now.

Dame. Sister, I pray you let's hear it.

Dow. Are you rhyme-given, too?

Mat. Mistress, I'll read it, if you please.

Brid. Pray you do, servant.

Dow. O, here's no foppery! Death, I can endure the stocks, better.   [*Exit.*

E. Kn. What ails thy brother? can he not hold his water at reading of a ballad?

Wel. O, no: a rhyme to him is worse than cheese or a bagpipe. But mark, you lose the protestation.

Mat. Faith, I did it in an humour; I know now how it is: but please you come near, sir. This gentleman has judgement, he knows how to censure of a—pray you sir, you can judge.

Ste. Not I, sir: upon my reputation and by the foot of Pharaoh.

Wel. O, chide your cousin for swearing.

E. Kn. Not I, so long as he do's not forswear himself.

Bob. Master Matthew, you abuse the expectation of your dear mistress, and her fair sister: Fie, while you live, avoid this prolixity.

Mat. I shall, sir: well, *Incipere dulce.*

E. Kn. How! *Insipere dulce?* a sweet thing to be a fool, indeed.

Wel. What, do you take *Incipere,* in that sense?

E. Kn. You do not? you? This was your villany to gull him with a *motte.*

Wel. O, the Benchers' phrase: *pauca verba, pauca verba.*

Mat. *Rare creature, let me speak without offence,*
Would God my rude words had the influence,
To rule thy thoughts, as thy fair looks do mine,
Then should'st thou be his prisoner, who is thine.

E. Kn. This is in *Hero and Leander*?

Wel. O, aye! peace, we shall have more of this.

Mat. Be not unkind, and fair, misshapen stuff
Is of behaviour boisterous, and rough:

Wel. How like you that, sir?

[*Master Stephen answers with shaking his head.*

E. Kn. 'Slight, he shakes his head like a bottle, to feel and there be any brain in it!

Mat. But observe the catastrophe, now,
And I in duty will exceed all other,
As you in beauty do excel love's mother.

E. Kn. Well, I'll have him free of the wit-brokers, for he utters nothing but stolen remnants.

Wel. O, forgive it him.

E. Kn. A filching rogue? hang him. And from the dead? it's worse than sacrilege.

Wel. Sister, what ha' you here? verses? pray you, let's see. Who made these verses? they are excellent good!

Mat. O, master Wellbred, 'tis your disposition to say so, sir. They were good i' the morning, I made 'em, *extempore*, this morning.

Wel. How? *extempore*?

Mat. Aye, would I might be hang'd else; ask Captain Bobadil. He saw me write them, at the—(pox on it) the Star, yonder.

Bra. Can he find, in his heart, to curse the stars, so?

E. Kn. Faith, his are even with him: they ha' curs'd him enough already.

Ste. Cousin, how do you like this gentleman's verses?

E. Kn. O, admirable! the best that ever I heard, coz.

Ste. Body o' Caesar! they are admirable!
The best that ever I heard, as I am a soldier.

Re-enter Downright.

Dow. I am vex'd, I can hold ne'er a bone of me still!
Heart, I think they mean to build and breed here!

Wel. Sister, you have a simple servant here, that crowns your beauty with such encomions and devices you may see what it is to be the mistress of a wit! that can make your

62

perfections so transparent, that every bleary eye may look through them, and see him drown'd over head and ears, in the deep well of desire. Sister Kitely, I marvel you get you not a servant that can rhyme and do tricks too.

Dow. O monster! impudence itself! tricks?

Dame. Tricks, brother? what tricks?

Brid. Nay, speak, I pray you, what tricks?

Dame. Aye, never spare anybody here: but say, what tricks?

Brid. Passion of my heart! do tricks?

Wel. 'Slight, here's a trick vied, and revied! why, you monkey, you? what a caterwauling do you keep? has he not given you rhymes, and verses, and tricks?

Dow. O, the fiend!

Wel. Nay, you lamp of virginity, that take it in snuff so! come and cherish this tame *poetical fury* in your servant, you'll be begg'd else, shortly, for a concealment: go to, reward his muse. You cannot give him less than a shilling, in conscience, for the book he had it out of cost him a teston at least. How now, gallants? Mr. Matthew? Captain? What? all sons of silence? no spirit?

Dow. Come, you might practise your ruffian-tricks somewhere else, and not here, I wish; this is no tavern, nor drinking school, to vent your exploits in.

Wel. How now! whose cow has calv'd?

Dow. Marry, that has mine, sir. Nay, boy, never look askance at me for the matter; I'll tell you of it, aye, sir, you, and your companions; mend yourselves when I ha' done.

Wel. My companions?

Dow. Yes, sir, your companions, so I say; I am not afraid of you, nor them neither: your hang-byes here. You must have your poets, and your potlings, your *soldado's*, and *foolado's*, to follow you up and down the City, and here they must come to domineer and swagger. Sirrah, you, ballad-singer, and slops, your fellow there; get you out; get you home: or by this steel I'll cut off your ears, and that presently.

Wel. 'Slight, stay, let's see what he dare do: cut off his ears? cut a whetstone. You are an ass, do you see? touch any man here, and by this hand, I'll run my rapier to the hilts in you.

Dow. Yea, that would I fain see, boy.

They all draw, and they of the house make out to part them.

Dame. O Jesu! murder. Thomas, Gaspar!

Brid. Help, help, Thomas.

E. Kn. Gentlemen, forbear, I pray you.

Bob. Well, sirrah, you, Holofernes: by my hand, I will pink your flesh full of holes with my rapier for this; I will, by this good heaven: [*They offer to fight again and are parted by* Cash *and* Servants *who have entered.*] Nay, let him come, let him come, gentlemen, by the body of St. George, I'll not kill him.

Cas. Hold, hold, good gentlemen.

Dow. You whorson, bragging coystrill!

Enter Kitely.

Kit. [*To them.*] Why, how now? what's the matter? what's the stir here?
Whence springs the quarrel? Thomas! where is he?
Put up your weapons, and put off this rage.
My wife and sister, they are cause of this,
What, Thomas, where is this knave?

Cas. Here, sir.

Wel. Come, let's go: this is one of my brother's ancient humours, this.

Ste. I am glad nobody was hurt by his ancient humour.
[*Exeunt* Wellbred, Bobadil, Stephen, Matthew, Brainworm, *and* Ed. Knowell.

Kit. Why, how now, brother, who enforc'd this brawl?

Dow. A sort of lewd rake-hells, that care neither for God, nor the Devil! And they must come here to read ballads, and roguery, and trash! I'll mar the knot of 'em ere I sleep, perhaps: especially Bob there: he that's all manner of shapes! and *Songs and sonnets,* his fellow.

Brid. Brother, indeed you are too violent,
Too sudden, in your humour: and you know

64

My brother Wellbred's temper will not bear
Any reproof, chiefly in such a presence,
Where every slight disgrace he should receive,
Might wound him in opinion and respect.

Dow. Respect? what talk you of respect 'mong such,
As ha' nor spark of manhood nor good manners?
'Sdeynes I am asham'd to hear you! respect?   [*Exit.*

Brid. Yes, there was one a civil gentleman,
And very worthily demean'd himself!

Kit. O, that was some love of yours, sister!

Brid. A love of mine? I would it were no worse, brother.
You'd pay my portion sooner than you think for.

Dame. Indeed, he seem'd to be a gentleman of an ex-
ceeding fair disposition, and of very excellent good parts!

               [*Exeunt* Dame Kitely *and* Bridget.

Kit. Her love, by heaven! my wife's minion!
Fair disposition? excellent good parts?
Death, these phrases are intolerable!
Good parts? how should she know his parts?
His parts? Well, well, well, well, well, well!
It is too plain, too clear: Thomas, come hither.
What, are they gone?

Cas.   Aye, sir, they went in.
My mistress, and your sister——

Kit. Are any of the gallants within?

Cas. No, sir, they are all gone.

Kit. Art thou sure of it?

Cas. I can assure you, sir.

Kit. What gentleman was that they prais'd so, Thomas?

Cas. One, they call him master Knowell, a handsome
young gentleman, sir.

Kit. Aye, I thought so: my mind gave me as much.
I'll die, but they have hid him i' the house,
Somewhere; I'll go and search: go with me, Thomas.
Be true to me, and thou shalt find me a master.   [*Exeunt.*

ACT IV. SCENE II

The lane before Cob's house.

Enter Cob.

Cob. [*Knocks.*] What, Tib, Tib, I say.

Tib. [*Within.*] How now, what cuckold is that knocks so hard? [*Enter* Tib.] O, husband, is't you? what's the news?

Cob. Nay, you have stunn'd me, i' faith! you ha' given me a knock o' the forehead will stick by me! cuckold? 'Slid, cuckold?

Tib. Away, you fool, did I know it was you that knock'd? Come, come, you may call me as bad when you list.

Cob. May I? Tib, you are a whore.

Tib. You lie in your throat, husband.

Cob. How, the lie? and in my throat too? do you long to be stabb'd, ha?

Tib. Why, you are no soldier, I hope?

Cob. O, must you be stabb'd by a soldier? Mass, that's true! when was Bobadil here? your Captain? that rogue, that foist, that fencing Burgullian? I'll tickle him, i' faith

Tib. Why, what's the matter? trow!

Cob. O, he has basted me, rarely, sumptiously! but I have it here in black and white for his black and blue: shall pay him. O, the Justice! the honestest old brave Trojan in London! I do honour the very flea of his dog. A plague on him though, he put me once in a villanous filthy fear; marry, it vanish'd away like the smoke of tobacco; but I was smok'd soundly first. I thank the devil, and his good angel, my guest. Well, wife, or Tib (which you will) get you in, and lock the door, I charge you, let nobody in to you; wife, nobody in to you: those are my words. Not Captain Bob himself, nor the fiend in his likeness; you are a woman; you have flesh and blood enough in you to be tempted: therefore keep the door shut upon all comers.

Tib. I warrant you there shall nobody enter here without my consent.

Cob. Nor with your consent, sweet Tib, and so I leave you.

Tib. It's more than you know whether you leave me so.

Cob. How?

Tib. Why, sweet.

Cob. Tut, sweet or sour, thou art a flower,
Keep close thy door, I ask no more.   [*Exeunt.*

ACT IV. SCENE III

A room in the Windmill Tavern.

Enter Ed. Knowell, Wellbred, Stephen, *and* Brainworm,
disguised as before.

E. Kn. Well, Brainworm, perform this business happily, and thou makest a purchase of my love, for ever.

Wel. I' faith, now let thy spirits use their best faculties. But, at any hand, remember the message to my brother: for there's no other means to start him.

Bra. I warrant you, sir, fear nothing: I have a nimble soul has wak'd all forces of my fancy by this time, and put 'em in true motion. What you have possess'd me withal, I'll discharge it amply, sir. Make it no question.   [*Exit.*

Wel. Forth, and prosper, Brainworm. Faith, Ned, how dost thou approve of my abilities in this device?

E. Kn. Troth, well, howsoever: but it will come excellent, if it take.

Wel. Take, man? why, it cannot choose but take, if the circumstances miscarry not: but, tell me, ingenuously, dost thou affect my sister Bridget, as thou pretend'st?

E. Kn. Friend, am I worth belief?

Wel. Come, do not protest. In faith, she is a maid of good ornament, and much modesty: and, except I conceiv'd very worthily of her, thou shouldest not have her.

E. Kn. Nay, that I am afraid will be a question yet, whether I shall have her, or no.

Wel. 'Slid, thou shalt have her; by this light, thou shalt.

E. Kn. Nay, do not swear.

Wel. By this hand, thou shalt have her: I'll go fetch her, presently. 'Point but where to meet, and as I am an honest man, I'll bring her.

E. Kn. Hold, hold, be temperate.

Wel. Why, by——what shall I swear by? thou shalt have her, as I am——

E. Kn. 'Pray thee, be at peace, I am satisfied: and do believe thou wilt omit no offered occasion to make my desires complete.

Wel. Thou shalt see, and know, I will not.   [*Exeunt.*

ACT IV. SCENE IV

A street in the Old Jewry.

Enter Formal *and* Knowell.

For. Was your man a soldier, sir?

Kno. Aye, a knave, I took him begging o' the way,
This morning, as I came over Moorfields!

Enter Brainworm, *disguised as before.*

O, here he is! yo' have made fair speed, believe me:
Where, i' the name of sloth, could you be thus——

Bra. Marry, peace be my comfort, where I thought I should have had little comfort of your worship's service.

Kno. How so?

Bra. O, sir! your coming to the City, your entertainment of me, and your sending me to watch—indeed, all the circumstances either of your charge, or my employment, are as open to your son as to yourself!

Kno. How should that be! unless that villain, Brainworm,
Have told him of the letter, and discover'd
All that I strictly charg'd him to conceal? 'tis so!

Bra. I am, partly, o' the faith 'tis so indeed.

Kno. But how should he know thee to be my man?

Bra. Nay, sir, I cannot tell; unless it be by the black art! Is not your son a scholar, sir?

Kno. Yes, but I hope his soul is not allied
Unto such hellish practice: if it were,
I had just cause to weep my part in him,
And curse the time of his creation.
But where didst thou find them, Fitz-Sword?

Bra. You should rather ask, where they found me, sir, for, I'll be sworn I was going along in the street, thinking nothing, when (of a sudden) a voice calls, Mr. Knowell's man; another cries, soldier: and thus half a dozen of 'em, till they had call'd me within a house where I no sooner came, but they seem'd men, and out flew all their rapiers at my bosom, with some three or four score oaths to accompany 'em, and all to tell me I was but a dead man if I did not confess where you were, and how I was employed, and about what; which, when they could not get out of me (as I protest, they must ha' dissected and made an anatomy o' me, first, and so I told 'em) they lock'd me up into a room i' the top of a high house, whence, by great miracle (having a light heart) I slid down by a bottom of pack-thread into the street, and so 'scap'd. But, sir, thus much I can assure you, for I heard it while I was lock'd up, there were a great many rich merchants, and brave citizens' wives with 'em at a feast, and your son, Mr. Edward, withdrew with some of 'em, and has 'pointed to meet her anon, at one Cob's house, a water-bearer that dwells by the wall. Now, there your worship shall be sure to take him, for there he preys, and fail he will not.

Kno. Nor will I fail to break his match, I doubt not.
Go thou, along with Justice Clement's man,
And stay there for me. At one Cob's house, sayest thou?

Bra. Aye sir, there you shall have him.   [*Exit* Knowell.
Yes? Invisible? Much wench, or much son! 'Slight, when he has stay'd there three or four hours, travailing with the expectation of wonders, and at length be deliver'd of air: O, the sport that I should then take to look on him, if I durst! But now I mean to appear no more afore him in this shape. I have another trick to act yet. O, that I were so

happy as to light on a nupson, now, of this Justice's novice. Sir, I make you stay somewhat long.

For. Not a whit, sir. 'Pray you, what do you mean, sir?

Bra. I was putting up some papers——

For. You ha' been lately in the wars, sir, it seems.

Bra. Marry have I, sir; to my loss: and expense of all, almost——

For. Troth, sir, I would be glad to bestow a bottle of wine o' you, if it please you to accept it——

Bra. O, sir——

For. But to hear the manner of your services, and your devices in the wars; they say they be very strange, and not like those a man reads in the Roman histories, or sees at Mile End.

Bra. No, I assure you, sir; why, at any time when it please you, I shall be ready to discourse to you all I know: and more too, somewhat.

For. No better time than now, sir; we'll go to the Windmill: there we shall have a cup of neat grist, we call it. I pray you, sir, let me request you to the Windmill.

Bra. I'll follow you, sir,——and make grist o' you, if I have good luck.   [*Exeunt.*

ACT IV. SCENE V

Moorfields.

Enter Matthew, Ed. Knowell, Bobadil, *and* Stephen.

Mat. Sir, did your eyes ever taste the like clown of him, where we were today, Mr. Wellbred's half-brother? I think the whole earth cannot show his parallel, by this daylight.

E. Kn. We were now speaking of him: Captain Bobadil tells me he is fall'n foul o' you, too.

Mat. O, aye, sir, he threatened me with the bastinado.

Bob. Aye, but I think I taught you prevention, this morning, for that——. You shall kill him, beyond question: if you be so generously minded.

Mat. Indeed, it is a most excellent trick!

He practises at a post.

Bob. Oh, you do not give spirit enough to your motion, you are too tardy, too heavy! O, it must be done like lightning, hey?

Mat. Rare, Captain!

Bob. Tut, 'tis nothing, an't be not done in a——*punto*!

E. Kn. Captain, did you ever prove yourself upon any of our masters of defence here?

Mat. O, good sir! yes, I hope he has.

Bob. I will tell you, sir. Upon my first coming to the City after my long travel for knowledge (in that mystery only), there came three or four of 'em to me, at a gentleman's house, where it was my chance to be resident at that time, to entreat my presence at their schools, and withal so much importun'd me, that (I protest to you as I am a gentleman) I was asham'd of their rude demeanour out of all measure: well, I told 'em that to come to a public school, they should pardon me, it was opposite (in *diameter*) to my humour, but, if so they would give their attendance at my lodging, I protested to do them what right or favour I could, as I was a gentleman, and so forth.

E. Kn. So, sir, then you tried their skill?

Bob. Alas, soon tried! you shall hear, sir. Within two or three days after, they came; and, by honesty, fair sir, believe me, I grac'd them exceedingly, show'd them some two or three tricks of prevention have purchas'd 'em, since, a credit to admiration! they cannot deny this: and yet now they hate me, and why? because I am excellent, and for no other vile reason on the earth.

E. Kn. This is strange, and barbarous as ever I heard!

Bob. Nay, for a more instance of their preposterous natures but note, sir. They have assaulted me some three, four, five, six of them together, as I have walk'd alone in divers 'skirts i' the town, as Turnbull, Whitechapel, Shoreditch, which were then my quarters, and since upon the Exchange, at my lodging, and at my ordinary: where I have driven them afore me the whole length of a street, in the open view of all our gallants, pitying to hurt them, believe me. Yet all this lenity will not o'ercome their spleen: they will be doing with a pismire, raising a hill a man may spurn abroad with his foot at pleasure. By myself, I could have slain them all, but I delight not in murder. I am loth to bear any other than this bastinado for 'em: yet I hold it good policy not to go disarm'd, for though I be skilful, I may be oppress'd with multitudes.

E. Kn. Aye, believe me, may you, sir: and (in my conceit) our whole nation should sustain the loss by it, if it were so.

Bob. Alas, no: what's a peculiar man to a nation? not seen.

E. Kn. Oh, but your skill, sir!

Bob. Indeed, that might be some loss; but who respects it? I will tell you, sir, by the way of private, and under seal; I am a gentleman, and live here obscure, and to myself: but, were I known to her Majesty and the Lords (observe me) I would undertake (upon this poor head and life) for the public benefit of the state, not only to spare the entire lives of her subjects in general but to save the one half, nay, three parts of her yearly charge, in holding war, and against what enemy soever. And, how would I do it, think you?

E. Kn. Nay, I know not, nor can I conceive.

Bob. Why thus, sir. I would select nineteen more to myself throughout the land; gentlemen they should be of good spirit, strong, and able constitution, I would choose them by an instinct, a character, that I have: and I would teach these nineteen the special rules, as your *Punto*, your *Reverso*, your *Stoccata*, your *Imbroccata*, your *Passada*, your *Montanto*: till they could all play very near, or altogether, as well as myself. This done, say the enemy were forty thousand strong, we twenty would come into the field, the tenth of March or thereabouts; and we would challenge twenty of the enemy; they could not, in their honour, refuse us; well, we would kill them: challenge twenty more, kill them; twenty more, kill them; twenty more, kill them too; and thus would we kill, every man, his twenty a day, that's twenty score; twenty score, that's two hundred; two hundred a day, five days a thousand;

forty thousand; forty times five, five times forty, two hundred days kills them all up, by computation. And this will I venture my poor gentlemanlike carcass to perform (provided there be no treason practis'd upon us) by fair and discreet manhood, that is, civilly by the sword.

E. Kn. Why, are you so sure of your hand, Captain, at all times?

Bob. Tut, never miss thrust, upon my reputation with you.

E. Kn. I would not stand in Downright's state, then, an' you meet him, for the wealth of any one street in London.

Bob. Why, sir, you mistake me! if he were here now, by this welkin, I would not draw my weapon on him! let this gentleman do his mind: but I will bastinado him (by the bright sun) wherever I meet him.

Mat. Faith, and I'll have a fling at him, at my distance.

[*Downright walks over the stage.*

E. Kn. Gods so', look, where he is: yonder he goes.

Dow. What peevish luck have I, I cannot meet with these bragging rascals.

Bob. It's not he? is it?

E. Kn. Yes faith, it is he.

Mat. I'll be hang'd, then, if that were he.

E. Kn. Sir, keep your hanging good for some greater matter, for I assure you that was he.

Ste. Upon my reputation, it was he.

Bob. Had I thought it had been he, he must not have gone so: but I can hardly be induc'd to believe it was he, yet.

E. Kn. That I think, sir.   [*Downright returns.*
But see he is come again!

Dow. O, Pharaoh's foot, have I found you? Come, draw, to your tools: draw, gypsy, or I'll thrash you.

Bob. Gentleman of valour, I do believe in thee, hear me——

Dow. Draw your weapon, then.

Bob. Tall man, I never thought on it till now (body of me) I had a warrant of the peace served on me, even now, as I came along, by a water-bearer; this gentleman saw it, Mr. Matthew.

Dow. 'Sdeath, you will not draw, then?

[*He beats him, and disarms him.*

Bob. Hold, hold, under thy favour, forbear.

Dow. Prate again, as you like this, you whorson foist you. You'll control the point, you? [*Matthew runs away.*] Your consort is gone? had he stay'd, he had shar'd with you, sir. [*Exit* Downright.

Bob. Well, gentlemen, bear witness, I was bound to the peace, by this good day.

E. Kn. No faith, it's an ill day, Captain, never reckon it other: but, say you were bound to the peace, the law allows you to defend yourself: that'll prove but a poor excuse.

Bob. I cannot tell, sir. I desire good construction, in fair sort. I never sustain'd the like disgrace (by heaven), sure I was struck with a planet thence, for I had no power to touch my weapon.

E. Kn. Aye, like enough, I have heard of many that have been beaten under a planet: go, get you to a surgeon. 'Slid, an' these be your tricks, your *Passadas*, and your *Mountantos*, I'll none of them. [*Exit* Bobadil.] O, manners! that this age should bring forth such creatures! that Nature should be at leisure to make 'em! Come, coz.

Ste. Mass, I'll ha' this cloak.

E. Kn. God's will, 'tis Downright's.

Ste. Nay, it's mine now, another might have ta'en up, as well as I: I'll wear it, so I will.

E. Kn. How, an' he see it? he'll challenge it, assure yourself.

Ste. Aye, but he shall not ha' it; I'll say I bought it.

E. Kn. Take heed you buy it not too dear, coz. [*Exeunt.*

74

ACT IV. SCENE VI

A room in Kitely's *house.*

Enter Kitely, Wellbred, Dame Kitely, *and* Bridget.

Kit. Now, trust me, brother, you were much to blame,
T" incense his anger, and disturb the peace
Of my poor house, where there are sentinels
That every minute watch, to give alarms,
Of civil war, without adjection
Of your assistance, or occasion.

Wel. No harm done, brother, I warrant you: since there
is no harm done. Anger costs a man nothing: and a tall man
is never his own man 'till he be angry. To keep his valour
in obscurity is to keep himself, as it were, in a cloak-bag.
What's a musician, unless he play? what's a tall man, unless
he fight? For, indeed, all this my wise brother stands upon
absolutely: and that made me fall in with him so resolutely.

Dame. Aye, but what harm might have come of it,
brother?

Wel. Might, sister? so might the good warm clothes
your husband wears be poison'd, for anything he knows:
or the wholesome wine he drunk, even now, at the table——

Kit. Now, God forbid: O me! Now, I remember,
My wife drunk to me last; and chang'd the cup:
And bade me wear this cursed suit to-day.
See, if heav'n suffer murder undiscover'd!
I feel me ill; give me some *mithridate*,
Some *mithridate* and oil, good sister, fetch me;
Oh, I am sick at heart! I burn, I burn.
If you will save my life, go, fetch it me.

Wel. O, strange humour! my very breath has poison'd
him.

Brid. Good brother, be content; what do you mean?
The strength of these extreme conceits will kill you.

Dame. Beshrew your heart-blood, brother Wellbred,
now;
For putting such a toy into his head.

Wel. Is a fit simile, a toy? will he be poison'd with a simile? Brother Kitely, what a strange and idle imagination is this? For shame, be wiser. O' my soul, there's no such matter.

Kit. Am I not sick? how am I, then, not poison'd?
Am I not poison'd? how am I, then, so sick?

Dame. If you be sick, your own thoughts make you sick.

Wel. His jealousy is the poison he has taken.

Brainworm *comes disguis'd like* Justice Clement's *man.*

Bra. Mr. Kitely, my master, Justice Clement, salutes you; and desires to speak with you with all possible speed.

Kit. No time but now? when I think I am sick? very sick! well, I will wait upon his worship. Thomas, Cob, I must seek them out, and set 'em sentinels, till I return. Thomas, Cob, Thomas. [*Exit* Kitely.

Wel. This is perfectly rare, Brainworm! [*takes him aside.*] but how got'st thou this apparel of the Justice's man?

Bra. Marry, sir, my proper fine penman would needs bestow the grist o' me, at the Windmill, to hear some martial discourse; where so I marshal'd him that I made him drunk with admiration! and, because too much heat was the cause of his distemper, I stripp'd him stark naked, as he lay along asleep, and borrowed his suit, to deliver this counterfeit message in, leaving a rusty armour and an old brown bill to watch him, till my return: which shall be when I ha' pawn'd his apparel, and spent the better part o' the money, perhaps.

Wel. Well, thou art a successful merry knave, Brainworm, his absence will be a good subject for more mirth. I pray thee, return to thy young master, and will him to meet me and my sister Bridget at the Tower instantly: for here, tell him, the house is so stor'd with jealousy there is no room for love to stand upright in. We must get our fortunes committed to some larger prison, say; and than the Tower I know no better air: nor where the liberty of the house may do us more present service. Away.

[*Exit* Brainworm.

Enter Kitely *and* Cash.

Kit. Come hither, Thomas. Now, my secret's ripe,
And thou shalt have it: lay to both thine ears.
Hark, what I say to thee. I must go forth, Thomas.
Be careful of thy promise, keep good watch,
Note every gallant, and observe him well,
That enters in my absence to thy mistress:
If she would show him rooms, the jest is stale,
Follow 'em, Thomas, or else hang on him,
And let him not go after; mark their looks;
Note, if she offer but to see his band
Or any other amorous toy about him;
But praise his leg; or foot; or if she say,
The day is hot, and bid him feel her hand,
How hot it is; and, that's a monstrous thing!
Note me all this, good Thomas, mark their sighs,
And, if they do but whisper, break 'em off:
I'll bear thee out in it. Wilt thou do this?
Wilt thou be true, my Thomas?
Cas.   As truth's self, sir.
Kit. Why, I believe thee: where is Cob, now? Cob?
                                        [*Exit* Kitely.
Dame. He's ever calling for Cob! I wonder how he employs Cob so!
Wel. Indeed, sister, to ask how he employs Cob, is a necessary question for you, that are his wife, and a thing not very easy for you to be satisfied in: but this I'll assure you, Cob's wife is an excellent bawd, sister, and oftentimes your husband haunts her house, marry, to what end I cannot altogether accuse him, imagine you what you think convenient. But I have known fair hides have foul hearts ere now, sister.
Dame. Never said you truer than that, brother, so much I can tell you for your learning. Thomas, fetch your cloak, and go with me, [*Exit* Cash.] I'll after him presently: I would to fortune I could take him there i' faith, Id return him his own, I warrant him.   [*Exit* Dame Kitely.

Wel. So, let 'em go: this may make sport anon. Now, my fair sister-in-law, that you knew but how happy a thing it were to be fair and beautiful?

Brid. That touches not me, brother.

Wel. That's true; that's even the fault of it: for, indeed, beauty stands a woman in no stead, unless it procure her touching. But, sister, whether it touch you or no, it touches your beauties; and, I am sure, they will abide the touch; an' they do not, a plague of all ceruse, say I: and, it touches me too in part, though not in the——. Well, there's a dear and respected friend of mine, sister, stands very strongly, and worthily affected toward you, and hath vow'd to inflame whole bonfires of zeal at his heart, in honour of your perfections. I have already engag'd my promise to bring you where you shall hear him confirm much more. Ned Knowell is the man, sister. There's no exception against the party. You are ripe for a husband; and a minute's loss to such an occasion is a great trespass in a wise beauty. What say you, sister? On my soul, he loves you. Will you give him the meeting?

Brid. Faith, I had very little confidence in mine own constancy, brother, if I durst not meet a man: but this motion of yours savours of an old knight-adventurer's servant a little too much, methinks.

Wel. What's that, sister?

Brid. Marry, of the squire.

Wel. No matter if it did, I would be such a one for my friend, but see! who is return'd to hinder us?

Re-enter Kitely.

Kit. What villany is this? call'd out on a false message?
This was some plot! I was not sent for. Bridget,
Where's your sister?

Brid.   I think she be gone forth, sir.

Kit. How! is my wife gone forth? whither for God's sake?

Brid. She's gone abroad with Thomas.

Kit. Abroad with Thomas, oh, that villain dors me.
He hath discover'd all unto my wife!

Beast that I was to trust him: whither, I pray you,
Went she?

Brid.   I know not, sir.

Wel.   I'll tell you, brother,
Whither I suspect she 's gone.

Kit.   Whither, good brother?

Wel. To Cob's house, I believe: but, keep my counsel.

Kit. I will, I will: to Cob's house? doth she haunt Cob's?
She 's gone a' purpose, now, to cuckold me,
With that lewd rascal, who, to win her favour,
Hath told her all.   [*Exit* Kitely.

Wel.   Come, he 's once more gone.
Sister, let 's lose no time; th' affair is worth it.   [*Exeunt.*

ACT IV. SCENE VII

A street.

Enter Matthew *and* Bobadil.

Mat. I wonder, Captain, what they will say of my going
away? ha?

Bob. Why, what should they say? but as of a discreet
gentleman? Quick, wary, respectful of nature's fair linea-
ments: and that 's all?

Mat. Why, so! but what can they say of your beating?

Bob. A rude part, a touch with soft wood, a kind of
gross battery us'd, laid on strongly, born most patiently:
and that 's all?

Mat. Aye, but would any man have offered it in Venice
as you say?

Bob. Tut, I assure you, no: you shall have there your
Nobilis, your *Gentelezza*, come in bravely upon your
reverse, stand you close, stand you firm, stand you fair,
save your *retricato* with his left leg, come to the *assalto*
with the right, thrust with brave steel, defy your base
wood! But, wherefore do I awake this remembrance? I
was fascinated, by Jupiter: fascinated: but I will be un-
witch'd, and reveng'd, by law.

Mat. Do you hear? is it not best to get a warrant, and have him arrested, and brought before Justice Clement?

Bob. It were not amiss, would we had it.

Enter Brainworm *disguised as* Formal.

Mat. Why, here comes his man, let's speak to him.

Bob. Agreed, do you speak.

Mat. Save you, sir.

Bra. With all my heart, sir.

Mat. Sir, there is one Downright hath abus'd this gentleman and myself, and we determine to make our amends by law; now, if you would do us the favour to procure a warrant to bring him afore your master, you shall be well considered, I assure you, sir.

Bra. Sir, you know my service is my living, such favours as these, gotten of my master, is his only preferment, and therefore, you must consider me, as I may make benefit of my place.

Mat. How is that, sir?

Bra. Faith, sir, the thing is extraordinary, and the gentleman may be of great accompt: yet, be what he will, if you will lay me down a brace of angels in my hand you shall have it, otherwise not.

Mat. How shall we do, Captain? he asks a brace of angels, you have no money?

Bob. Not a cross, by fortune.

Mat. Nor I, as I am a gentleman, but two pence, left of my two shillings in the morning for wine and radish: let's find him some pawn.

Bob. Pawn? we have none to the value of his demand.

Mat. O, yes. I'll pawn this jewel in my ear, and you may pawn your silk stockings, and pull up your boots, they will ne'er be missed. It must be done, now.

Bob. Well, an' there be no remedy: I'll step aside, and pull 'em off. [*Withdraws.*

Mat. Do you hear, sir? we have no store of money at this time, but you shall have good pawns: look you, sir, this jewel, and that gentleman's silk stockings, because we would have it dispatched e'er we went to our chambers.

Bra. I am content, sir; I will get you the warrant presently, what's his name, say you? Downright?

Mat. Aye, aye, George Downright.

Bra. What manner of man is he?

Mat. A tall big man, sir; he goes in a cloak, most commonly, of silk russet, laid about with russet lace.

Bra. 'Tis very good, sir.

Mat. Here sir, here's my jewel.

Bob. [*Returning.*] And here are stockings.

Bra. Well, gentlemen, I'll procure you this warrant, presently, but who will you have to serve it?

Mat. That's true, Captain: that must be consider'd.

Bob. Body o' me, I know not! 'tis service of danger!

Bra. Why, you were best get one o' the varlets o' the City, a serjeant. I'll appoint you one, if you please

Mat. Will you, sir? why, we can wish no better.

Bob. We'll leave it to you, sir.   [*Exeunt* Bob. *and* Mat.

Bra. This is rare! now will I go pawn this cloak of the Justice's man's at the brokers for a varlet's suit, and be the varlet myself; and get either more pawns, or more money off Downright, for the arrest.   [*Exit.*

ACT IV. SCENE VIII

The lane before Cob's *house.*

Enter Knowell.

Kno. O, here it is, I am glad: I have found it now. Ho? who is within here?

Tib. [*Within.*] I am within sir, what's your pleasure?

Kno. To know who is within besides yourself.

Tib. Why, sir, you are no constable, I hope?

Kno. O, fear you the constable? then, I doubt not You have some guests within deserve that fear, I'll fetch him straight.

Enter Tib.

Tib.   O' God's name, sir.

Kno. Go to. Come, tell me, is not young Knowell, here?

Tib. Young Knowell? I know none such, sir, o' mine honesty!

Kno. Your honesty? dame, it flies too lightly from you:
There is no way but fetch the constable.

Tib. The constable? the man is mad, I think.   [*Exit.*

Enter Dame Kitely *and* Cash.

Cas. Ho, who keeps house here?

Kno. O, this is the female copes-mate of my son?
Now shall I meet him straight.

Dame.   Knock, Thomas, hard.

Cas. Ho, good wife?

Re-enter Tib.

Tib.   Why, what's the matter with you?

Dame. Why, woman, grieves it you to ope your door?
Belike you get something to keep it shut.

Tib. What mean these questions, pray ye?

Dame. So strange you make it? is not my husband here?

Kno. Her husband!

Dame.   My tried husband, master Kitely.

Tib. I hope he needs not to be tried here.

Dame. No, dame: he does it not for need, but pleasure.

Tib. Neither for need, nor pleasure, is he here.

Kno. This is but a device to baulk me withal.
Soft, who is this?

Enter Kitely *muffled in his cloak.*

'Tis not my son, disguised?

[*Dame Kitely* spies her husband coming and runs to him.

Dame. O, sir, have I forestalled your honest market?
Found your close walks? you stand amaz'd now, do you?
I' faith (I am glad) I have smoked you yet at last:
What is your jewel, trow? In: come, let's see her;
Fetch forth your housewife, dame; if she be fairer,
In any honest judgement, than myself,
I'll be content with it: but, she is change,
She feeds you fat, she soothes your appetite,

82

And you are well? your wife, an honest woman,
Is meat twice sod to you, sir? O, you treacher!

Kno. She cannot counterfeit thus palpably.

Kit. Out on thy more than strumpet's impudence!
Steal'st thou thus to thy haunts? and have I taken
Thy bawd, and thee, and thy companion,
This hoary-headed lecher, this old goat,

[*Pointing to* Old Knowell.

Close at your villany, and would'st thou 'scuse it,
With this stale harlot's jest accusing me?

[*To him.*] O, old incontinent, do'st not thou shame,
When all thy powers in chastity is spent,
To have a mind so hot? and to entice,
And feed th' enticements of a lustful woman?

Dame. Out, I defy thee, aye, dissembling wretch.

Kit. Defy me, strumpet? ask thy pandar here,
Can he deny it? or that wicked elder?

Kno. Why, hear you, sir.

Kit.   Tut, tut, tut: never speak.
Thy guilty conscience will discover thee.

Kno. What lunacy is this that haunts this man?

Kit. Well, good-wife bawd, Cob's wife; and you,
That make your husband such a hoddie-doddie;
And you, young apple-squire; and old cuckold-maker;
I'll ha' you every one before a Justice:
Nay, you shall answer it, I charge you go.

Kno. Marry, with all my heart, sir: I go willingly.
Though I do taste this as a trick put on me
To punish my impertinent search; and justly:
And half forgive my son for the device.

Kit. Come, will you go?

Dame.   Go? to thy shame, believe it.

Enter Cob.

Cob. Why, what's the matter, here? What's here to do?

Kit. O, Cob, art thou come? I have been abus'd,
And i' thy house. Never was man so wrong'd!

Cob. 'Slid, in my house? my master Kitely? Who
wrongs you in my house?

Kit. Marry, young lust in old; and old in young, here:
Thy wife's their bawd, here have I taken 'em.

Cob. How? bawd? Is my house come to that? Am I
prefer'd thither? Did I charge you to keep your doors
shut, Is'bel? and do you let 'em lie open for all comers?
[*He falls upon his wife and beats her.*

Kno. Friend, know some cause, before thou beat'st thy
wife,
This's madness in thee.

Cob.   Why, is there no cause?

Kit. Yes, I'll show cause before the Justice, Cob:
Come, let her go with me.

Cob.   Nay, she shall go.

Tib. Nay, I will go. I'll see an' you may be allow'd to
make a bundle o' hemp o' your right and lawful wife thus,
at every cuckoldly knave's pleasure. Why do you not go?

Kit. A bitter quean. Come, we'll ha' you tam'd. [*Exeunt.*

ACT IV. SCENE IX

A street. Enter Brainworm, *disguised as a city serjeant.*

Bra. Well, of all my disguises yet now am I most like
myself: being in this serjeant's gown. A man of my present
profession never counterfeits till he lays hold upon a debtor
and says he 'rests him, for then he brings him to all manner
of unrest. A kind of little kings we are, bearing the diminu-
tive of a mace, made like a young artichoke, that always
carries pepper and salt in itself. Well, I know not what
danger I undergo by this exploit, pray heaven, I come
well off.

Enter Matthew *and* Bobadil.

Mat. See, I think yonder is the varlet by his gown.

Bob. Let's go in quest of him.

Mat. 'Save you, friend, are not you here by appointment
of Justice Clement's man?

Bra. Yes, an't please you, sir: he told me two gentlemen
had will'd him to procure a warrant from his master (which
I have about me) to be serv'd on one Downright.

Mat. It is honestly done of you both; and see where the party comes you must arrest: serve it upon him, quickly, afore he be aware——

Bob. Bear back, master Matthew.

Enter Stephen *in* Downright's *cloak.*

Bra. Master Downright, I arrest you i' the Queen's name, and must carry you afore a Justice, by virtue of this warrant.

Ste. Me, friend? I am no Downright, I. I am master Stephen, you do not well to arrest me, I tell you truly: I am in nobody's bonds, nor books, I would you should know it. A plague on you heartily, for making me thus afraid afore my time.

Bra. Why, now are you deceived, gentlemen?

Bob. He wears such a cloak, and that deceived us: But see, here a comes, indeed! this is he, officer.

Enter Downright.

Dow. Why, how now, signior gull! are you turn'd filcher of late? come, deliver my cloak.

Ste. Your cloak, sir? I bought it, even now, in open market.

Bra. Master Downright, I have a warrant I must serve upon you, procur'd by these two gentlemen.

Dow. These gentlemen? these rascals?

Bra. Keep the peace, I charge you in her Majesty's name.

Dow. I obey thee. What must I do, officer?

Bra. Go before master Justice Clement, to answer what they can object against you, sir. I will use you kindly, sir.

Mat. Come, let's before, and make the Justice, Captain——

Bob. The varlet's a tall man! afore heaven!

[*Exeunt* Matthew *and* Bobadil.

Dow. Gull, you'll gi' me my cloak?

Ste. Sir, I bought it, and I'll keep it.

Dow. You will.

Ste. Aye, that I will.

Dow. Officer, there's thy fee, arrest him.

Bra. Master Stephen, I must arrest you.

Ste. Arrest me, I scorn it. There, take your cloak, I'll none on 't.

Dow. Nay, that shall not serve your turn, now, sir. Officer, I'll go with thee to the Justice's: bring him along.

Ste. Why, is not here your cloak? what would you have?

Dow. I'll ha' you answer it, sir.

Bra. Sir, I'll take your word; and this gentleman's, too, for his appearance.

Dow. I'll ha' no words taken. Bring him along.

Bra. Sir, I may choose to do that: I may take bail.

Dow. 'Tis true, you may take bail, and choose, at another time; but you shall not now, varlet. Bring him along, or I'll swinge you.

Bra. Sir, I pity the gentleman's case. Here's your money again.

Dow. 'Sdeynes, tell not me of my money; bring him away, I say.

Bra. I warrant you he will go with you of himself, sir.

Dow. Yet more ado?

Bra. I have made a fair mash on 't. [*Aside.*

Ste. Must I go?

Bra. I know no remedy, master Stephen.

Dow. Come along, afore me, here. I do not love your hanging look behind.

Ste. Why, sir. I hope you cannot hang me for it. Can he, fellow?

Bra. I think not, sir. It is but a whipping matter, sure!

Ste. Why, then, let him do his worst, I am resolute.

[*Exeunt.*

ACT V. SCENE I

Colman-street. A Hall in Justice Clement's *house.*

Enter Clement, Knowell, Kitely, Dame Kitely, Tib, Cash, Cob, *and* Servants.

Clem. Nay, but stay, stay, give me leave: my chair, sirrah. You, master Knowell, say you went thither to meet your son.

Kno. Aye, sir.

Clem. But who directed you thither?

Kno. That did mine own man, sir.

Clem. Where is he?

Kno. Nay, I know not, now; I left him with your clerk: and appointed him to stay here for me.

Clem. My clerk? about what time was this?

Kno. Marry, between one and two, as I take it.

Clem. And what time came my man with the false message to you, master Kitely?

Kit. After two, sir.

Clem. Very good: but, mistress Kitely, how that you were at Cob's? ha?

Dame. An' please you, sir, I'll tell you: my brother, Wellbred, told me that Cob's house was a suspected place——

Clem. So it appears, methinks: but on.

Dame. And that my husband us'd thither, daily.

Clem. No matter, so he us'd himself well, mistress.

Dame. True sir, but you know what grows by such haunts often-times.

Clem. I see, rank fruits of a jealous brain, mistress Kitely: but did you find your husband there, in that case, as you suspected?

Kit. I found her there, sir.

Clem. Did you so? that alters the case. Who gave you knowledge of your wife's being there?

Kit. Marry, that did my brother Wellbred.

Clem. How? Wellbred first tell her? then tell you, after? where is Wellbred?

Kit. Gone with my sister, sir, I know not whither.

Clem. Why, this is a mere trick, a device; you are gull'd in this most grossly, all! alas, poor wench, wert thou beaten for this?

Tib. Yes, most pitifully, and 't please you.

Cob. And worthily, I hope: if it shall prove so.

Clem. Aye, that's like, and a piece of a sentence.

Enter Servant.

How now, sir? what's the matter?

Serv. Sir, there's a gentleman i' the court without, desires to speak with your worship.

Clem. A gentleman? what's he?

Serv. A soldier, sir, he says.

Clem. A soldier? take down my armour, my sword, quickly: a soldier speak with me! why, when knaves? come on, come on, hold my cap there, so; give me my gorget, my sword: [*He arms himself.*] stand by, I will end your matters, anon——Let the soldier enter.

[*Exit* Servant.

Enter Bobadil *and* Matthew.

Now, sir, what ha' you to say to me?

Bob. By your worship's favour——

Clem. Nay, keep out, sir, I know not your pretence; you send me word, sir, you are a soldier: why, sir, you shall be answer'd here; here be them have been amongst soldiers. Sir, your pleasure.

Bob. Faith, sir, so it is this gentleman and myself, have been most uncivilly wrong'd and beaten, by one Downright, a coarse fellow about the town, here; and for mine own part, I protest, being a man in no sort given to this filthy humour of quarrelling, he hath assaulted me in the way of my peace; dispoil'd me of mine honour; disarm'd me of my weapons; and rudely laid me along in the open streets: when I not so much as once offer'd to resist him.

Clem. O, god's precious! is this the soldier? here, take my armour off quickly, 'twill make him swoon, I fear; he is not fit to look on't that will put up a blow.

Mat. An't please your worship, he was bound to the peace.

Clem. Why, and he were sir, his hands were not bound, were they?

Re-enter Servant.

Serv. There's one of the varlets of the city, sir, has brought two gentlemen, here, one upon your worship's warrant.

Clem. My warrant?

88

Serv. Yes, sir. The officer says, procur'd by these two.

Clem. Bid him come in. Set by this picture. What, Mr. Downright! are you brought at Mr. Freshwater's suit, here!

Enter Downright, Stephen, *and* Brainworm *disguised as before.*

Dow. I' faith, sir. And here's another brought at my suit.

Clem. What are you, sir?

Ste. A gentleman, sir. Oh, uncle!

Clem. Uncle? who? master Knowell?

Kno. Aye, sir! this is a wise kinsman of mine.

Ste. God's my witness, uncle, I am wrong'd here monstrously; he charges me with stealing of his cloak, and would I might never stir, if I did not find it in the street, by chance.

Dow. O, did you find it now? you said you bought it, erewhile.

Ste. And you said I stole it; nay, now my uncle is here, I'll do well enough with you.

Clem. Well, let this breathe a while; you that have cause to complain there, stand forth: had you my warrant for this gentleman's apprehension?

Bob. Aye, an't please your worship.

Clem. Nay, do not speak in passion so: where had you it?

Bob. Of your clerk, sir.

Clem. That's well! an' my clerk can make warrants, and my hand not at 'em! Where is the warrant? Officer, have you it?

Bra. No, sir, your worship's man, master Formal, bid me do it for these gentlemen, and he would be my discharge.

Clem. Why, master Downright, are you such a novice, to be serv'd, and never see the warrant?

Dow. Sir. He did not serve it on me.

Clem. No? how then?

Dow. Marry, sir, he came to me and said he must serve it, and he would use me kindly, and so——

Clem. O, God's pity, was it so, sir? he must serve it? give me my long-sword there, and help me off, so. Come on, sir varlet, I must cut off your legs, sirrah: [*He flourishes over him with his long sword.*] nay, stand up, I'll use you kindly: I must cut off your legs, I say.

Bra. O, good sir, I beseech you; nay, good master Justice.

Clem. I must do it; there is no remedy. I must cut off your legs, sirrah; I must cut off your ears, you rascal; I must do it; I must cut off your nose, I must cut off your head.

Bra. O, good your worship.

Clem. Well, rise, how dost thou do, now? dost thou feel thyself well? hast thou no harm?

Bra. No, I thank your good worship, sir.

Clem. Why, so! I said, I must cut off thy legs, and I must cut off thy arms, and I must cut off thy head; but I did not do it: so you said you must serve this gentleman, with my warrant, but. you did not serve him. You knave, you slave, you rogue, do you say you must? sirrah, away with him, to the jail; I'll teach you a trick for your must, sir.

Bra. Good sir, I beseech you, be good to me.

Clem. Tell him he shall to the jail, away with him, I say.

Bra. Nay, sir, if you will commit me, it shall be for committing more than this: I will not lose, by my travail, any grain of my fame certain. [*Throws off his disguise.*]

Clem. How is this!

Kno. My man, Brainworm!

Ste. O yes, uncle. Brainworm has been with my cousin Edward and me, all this day.

Clem. I told you all there was some device!

Bra. Nay, excellent Justice, since I have laid myself thus open to you; now stand strong for me: both with your sword, and your balance.

Clem. Body o' me, a merry knave! Give me a bowl of sack: If he belong to you, master Knowell, I bespeak your patience.

Bra. That is it I have most need of. Sir, if you'll pardon me only; I'll glory in all the rest of my exploits.

Kno. Sir, you know I love not to have my favours come hard from me. You have your pardon: though I suspect you shrewdly for being of counsel with my son against me.

Bra. Yes, faith, I have, sir; though you retain'd me doubly this morning, for yourself: first, as Brainworm; after, as Fitz-Sword. I was your reform'd soldier, sir. 'Twas I sent you to Cob's upon the errand without end.

Kno. Is it possible! or that thou should'st disguise thy language so, as I should not know thee?

Bra. O, sir, this has been the day of my metamorphosis! It is not that shape alone that I have run through today. I brought this gentleman, master Kitely, a message too, in the form of master Justice's man, here, to draw him out o' the way, as well as your worship: while master Wellbred might make a conveyance of mistress Bridget to my young master.

Kit. How! my sister stolen away?

Kno. My son is not married, I hope!

Bra. Faith, sir, they are both as sure as love, a priest, and three thousand pounds (which is her portion) can make 'em: and by this time are ready to bespeak their wedding supper at the Windmill, except some friend, here, prevent 'em, and invite 'em home.

Clem. Marry, that will I (I thank thee, for putting me in mind on't). Sirrah, go you, and fetch 'em hither, upon my warrant. Neither's friends have cause to be sorry if I know the young couple, aright. Here, I drink to thee, for thy good news. But, I pray thee, what hast thou done with my man Formal?

Bra. Faith, sir, after some ceremony past, as making him drunk, first with story, and then with wine (but all in kindness) and stripping him to his shirt: I left him in that cool vein, departed, sold your worship's warrant to these two, pawn'd his livery for that varlet's gown, to serve it in; and thus have brought myself, by my activity, to your worship's consideration.

Clem. And I will consider thee in another cup of sack. Here's to thee, which having drunk of, this is my sentence. Pledge me. Thou hast done, or assisted to nothing, in my judgement, but deserves to be pardon'd for the wit o' the offence. If thy master, or any man, here, be angry with

thee, I shall suspect his ingine, while I know him for't.
How now? what noise is that!

Enter Servant.

Serv. Sir, it is Roger is come home.

Clem. Bring him in, bring him in. What! drunk in arms,
against me? Your reason, your reason for this.

Enter Formal *in armour.*

For. I beseech your worship to pardon me; I happen'd
into ill company by chance, that cast me into a sleep, and
stripped me of all my clothes——

Clem. Well, tell him I am Justice Clement and do pardon
him: but, what is this to your armour! what may that
signify?

For. And't please you, sir, it hung up i' the room where
I was stripped; and I borrow'd it of one o' the drawers to
come home in, because I was loth to do penance through
the street i' my shirt.

Enter Ed. Knowell, Wellbred, *and* Bridget.

Clem. Well, stand by a while. Who be these? O, the
young company, welcome, welcome. Gi' you joy. Nay,
mistress Bridget, blush not; you are not so fresh a bride but
the news of it is come hither afore you. Master Bride-
groom, I ha' made your peace, give me your hand: so will
I for all the rest, ere you forsake my roof.

E. Kn. We are the more bound to your humanity, sir.

Clem. Only these two have so little of man in 'em, they
are no part of my care.

Wel. Yes, sir, let me pray you for this gentleman, he
belongs to my sister, the bride.   [*Points to* Matthew.

Clem. In what place, sir?

Wel. Of her delight, sir, below the stairs, and in public:
her *poet*, sir.

Clem. A *poet*? I will challenge him myself, presently, at
extempore.

 Mount up thy Phlegon muse, and testify
 How Saturne, *sitting in an ebon cloud,*
 Disrob'd his podex white as ivory
 And, through the welkin, thundered all aloud.

Wel. He is not for *extempore*, sir. He is all for the pocket-muse, please you command a sight of it.

Clem. Yes, yes, search him for a taste of his vein.

[*They search* Matthew's *pockets.*

Wel. You must not deny the Queen's Justice, sir, under a writ o' rebellion.

Clem. What! all this verse? Body o' me, he carries a whole realm, a commonwealth of paper, in 's hose! let's see some of his subjects!

Unto the boundless Ocean of thy face,
Runs this poor river charg'd with streams of eyes.
How? this is stolen!

E. Kn. A parody! a parody! with a kind of miraculous gift to make it absurder than it was.

Clem. Is all the rest of this batch? Bring me a torch; lay it together, and give fire. Cleanse the air. [*Sets the papers on fire.*] Here was enough to have infected the whole city if it had not been taken in time! See, see, how our poet's glory shines! brighter and brighter! still it increases! and now, it's at the highest: and now it declines as fast. You may see. *Sic transit gloria mundi.*

Kno. There's an *emblem* for you, son, and your studies!

Clem. Nay, no speech, or act of mine be drawn against such as profess it worthily. They are not born every year, as an alderman. There goes more to the making of a good poet, than a sheriff, Mr. Kitely. You look upon me! though I live i' the City here, amongst you, I will do more reverence to him, when I meet him, than I will to the mayor, out of his year. But, these paper-pedlars! these ink-dabblers! They cannot expect reprehension, or reproach. They have it with the fact.

E. Kn. Sir, you have sav'd me the labour of a defence.

Clem. It shall be discourse for supper; between your father and me, if he dare undertake me. But, to dispatch away these, you sign o' the soldier, and picture o' the poet (but, both so false, I will not ha' you hang'd out at my door till midnight), while we are at supper, you two shall penitently fast it out in my court, without; and, if you will, you may pray there that we may be so merry within as to

93

forgive or forget you when we come out. Here's a third, because we tender your safety, shall watch you, he is provided for the purpose. Look to your charge, sir.

Ste. And what shall I do?

Clem. O! I had lost a sheep, an he had not bleated! Why, sir, you shall give Mr. Downright his cloak: and I will entreat him to take it. A trencher and a napkin you shall have i' the buttery and keep Cob and his wife company here; whom I will entreat first to be reconcil'd: and you to endeavour with your wit, to keep 'em so.

Ste. I'll do my best.

Cob. Why, now I see thou art honest, Tib, I receive thee as my dear and mortal wife again.

Tib. And I you, as my loving and obedient husband.

Clem. Good complement! It will be their bridal night too. They are married anew. Come, I conjure the rest to put off all discontent. You, Mr. Downright, your anger; you, master Knowell, your cares; master Kitely and his wife, their jealousy.

For, I must tell you both, while that is fed,
Horns i' the mind are worse than o' the head.

Kit. Sir, thus they go from me, kiss me, sweetheart.

See, what a drove of horns fly in the air
Wing'd with my cleansed and my credulous breath!
Watch 'em, suspicious eyes, watch, where they fall.
See, see! on heads that think th' have none at all!
O, what a plenteous world of this will come!
When air rains horns, all may be sure of some.

I ha' learned so much verse out of a jealous man's part, in a play.

Clem. 'Tis well, 'tis well! This night we'll dedicate to friendship, love and laughter. Master Bridegroom, take your bride, and lead; everyone, a fellow. Here is my mistress. Brainworm! to whom all my addresses of courtship shall have their reference. Whose adventures, this day, when our grandchildren shall hear to be made a fable, I doubt not, but it shall find both spectators, and applause.

[*Exeunt.*

THE END

SEJANUS
HIS FALL

SEJANUS
HIS FALL

SEIANVS

HIS FALL.

Written

by

BEN: IONSON.

Mart. Non hîc *Centauros*, non *Gorgonas, Harpyasq̃*,
Inuenies : Hominem pagina noſtra ſapit.

AT LONDON
Printed by *G. Elld*, for *Thomas
Thorpe*. 1605.

SEIANVS

HIS FALL.

Written
Printed by G. Elld, for Thomas

TO THE NO LESS NOBLE, BY VIRTUE THAN BLOOD:

Esme, Lord Aubigne.

MY LORD,

IF ever any ruin were so great as to survive, I think this be one I send you: The Fall of Sejanus. It is a poem, that (if I well remember) in your Lordship's sight, suffer'd no less violence from our people here than the subject of it did from the rage of the people of Rome; but with a different fate, as (I hope) merit: For this hath out-liv'd their malice, and begot itself a greater favour than he lost, the love of good men. Amongst whom, if I make your Lordship the first it thanks, it is not without a just confession of the bond your benefits have, and ever shall hold upon me.

Your Lordship's most faithful honourer,

BEN. JONSON.

To the Readers

The following and voluntary labours of my friends, pre-fix'd to my book, have relieved me in much, whereat (without them) I should necessarily have touched: Now I will only use three or four short and needful notes; and so rest.

First, if it be objected that what I publish is no true poem, in the strict laws of time, I confess it: as also in the want of a proper chorus, whose habit and moods are such and so difficult as not any whom I have seen since the ancients (no, not they who have most presently affected laws) have yet come in the way of. Nor is it needful, or almost possible, in these our times, and to such auditors as commonly things are presented, to observe the old state and splendour of dramatic poems, with preservation of any popular delight. But of this I shall take more seasonable cause to speak, in my observations upon Horace his Art of Poetry which (with the text translated) I intend shortly to publish. In the meantime, if in truth of argument, dignity of persons, gravity and height of elocution, fullness and frequency of sentence, I have discharg'd the other offices of a tragic writer, let not the absence of these Forms be imputed to me, wherein I shall give you occasion hereafter (and without my boast) to think I could better prescribe, than omit the due use for want of a convenient knowledge.

The next is, lest in some nice nostril the quotations might savour affected, I do let you know that I abhor nothing more; and have only done it to show my integrity in the story, and save myself in those common torturers, that bring all wit to the rack: whose noses are ever like swine spoiling and rooting up the Muses' gardens, and their whole bodies, like moles, as blindly working under earth to cast any, the least, hills upon virtue.

Whereas they are in Latin, and the work in English, it was presuppos'd none but the learned would take the pains to confer them, the authors themselves being all in the learned tongues, save one, with whose English side I have had little to do: To which it may be required, since I have quoted the page, to name what edition I follow'd. *Tacit. Lips.* in 4°. *Antwerp. edit* 1600. *Dio. Folio Hen. Step.* 92. For the rest, as *Sueton. Seneca.* &c. the chapter doth sufficiently direct, or the edition is not varied.

Lastly, I would inform you that this book, in all numbers, is not the same with that which was acted on the public stage, wherein a second pen had good share: in place of which I have rather chosen to put weaker (and no doubt less pleasing) of mine own, than to defraud so happy a genius of his right, by my loathed usurpation.

Fare you well, and if you read farther of me, and like, I shall not be afraid of it, though you praise me out.

Neque enim mihi cornea fibra est.

But that I should plant my felicity in your general saying *Good*, or *Well*, &c., were a weakness which the better sort of you might worthily contemn, if not absolutely hate me for.

BEN. JONSON. and no such,
Quem Palma negata macrum, donata reducit opimum.

The Argument

AELIUS SEJANUS, son to Sejus Strabo, a gentleman of Rome, and born at Vulsinium, after his long service in court, first under Augustus; afterward, Tiberius: grew into that favour with the latter, and won him by those arts, as there wanted nothing but the name to make him a co-partner of the Empire. Which greatness of his, Drusus, the Emperor's son, not brooking, after many smother'd dislikes (it one day breaking out), the Prince struck him publicly on the face. To revenge which disgrace, Livia, the wife of Drusus (being before corrupted by him to her dishonour, and the discovery of her husband's counsels) Sejanus practiseth with, together with her physician, called Eudemus, and one Lygdus, an eunuch, to poison Drusus. This, their inhuman act, having successful and unsuspected passage, it emboldeneth Sejanus to further more insolent projects, even the ambition of the Empire: where finding the lets he must encounter to be many and hard, in respect of the issue of Germanicus (who were next in hope for the succession) he deviseth to make Tiberius' self his means: and instils into his ears many doubts and suspicions, both against the Princes and their mother Agrippina: which Cæsar jealously hearkening to, as covetously consenteth to their ruin, and their friends'. In this time, the better to mature and strengthen his design, Sejanus labours to marry Livia, and worketh (with all his ingine) to remove Tiberius from the knowledge of public business, with allurements of a quiet and retired life: the latter of which, Tiberius (out of a proneness to lust, and a desire to hide those unnatural pleasures which he could not so publicly practise) embraceth: the former enkindleth his fears, and there gives him first cause of doubt or suspect toward Sejanus, against whom he raiseth (in private) a new instrument, one Sertorius Macro, and by him underworketh, discovers the other's counsels, his means, his ends, sounds the affections of the senators, divides, distracts them: at last, when Sejanus

102

least looketh, and is most secure (with pretext of doing him an unwonted honour in the senate) he trains him from his guards, and with a long doubtful letter, in one day hath him suspected, accused, condemned, and torn in pieces, by the rage of the people.

The Persons of the Play

TIBERIUS.	SEJANUS.
DRUSUS, *senior.*	LATIARIS.
NERO.	VARRO.
DRUSUS, *junior.*	MACRO.
CALIGULA.	COTTA.
ARRUNTIUS.	AFER.
SILIUS.	HATERIUS.
SABINUS.	SANQUINIUS.
LEPIDUS.	POMPONIUS.
CORDUS.	POSTHUMUS
GALLUS.	TRIO.
REGULUS.	MINUTIUS.
TERENTIUS.	SATRIUS.
LACO.	NATTA.
EUDEMUS.	OPSIUS.
RUFUS.	NUNTIUS.
AGRIPPINA.	LIVIA.
	SOSIA.
PRAECONES.	LICTORES.
FLAMEN.	MINISTRI.
TUBICINES.	TIBICINES.
TRIBUNI.	SERVUS.

The Scene
ROME

SEJANUS

ACT I. SCENE I

A state room in the palace.

Enter Sabinus *and* Silius, *followed by* Latiaris.

Sab. Hail, Caius Silius.

Sil.   Titius Sabinus, hail.
You're rarely met in court!

Sab.   Therefore, well met.

Sil. 'Tis true: Indeed, this place is not our sphere.

Sab. No, Silius, we are no good inginers;
We want the fine arts, and their thriving use
Should make us grac'd, or favour'd of the times:
We have no shift of faces, no cleft tongues,
No soft and glutinous bodies, that can stick
Like snails on painted walls; or, on our breasts,
Creep up, to fall from that proud height, to which
We did by slavery, not by service, climb:
We are no guilty men, and then no great;
We have no place in court, office in state,
That we can say we owe unto our crimes:
We burn with no black secrets, which can make
Us dear to the authors; or live fear'd
Of their still waking jealousies, to raise
Ourselves a fortune, by subverting theirs.
We stand not in the lines, that do advance
To that so courted point.

Enter Satrius *and* Natta.

Sil.   But yonder lean
A pair that do.

Sab.   Good cousin Latiaris.

Sil. Satrius Secundus, and Pinnarius Natta,
The great Sejanus' clients: There be two,
Know more than honest counsels: whose close breasts
Were they ripp'd up to light, it would be found

105

A poor and idle sin, to which their trunks
Had not been made fit organs. These can lie,
Flatter, and swear, forswear, deprave, inform,
Smile, and betray; make guilty men; then beg
The forfeit lives, to get the livings; cut
Men's throats with whisperings; sell to gaping suitors
The empty smoke that flies about the palace;
Laugh when their patron laughs; sweat, when he sweats;
Be hot and cold with him; change every mood,
Habit and garb, as often as he varies;
Observe him, as his watch observes his clock;
And, true as turquoise in the dear lord's ring,
Look well or ill with him: ready to praise
His lordship if he spit, or but piss fair,
Have an indifferent stool, or break wind well,
Nothing can scape their catch.

    Sab.   Alas! these things
Deserve no note, conferr'd with other vile
And filthier flatteries that corrupt the times:
When, not alone our gentries chief are fain
To make their safety from such sordid acts,
But all our consuls, and no little part
Of such as have been prætors, yea, the most
Of senators (that else not use their voices)
Start up in public senate, and there strive
Who shall propound most abject things, and base.
So much, as oft Tiberius hath been heard,
Leaving the court, to cry, O race of men,
Prepar'd for servitude! which show'd that he,
Who least the public liberty could like,
As lothly brook'd their flat servility.

    Sil. Well, all is worthy of us, were it more,
Who with our riots, pride, and civil hate,
Have so provok'd the justice of the gods.
We, that (within these fourscore years) were born
Free, equal lords of the triumphed world,
And knew no masters but affections,
To which betraying first our liberties,
We since became the slaves to one man's lusts;

And now to many: every ministering spy
That will accuse and swear, is lord of you,
Of me, of all, our fortunes and our lives.
Our looks are call'd to question, and our words,
How innocent soever, are made crimes;
We shall not shortly dare to tell our dreams,
Or think, but 'twill be treason.

Sab.   Tyrant's arts
Are to give flatterers, grace; accusers, power;
That those may seem to kill whom they devour.

Enter Cordus *and* Arruntius.

Now good Cremutius Cordus.

Cor.   Hail to your lordship.

Nat. Who's that salutes your cousin?   [*They whisper.*

Lat.   'Tis one Cordus,
A gentleman of Rome: one that has writ
Annals of late, they say, and very well.

Nat. Annals? of what times?

Lat.   I think of Pompey's.
And Caius Cæsar's; and so down to these.

Nat. How stands h' affected to the present state?
Is he or Drusian? or Germanican?
Or ours? or neutral?

Lat.   I know him not so far.

Nat. Those times are somewhat queasy to be touch'd.
Have you or seen or heard part of his work?

Lat. Not I, he means they shall be public shortly.

Nat. O, Cordus do you call him?

Lat.   Aye.

                                [*Exeunt* Natta *and* Satrius.

Sab.   But these our times
Are not the same, Arruntius.

Arr.   Times? the men,
The men are not the same: 'tis we are base,
Poor, and degenerate from th' exalted strain
Of our great fathers. Where is now the soul
Of god-like Cato? he, that durst be good,
When Cæsar durst be evil; and had power,

107

As not to live his slave, to die his master.
Or where the constant Brutus, that (being proof
Against all charm of benefits) did strike
So brave a blow into the monster's heart
That sought unkindly to captive his country?
O, they are fled the light. Those mighty spirits
Lie rak'd up with their ashes in their urns,
And not a spark of their eternal fire
Glows in a present bosom. All's but blaze,
Flashes, and smoke, wherewith we labour so,
There's nothing Roman in us; nothing good,
Gallant, or great: 'Tis true that Cordus says,
'Brave Cassius was the last of all that race.'

    Sab. Stand by, Lord Drusus.

                       [*Drusus passeth by, attended by* Haterius.

    Hat.   Th' Emp'ror's son, give place.

    Sil. I like the prince well.

    Arr.   A riotous youth,
There's little hope of him.

    Sab.   That fault his age
Will, as it grows, correct. Methinks he bears
Himself, each day, more nobly than other:
And wins no less on men's affections,
Than doth his father lose. Believe me, I love him;
And chiefly for opposing to Sejanus.

    Sil. And I, for gracing his young kinsmen so,
The sons of Prince Germanicus: It shows
A gallant clearness in him, a straight mind,
That envies not, in them, their father's name.

    Arr. His name was, while he liv'd, above all envy;
And being dead, without it. O, that man!
If there were seeds of the old virtue left,
They liv'd in him.

    Sil.   He had the fruits, Arruntius,
More than the seeds: Sabinus, and myself
Had means to know him, within; and can report him.
We were his followers, he would call us friends.
He was a man most like to virtue; in all
And every action, nearer to the gods

Than men, in nature; of a body as fair
As was his mind; and no less reverend
In face, than fame: he could so use his state,
Temp'ring his greatness with his gravity,
As it avoided all self-love in him,
And spite in others. What his funerals lack'd
In images and pomp, they had suppli'd
With honourable sorrow, soldiers' sadness,
A kind of silent mourning, such as men
(Who know no tears, but from their captives) use
To show in so great losses.

Cor.   I thought once,
Considering their forms, age, manner of deaths,
The nearness of the places where they fell,
T' have parallel'd him with great Alexander:
For both were of best feature, of high race,
Year'd but to thirty and, in foreign lands,
By their own people, alike made away.

Sab. I know not, for his death, how you might wrest it:
But, for his life, it did as much disdain
Comparison, with that voluptuous, rash,
Giddy, and drunken Macedon's, as mine
Doth with my bondman's. All the good in him
(His valour and his fortune) he made his;
But he had other touches of late Romans,
That more did speak him: Pompey's dignity,
The innocence of Cato, Cæsar's spirit,
Wise Brutus' temperance, and every virtue,
Which, parted unto others, gave them name,
Flow'd mixed in him. He was the soul of goodness:
And all our praises of him are like streams
Drawn from a spring that still rise full, and leave
The part remaining greatest.

Arr.   I am sure
He was too great for us, and that they knew
Who did remove him hence.

Sab.   When men grow fast
Honour'd and lov'd, there is a trick in state
(Which jealous princes never fail to use)

How to decline that growth with fair pretext,
And honourable colours of employment,
Either by embassy, the war, or such,
To shift them forth into another air,
Where they may purge, and lessen; so was he:
And had his seconds there, sent by Tiberius,
And his more subtle dam, to discontent him;
To breed and cherish mutinies; detract
His greatest actions; give audacious check
To his commands; and work to put him out
In open act of treason. All which snares
When his wise cares prevented, a fine poison
Was thought on to mature their practices.

Enter Sejanus, *with* Terentius, Satrius, *and* Natta.

Cor. Here comes Sejanus.
    Sil.   Now observe the stoops,
The bendings, and the falls.
    Arr.   Most creeping base!
    Sej. [*To* Natta.] I note 'em well: No more. Say you?
    Sat.   My lord,
There is a gentleman of Rome would buy——
    Sej. How call you him you talk'd with?
    Sat.   'Please your lordship,
It is Eudemus, the physician
To Livia, Drusus' wife.
    Sej.   On with your suit.
Would buy, you said——
    Sat.   A tribune's place, my lord.
    Sej. What will he give?
    Sat.   Fifty sestertia.
    Sej. Livia's physician, say you, is that fellow?
    Sat. It is, my lord; your lordship's answer?
    Sej.   To what?
    Sat. The place, my lord. 'Tis for a gentleman
Your lordship will well like of, when you see him;
And one you may make yours, by the grant.
    Sej. Well, let him bring his money, and his name.
    Sat. Thank your lordship. He shall, my lord.

Sej.   Come hither.
Know you this same Eudemus? Is he learn'd?

Sat. Reputed so, my lord: and of deep practice.

Sej. Bring him in to me, in the gallery;
And take you cause to leave us there together:
I would confer with him about a grief.——On.

[*Exeunt* Sejanus, Terentius, Satrius, *and* Natta.

Arr. So yet! another? yet? O desperate state
Of grovelling honour! Seest thou this, O sun,
And do we see thee after? Methinks, day
Should lose his light, when men do lose their shames,
And, for the empty circumstance of life,
Betray their cause of living.

Sil.   Nothing so.
Sejanus can repair if Jove should ruin.
He is the now court-god; and well applied
With sacrifice of knees, of crooks, and cringe,
He will do more than all the house of heav'n
Can for a thousand hecatombs. 'Tis he
Makes us our day, or night; Hell, and Elysium
Are in his look: We talk of Rhadamanth,
Furies, and firebrands; But 'tis his frown
That is all these, where, on the adverse part,
His smile is more, than e'er yet poets feign'd
Of bliss, and shades, nectar——

Arr.   A serving boy?
I knew him, at Caius' trencher, when for hire,
He prostituted his abused body
To that great gourmand, fat Apicius;
And was the noted pathic of the time.

Sab. And, now, the second face of the whole world.
The partner of the empire, hath his image
Rear'd equal with Tiberius, born in ensigns,
Commands, disposes every dignity.
Centurions, tribunes, heads of provinces
Prætors, and consuls, all that heretofore
Rome's general suffrage gave, is now his sale.
The gain or rather spoil of all the earth,
One, and his house, receives.

Sil.   He hath of late
Made him a strength too, strangely, by reducing
All the Prætorian bands into one camp,
Which he commands: pretending, that the soldier
By living loose and scattered, fell to riot;
And that if any sudden enterprise
Should be attempted, their united strength
Would be far more than sever'd; and their life
More strict, if from the city more remov'd.

Sab. Where now he builds what kind of forts he please,
Is heard to court the soldier by his name,
Woos, feasts the chiefest men of action,
Whose wants, not loves, compel them to be his.
And, though he ne'er were liberal by kind,
Yet to his own dark ends, he's most profuse,
Lavish, and letting fly, he cares not what
To his ambition.

Arr.   Yet, hath he ambition?
Is there that step in state can make him higher?
Or more? or anything he is, but less?

Sil. Nothing, but Emperor.

Arr.   The name Tiberius,
I hope, will keep; howe'er he hath forgone
The dignity and power.

Sil.   Sure, while he lives.

Arr. And dead, it comes to Drusus. Should he fail,
To the brave issue of Germanicus
And they are three: Too many (ha?) for him
To have a plot upon?

Sab.   I do not know
The heart of his designs; but, sure, their face
Looks farther than the present.

Arr.   By the gods,
If I could guess he had but such a thought,
My sword should cleave him down from head to heart,
But I would find it out: and with my hand
I'd hurl his panting brain about the air,
In mites as small as *atomi*, to undo
The knotted bed——

Sab. You are observed, Arruntius.

Arr. [*Turns to* Sejanus' *client.*] Death! I dare tell him
so; and all his spies:
You, sir, I would, do you look? and you.

Sab. Forbear.

ACT I. SCENE II

A gallery opening into the state room.

Enter Satrius *with* Eudemus.

Sat. Here he will instant be; let's walk a turn.
You're in a muse, Eudemus?

Eud. Not I, sir.
I wonder he should mark me out so! well,
Jove and Apollo form it for the best. [*Aside.*

Sat. Your fortune's made unto you now, Eudemus,
If you can but lay hold upon the means;
Do but observe his humour, and—believe it—
He's the noblest Roman, where he takes——

Enter Sejanus.

Here comes his lordship.

Sej. Now, good Satrius.

Sat. This is the gentleman, my lord.

Sej. Is this?
Give me your hand, we must be more acquainted.
Report, sir, hath spoke out your art and learning:
And I am glad I have so needful cause
(However in itself painful and hard)
To make me known to so great virtue. Look,
Who's that, Satrius? [*Exit Satrius.*

I have a grief, sir,
That will desire your help. Your name's Eudemus?

Eud. Yes.

Sej. Sir?

Eud.   It is, my lord.

Sej.   I hear, you are
Physician to Livia the princess?

   Eud. I minister unto her, my good lord.

   Sej. You minister to a royal lady, then.

   Eud. She is, my lord, and fair.

   Sej.   That's understood
Of all their sex, who are or would be so;
And those that would be, physic soon can make 'em:
For those that are, their beauties fear no colours.

   Eud. Your lordship is conceited.

   Sej.   Sir, you know it,
And can (if need be) read a learned lecture,
On this, and other secrets. Pray you tell me,
What more of ladies, besides Livia,
Have you your patients?

   Eud.   Many, my good lord.
The great Augusta Urgulania,
Mutilia Prisca and Plancina, divers——

   Sej. And all these tell you the particulars
Of every several grief? how first it grew,
And then increas'd, what action caused that;
What passion that: and answer to each point
That you will put 'em.

   Eud.   Else, my lord, we know not
How to prescribe the remedies.

   Sej.   Go to,
You are a subtle nation, you physicians!
And grown the only cabinets in court,
To ladies' privacies. Faith, which of these
Is the most pleasant lady, in her physic?
Come, you are modest now.

   Eud.   'Tis fit, my lord.

   Sej. Why, sir, I do not ask you of their urines,
Whose smells most violet? or whose siege is best?
Or who makes hardest faces on her stool?
Which lady sleeps with her own face, at nights?
Which puts her teeth off, with her clothes, in court?
Or which her hair? which her complexion?

And, in which box she puts it? These were questions
That might, perhaps, have put your gravity
To some defence of blush. But I enquir'd,
Which was the wittiest? merriest? wantonest?
Harmless interrogatories, but conceits.
Methinks, Augusta should be most perverse,
And froward in her fit?

Eud.　　　　　　　She's so, my lord.

Sej. I knew it. And Mutilia the most jocund?

Eud. 'Tis very true, my lord.

Sej.　　　　　　　And why would you
Conceal this from me, now? Come, what's Livia?
I know she's quick, and quaintly spirited,
And will have strange thoughts, when she's at leisure;
She tells 'em all to you?

Eud.　　　　　My noblest lord,
He breathes not in the empire, or on earth,
Whom I would be ambitious to serve
In any act, that may preserve mine honour,
Before your lordship.

Sej.　　　　　Sir, you can lose no honour,
By trusting ought to me. The coarsest act
Done to my service, I can so requite,
As all the world shall style it honourable:
Your idle, virtuous definitions
Keep honour poor, and are as scorn'd as vain:
Those deeds breathe honour that do suck in gain.

Eud. But, good my lord, if I should thus betray
The counsels of my patient, and a lady's
Of her high place, and worth; what might your lordship,
Who presently are to trust me with your own,
Judge of my faith?

Sej.　　　　　Only the best, I swear.
Say now, that I should utter you my grief;
And with it, the true cause; that it were love;
And love to Livia: you should tell her this?
Should she suspect your faith? I would you could
Tell me as much, from her; see, if my brain
Could be turn'd jealous.

115

Eud.   Happily, my lord,
I could, in time, tell you as much, and more;
So I might safely promise but the first,
To her, from you.

Sej.   As safely, my Eudemus,
(I now dare call thee so) as I have put
The secret into thee.

Eud.   My lord——

Sej.   Protest not.
Thy looks are vows to me, use only speed,
And but affect her with Sejanus' love,
Thou art a man made to make consuls. Go.

Eud. My lord, I'll promise you a private meeting
This day, together.

Sej.   Canst thou?

Eud.   Yes.

Sej.   The place?

Eud. My gardens, whither I shall [fetch] your lordship.

Sej. Let me adore my Æsculapius.
Why, this indeed is physic! and outspeaks
The knowledge of cheap drugs, or any use
Can be made out of it! more comforting
Than all your opiates, juleps, apozems,
Magistral syrups, or—Begone, my friend,
Not barely styled, but created so;
Expect things greater than thy largest hopes,
To overtake thee: Fortune shall be taught
To know how ill she hath deserv'd thus long,
To come behind thy wishes. Go, and speed.

                                    [*Exit* Eudemus.

Ambition makes more trusty slaves, than need.
These fellows, by the favour of their art,
Have still the means to tempt, oft-times, the power.
If Livia will now be corrupted, then
Thou hast the way, Sejanus, to work out
His secrets, who (thou knowest) endures thee not,
Her husband Drusus: and to work against them.
Prosper it, Pallas, thou, that betterest wit;
For Venus hath the smallest share in it.

Enter Tiberius *and* Drusus, *attended.*

Tib. [*One kneels to him.*] We not endure these flat-
teries; let him stand;
Our empire, ensigns, axes, rods, and state
Take not away our human nature from us:
Look up on us, and fall away before the gods.

Sej. How like a god speaks Cæsar!

Arr.   There, observe!
He can endure that second, that's no flattery.
O, what is it, proud slime will not believe
Of his own worth, to hear it equal prais'd
Thus with the gods?

Cor.   He did not hear it, sir.

Arr. He did not? Tut, he must not, we think meanly.
'Tis your most courtly, known confederacy,
To have your private parasite redeem
What he, in public subtlety, will lose
To making him a name.

Hat.   Right mighty lord——
                              [*Gives him letters.*

Tib. We must make up our ears 'gainst these assaults
Of charming tongues; we pray you use no more
These contumelies to us: style not us
Or lord, or mighty, who profess ourself
The servant of the senate, and are proud
T' enjoy them our good, just, and favouring lords.

Cor. Rarely dissembled.

Arr.   Prince-like, to the life.

Sab. When power, that may command, so much descends,
Their bondage, whom it stoops to, it intends.

Tib. Whence are these letters?

Hat.   From the senate.

Tib.   So.
                         [*Latiaris gives him letters.*
Whence these?

Lat.   From thence too.

Tib.   Are they sitting now?

Lat. They stay thy answer, Cæsar.

Sil.   If this man
Had but a mind allied unto his words,
How bless'd a fate were it to us, and Rome?
We could not think that state for which to change,
Although the aim were our old liberty:
The ghosts of those that fell for that, would grieve
Their bodies liv'd not, now, again to serve.
Men are deceiv'd, who think there can be thrall
Beneath a virtuous prince. Wish'd liberty
Ne'er lovelier looks, than under such a crown.
But, when his grace is merely but lip-good,
And that, no longer than he airs himself
Abroad in public, there, to seem to shun
The stroke and stripes of flatterers, which within
Are lechery unto him, and so feed
His brutish sense with their afflicting sound,
As (dead to virtue) he permits himself
Be carried like a pitcher, by the ears,
To every act of vice: this is a case
Deserves our fear, and doth presage the nigh
And close approach of blood and tyranny.
Flattery is midwife unto princes' rage:
And nothing sooner doth help forth a tyrant,
Than that and whisperers' grace, who have the time,
The place, the power, to make all men offenders.

   Arr. He should be told this: and be bid dissemble
With fools, and blind men: we that know the evil
Should hunt the palace-rats, or give them bane;
Fright hence these worse than ravens, that devour
The quick, where they but prey upon the dead:
He shall be told of it.

   Sab.   Stay, Arruntius,
We must abide our opportunity:
And practise what is fit, as what is needful.
It is not safe t' enforce a sovereign's ear:
Princes hear well, if they at all will hear.

   Arr. Ha? Say you so? well. In the meantime, Jove
(Say not but I do call upon thee now),
Of all wild beasts, preserve me from a tyrant;

And of all tame, a flatterer.

   Sil.   'Tis well pray'd.

   Tib. Return the lords this voice, we are their creature:
And it is fit a good and honest prince,
Whom they, out of their bounty, have instructed
With so dilate and absolute a power,
Should owe the office of it to their service,
And good of all and every citizen.
Nor shall it e'er repent us to have wish'd
The senate just, and fav'ring lords unto us,
Since their free loves do yield no less defence
T' a prince's state, than his own innocence.
Say then there can be nothing in their thought
Shall want to please us, that hath pleased them;
Our suffrage rather shall prevent, than stay
Behind their wills: 'tis empire, to obey
Where such, so great, so grave, so good determine.
Yet, for the suit of Spain t' erect a temple
In honour of our mother, and ourself,
We must (with pardon of the senate) not
Assent thereto. Their lordships may object
Our not denying the same late request
Unto the Asian cities: We desire
That our defence, for suffering that, be known
In these brief reasons, with our after purpose.
Since deified Augustus hindered not
A temple to be built at Pergamum,
In honour of himself and sacred Rome
We, that have all his deeds and words observ'd
Ever, in place of laws, the rather follow'd
That pleasing precedent, because, with ours,
The senate's reverence, also, there was join'd.
But as, t' have once receiv'd it, may deserve
The gain of pardon, so to be ador'd
With the continu'd style and note of gods,
Through all the provinces, were wild ambition,
And no less pride: Yea, ev'n Augustus' name
Would early vanish, should it be profan'd
With such promiscuous flatteries. For our part,

We here protest it, and are covetous
Posterity should know it, we are mortal:
And can but deeds of men: 'twere glory enough,
Could we be truly a prince. And, they shall add
Abounding grace unto our memory,
That shall report us worthy our forefathers,
Careful of your affairs, constant in dangers,
And not afraid of any private frown
For public good. These things shall be to us
Temples, and statues, reared in your minds,
The fairest, and most during imagery:
For those of stone, or brass, if they become
Odious in judgement of posterity
Are more contemn'd as dying sepulchres,
Than ta'en for living monuments. We then
Make here our suit, alike to gods and men,
The one, until the period of our race,
T' inspire us with a free and quiet mind,
Discerning both divine and human laws;
The other, to vouchsafe us after death,
An honourable mention, and fair praise,
T' accompany our actions and our name:
The rest of greatness princes may command,
And (therefore) may neglect; only, a long,
A lasting, high, and happy memory
They should, without being satisfied, pursue.
Contempt of fame begets contempt of virtue.

   Nat. Rare!

   Sat.   Most divine!

   Sej.   The oracles are ceas'd,
That only Cæsar, with their tongue, might speak.

   Arr. Let me be gone, most felt and open this!

   Cor. Stay.

   Arr.   What? to hear more cunning and fine words,
With their sound flatter'd ere their sense be meant?

   Tib. Their choice of Antium, there to place the gift
Vow'd to the goddess, for our mother's health,
We will the senate know, we fairly like;
As also, of their grant to Lepidus

For his repairing the Æmilian place,
And restoration of those monuments:
Their grace too in confining of Silanus
To th' other isle Cithera at the suit
Of his religious sister, much commends
Their policy so temp'red with their mercy.
But, for the honours, which they have decreed
To our Sejanus, to advance his statue
In Pompey's theatre (whose ruining fire
His vigilance and labour kept restrain'd
In that one loss), they have, therein, outgone
Their own great wisdoms, by their skilful choice,
And placing of their bounties on a man,
Whose merit more adorns the dignity
Than that can him: and gives a benefit
In taking, greater than it can receive.
Blush not, Sejanus, thou great aid of Rome,
Associate of our labours, our chief helper
Let us not force thy simple modesty
With offering at thy praise, for more we cannot,
Since there's no voice can take it. No man here
Receive our speeches as hyperboles;
For we are far from flattering our friend
(Let envy know) as from the need to flatter
Nor let them ask the causes of our praise;
Princes have still their grounds rear'd with themselves,
Above the poor low flats of common men,
And who will search the reasons of their acts,
Must stand on equal bases. Lead, away.
Our loves unto the senate.

           [*Exeunt* Tib., Sejan., Natta, Hat., Lat., *etc.*

  Arr.   Cæsar.
  Sab.   **Peace.**
  Cor. Great Pompey's theatre was never ruin'd
Till now, that proud Sejanus hath a statue
Rear'd on his ashes.
  Arr.   Place the shame of soldiers,
Above the best of generals? crack the world,
And bruise the name of Romans into dust,

Ere we behold it!

Sil.   Check your passion;
Lord Drusus tarries.

Dru.   Is my father mad?
Weary of life and rule, lords? thus to heave
An idol up with praise! make him his mate!
His rival in the empire!

Arr.   O, good prince!

Dru. Allow him statues? titles? honours? such,
As he himself refuseth?

Arr.   Brave, brave Drusus!

Dru. The first ascents to sovereignty are hard,
But, entered once, there never wants or means,
Or ministers, to help th' aspirer on.

Arr. True, gallant Drusus.

Dru.   We must shortly pray
To Modesty, that he will rest contented——

Arr. Aye, where he is, and not write emperor.

Re-enter Sejanus, Satrius, Latiaris, *etc.*

Sej. There is your bill. and yours: bring you your man:
[*To* Satrius.]
I' have mov'd for you, too, Latiaris.

Dru.   What?
Is your vast greatness grown so blindly bold,
That you will over us?

Sej.   Why, then give way.

Dru. Give way, Colossus? Do you lift? Advance you?
Take that.   [Drusus *strikes him.*

Arr. Good! brave! excellent brave prince!

Dru. Nay, come, approach. [*Draws his sword.*] What?
          stand you off? at gaze?
It looks too full of death for thy cold spirits.
Avoid mine eye, dull camel, or my sword
Shall make thy bravery fitter for a grave
Than for a triumph. I'll advance a statue
O' your own bulk; but't shall be on the cross:
Where I will nail your pride, at breadth, and length,
And crack those sinews, which are yet but stretch'd

122

With your swollen fortune's rage.

   Arr.   A noble prince!

   All. A Castor, a Castor, a Castor, a Castor!

                       [Exeunt all but Sejanus.

   Sej. He that with such wrong moved, can bear it through
With patience, and an even mind, knows how
To turn it back. Wrath, cover'd, carries fate:
Revenge is lost, if I profess my hate.
What was my practice late, I'll now pursue
As my fell justice. This hath styled it new.   *[Exit.*

ACT II. SCENE I

The garden of Eudemus.

Enter Sejanus, Livia, *and* Eudemus.

   Sej. Physician, thou art worthy of a province,
For the great favours done unto our loves;
And, but that greatest Livia bears a part
In the requital of thy services,
I should alone despair of aught, like means,
To give them worthy satisfaction.

   Liv. Eudemus (I will see it) shall receive
A fit and full reward for his large merit.
But for this potion, we intend to Drusus,
(No more our husband, now) whom shall we choose
As the most apt and abled instrument,
To minister it to him?

   Eud.   I say, Lygdus.

   Sej. Lygdus? what's he?

   Liv.   An eunuch Drusus loves.

   Eud. Aye, and his cup-bearer.

   Sej.   Name not a second.
If Drusus love him, and he have that place,
We cannot think a fitter.

   Eud.   True, my lord,
For free access and trust are two main aids.

   Sej. Skilful physician!

Liv.   But he must be wrought
To th' undertaking, with some labour'd art.

   Sej. Is he ambitious?

   Liv.   No.

   Sej.   Or covetous?

   Liv. Neither.

   Eud.   Yet, gold is a good general charm.

   Sej. What is he then?

   Liv.   'Faith, only wanton, light.

   Sej. How! Is he young? and fair?

   Eud.   A delicate youth.

   Sej. Send him to me, I'll work him. Royal lady,
Though I have lov'd you long, and with that height
Of zeal and duty (like the fire, which more
It mounts, it trembles) thinking nought could add
Unto the fervour, which your eye had kindled;
Yet, now I see your wisdom, judgement, strength,
Quickness, and will to apprehend the means
To your own good and greatness, I protest
Myself through rarified, and turn'd all flame
In your affection: Such a spirit as yours,
Was not created for the idle second
To a poor flesh, as Drusus; but to shine
Bright as the Moon among the lesser lights,
And share the sov'reignty of all the world.
Then Livia triumphs in her proper sphere,
When she and her Sejanus shall divide
The name of Cæsar; and Augusta's star
Be dimm'd with glory of a brighter beam:
When Agrippina's fires are quite extinct,
And the scarce-seen Tiberius borrows all
His little light from us, whose folded arms
Shall make one perfect orb. [*Knocking within.*] Who's
        that? Eudemus,
Look. [*Exit* Eudemus.] 'Tis not Drusus? Lady, do not fear.

   Liv. Not I, my lord. My fear and love of him
Left me at once.

   Sej.   Illustrious lady! stay——

   Eud. [*Within.*] I'll tell his lordship.

Re-enter Eudemus.

Sej. Who is't, Eudemus?

Eud. One of your lordship's servants brings you word
The Emp'ror hath sent for you.

Sej.   O! where is he?
With your fair leave, dear Princess, I'll but ask
A question, and return.   [*He goes out.*

Eud.   Fortunate Princess!
How are you blessed in the fruition
Of this unequalled man, this soul of Rome,
The empire's life, and voice of Cæsar's world!

Liv. So blessed, my Eudemus, as to know
The bliss I have, with what I ought to owe
The means that wrought it. How do I look to-day?

Eud. Excellent clear, believe it. This same fucus
Was well laid on.

Liv.   Methinks, 'tis here not white.

Eud. Lend me your scarlet, lady. 'Tis the sun
Hath giv'n some little taint unto the ceruse,
You should have us'd of the white oil I gave you.
Sejanus, for your love! his very name
Commandeth above Cupid, or his shafts——

                                   [*Paints her cheeks.*

Liv. Nay, now yo' have made it worse.

Eud.   I'll help it straight——
And, but pronounc'd, is a sufficient charm
Against all rumour; and of absolute power
To satisfy for any lady's honour.

Liv. What do you now, Eudemus?

Eud.   Make a light fucus,
To touch you o'er withall. Honour'd Sejanus!
What act (though ne'er so strange and insolent)
But that addition will at least bear out,
If 't do not expiate?

Liv.   Here, good physician.

Eud. I like this study to preserve the love
Of such a man, that comes not every hour
To greet the world. ('Tis now well, lady, you should

125

Use of the dentifrice I prescrib'd you, too,
To clear your teeth, and the prepar'd pomatum,
To smoothe the skin:) A lady cannot be
Too curious of her form, that still would hold
The heart of such a person, made her captive,
As you have his: who, to endear him more
In your clear eye, hath put away his wife,
The trouble of his bed, and your delights,
Fair Apicata, and made spacious room
To your new pleasures.

  Liv.   Have not we return'd
That with our hate of Drusus, and discovery
Of all his counsels?

  Eud.   Yes, and wisely, lady,
The ages that succeed, and stand far off
To gaze at your high prudence, shall admire
And reckon it an act without your sex:
It hath that rare appearance. Some will think
Your fortune could not yield a deeper sound,
Than mix'd with Drusus; but, when they shall hear
That, and the thunder of Sejanus meet,
Sejanus, whose high name doth strike the stars,
And rings about the concave, great Sejanus,
Whose glories, style, and titles are himself,
The often iterating of Sejanus:
They then will lose their thoughts, and be asham'd
To take acquaintance of them.

     Re-enter Sejanus.

  Sej.   I must make
A rude departure, lady. Cæsar sends
With all his haste both of command and prayer.
Be resolute in our plot; you have my soul,
As certain yours as it is my body's.
And, wise physician, so prepare the poison
As you may lay the subtile operation
Upon some natural disease of his.
Your eunuch send to me. I kiss your hands,
Glory of ladies, and commend my love

To your best faith and memory.

    Liv.   My lord,
I shall but change your words. Farewell. Yet, this
Remember for your heed, he loves you not;
You know what I have told you: his designs
Are full of grudge and danger: we must use
More than a common speed.

    Sej.   Excellent lady,
How you do fire my blood!

    Liv.   Well, you must go?
The thoughts be best, are least set forth to show.

                              [Exit Sejanus.

    Eud. When will you take some physic, lady?

    Liv.   When
I shall, Eudemus: but let Drusus' drug
Be first prepar'd.

    Eud.   Were Lygdus made, that's done;
I have it ready. And to-morrow morning,
I'll send you a perfume, first to resolve,
And procure sweat, and then prepare a bath
To cleanse, and clear the cutis; against when
I'll have an excellent new fucus made,
Resistive 'gainst the sun, the rain, or wind,
Which you shall lay on with a breath, or oil,
As you best like, and last some fourteen hours.
This change came timely, lady, for your health;
And the restoring your complexion,
Which Drusus' choler had almost burnt up:
Wherein your fortune hath prescrib'd you better
Than art could do.

    Liv.   Thanks, good physician,
I'll use my fortune (you shall see) with reverence.
Is my coach ready?

    Eud.   It attends your highness.   *[Exeunt*

ACT II. SCENE II

An apartment in the palace.

Enter Sejanus.

   Sej. If this be not revenge, when I have done
And made it perfect, let Egyptian slaves,
Parthians and barefoot Hebrews brand my face,
And print my body full of injuries.
Thou lost thyself, child Drusus, when thou thought'st
Thou could'st outskip my vengeance: or outstand
The power I had to crush thee into air.
Thy follies now shall taste what kind of man
They have provok'd, and this thy father's house
Crack in the flame of my incensed rage,
Whose fury shall admit no shame, or mean.
Adultery? it is the lightest ill
I will commit. A race of wicked acts
Shall flow out of my anger, and o'erspread
The world's wide face, which no posterity
Shall e'er approve, nor yet keep silent: things,
That for their cunning, close and cruel mark,
Thy father would wish his; and shall (perhaps)
Carry the empty name, but we the prize.
On then, my soul, and start not in thy course;
Though heav'n drop sulphur, and hell belch out fire,
Laugh at the idle terrors: tell proud Jove,
Between his power and thine, there is no odds.
'Twas only fear first in the world made gods.

           Enter Tiberius, *attended.*

  Tib. Is yet Sejanus come?
  Sej.   He's here, dread Cæsar.
  Tib. Let all depart that chamber, and the next:
                              [*Exeunt* Attendants.
Sit down, my comfort. When the master prince
Of all the world, Sejanus, saith he fears;
Is it not fatal?
  Sej.   Yes, to those are fear'd.

Tib. And not to him?

Sej.   Not, if he wisely turn
That part of fate he holdeth, first on them.

Tib. That nature, blood, and laws of kind forbid.

Sej. Do policy and state forbid it?

Tib.   No.

Sej. The rest of poor respects, then, let go by:
State is enough to make th' act just, them guilty.

Tib. Long hate pursues such acts.

Sej.   Whom hatred frights,
Let him not dream on sov'reignty.

Tib.   Are rites
Of faith, love, piety, to be trod down?
Forgotten? and made vain?

Sej.   All for a crown.
The prince who shames a tyrant's name to bear,
Shall never dare do anything but fear;
All the command of sceptres quite doth perish
If it begin religious thoughts to cherish:
Whole empires fall, swayed by those nice respects;
It is the licence of dark deeds protects
Ev'n states most hated: when no laws resist
The sword, but that it acteth what it list.

Tib. Yet so, we may do all things cruelly,
Not safely.

Sej.   Yes, and do them thoroughly.

Tib. Knows yet Sejanus whom we point at?

Sej.   Aye,
Or else my thought, my sense, or both do err:
'Tis Agrippina?

Tib.   She; and her proud race.

Sej. Proud? dangerous, Cæsar. For in them apace
The father's spirit shoots up. Germanicus
Lives in their looks, their gait, their form, t' upbraid us
With his close death, if not revenge the same.

Tib. The act's not known.

Sej.   Not prov'd. But whispering fame
Knowledge and proof doth to the jealous give,
Who, than to fail, would their own thought believe.

It is not safe the children draw long breath,
That are provoked by a parent's death.
   Tib. It is as dangerous to make them hence,
If nothing but their birth be their offence.
   Sej. Stay, till they strike at Cæsar: then their crime
Will be enough, but late, and out of time
For him to punish.
   Tib.   Do they purpose it?
   Sej. You know, sir, thunder speaks not till it hit
Be not secure: none swiftlier are oppress'd
Than they whom confidence betrays to rest.
Let not your daring make your danger such:
All power 's to be fear'd, where 'tis too much.
The youths are (of themselves) hot, violent,
Full of great thought; and that male-spirited dame,
Their mother, slacks no means to put them on,
By large allowance, popular presentings,
Increase of train and state, suing for titles,
Hath them commended with like prayers, like vows,
To the same gods, with Cæsar: days and nights
She spends in banquets and ambitious feasts
For the nobility; where Caius Silius,
Titius Sabinus, old Arruntius,
Asinius Gallus, Furnius, Regulus,
And others of that discontented list,
Are the prime guests. There, and to these she tells
Whose niece she was, whose daughter, and whose wife.
And then must they compare her with Augusta,
Aye, and prefer her too; commend her form,
Extol her fruitfulness; at which a shower
Falls for the memory of Germanicus,
Which they blow over straight, with windy praise
And puffing hopes of her aspiring sons:
Who, with these hourly ticklings, grow so pleas'd
And wantonly conceited of themselves,
As now, they stick not to believe they're such
As these do give 'em out: and would be thought
(More than competitors) immediate heirs.
Whilst to their thirst of rule they win the rout

(That's still the friend of novelty) with hope
Of future freedom, which on every change
That greedily, though emptily, expects.
Cæsar, 'tis age in all things breeds neglects,
And princes that will keep old dignity
Must not admit too youthful heirs stand by;
Not their own issue: but so darkly set
As shadows are in picture, to give height,
And lustre to themselves.

 Tib.   We will command
Their rank thoughts down, and with a stricter hand
Than we have yet put forth, their trains must bate,
Their titles, feasts and factions.

 Sej.   Or your state.
But how sir, will you work?

 Tib.   Confine 'em.

 Sej.   No.
They are too great, and that too faint a blow
To give them now: it would have serv'd at first,
When, with the weakest touch, their knot had burst.
But now your care must be not to detect
The smallest cord or line of your suspect,
For such who know the weight of princes' fear,
Will, when they find themselves discover'd, rear
Their forces, like seen snakes, that else would lie
Rotted in their circles, close: nought is more high,
Daring, or desperate, than offenders found;
Where guilt is, rage and courage both abound.
The course must be to let 'em still swell up,
Riot, and surfeit on blind fortune's cup;
Give 'em more place, more dignities, more style,
Call 'em to court, to senate: in the while,
Take from their strength some one or twain or more
Of the main fautors (it will fright the store)
And, by some by-occasion. Thus, with slight
You shall disarm them first, and they (in night
Of their ambition) not perceive the train,
Till in the engine they are caught and slain.

 Tib. We would not kill, if we knew how to save;

Yet, than a throne, 'tis cheaper give a grave.
Is there no way to bind them by deserts?

Sej. Sir, wolves do change their hair, but not their hearts.
While thus your thought unto a mean is tied,
You neither dare enough, nor do provide.
All modesty is fond; and chiefly where
The subject is no less compelled to bear,
Than praise his sov'reign's acts.

Tib.   We can no longer
Keep on our mask to thee, our dear Sejanus;
Thy thoughts are ours, in all, and we but prov'd
Their voice, in our designs, which by assenting
Hath more confirm'd us, than if heartening Jove
Had, from his hundred statues, bid us strike,
And at the stroke clicked all his marble thumbs.
But, who shall first be struck?

Sej.   First, Caius Silius;
He is the most of mark, and most of danger:
In power and reputation equal strong,
Having commanded an imperial army
Seven years together, vanquish'd Sacrovir
In Germany and thence obtain'd to wear
The ornaments triumphal. His steep fall,
By how much it doth give the weightier crack,
Will send more wounding terror to the rest,
Command them stand aloof, and give more way
To our surprising of the principal.

Tib. But what, Sabinus?

Sej.   Let him grow awhile,
His fate is not yet ripe: we must not pluck
At all together, lest we catch ourselves.
And there's Arruntius too, he only talks.
But Sosia, Silius' wife, would be wound in
Now, for she hath a fury in her breast
More than hell ever knew; and would be sent
Thither in time. Then, is there one Cremutius
Cordus, a writing fellow they have got
To gather notes of the precedent times,
And make them into Annals; a most tart

And bitter spirit (I hear) who under colour
Of praising those, doth tax the present state,
Censures the men, the actions, leaves no trick,
No practice un-examin'd, parallels
The times, the governments, a profess'd champion
For the old liberty——

   Tib.   A perishing wretch.
As if there were that chaos bred in things,
That laws and liberty would not rather choose
To be quite broken, and ta'en hence by us,
Than have the stain to be preserv'd by such.
Have we the means to make these guilty, first?

   Sej. Trust that to me: let Cæsar, by his power,
But cause a formal meeting of the senate,
I will have matter and accusers ready.

   Tib. But how? let us consult.

   Sej.   We shall misspend
The time of action. Counsels are unfit
In business, where all rest is more pernicious
Than rashness can be. Acts of this close kind
Thrive more by execution than advice.
There is no lingering in that work begun,
Which cannot praised be, until through done.

   Tib. Our edict shall forthwith command a court.
While I can live, I will prevent earth's fury:
᾽Εμοῦ Θανόντος γαῖα μιχ θήτω πυρί.   [*Exit.*

Enter Posthumus.

   Pos. My lord Sejanus——

   Sej.   Julius Posthumus,
Come with my wish! what news from Agrippina's?

   Pos. 'Faith, none. They all lock up themselves a'late;
Or talk in character: I have not seen
A company so chang'd. Except they had
Intelligence by augury of our practice.

   Sej. When were you there?

   Pos.   Last night.

   Sej.   And what guests found you?

Pos. Sabinus, Silius (the old list,) Arruntius,
Furnius, and Gallus.

    Sej.   Would not these talk?

    Pos.   Little.

And yet we offer'd choice of argument.
Satrius was with me.

    Sej.   Well: 'tis guilt enough

Their often meeting. You forgot t' extol
The hospitable lady?

    Pos.   No, that trick

Was well put home, and had succeeded too,
But that Sabinus coughed a caution out;
For she began to swell.

    Sej.   And may she burst!

Julius, I would have you go instantly
Unto the palace of the great Augusta
And (by your kindest friend) get swift access;
Acquaint her with these meetings: Tell the words
You brought me (th' other day) of Silius.
Add somewhat to 'em. Make her understand
The danger of Sabinus, and the times,
Out of his closeness. Give Arruntius words
Of malice against Cæsar; so, to Gallus:
But (above all) to Agrippina. Say
(As you may truly) that her infinite pride,
Propt with the hopes of her too fruitful womb,
With popular studies gapes for sovereignty;
And threatens Cæsar. Pray Augusta then,
That for her own, great Cæsar's, and the pub-
lic safety she be pleas'd to urge these dangers.
Cæsar is too secure, he must be told,
And best he'll take it from a mother's tongue,
Alas! what is't for us to sound, t' explore,
To watch, oppose, plot, practise, or prevent,
If he, for whom it is so strongly labour'd,
Shall, out of greatness and free spirit, be
Supinely negligent? Our city's now
Divided as in time o' th' civil war,
And men forbear not to declare themselves

Of Agrippina's party. Every day,
The faction multiplies; and will do more
If not resisted: you can best enlarge it
As you find audience. Noble Posthumus,
Commend me to your Prisca: and pray her
She will solicit this great business
To earnest and most present execution,
With all her utmost credit with Augusta.

Pos. I shall not fail in my instructions.   [*Exit.*

Sej. This second (from his mother) will well urge
Our late design, and spur on Cæsar's rage:
Which else might grow remiss. The way to put
A prince in blood, is to present the shapes
Of dangers greater than they are (like late
Or early shadows) and, sometimes, to feign
Where there are none, only to make him fear;
His fear will make him cruel: and once entered,
He doth not easily learn to stop, or spare
Where he may doubt. This have I made my rule,
To thrust Tiberius into tyranny.
And make him toil to turn aside those blocks,
Which I alone could not remove with safety.
Drusus once gone, Germanicus' three sons
Would clog my way; whose guards have too much faith
To be corrupted: and their mother known
Of too too unreprov'd a chastity
To be attempted, as light Livia was.
Work then, my art, on Cæsar's fears, as they
On those they fear, till all my lets be clear'd:
And he in ruins of his house, and hate
Of all his subjects, bury his own state:
When, with my peace and safety, I will rise,
By making him the public sacrifice.   [*Exit.*

135

ACT II. SCENE III

A room in Agrippina's house.

Enter Satrius *and* Natta.

Sat. They are grown exceeding circumspect, and wary.

Nat. They have us in the wind: And yet Arruntius
Cannot contain himself.

Sat.   Tut, he's not yet
Look'd after, there are others more desir'd
That are more silent.

Nat.   Here he comes. Away.   [*Exeunt.*

Enter Sabinus, Arruntius, *and* Cordus.

Sab. How is it that these beagles haunt the house
Of Agrippina?

Arr.   O, they hunt, they hunt,
There is some game here lodg'd, which they must rouse
To make the great ones sport.

Cor.   Did you observe
How they inveigh'd 'gainst Cæsar?

Arr.   Aye, baits, baits,
For us to bite at: would I have my flesh
Torn by the public hook, these qualified hangmen
Should be my company.

Cor.   Here comes another.

Arr. Aye, there's a man, Afer the orator!
                                        [*Afer passeth by.*
One that hath phrases, figures, and fine flowers,
To strew his rhetoric with, and doth make haste
To get him note or name by any offer
Where blood or gain be objects; steeps his words,
When he would kill, in artificial tears:
The crocodile of Tiber! him I love,
That man is mine. He hath my heart and voice,
When I would curse! he, he.

Sab.   Contemn the slaves,
Their present lives will be their future graves.   [*Exeunt.*

ACT II. SCENE IV

Another apartment in the same.

Enter Silius, Agrippina, Nero, *and* Sosia.

 Sil. May't please your highness not forget yourself,
I dare not, with my manners, to attempt
Your trouble farther.
 Agr.   Farewell, noble Silius.
 Sil. Most royal princess.
 Agr.   Sosia stays with us?
 Sil. She is your servant, and doth owe your grace
An honest but unprofitable love.
 Agr. How can that be, when there's no gain but virtue's?
 Sil. You take the moral not the politic sense.
I meant, as she is bold and free of speech,
Earnest to utter what her zealous thought
Travails withal, in honour of your house;
Which act, as it is simply born in her,
Partakes of love and honesty, but may,
By th' over-often and unseason'd use,
Turn to your loss and danger: For your state
Is waited on by envies, as by eyes;
And every second guest your tables take,
Is a fee'd spy, t' observe who goes, who comes,
What conference you have, with whom, where, when,
What the discourse is, what the looks, the thoughts
Of ev'ry person there, they do extract,
And make into a substance.
 Agr.   Hear me, Silius.
Were all Tiberius' body stuck with eyes,
And ev'ry wall and hanging in my house
Transparent, as this lawn I wear, or air;
Yea, had Sejanus both his ears as long
As to my inmost closet: I would hate
To whisper any thought, or change an act,
To be made Juno's rival. Virtue's forces
Show ever noblest in conspicuous courses.

Sil. 'Tis great, and bravely spoken, like the spirit
Of Agrippina: yet, your highness knows,
There is nor loss nor shame in providence:
Few can, what all should do, beware enough.
You may perceive with what officious face,
Satrius and Natta, Afer, and the rest
Visit your house, of late, t' enquire the secrets;
And with what bold and privileg'd art they rail
Against Augusta: yea, and at Tiberius.
Tell tricks of Livia and Sejanus, all
T' excite and call your indignation on,
That they might hear it at more liberty.

   Agr. You're too suspicious, Silius.

   Sil.   Pray the gods,
I be so, Agrippina: but I fear
Some subtle practice. They that durst to strike
At so examples and unblam'd a life
As that of the renown'd Germanicus,
Will not sit down with that exploit alone:
He threatens many, that hath injur'd one.

   Nero. 'Twere best rip forth their tongues, sear out their
      eyes,
When next they come.

   Sos.   A fit reward for spies.

             Enter Drusus, junior.

   Dru. Hear you the rumour?

   Agr.   What?

   Dru.   Drusus is dying.

   Agr. Dying?

   Nero.   That's strange?

   Agr.   Yo' were with him, yesternight.

   Dru. One met Eudemus the physician,
Sent for but now, who thinks he cannot live.

   Sil. Thinks? if 't be arriv'd at that, he knows,
Or none.

   Agr. This's quick! what should be his disease?

   Sil. Poison. Poison——

   Agr.   How, Silius!

Nero.   What's that?

Sil. Nay, nothing. There was (late) a certain blow
Giv'n o' the face.

Nero.   Aye, to Sejanus?

Sil.   True.

Dru. And, what of that?

Sil.   I am glad I gave it not.

Nero. But there is somewhat else?

Sil.   Yes, private meetings.
With a great lady, at a physician's,
And, a wife turn'd away——

Nero.   Ha!

Sil.   Toys, mere toys:
What wisdom's now i' th' streets? i' th' common mouth?

Dru. Fears, whisp'rings, tumults, noise, I know not what:
They say the senate sit.

Sil.   I'll thither, straight;
And see what's in the forge.

Agr.   Good Silius, do.
Sosia and I will in.

Sil.   Haste you, my lords,
To visit the sick prince: tender your loves
And sorrows to the people. This Sejanus
(Trust my divining soul) hath plots on all:
No tree that stops his prospect but must fall.   [*Exeunt.*

ACT III. SCENE I

The Senate.

Enter Sejanus, Varro, Latiaris, Cotta, Afer, Præcones, *and* Lictores.

Sej. 'Tis only you must urge against him, Varro;
Nor I nor Cæsar may appear therein,
Except in your defence, who are the Consul:
And, under colour of late en'mity
Between your father and his, may better do it,
As free from all suspicion of a practice.

Here be your notes, what points to touch at; read:
Be cunning in them. Afer has them too.

    Var. But is he summon'd?

    Sej.   No. It was debated
By Cæsar and concluded as most fit
To take him unprepar'd.

    Afer.   And prosecute
All under name of treason.

    Var.   I conceive.

       Enter Sabinus, Gallus, Lepidus, *and* Arruntius.

    Sab. Drusus being dead, Cæsar will not be here.

    Gal. What should the business of this senate be?

    Arr. That can my subtile whisperers tell you: We,
That are the good-dull-noble lookers on,
Are only call'd to keep the marble warm.
What should we do with those deep mysteries,
Proper to these fine heads? let them alone.
Our ignorance may, perchance, help us be sav'd
From whips and furies.

    Gal.   See, see, see, their action!

    Arr. Aye, now their heads do travail, now they work;
Their faces run like shuttles, they are weaving
Some curious cobweb to catch flies.

    Sab.   Observe,
They take their places.

    Arr.   What, so low?

    Gal.   O yes,
They must be seen to flatter Cæsar's grief
Though but in sitting.

    Var.   Bid us silence.

    Præ.   Silence.

    Var. 'Fathers Conscript, may this our present meeting
Turn fair, and fortunate to the commonwealth.'

       Enter Silius *and other* senators.

    Sej. See, Silius enters.

    Sil.   Hail, grave Fathers.

    Lic.   Stand.
Silius, forbear thy place.

Sen. How!

Præ. Silius, stand forth,
The Consul hath to charge thee.

Lic. Room for Cæsar.

Arr. Is he come too? nay, then, expect a trick.

Sab. Silius accus'd? sure he will answer nobly.

Enter Tiberius *attended.*

Tib. We stand amazed, fathers, to behold
This general dejection. Wherefore sit
Rome's consuls thus dissolv'd, as they had lost
All the remembrance both of style and place?
It not becomes. No woes are of fit weight,
To make the honour of the empire stoop:
Though I, in my peculiar self, may meet
Just reprehension, that so suddenly,
And in so fresh a grief, would greet the senate,
When private tongues of kinsmen and allies
(Inspir'd with comforts) lothly are endur'd,
The face of men not seen, and scarce the day,
To thousands that communicate our loss.
Nor can I argue these of weakness; since
They take but natural ways: yet I must seek
For stronger aids, and those fair helps draw out
From warm embraces of the commonwealth.
Our mother, great Augusta, is struck with time,
Ourself impress'd with aged characters;
Drusus is gone, his children young, and babes,
Our aims must now reflect on those that may
Give timely succour to these present ills,
And are our only glad-surviving hopes,
The noble issue of Germanicus,
Nero, and Drusus: might it please the Consul
Honour them in, (they both attend without.)
I would present them to the senate's care,
And raise those suns of joy, that should drink up
These floods of sorrow, in your drowned eyes.

Arr. By Jove, I am not Œdipus enough
To understand this Sphinx.

SEJANUS

Sab.   The princes come.

Enter Nero *and* Drusus, junior.

  Tib. Approach, you noble Nero, noble Drusus,
These princes, fathers, when their parent died,
I gave unto their uncle with this prayer,
That, though he had proper issue of his own,
He would no less bring up and foster these,
Than that self-blood; and by that act confirm
Their worths to him and to posterity:
Drusus ta'en hence, I turn my prayers to you,
And, 'fore our country and our gods, beseech
You take and rule Augustus' nephew's sons,
Sprung of the noblest ancestors; and so
Accomplish both my duty and your own.
Nero and Drusus, these shall be to you
In place of parents, these your fathers, these,
And not unfitly: for you are so born,
As all your good or ill's the commonwealth's.
Receive them, you strong guardians; and, blest gods,
Make all their actions answer to their bloods:
Let their great titles find increase by them,
Not they by titles. Set them, as in place
So in example, above all the Romans:
And may they know no rivals but themselves.
Let Fortune give them nothing; but attend
Upon their virtue: and that still come forth
Greater than hope, and better than their fame.
Relieve me, fathers, with your general voice.
  Sen. 'May all the gods consent to Cæsar's wish,
And add to any honours that may crown
The hopeful issue of Germanicus.'
  Tib. We thank you, reverend fathers, in their right.
  Arr. If this were true now! but the space, the space
Between the breast and lips—Tiberius' heart
Lies a thought farther than another man's.   [*Aside.*
  Tib. My comforts are so flowing in my joys,
As, in them, all my streams of grief are lost,
No less than are land-waters in the sea,

Or showers in rivers; though their cause was such,
As might have sprinkled ev'n the gods with tears:
Yet since the greater doth embrace the less,
We covetously obey.

Arr.　　　　　　Well acted, Cæsar. 　　　[*Aside.*

Tib. And now I am the happy witness made
Of your so much desir'd affections,
To this great issue, I could wish, the fates
Would here set peaceful period to my days;
However to my labours, I entreat
And beg it of this senate, some fit ease.

Arr. Laugh, fathers, laugh: Ha' you no spleens about
you? 　　　　　　　　　　　　　　　[*Aside.*

Tib. The burden is too heavy I sustain
On my unwilling shoulders; and I pray
It may be taken off, and re-conferr'd
Upon the consuls, or some other Roman,
More able, and more worthy.

Arr.　　　　　　Laugh on, still. 　　　[*Aside.*

Sab. Why, this doth render all the rest suspected!

Gal. It poisons all.

Arr.　　　　O, do you taste it then?

Sab. It takes away my faith to anything
He shall hereafter speak.

Arr.　　　　　　Aye, to pray that
Which would be to his head as hot as thunder,
('Gainst which he wears that charm) should but the court
Receive him at his word.

Gal.　　　　　　Hear!

Tib.　　　　　　For myself,
I know my weakness, and so little covet
(Like some gone past) the weight that will oppress me,
As my ambition is the counter-point.

Arr. Finely maintain'd; good still.

Sej.　　　　　　But Rome, whose blood,
Whose nerves, whose life, whose very frame relies
On Cæsar's strength, no less than heav'n on Atlas,
Cannot admit it but with general ruin.

Arr. Ah! are you there, to bring him off. 　　[*Aside.*

Sej.   Let Cæsar
No more than urge a point so contrary
To Cæsar's greatness, the griev'd senate's vows,
Or Rome's necessity.

    Gal.   He comes about.

    Arr. More nimbly then Vertumnus.

    Tib.   For the public
I may be drawn to show I can neglect
All private aims; though I affect my rest:
But, if the senate still command me serve,
I must be glad to practise my obedience.

    Arr. You must and will, sir. We do know it.   [*Aside.*

    Sen.   'Cæsar,
Live long and happy, great and royal Cæsar,
The gods preserve thee and thy modesty,
Thy wisdom, and thy innocence.'

    Arr.   Where is't?
The prayer's made before the subject.   [*Aside.*

    Sen.   'Guard
His meekness, Jove, his piety, his care,
His bounty'——

    Arr.   And his subtlety, I'll put in:
Yet he'll keep that himself, without the gods.
All prayers are vain for him.   [*Aside.*

    Tib.   We will not hold
Your patience, fathers, with long answer; but
Shall still contend to be what you desire,
And work to satisfy so great a hope:
Proceed to your affairs.

    Arr.   Now, Silius, guard thee;
The curtain's drawing. Afer advanceth.   [*Aside.*

    Præ.   Silence.

    Afer. Cite Caius Silius.

    Præ.   Caius Silius.

    Sil.   Here.

    Afer. The triumph that thou hadst in Germany
For thy late victory on Sacrovir,
Thou hast enjoy'd so freely, Caius Silius,
As no man it envied thee; nor would Cæsar

Or Rome admit that thou wert then defrauded
Of any honours thy deserts could claim
In the fair service of the commonwealth:
But now, if, after all their loves and graces
(Thy actions, and their courses being discover'd)
It shall appear to Cæsar, and this senate,
Thou hast defil'd those glories with thy crimes——

 Sil. Crimes?

 Afer.   Patience, Silius.

 Sil.   Tell thy mule of patience;
I am a Roman. What are my crimes? Proclaim them.
Am I too rich? too honest for the times?
Have I or treasure, jewels, land, or houses
That some informer gapes for? Is my strength
Too much to be admitted? Or my knowledge?
These now are crimes.

 Afer.   Nay, Silius, if the name
Of crime so touch thee, with what impotence
Wilt thou endure the matter to be search'd?

 Sil. I tell thee, Afer, with more scorn than fear:
Employ your mercenary tongue and art.
Where's my accuser?

 Var.   Here.

 Arr.   Varro? The consul?
Is he thrust in?   [*Aside.*

 Var.   'Tis I accuse thee, Silius.
Against the majesty of Rome and Cæsar,
I do pronounce thee here a guilty cause,
First, of beginning and occasioning,
Next, drawing out the war in Gallia,
For which thou late triumph'st; dissembling long
That Sacrovir to be an enemy,
Only to make thy entertainment more,
Whilst thou and thy wife Sosia poll'd the province;
Wherein, with sordid-base desire of gain,
Thou hast discredited thy actions' worth
And been a traitor to the state.

 Sil.   Thou liest.

Arr. I thank thee, Silius, speak so still and often.

Var. If I not prove it, Cæsar, but unjustly
Have call'd him into trial, here I bind
Myself to suffer, what I claim 'gainst him;
And yield to have what I have spoke, confirm'd
By judgement of the court and all good men.

Sil. Cæsar, I crave to have my name deferr'd,
Till this man's consulship be out.

Tib.   We cannot,
Nor may we grant it.

Sil.   Why? shall he design
My day of trial? is he my accuser?
And must he be my judge?

Tib.   It hath been usual
And is a right, that custom hath allow'd
The magistrate to call forth private men;
And to appoint their day: which privilege
We may not in the consul see infring'd,
By whose deep watches and industrious care
It is so labour'd, as the commonwealth
Receive no loss by any oblique course.

Sil. Cæsar, thy fraud is worse than violence.

Tib. Silius, mistake us not, we dare not use
The credit of the consul to thy wrong,
But only do preserve his place and power,
So far as it concerns the dignity
And honour of the state.

Arr.   Believe him, Silius.

Cot. Why, so he may, Arruntius.

Arr.   I say so.
And he may choose too.

Tib.   By the Capitol
And all our gods, but that the dear republic,
Our sacred laws, and just authority
Are interested therein, I should be silent.

Afer. Please Cæsar to give way unto his trial.
He shall have justice.

Sil.   Nay, I shall have law;
Shall I not, Afer? speak.

Afer.   Would you have more?

Sil. No, my well-spoken man, I would no more;
Nor less: might I enjoy it natural,
Not taught to speak unto your present ends,
Free from thine, his, and all your unkind handling,
Furious enforcing, most unjust presuming,
Malicious, and manifold applying,
Foul wresting, and impossible construction.

Afer. He raves, he raves.

Sil.   Thou durst not tell me so
Had'st thou not Cæsar's warrant. I can see
Whose power condemns me.

Var.   This betrays his spirit.
This doth enough declare him what he is.

Sil. What am I? speak.

Var.   An enemy to the state.

Sil. Because I am an enemy to thee,
And such corrupted ministers o' the state,
That here art made a present instrument
To gratify it with thine own disgrace.

Sej. This, to the consul, is most insolent!
And impious!

Sil.   Aye, take part. Reveal yourselves.
Alas, I scent not your confed'racies,
Your plots, and combinations! I not know
Minion Sejanus hates me; and that all
This boast of law, and law, is but a form,
A net of Vulcan's filing, a mere ingine,
To take that life by a pretext of justice,
Which you pursue in malice? I want brain
Or nostril to persuade me that your ends
And purposes are made to what they are,
Before my answer? O, you equal gods,
Whose justice not a world of wolf-turn'd men
Shall make me to accuse howe'er provoked;
Have I for this so oft engag'd myself?
Stood in the heat and fervour of a fight,
When Phœbus sooner hath forsook the day
Than I the field? Against the blue-ey'd Gauls?

And crisped Germans? when our Roman eagles
Have fann'd the fire with their labouring wings,
And no blow dealt that left not death behind it?
When I have charg'd, alone, into the troops
Of curl'd Sicambrians, routed them, and came
Not off with backward ensigns of a slave,
But forward marks, wounds on my breast and face,
Were meant to thee, O Cæsar, and thy Rome?
And have I this return? did I, for this,
Perform so noble and so brave defeat
On Sacrovir? O Jove, let it become me
To boast my deeds, when he, whom they concern,
Shall thus forget them.

    Afer.   Silius, Silius,
These are the common customs of thy blood,
When it is high with wine, as now with rage:
This well agrees with that intemperate vaunt
Thou lately mad'st at Agrippina's table,
That when all other of the troops were prone
To fall into rebellion, only yours
Remain'd in their obedience. You were he
That sav'd the empire; which had then been lost,
Had but your legions there, rebell'd or mutin'd.
Your virtue met, and fronted every peril.
You gave to Cæsar and to Rome their surety.
Their name, their strength, their spirit, and their state,
Their being was a donative from you.

    Arr. Well worded, and most like an orator.

    Tib. Is this true, Silius?

    Sil.   Save thy question, Cæsar.
Thy spy of famous credit hath affirm'd it.

    Arr. Excellent Roman!

    Sab.   He doth answer stoutly.

    Sej. If this be so, there needs no farther cause
Of crime against him.

    Var.   What can more impeach
The royal dignity, and state of Cæsar,
Than to be urged with a benefit
He cannot pay?

Cot. In this, all Cæsar's fortune
Is made unequal to the courtesy.
   Lat. His means are clean destroy'd that should requite.
   Gal. Nothing is great enough for Silius' merit.
   Arr. Gallus on that side too?   [*Aside.*
   Sil.   Come, do not hunt
And labour so about for circumstance,
To make him guilty whom you have foredoom'd:
Take shorter ways, I'll meet your purposes.
The words were mine, and more I now will say:
Since I have done thee that great service, Cæsar,
Thou still hast fear'd me; and, in place of grace,
Return'd me hatred: so soon all best turns,
With doubtful princes, turn deep injuries
In estimation, when they greater rise
Than can be answer'd. Benefits, with you,
Are of no longer pleasure, than you can
With ease restore them; that transcended once,
Your studies are not how to thank, but kill.
It is your nature, to have all men slaves
To you, but you acknowledging to none.
The means that makes your greatness must not come
In mention of it; if it do, it takes
So much away, you think: and that which help'd,
Shall soonest perish, if it stand in eye,
Where it may front, or but upbraid the high.
   Cot. Suffer him speak no more.
   Var.   Note but his spirit.
   Afer. This shows him in the rest.
   Lat.   Let him be censur'd.
   Sej. He hath spoke enough to prove him Cæsar's foe.
   Cot. His thoughts look through his words.
   Sej.   A censure.
   Sil.   Stay,
Stay, most officious senate, I shall straight
Delude thy fury. Silius hath not plac'd
His guards within him, against fortune's spite,
So weakly but he can escape your gripe
That are but hands of fortune: she herself

When virtue doth oppose, must lose her threats.
All that can happen in humanity,
The frown of Cæsar, proud Sejanus' hatred,
Base Varro's spleen, and Afer's bloodying tongue,
The senate's servile flattery, and these
Mustered to kill, I am fortified against;
And can look down upon: they are beneath me.
It is not life whereof I stand enamour'd:
Nor shall my end make me accuse my fate.
The coward and the valiant man must fall,
Only the cause and manner how, discerns them:
Which then are gladdest, when they cost us dearest.
Romans, if any here be in this senate,
Would know to mock Tiberius' tyranny,
Look upon Silius, and so learn to die.   [*Stabs himself.*

  Var. O, desperate act!
  Arr.   An honorable hand!
  Tib. Look, is he dead?
  Sab.   'Twas nobly struck, and home.
  Arr. My thought did prompt him to it. Farewell, Silius.
Be famous ever for thy great example.
  Tib. We are not pleas'd in this sad accident,
That thus hath stalled and abus'd our mercy,
Intended to preserve thee, noble Roman:
And to prevent thy hopes.
  Arr.   Excellent wolf!
Now he is full, he howls.   [*Aside.*
  Sej.   Cæsar doth wrong
His dignity and safety thus to mourn
The deserv'd end of so profess'd a traitor,
And doth, by this his lenity, instruct
Others as factious to the like offence.
  Tib. The confiscation merely of his state
Had been enough.
  Arr.   O, that was gap'd for then?   [*Aside.*
  Var. Remove the body.
  Sej.   Let citation
Go out for Sosia.
  Gal.   Let her be proscrib'd.

And for the goods, I think it fit that half
Go to the treasure, half unto the children.

Lep. With leave of Cæsar, I would think that fourth
Part, which the law doth cast on the informers,
Should be enough; the rest go to the children:
Wherein the prince shall show humanity,
And bounty not to force them by their want
(Which in their parents' trespass they deserv'd)
To take ill courses.

Tib.   It shall please us.

Arr.   Aye,
Out of necessity. This Lepidus
Is grave and honest, and I have observ'd
A moderation still in all his censures.

Sab. And bending to the better——. Stay, who's this?
Cremutius Cordus? what? is he brought in?

Arr. More blood unto the banquet? Noble Cordus,
I wish thee good: Be as thy writings, free,
And honest.

Tib.   What is he?

Sej.   For th' Annals, Cæsar.

Enter Satrius *and* Natta, *with* Cordus, *guarded.*

Præ. Cremutius Cordus.

Cor.   Here.

Præ.   Satrius Secundus,
Pinnarius Natta, you are his accusers.

Arr. Two of Sejanus' bloodhounds, whom he breeds
With human flesh, to bay at citizens.

Afer. Stand forth before the senate and confront him.

Sat. I do accuse thee here, Cremutius Cordus,
To be a man factious and dangerous,
A sower of sedition in the state,
A turbulent and discontented spirit,
Which I will prove from thine own writings, here,
The Annals thou hast publish'd; where thou bit'st
The present age, and with a viper's tooth,
Being a member of it, dar'st that ill
Which never yet degenerous bastard did

Upon his parent.

Nat.　　　　　To this, I subscribe;
And, forth a world of more particulars,
Instance in only one: comparing men,
And times, thou praisest Brutus, and affirm'st
That Cassius was the last of all the Romans,

Cot. How! what are we then?

Var.　　　　　What is Cæsar? nothing?

Afer. My lords, this strikes at every Roman's private,
In whom reigns gentry and estate of spirit,
To have a Brutus brought in parallel,
A parricide, an enemy of his country,
Rank'd, and preferr'd to any real worth
That Rome now holds. This is most strangely invective.
Most full of spite, and insolent upbraiding.
Nor is't the time alone is here dispris'd,
But the whole man of time yea, Cæsar's self
Brought in disvalue; and he aim'd at most
By oblique glance of his licentious pen.
Cæsar, if Cassius were the last of Romans,
Thou hast no name.

Tib.　　　　　Let's hear him answer. Silence.

Cor. So innocent I am of fact, my lords,
As but my words are argu'd; yet those words
Not reaching either prince, or prince's parent:
The which your law of treason comprehends.
Brutus and Cassius, I am charg'd t' have prais'd:
Whose deeds, when many more, besides myself,
Have writ, not one hath mention'd without honour.
Great Titus Livius, great for eloquence
And faith, amongst us, in his history,
With so great praises Pompey did extol
As oft Augustus call'd him a Pompeian:
Yet this not hurt their friendship. In his book
He often names Scipio, Afranius,
Yea, the same Cassius, and this Brutus too,
As worthiest men; not thieves and parricides,
Which notes upon their fames are now impos'd.
Asinius Pollio's writings quite throughout

Give them a noble memory; so Messalla
Renown'd his general Cassius: yet both these
Liv'd with Augustus full of wealth and honours.
To Cicero's book, where Cato was heav'd up
Equal with heav'n, what else did Cæsar answer,
Being then dictator, but with a penn'd oration,
As if before the judges? Do but see
Antonius' letters; read but Brutus' pleadings:
What vile reproach they hold against Augustus,
False I confess, but with much bitterness.
The epigrams of Bibaculus and Catullus
Are read, full stuff'd with spite of both the Cæsars;
Yet deified Julius, and no less Augustus!
Both bore them, and contemn'd them: I not know
Promptly to speak it, whether done with more
Temper, or wisdom; for such obloquies
If they despised be, they die suppress'd;
But, if with rage acknowledg'd, they are confess'd.
The Greeks I slip, whose licence not alone,
But also lust did scape unpunished:
Or where some one (by chance) exception took,
He words with words reveng'd. But, in my work,
What could be aim'd more free, or farther off
From the time's scandal, than to write of those
Whom death from grace or hatred had exempted?
Did I, with Brutus and with Cassius,
Arm'd, and possess'd of the Philippi fields,
Incense the people in the civil cause,
With dangerous speeches? or do they, being slain
Seventy years since, as by their images
(Which not the conqueror hath defac'd) appears,
Retain that guilty memory with writers?
Posterity pays every man his honour.
Nor shall there want, though I condemned am,
That will not only Cassius well approve,
And of great Brutus' honour mindful be,
But that will, also, mention make of me.

  Arr. Freely and nobly spoken.
  Sab.   With good temper,

I like him, that he is not mov'd with passion.

Arr. He puts 'em to their whisper.

Tib.   Take him hence,
We shall determine of him at next sitting.

              [*Exeunt guards with* Cordus.

Cot. Meantime, give order that his books be burnt,
To the ædiles.

Sej.   You have well advis'd.

Afer. It fits not such licentious things should live
T' upbraid the age.

Arr.   If th' age were good, they might.

Lat. Let 'em be burnt.

Gal.   All sought, and burnt, today.

Præ. The court is up, lictors, resume the fasces.

              [*Exeunt all but* Arruntius, Sabinus, *and* Lepidus.

Arr. Let 'em be burnt! O, how ridiculous
Appears the senate's brainless diligence,
Who think they can, with present power, extinguish
The memory of all succeeding times!

Sab. 'Tis true, when, contrary, the punishment
Of wit, doth make th' authority increase.
Nor do they aught that use this cruelty
Of interdiction, and this rage of burning,
But purchase to themselves rebuke, and shame,
And to the writers an eternal name.

Lep. It is an argument the times are sore,
When virtue cannot safely be advanc'd;
Nor vice reprov'd.

Arr.   Aye, noble Lepidus,
Augustus well foresaw what we should suffer
Under Tiberius, when he did pronounce
The Roman race most wretched, that should live
Between so slow jaws, and so long a bruising.   [*Exeunt.*

ACT III. SCENE II

A room in the palace.

Enter Tiberius *and* Sejanus.

Tib. This business hath succeeded well, Sejanus:
And quite remov'd all jealousy of practice
'Gainst Agrippina and our nephews. Now,
We must bethink us how to plant our ingines
For th' other pair, Sabinus and Arruntius,
And Gallus too; howe'er he flatter us,
His heart we know.

Sej.　　　　　Give it some respite, Cæsar.
Time shall mature, and bring to perfect crown,
What we, with so good vultures, have begun:
Sabinus shall be next.

Tib.　　　　　Rather Arruntius.

Sej. By any means, preserve him. His frank tongue
Being lent the reins, will take away all thought
Of malice in your course against the rest.
We must keep him to stalk with.

Tib.　　　　　Dearest head,
To thy most fortunate design I yield it.

Sej. Sir—I have been so long train'd up in grace,
First, with your father, great Augustus, since
With your most happy bounties so familiar,
As I not sooner would commit my hopes
Or wishes to the gods, than to your ears.
Nor have I ever yet been covetous
Of over-bright and dazzling honours: rather
To watch, and travail in great Cæsar's safety,
With the most common soldier.

Tib.　　　　　'Tis confess'd.

Sej. The only gain, and which I count most fair
Of all my fortunes, is that mighty Cæsar
Hath thought me worthy his alliance. Hence
Begin my hopes.

Tib.　　　　　H'mh?

Sej.   I have heard, Augustus
In the bestowing of his daughter, thought
But even of gentlemen of Rome: if so
(I know not how to hope so great a favour),
But if a husband should be sought for Livia,
And I be had in mind, as Cæsar's friend,
I would but use the glory of the kindred.
It should not make me slothful or less caring
For Cæsar's state; it were enough to me
It did confirm and strengthen my weak house,
Against the now unequal opposition
Of Agrippina; and for dear regard
Unto my children, this I wish: myself
Have no ambition farther than to end
My days in service of so dear a master.

Tib. We cannot but commend thy piety,
Most lov'd Sejanus, in acknowledging
Those bounties, which we, faintly, such remember——
But to thy suit. The rest of mortal men,
In all their drifts and counsels, pursue profit:
Princes, alone, are of a different sort,
Directing their main actions still to fame.
We therefore will take time to think, and answer.
For Livia, she can best herself resolve
If she will marry after Drusus, or
Continue in the family; besides
She hath a mother and a grandam yet,
Whose nearer counsels she may guide her by:
But I will simply deal. That enmity
Thou fear'st in Agrippina, would burn more,
If Livia's marriage should, as 'twere in parts,
Divide th' imperial house; an emulation
Between the women might break forth: and discord
Ruin the sons and nephews on both hands.
What if it cause some present difference?
Thou art not safe, Sejanus, if thou prove it.
Canst thou believe, that Livia, first the wife
To Caius Cæsar, then my Drusus, now
Will be contented to grow old with thee,

Born but a private gentleman of Rome?
And raise thee with her loss, if not her shame?
Or say, that I should wish it, canst thou think
The senate, or the people (who have seen
Her brother, father, and our ancestors,
In highest place of empire) will endure it?
The state thou hold'st already is in talk;
Men murmur at thy greatness; and the nobles
Stick not in public to upbraid thy climbing
Above our father's favours, or thy scale:
And dare accuse me, from their hate to thee.
Be wise, dear friend. We would not hide these things
For friendship's dear respect. Nor will we stand
Adverse to thine or Livia's designments.
What we had purpos'd to thee, in our thought,
And with what near degrees of love to bind thee,
And make thee equal to us; for the present,
We will forbear to speak. Only, thus much
Believe, our lov'd Sejanus, we not know
That height in blood, or honour, which thy virtue,
And mind to us, may not aspire with merit.
And this we'll publish, on all watch'd occasion
The senate or the people shall present.

    Sej. I am restor'd, and to my sense again,
Which I had lost in this so blinding suit.
Cæsar hath taught me better to refuse,
Than I knew how to ask. How pleaseth Cæsar
T' embrace my late advice, for leaving Rome?

    Tib. We are resolv'd.

    Sej.   Here are some motives more,
                                [Gives him a paper.
Which I have thought on since, may more confirm.

    Tib. Careful Sejanus! we will straight peruse them:
Go forward in our main design and prosper.   *[Exit.*

    Sej. If those but take, I shall: dull, heavy Cæsar!
Would'st thou tell me thy favours were made crimes?
And that my fortunes were esteem'd thy faults?
That thou, for me, wert hated? and not think
I would with winged haste prevent that change,

When thou might'st win all to thyself again,
By forfeiture of me? Did those fond words
Fly swifter from thy lips, than this my brain,
This sparkling forge, created me an armour
T' encounter chance, and thee? Well, read my charms,
And may they lay that hold upon thy senses,
As thou had'st snuft up hemlock, or ta'en down
The juice of poppy and of mandrakes. Sleep,
Voluptuous Cæsar, and security
Seize on thy stupid powers, and leave them dead
To public cares, awake but to thy lusts.
The strength of which makes thy libidinous soul
Itch to leave Rome; and I have thrust it on:
With blaming of the city business,
The multitude of suits, the confluence
Of suitors, then their importunacies,
The manifold distractions he must suffer,
Besides ill rumours, envies, and reproaches
All which, a quiet and retired life,
Larded with ease and pleasure, did avoid;
And yet, for any weighty and great affair,
The fittest place to give the soundest counsels.
By this, shall I remove him both from thought
And knowledge of his own most dear affairs;
Draw all dispatches through my private hands;
Know his designments, and pursue mine own;
Make mine own strengths by giving suits and places,
Conferring dignities and offices:
And these, that hate me now, wanting access
To him, will make their envy none, or less.
For when they see me arbiter of all,
They must observe: or else, with Cæsar fall.   [*Exit.*

ACT III. SCENE III

Another room in the palace.

Enter Tiberius.

Tib. To marry Livia? will no less, Sejanus,
Content thy aims? no lower object? well!
Thou know'st how thou art wrought into our trust;
Woven in our design; and think'st we must
Now use thee, whatsoever thy projects are:
'Tis true. But yet with caution and fit care.
And, now we better think——who's there, within?

Enter Servus.

Ser. Cæsar?
Tib.   To leave our journey off, were sin
'Gainst our decree'd delights; and would appear
Doubt: or (what less becomes a prince) low fear.
Yet, doubt hath law, and fears have their excuse,
Where princes' states plead necessary use;
As ours doth now: more in Sejanus' pride,
Than all fell Agrippina's hates beside.
Those are the dreadful enemies we raise
With favours, and make dangerous with praise;
The injur'd by us may have will alike,
But 'tis the favourite hath the power to strike:
And fury ever boils more high and strong,
Heat with ambition, than revenge of wrong.
'Tis then a part of supreme skill, to grace
No man too much; but hold a certain space
Between th' ascender's rise and thine own flat,
Lest, when all rounds be reach'd, his aim be that.
'Tis thought—Is Macro in the palace? See:
If not, go seek him, to come to us.   [*Exit* Servus.
                                        He
Must be the organ we must work by now;
Though none less apt for trust: need doth allow
What choice would not. I have heard that aconite,

159

Being timely taken, hath a healing might
Against the scorpion's stroke; the proof we'll give:
That, while two poisons wrestle, we may live.
He hath a spirit too working, to be us'd
But to th' encounter of his like; excus'd
Are wiser sov'reigns then, that raise one ill
Against another, and both safely kill:
The prince that feeds great natures, they will sway him;
Who nourisheth a lion, must obey him.

Re-enter Servus *with* Macro.

Macro, we sent for you.
   Mac.   I heard so, Cæsar.
   Tib. Leave us awhile.   [*Exit* Servus.
                When you shall know, good Macro;
The causes of our sending, and the ends;
You then will harken nearer: and be pleas'd
You stand so high both in our choice and trust.
   Mac. The humblest place in Cæsar's choice or trust,
May make glad Macro proud; without ambition,
Save to do Cæsar service.
   Tib.   Leave your courtings.
We are in purpose, Macro, to depart
The city for a time, and see Campania;
Not for our pleasures, but to dedicate
A pair of temples, one to Jupiter
At Capua; th' other at Nola, to Augustus:
In which great work, perhaps your stay will be
Beyond our will produc'd. Now, since we are
Not ignorant what danger may be born
Out of our shortest absence in a state
So subject unto envy and embroil'd
With hate and faction; we have thought on thee,
Amongst a field of Romans, worthiest Macro,
To be our eye and ear, to keep strict watch
On Agrippina, Nero, Drusus; aye,
And on Sejanus: not that we distrust
His loyalty or do repent one grace
Of all that heap we have confer'd on him.

For that were to disparage our election,
And call that judgement now in doubt, which then
Seem'd as unquestion'd as an oracle—
But greatness hath his cankers. Worms and moths
Breed out of too fit matter in the things
Which after they consume, transferring quite
The substance of their makers, int' themselves.
Macro is sharp, and apprehends. Besides,
I know him subtle, close, wise, and well read
In man and his large nature. He hath studied
Affections, passions, knows their springs, their ends,
Which way, and whether they will work: 'tis proof
Enough of his great merit that we trust him.
Then, to a point; because our conference
Cannot be long without suspicion—
Here, Macro, we assign thee, both to spy,
Inform, and chastise; think, and use thy means,
Thy ministers, what, where, on whom thou wilt;
Explore, plot, practise: All thou dost in this,
Shall be, as if the senate or the laws
Had giv'n it privilege, and thou thence styl'd
The saviour both of Cæsar and of Rome.
We will not take thy answer but in act:
Whereto, as thou proceed'st, we hope to hear
By trusted messengers. If't be enquir'd
Wherefore we call'd you, say you have in charge
To see our chariots ready and our horse:
Be still our lov'd, and shortly honor'd Macro.   [*Exit.*

  Mac. I will not ask, why Cæsar bids do this:
But joy, that he bids me. It is the bliss
Of courts to be employ'd; no matter how:
A prince's power makes all his actions virtue.
We, whom he works by, are dumb instruments,
To do, but not enquire: his great intents
Are to be serv'd, not search'd. Yet, as that bow
Is most in hand whose owner best doth know
T' affect his aims, so let that statesman hope
Most use, most price, can hit his prince's scope.
Nor must he look at what or whom to strike,

But loose at all; each mark must be alike.
Were it to plot against the fame, the life
Of one with whom I twinn'd; remove a wife
From my warm side, as lov'd as is the air;
Practise away each parent; draw mine heir
In compass, though but one; work all my kin
To swift perdition; leave no untrain'd engin,
For friendship, or for innocence; nay, make
The gods all guilty: I would undertake
This, being impos'd me, both with gain and ease.
The way to rise is to obey and please.
He that will thrive in state, he must neglect
The trodden paths, that truth and right respect;
And prove new, wilder ways: for virtue, there,
Is not that narrow thing she is elsewhere.
Men's fortune there is virtue; reason, their will:
Their licence, law; and their observance, skill.
Occasion is their foil; conscience, their stain;
Profit, their lustre: and what else is, vain.
If then it be the lust of Cæsar's power,
T' have rais'd Sejanus up, and in an hour
O'erturn him, tumbling down from height of all;
We are his ready engine: and his fall
May be our rise. It is no uncouth thing
To see fresh buildings from old ruins spring.   [*Exit.*

ACT IV. SCENE I

An apartment in Agrippina's *house.*

Enter Gallus *and* Agrippina.

Gal. You must have patience, royal Agrippina.
Agr. I must have vengeance, first: and that were nectar
Unto my famish'd spirits. O, my fortune,
Let it be sudden thou prepar'st against me;
Strike all my powers of understanding blind,
And ignorant of destiny to come:
Let me not fear, that cannot hope.

Gal.   Dear princess,
These tyrannies on yourself are worse than Cæsar's.
   Agr. Is this the happiness of being born great?
Still to be aim'd at? still to be suspected?
To live the subject of all jealousies?
At the least colour made, if not the ground
To every painted danger? who would not
Choose once to fall, than thus to hang for ever?
   Gal. You might be safe, if you would——
   Agr.   What, my Gallus?
Be lewd Sejanus' strumpet? Or the bawd
To Cæsar's lusts, he now is gone to practise?
Not these are safe, where nothing is. Yourself,
While you thus stand but by me, are not safe.
Was Silius safe? or the good Sosia safe?
Or was my niece, dear Claudia Pulchra, safe?
Or innocent Furnius? They, that latest have
(By being made guilty) added reputation
To Afer's eloquence? O, foolish friends,
Could not so fresh example warn your loves,
But you must buy my favours with that loss
Unto yourselves: and when you might perceive
That Cæsar's cause of raging must forsake him,
Before his will? Away, good Gallus, leave me.
Here to be seen, is danger; to speak, treason:
To do me least observance, is call'd faction.
You are unhappy in me, and I in all.
Where are my sons? Nero? and Drusus? We
Are they, be shot at; let us fall apart:
Not in our ruins sepulchre our friends.
Or shall we do some action like offence,
To mock their studies, that would make us faulty,
And frustrate practice, by preventing it?
The danger's like: for, what they can contrive,
They will make good. No innocence is safe,
When power contests. Nor can they trespass more,
Whose only being was all crime before.

       Enter Nero, Drusus, *and* Caligula.

   Nero. You hear Sejanus is come back from Cæsar?

Gal. No. How? Disgrac'd?

Dru.   More graced now, than ever.

Gal. By what mischance?

Cal.   A fortune like enough
Once to be bad.

Dru.   But turn'd too good, to both.

Gal. What was't?

Nero.   Tiberius sitting at his meat,
In a farm-house they call Spelunca, sited
By the sea-side, among the Fundane hills,
Within a natural cave, part of the grot
About the entry fell, and overwhelm'd
Some of the waiters; others ran away:
Only Sejanus, with his knees, hands, face,
O'erhanging Cæsar, did oppose himself
To the remaining ruins, and was found
In that so labouring posture by the soldiers
That came to succour him. With which adventure,
He hath so fix'd himself in Cæsar's trust,
As thunder cannot move him, and is come
With all the height of Cæsar's praise, to Rome.

Agr. And power to turn those ruins all on us;
And bury whole posterities beneath them.
Nero, and Drusus, and Caligula,
Your places are the next, and therefore most
In their offence. Think on your birth and blood,
Awake your spirits, meet their violence;
'Tis princely when a tyrant doth oppose;
And is a fortune sent to exercise
Your virtue, as the wind doth try strong trees,
Who by vexation grow more sound and firm.
After your father's fall, and uncle's fate,
What can you hope, but all the change of stroke
That force or sleight can give? then stand upright;
And though you do not act, yet suffer nobly:
Be worthy of my womb, and take strong cheer;
What we do know will come, we should not fear. [*Exeunt.*

ACT IV. SCENE II

The street.

Enter Macro.

Mac. Return'd so soon? renew'd in trust and grace?
Is Cæsar then so weak? or hath the place
But wrought this alteration, with the air;
And he, on next remove, will all repair?
Macro, thou art engag'd: and what before
Was public; now, must be thy private, more.
The weal of Cæsar, fitness did imply;
But thine own fate confers necessity
On thy employment: and the thoughts born nearest
Unto ourselves, move swiftest still, and dearest.
If he recover, thou art lost: yea, all
The weight of preparation to his fall
Will turn on thee, and crush thee. Therefore, strike
Before he settle, to prevent the like
Upon thyself. He doth his vantage know,
That makes it home, and gives the foremost blow. [*Exit.*

ACT IV. SCENE III

An upper room of Agrippina's *house.*

Enter Latiaris, Rufus, *and* Opsius.

Lat. It is a service, great Sejanus will
See well requited, and accept of nobly.
Here place yourselves, between the roof, and ceiling
And when I bring him to his words of danger,
Reveal yourselves, and take him.
Ruf.   Is he come?
Lat. I'll now go fetch him.   [*Exit.*
Ops.   With good speed. I long
To merit from the state, in such an action.
Ruf. I hope it will obtain the consulship
For one of us.

Ops. We cannot think of less,
To bring in one so dangerous as Sabinus.

 Ruf. He was a follower of Germanicus,
And still is an observer of his wife
And children, though they be declin'd in grace;
A daily visitant, keeps them company
In private and in public; and is noted
To be the only client of the house:
Pray Jove he will be free to Latiaris:

 Ops. He's allied to him, and doth trust him well.

 Ruf. And he'll requite his trust?

 Ops.   To do an office
So grateful to the state, I know no man
But would strain nearer bands than kindred——

 Ruf.   List,
I hear them come.

 Ops.   Shift to our holes with silence. [*They retire.*

Re-enter Latiaris *with* Sabinus.

 Lat. It is a noble constancy you show
To this afflicted house: that not like others
(The friends of season) you do follow fortune,
And, in the winter of their fate, forsake
The place whose glories warm'd you. You are just,
And worthy such a princely patron's love,
As was the world's renown'd Germanicus:
Whose ample merit when I call to thought,
And see his wife and issue, objects made
To so much envy, jealousy and hate;
It makes me ready to accuse the gods
Of negligence, as men of tyranny.

 Sab. They must be patient, so must we.

 Lat.   O Jove.
What will become of us, or of the times,
When to be high or noble, are made crimes?
When land and treasure are most dangerous faults?

 Sab. Nay, when our table, yea our bed, assaults
Our peace and safety? when our writings are,
By any envious instruments that dare

Apply them to the guilty, made to speak
What they will have, to fit their tyrannous wreak?
When ignorance is scarcely innocence:
And knowledge made a capital offence?
When not so much, but the bare empty shade
Of liberty is reft us? and we made
The prey to greedy vultures, and vile spies,
That first transfix us with their murdering eyes?

   Lat. Methinks, the genius of the Roman race
Should not be so extinct, but that bright flame
Of liberty might be reviv'd again,
Which no good man but with his life should lose,
And we not sit like spent and patient fools,
Still puffing in the dark at one poor coal,
Held on by hope, till the last spark is out.
The cause is public, and the honour, name,
The immortality of every soul
That is not bastard, or a slave in Rome,
Therein concern'd: Whereto, if men would change
The wearied arm, and for the weighty shield
So long sustain'd, employ the ready sword,
We might have some assurance of our vows.
This ass's fortitude doth tire us all.
It must be active valour must redeem
Our loss, or none. The rock and our hard steel
Should meet t' enforce those glorious fires again,
Whose splendour cheer'd the world, and heat gave life
No less than doth the sun's.

   Sab.   'Twere better stay
In lasting darkness and despair of day.
No ill should force the subject undertake
Against the sovereign more than hell should make
The gods do wrong. A good man should and must
Sit rather down with loss than rise unjust.
Though, when the Romans first did yield themselves
To one man's power, they did not mean their lives,
Their fortunes, and their liberties, should be
His absolute spoil, as purchas'd by the sword.

   Lat. Why, we are worse, if to be slaves, and bond

To Cæsar's slave, be such, the proud Sejanus!
He that is all, does all, gives Cæsar leave
To hide his ulcerous and anointed face,
With his bald crown at Rhodes, while he here stalks
Upon the heads of Romans and their princes,
Familiarly to empire.

   Sab.   Now you touch
A point indeed, wherein he shows his art,
As well as power.

   Lat.   And villainy in both.
Do you observe where Livia lodges? How
Drusus came dead? What men have been cut off?

   Sab. Yes, those are things remov'd: I nearer look'd,
Into his later practice, where he stands
Declar'd a master in his mystery.
First, ere Tiberius went, he wrought his fear
To think that Agrippina sought his death.
Then put those doubts in her; sent her oft word,
Under the show of friendship, to beware
Of Cæsar, for he laid to poison her:
Drave them to frowns, to mutual jealousies,
Which, now, in visible hatred are burst out.
Since, he hath had his hired instruments
To work on Nero, and to heave him up;
To tell him Cæsar's old; that all the people,
Yea, all the army have their eyes on him;
That both do long to have him undertake
Something of worth, to give the world a hope:
Bids him to court their grace: The easy youth,
Perhaps, gives ear, which straight he writes to Cæsar;
And with this comment; See yon dangerous boy;
Note but the practice of the mother, there;
She's tying him, for purposes at hand,
With men of sword. Here's Cæsar put in fright
'Gainst son and mother. Yet, he leaves not thus.
The second brother Drusus (a fierce nature,
And fitter for his snares, because ambitious,
And full of envy), him he clasps, and hugs,
Poisons with praise, tells him what hearts he wears,

How bright he stands in popular expectance;
That Rome doth suffer with him in the wrong
His mother does him by preferring Nero:
Thus sets he them asunder, each 'gainst other,
Projects the course that serves him to condemn,
Keeps in opinion of a friend to all,
And all drives on to ruin.

Lat.   Cæsar sleeps,
And nods at this?

Sab.   Would he might ever sleep,
Bogg'd in his filthy lusts.

Opsius *and* Rufus *rush in.*

Ops.   Treason to Cæsar.
Ruf. Lay hands upon the traitor, Latiaris,
Or take the name thyself.

Lat.   I am for Cæsar.
Sab. Am I then catch'd?

Ruf.   How think you, sir? you are.
Sab. Spies of this head! so white! so full of years!
Well, my most reverend monsters, you may live
To see yourselves thus snar'd.

Ops.   Away with him.
Lat. Hale him away.

Ruf.   To be a spy for traitors,
Is honorable vigilance.

Sab.   You do well,
My most officious instruments of state;
Men of all uses: Drag me hence, away.
The year is well begun, and I fall fit
To be an offering to Sejanus. Go.

Ops. Cover him with his garments, hide his face.
Sab. It shall not need. Forbear your rude assault,
The fault's not shameful, villainy makes a fault.   [*Exeunt.*

ACT IV. SCENE IV

The street before Agrippina's house.

Enter Macro *and* Caligula.

Mac. Sir, but observe how thick your dangers meet
In his clear drifts! Your mother, and your brothers,
Now cited to the senate! Their friend, Gallus,
Feasted today by Cæsar, since committed!
Sabinus here we met, hurried to fetters!
The senators all struck with fear and silence,
Save those whose hopes depend not on good means,
But force their private prey from public spoil!
And you must know, if here you stay, your state
Is sure to be the subject of his hate,
As now the object.

Cal.   What would you advise me?

Mac. To go for Capreæ presently: and there
Give up yourself, entirely, to your uncle.
Tell Cæsar (since your mother is accus'd
To fly for succours to Augustus' statue,
And to the army, with your brethren) you
Have rather chose to place your aids in him,
Than live suspected; or in hourly fear
To be thrust out by bold Sejanus' plots:
Which you shall confidently urge to be
Most full of peril to the state and Cæsar,
As being laid to his peculiar ends,
And not to be let run with common safety.
All which, upon the second, I'll make plain,
So both shall love and trust with Cæsar gain.

Cal. Away then, let's prepare us for our journey.

[*Exeunt.*

ACT IV. SCENE V

Another part of the street.

Enter Arruntius.

Arr. Still do'st thou suffer, heav'n? will no flame,
No heat of sin make thy just wrath to boil

In thy distemp'red bosom, and o'erflow
The pitchy blazes of impiety
Kindled beneath thy throne? Still canst thou sleep,
Patient, while vice doth make an antique face
At thy dread power, and blow dust and smoke
Into thy nostrils? Jove, will nothing wake thee?
Must vile Sejanus pull thee by the beard,
Ere thou wilt open thy black-lidded eye,
And look him dead? Well! Snore on, dreaming gods:
And let this last of that proud giant-race,
Heave mountain upon mountain 'gainst your state——
Be good unto me, Fortune, and you powers,
Whom I, expostulating, have profan'd;
I see (what's equal with a prodigy)
A great, a noble Roman, and an honest,
Live an old man! O, Marcus Lepidus,
When is our turn to bleed? Thyself, and I
(Without our boast) are almost all the few
Left to be honest, in these impious times.

Enter Lepidus.

Lep. What we are left to be, we will be, Lucius,
Though tyranny did stare, as wide as death,
To fright us from it.

Arr.   'T hath so, on Sabinus.

Lep. I saw him now drawn from the Gemonies.
And what increas'd the direness of the fact,
His faithful dog, upbraiding all us Romans
Never forsook the corpse, but, seeing it thrown
Into the stream, leap'd in, and drown'd with it.

Arr. O act! to be envied him of us men!
We are the next the hook lays hold on, Marcus:
What are thy arts, good patriot, teach them me
That have preserv'd thy hairs to this white dye,
And kept so reverend and so dear a head,
Safe on his comely shoulders?

Lep.   Arts, Arruntius?
None, but the plain and passive fortitude
To suffer and be silent; never stretch

171

These arms against the torrent; live at home,
With my own thoughts and innocence about me,
Not tempting the wolves' jaws: these are my arts.

Arr. I would begin to study 'em, if I thought
They would secure me. May I pray to Jove,
In secret, and be safe? Aye, or aloud?
With open wishes? so I do not mention
Tiberius, or Sejanus? yes, I must
If I speak out. 'Tis hard, that. May I think,
And not be racked? What danger is 't to dream?
Talk in one's sleep? or cough? who knows the law?
May I shake my head without a comment? say
It rains, or it holds up, and not be thrown
Upon the Gemonies? These now are things
Whereon men's fortune, yea, their fate depends.
Nothing hath privilege 'gainst the violent ear.
No place, no day, no hour we see is free,
Not our religious and most sacred times,
From some one kind of cruelty: all matter,
Nay, all occasion pleaseth. Madmen's rage,
The idleness of drunkards, women's nothing,
Jesters' simplicity, all, all is good
That can be catch'd at. Nor is now th' event
Of any person, or for any crime,
To be expected; for 'tis always one:
Death, with some little difference of place,
Or time—what's this? Prince Nero? guarded?

Enter Laco *and* Nero *with guards.*

Laco. On, lictors, keep your way: My lords, forbear.
On pain of Cæsar's wrath, no man attempt
Speech with the prisoner.

Nero.　　　　　Noble friends, be safe:
To lose yourselves for words, were as vain hazard,
As unto me small comfort: Fare you well.
Would all Rome's sufferings in my fate did dwell.

Laco. Lictors, away.

Lep.　　　　　Where goes he, Laco?

Laco.   Sir,
He's banish'd into Pontia, by the senate.

Arr. Do I see? and hear? and feel? May I trust sense?
Or doth my fancy form it?

Lep.   Where's his brother?

Laco. Drusus is prisoner in the palace.

Arr.   Ha?
I smell it now: 'tis rank. Where's Agrippina?

Laco. The princess is confin'd to Pandataria.

Arr. Bolts, Vulcan; bolts, for Jove! Phœbus, thy bow;
Stern Mars, thy sword; and blue-ey'd maid, thy spear;
Thy club, Alcides: all the armoury
Of heaven is too little!—Ha? to guard
The gods, I meant. Fine, rare dispatch! This same
Was swiftly born! confin'd? imprison'd? banish'd?
Most tripartite! The cause, sir?

Laco.   Treason.

Arr.   O?
The complement of all accusings? that
Will hit, when all else fails.

Lep.   This turn is strange!
But yesterday, the people would not hear
Far less objected, but cry'd, Cæsar's letters
Were false, and forg'd; that all these plots were malice:
And that the ruin of the prince's house
Was practis'd 'gainst his knowledge. Where are now
Their voices? now that they behold his heirs
Lock'd up, disgrac'd, led into exile?

Arr.   Hush'd,
Drown'd in their bellies. Wild Sejanus' breath
Hath, like a whirlwind, scatter'd that poor dust,
With this rude blast. We'll talk no treason, sir,

                    [*He turns to* Laco *and the rest.*
If that be it you stand for? Fare you well.
We have no need of horse-leeches. Good spy,
Now you are spied, begone.

                    [*Exeunt* Laco, Nero, *and guards.*
Lep.   I fear you wrong him.
He has the voice to be an honest Roman.

Arr. And trusted to this office? Lepidus.
I'd sooner trust Greek Sinon, than a man
Our state employs. He's gone: and being gone,
I dare tell you, whom I dare better trust,
That our night-ey'd Tiberius doth not see
His minion's drifts; or, if he do he's not
So arrant subtile as we fools do take him:
To breed a mongrel up, in his own house,
With his own blood, and, if the good gods please,
At his own throat flesh him to take a leap.
I do not beg it, heav'n: but if the fates
Grant it these eyes, they must not wink.

  Lep.   They must
Not see it, Lucius.

  Arr.   Who should let 'em?

  Lep.   Zeal,
And duty; with the thought he is our prince.

  Arr. He is our monster: forfeited to vice
So far, as no rack'd virtue can redeem him.
His loathed person fouler than all crimes:
An Emperor only in his lusts. Retir'd
From all regard of his own fame, or Rome's,
Into an obscure island; where he lives,
Acting his tragedies with a comic face
Amid'st his rout of Chaldees: spending hours,
Days, weeks, and months, in the unkind abuse
Of grave astrology to the bane of men,
Casting the scope of men's nativities,
And having found aught worthy in their fortune,
Kill, or precipitate them in the sea,
And boast he can mock fate. Nay, muse not: these
Are far from ends of evil, scarce degrees.
He hath his slaughter-house at Capreæ;
Where he doth study murder as an art:
And they are dearest in his grace that can
Devise the deepest tortures. Thither, too,
He hath his boys, and beauteous girls ta'en up,
Out of our noblest houses, the best form'd,
Best nurtur'd, and most modest: what's their good

174

Serves to provoke his bad. Some are allur'd,
Some threatened; others, by their friends detain'd,
Are ravish'd hence like captives, and, in sight
Of their most grieved parents, dealt away
Unto his spintries, sellaries, and slaves,
Masters of strange and new commented lusts,
For which wise nature hath not left a name.
To this (what most strikes us, and bleeding Rome)
He is, with all his craft, become the ward
To his own vassal, a stale catamite:
Whom he, upon our low and suffering necks,
Hath rais'd from excrement to side the gods,
And have his proper sacrifice in Rome:
Which Jove beholds, and yet will sooner rive
A senseless oak with thunder than his trunk.

Re-enter Laco *with* Pomponius *and* Minutius.

Laco. These letters make men doubtful what t' expect,
Whether his coming, or his death.
Pom.   Troth, both:
And which comes soonest, thank the gods for.
Arr.   List!
Their talk is Cæsar; I would hear all voices.
Min. One day he's well; and will return to Rome:
The next day, sick; and knows not when to hope it.
Laco. True, and today, one of Sejanus' friends
Honour'd by special writ; and on the morrow
Another punish'd——
Pom.   By more special writ.
Min. This man receives his praises of Sejanus,
A second, but slight mention: a third, none:
A fourth, rebukes. And thus he leaves the senate
Divided and suspended, all uncertain.
Laco. These forked tricks, I understand 'em not,
Would he would tell us whom he loves or hates,
That we might follow, without fear or doubt.
Arr. Good Heliotrope! Is this your honest man?
Let him be yours so still. He is my knave.

Pom. I cannot tell, Sejanus still goes on,
And mounts, we see: New statues are advanc'd,
Fresh leaves of titles, large inscriptions read,
His fortune sworn by, himself new gone out
Cæsar's colleague in the fifth consulship,
More altars smoke to him than all the gods:
What would we more?

  Arr.   That the dear smoke would choke him,
That would I more.

  Lep.   Peace, good Arruntius.

  Laco. But there are letters come, they say, ev'n now,
Which do forbid that last.

  Min.   Do you hear so?

  Laco.   Yes.

  Pom. By Pollux, that's the worst.

  Arr.   By Hercules, best.

  Min. I did not like the sign, when Regulus
Whom all we know no friend unto Sejanus,
Did, by Tiberius' so precise command,
Succeed a fellow in the consulship:
It boded somewhat.

  Pom.   Not a note. His partner,
Fulcinius Trio, is his own, and sure.
Here comes Terentius.

     Enter Terentius.

     He can give us more.
     [*They whisper with* Terentius.

  Lep. I'll ne'er believe but Cæsar hath some scent
Of bold Sejanus' footing. These cross points
Of varying letters, and opposing consuls,
Mingling his honours and his punishments,
Feigning now ill, now well, raising Sejanus,
And then depressing him, as now of late
In all reports we have it, cannot be
Empty of practice: 'Tis Tiberius' art.
For, having found his favourite grown too great,
And, with his greatness, strong; that all the soldiers
Are, with their leaders, made at his devotion;

That almost all the senate are his creatures,
Or hold on him their main dependences,
Either for benefit, or hope, or fear;
And that himself hath lost much of his own,
By parting unto him; and by th' increase
Of his rank lusts and rages, quite disarm'd
Himself of love, or other public means,
To dare an open contestation;
His subtilty hath chose this doubling line,
To hold him even in: not so to fear him,
As wholly put him out, and yet give check
Unto his farther boldness. In mean time,
By his employments, makes him odious
Unto the staggering rout, whose aid (in fine)
He hopes to use, as sure, who (when they sway)
Bear down, o'erturn all objects in their way.

 Arr. You may be a Lynceus, Lepidus: yet I
See no such cause, but that a politic tyrant
Who can so well disguise it, should have ta'en
A nearer way: feign'd honest, and come home
To cut his throat, by law.

 Lep.   Aye, but his fear
Would ne'er be mask'd, all-be his vices were.

 Pom. His lordship then is still in grace?

 Ter.   Assure you,
Never in more, either of grace or power.

 Pom. The gods are wise and just.

 Arr.   The fiends they are,
To suffer thee belie 'em!

 Ter.   I have here
His last and present letters where he writes him
'The partner of his cares', and 'his Sejanus'——

 Laco. But is that true, it is prohibited
To sacrifice unto him?

 Ter.   Some such thing
Cæsar makes scruple of, but forbids it not;
No more than to himself: says, he could wish
It were forlorn to all.

 Laco.   Is it no other?

Ter. No other, on my trust. For your more surety,
Here is that letter too.

    Arr.   How easily
Do wretched men believe what they would have!
Looks this like plot?

    Lep.   Noble Arruntius, stay.

    Laco. He names him here without his titles.

    Lep.   Note.

    Arr. Yes, and come off your notable fool. I will.

    Laco. No other, than Sejanus.

    Pom.   That's but haste
In him that writes. Here he gives large amends,

    Min. And with his own hand written?

    Pom.   Yes.

    Laco.   Indeed?

    Ter. Believe it, gentlemen, Sejanus' breast
Never receiv'd more full contentments in,
Than at this present.

    Pom.   Takes he well th' escape
Of young Caligula with Macro?

    Ter.   Faith,
At the first air, it somewhat troubled him.

    Lep. Observe you?

    Arr.   Nothing. Riddles. Till I see
Sejanus struck, no sound thereof strikes me.

                       [Exeunt Arruntius *and* Lepidus.

    Pom. I like it not. I muse he would not attempt
Somewhat against him in the consulship,
Seeing the people 'gin to favour him.

    Ter. He doth repent it, now; but he has employ'd
Pagonianus after him: and he holds
That correspondence, there, with all that are
Near about Cæsar, as no thought can pass
Without his knowledge, thence, in act to front him.

    Pom. I gratulate the news.

    Laco.   But, how comes Macro
So in trust and favour with Caligula?

    Pom. O, sir, he has a wife; and the young prince
An appetite: he can look up, and spy

Flies in the roof when there are fleas i' bed;
And hath a learned nose to assure his sleeps.
Who, to be favour'd of the rising sun,
Would not lend little of his waning moon?
'Tis the saf'st ambition. Noble Terentius!

Ter. The night grows fast upon us. At your service.

[*Exeunt.*

ACT V. SCENE I

An apartment in Sejanus' *house.*

Enter Sejanus.

Sej. Swell, swell, my joys: and faint not to declare
Yourselves as ample as your causes are.
I did not live, till now; this my first hour
Wherein I see my thoughts reach'd by my power.
But this, and gripe my wishes. Great and high,
The world knows only two, that's Rome and I.
My roof receives me not; 'tis air I tread:
And, at each step, I feel my advanced head
Knock out a star in heav'n! Rear'd to this height,
All my desires seem modest, poor and slight,
That did before sound impudent: 'tis place,
Not blood, discerns the noble and the base.
Is there not something more than to be Cæsar?
Must we rest there? It irks t' have come so far,
To be so near a stay. Caligula,
Would thou stood'st stiff, and many in our way.
Winds lose their strength when they do empty fly
Unmet of woods or buildings; great fires die,
That want their matter to withstand them; so,
It is our grief, and will be our loss, to know
Our power shall want opposites; unless
The gods, by mixing in the cause, would bless
Our fortune with their conquest. That were worth
Sejanus' strife: durst fates but bring it forth.

Enter Terentius.

Ter. Safety to great Sejanus.

Sej.   Now, Terentius?

Ter. Hears not my lord the wonder?

Sej.   Speak it; no.

Ter. I meet it violent in the people's mouths,
Who run in routs to Pompey's theatre,
To view your statue: which, they say, sends forth
A smoke, as from a furnace, black and dreadful.

Sej. Some traitor hath put fire in: you, go see.
And let the head be taken off, to look
What 'tis—[*Exit* Terentius.] Some slave hath practis'd an
     imposture,
To stir the people. How now? why return you?

     Re-enter Terentius *with* Satrius *and* Natta.

Sat. The head, my lord, already is ta'en off,
I saw it: and, at op'ning, there leapt out
A great and monstrous serpent!

Sej.   Monstrous! why?
Had it a beard? and horns? no heart? a tongue
Forked as flattery? look'd it of the hue,
To such as live in great men's bosoms? was
The spirit of it Macro's?

Nat.   May it please
The most divine Sejanus, in my days,
(And by his sacred fortune, I affirm it)
I have not seen a more extended, grown,
Foul, spotted, venomous, ugly——

Sej.   O, the fates!
What a wild muster's here of attributes,
T' express a worm, a snake?

Ter.   But how that should
Come there, my lord!

Sej.   What! and you too, Terentius?
I think you mean to make 't a prodigy
In your reporting?

Ter.   Can the wise Sejanus
Think heav'n hath meant it less?

Sej.   O, superstition!
Why, then the falling of our bed that brake

This morning, burd'ned with the populous weight
Of our expecting clients, to salute us;
Or running of the cat betwixt our legs,
As we set forth unto the Capitol,
Were prodigies.

   Ter.   I think them ominous!
And, would they had not happened. As, today,
The fate of some your servants; who, declining
Their way, not able, for the throng, to follow,
Slipt down the Gemonies, and brake their necks!
Besides, in taking your last augury
No prosperous bird appear'd, but croking ravens
Flagg'd up and down: and from the sacrifice
Flew to the prison, where they sat, all night,
Beating the air with their obstreperous beaks!
I dare not counsel, but I could entreat
That great Sejanus would attempt the gods
Once more with sacrifice.

   Sej.   What excellent fools,
Religion makes of men? Believes Terentius.
If these were dangers, as I shame to think them,
The gods could change the certain course of fate?
Or, if they could, they would, now in a moment,
For a beeve's fat, or less, be brib'd t' invert
Those long decrees? Then think the gods, like flies,
Are to be taken with the steam of flesh
Or blood, diffus'd about their altars: think
Their power as cheap, as I esteem it small.
Of all the throng, that fill th' Olympian hall,
And, without pity, laid poor Atlas' back,
I know not that one deity, but Fortune;
To whom I would throw up in begging smoke,
One grain of incense: or whose ear I'd buy
With thus much oil. Her I indeed adore;
And keep her grateful image in my house,
Sometime belonging to a Roman king,
But now call'd mine, as by the better style:
To her, I care not, if (for satisfying
Your scrupulous fancies) I go offer. Bid

Our priest prepare us honey, milk, and poppy,
His masculine odours and night-vestments: say,
Our rites are instant, which perform'd, you'll see
How vain and worthy laughter, your fears be.   [*Exeunt.*

ACT V. SCENE II

Another room in the same.

Enter Cotta *and* Pomponius.

Cot. Pomponius! whither in such speed?
Pom.   I go
To give my lord Sejanus notice——
Cot.   What?
Pom. Of Macro.
Cot.   Is he come?
Pom.   Enter'd but now
The house of Regulus.
Cot.   The opposite consul!
Pom. Some half-hour since.
Cot.   And, by night too! Stay, sir;
I'll bear you company.
Pom.   Along, then——   [*Exeunt.*

ACT V. SCENE III

A room in Regulus's house.

Enter Macro, Regulus, *and* attendant.

Mac. 'Tis Cæsar's will to have a frequent senate;
And therefore must your edict lay deep mulct
On such as shall be absent.
Reg. So it doth.
Bear it my fellow consul to adscribe.
Mac. And tell him it must early be proclaim'd;
The place, Apollo's temple.   [*Exit* attendant.
Reg.   That's remembered.
Mac. And at what hour.

Reg.   Yes.

Mac.   You do forget
To send one for the provost of the watch?

Reg. I have not: here he comes.

Enter Laco.

Mac.   Gracinus Laco,
You are a friend most welcome: by and by,
I'll speak with you. You must procure this list
Of the prætorian cohorts, with the names
Of the centurions, and their tribunes.

Reg. Aye.

Mac. I bring you letters and a health from Cæsar.

Laco. Sir, both come well.

Mac.   And hear you? with your note
Which are the eminent men, and most of action.

Reg. That shall be done you too.

Mac.   Most worthy Laco.
Cæsar salutes you. [*The consul goes out.*] Consul! death,
     and furies!
Gone now? the argument will please you, sir.
Ho! Regulus? The anger of the gods
Follow his diligent legs, and overtake 'em,
In likeness of the gout. [*The consul returns.*] O, good my
     lord,
We lack'd you present; I would pray you send
Another to Fulcinius Trio straight,
To tell him you will come and speak with him:
(The matter we'll devise) to stay him there,
While I, with Laco, do survey the watch.
                              [*The consul goes out again.*
What are your strengths, Gracinus?

Laco.   Seven cohorts.

Mac. You see, what Cæsar writes: and—Gone again?
H' has sure a vein of mercury in his feet.
Know you what store of the prætorian soldiers
Sejanus holds about him, for his guard?

Laco. I cannot the just number: but, I think,
Three centuries.

Mac.   Three? good.

Laco.   At most, not four.

Mac. And who be those centurions?

Laco.   That the consul
Can best deliver you.

Mac.   When he's away:
Spite on his nimble industry—Gracinus,
You find what place you hold there, in the trust
Of royal Cæsar?

Laco.   Aye, and I am——

Mac.   Sir,
The honours, there propos'd, are but beginnings
Of his great favours.

Laco.   They are more——

Mac.   I heard him
When he did study what to add——

Laco.   My life,
And all I hold——

Mac.   You were his own first choice;
Which doth confirm as much as you can speak:
And will (if we succeed) make more—Your guards
Are seven cohorts, you say?

Laco.   Yes.

Mac.   Those we must
Hold still in readiness, and undischarg'd.

Laco. I understand so much. But how it can——

Mac. Be done without suspicion, you'll object?

Re-enter Regulus.

Reg. What's that?

Laco.   The keeping of the watch in arms
When morning comes.

Mac.   The senate shall be met, and set
So early, in the temple, as all mark
Of that will be avoided.

Reg.   If we need,
We have commission to possess the palace,
Enlarge prince Drusus, and make him our chief.

Mac. That secret would have burnt his reverend mouth

Had he not spit it out now: by the gods,
You carry things too—let me borrow a man
Or two, to bear these—That of freeing Drusus,
Cæsar projected as the last and utmost;
Not else to be remembered.

Enter servants.

Reg.   Here are servants.
   Mac. These to Arruntius, these to Lepidus,
This bear to Cotta, this to Latiaris.
If they demand you of me: say I have ta'en
Fresh horse and am departed. You, my lord,
To your colleague, and be you sure to hold him
With long narration of the new fresh favours,
Meant to Sejanus, his great patron; I,
With trusted Laco here, are for the guards:
Then to divide. For night hath many eyes,
Whereof, though most do sleep, yet some are spies.

                             [Exeunt.

ACT V. SCENE IV

A chapel in Sejanus's *house.*

Enter Præcones, Tubicines, Tibicines, Flamen, Ministri,
Sejanus, Terentius, Satrius, Natta, *etc.*

   Præ. 'Be all profane far hence; Fly fly far off:
Be absent far. Far hence be all profane.'
          [Tub. Tib. sound while the Flamen *washeth.*
   Fla. We have been faulty but repent us now,
And bring pure hands, pure vestments, and pure minds.
   1 Min. Pure vessels.
   2 Min.   And pure offerings.
   3 Min.   Garlands pure.
   Fla. Bestow your garlands: and, with reverence, place
The vervin on the altar.
   Præ.   Favour your tongues.
   While they sound again, the Flamen *takes of the honey*

*with his finger and tastes, then ministers to all the rest:
so of the milk in an earthen vessel, he deals about: which
done, he sprinkleth, upon the altar, milk: then imposeth
the honey, and kindleth his guns, and after censing about
the altar placeth his censer thereon, into which they put
several branches of poppy, and, the music ceasing, pro-
ceeds.*

Fla. 'Great mother Fortune, Queen of human state,
Rectress of action, arbitress of fate,
To whom all sway, all power, all empire bows,
Be present, and propitious to our vows.'

Præ. Favour it with your tongues.

Min. Be present, and propitious to our vows.
Accept our offering, and be pleas'd, great goddess.

Ter. See, see, the image stirs!

Sat. And turns away!

Nat. Fortune averts her face!

Fla. Avert, you gods,
The prodigy. Still! still! Some pious rite
We have neglected. Yet! heav'n be appeas'd.
And be all tokens false, or void, that speak
Thy present wrath.

Sej. Be thou dumb, scrupulous priest:
And gather up thyself, with these thy wares,
Which I, in spite of thy blind mistress, or
Thy juggling mystery religion, throw
Thus, scorned on the earth.

[*Overturns the statue and the altar.*
Nay, hold thy look
Averted, till I woo thee, turn again;
And thou shalt stand to all posterity
Th' eternal game and laughter, with thy neck
Writh'd to thy tail, like a ridiculous cat.
Avoid these fumes, these superstitious lights,
And all these coz'ning ceremonies: you,
Your pure, and spiced conscience!

[*Exeunt all but* Sejanus, Terentius, Satrius, *and* Natta.
I, the slave,
And mock of fools, scorn on my worthy head!

That hath been titled and ador'd a god,
Yea, sacrific'd unto myself, in Rome,
No less than Jove: and I be brought to do
A peevish giglot rites? Perhaps the thought
And shame of that made Fortune turn her face,
Knowing herself the lesser deity,
And but my servant. Bashful queen, if so,
Sejanus thanks thy modesty.   Who's that?

Enter Pomponius *and* Minutius.

Pom. His fortune suffers, till he hears my news:
I have waited here too long. Macro, my lord——
    Sej. Speak lower, and withdraw.
    Ter.   Are these things true?
    Min. Thousands are gazing at it in the streets.
    Sej. What's that?
    Ter.   Minutius tells us here, my lord,
That a new head being set upon your statue,
A rope is since found wreath'd about it! and,
But now, a fiery meteor, in the form
Of a great ball, was seen to roll along
The troubled air, where yet it hangs, unperfect,
Th' amazing wonder of the multitude!
    Sej. No more. That Macro's come, is more than all!
    Ter. Is Macro come?
    Pom.   I saw him.
    Ter.   Where? with whom?
    Pom. With Regulus.
    Sej.   Terentius——
    Ter.   My lord?
    Sej. Send for the tribune, we will straight have up
More of the soldiers, for our guard. [*Exit* Terentius.]
    Minutius,
We pray you, go for Cotta, Latiaris,
Trio the consul, or what senators
You know are sure, and ours.   [*Exit* Minutius.
                        Now, my good Natta,
For Laco, provost of the watch.   [*Exit* Natta.
                        Now, Satrius,

524   187   G

The time of proof comes on. Arm all our servants,
And without tumult. [*Exit* Satrius.] You, Pomponius,
Hold some good correspondence with the consul:
Attempt him, noble friend. [*Exit* Pomponius.] These
 things begin
To look like dangers, now, worthy my fates.
Fortune, I see thy worst: let doubtful states
And things uncertain hang upon thy will:
Me surest death shall render certain still.
Yet, why is, now, my thought turn'd toward death,
Whom fates have let go on, so far in breath,
Uncheck'd or unreprov'd? I, that did help
To fell the lofty cedar of the world,
Germanicus; that, at one stroke, cut down
Drusus, that upright elm; wither'd his vine;
Laid Silius and Sabinus, two strong oaks,
Flat on the earth; besides those other shrubs,
Cordus, and Sosia, Claudia Pulchra,
Furnius and Gallus, which I have grubb'd up;
And since have set my axe so strong and deep
Into the root of spreading Agrippine;
Lopp'd off, and scatter'd her proud branches, Nero,
Drusus, and Caius too, although re-planted;
If you will, Destinies, that after all
I faint now ere I touch my period,
You are but cruel: and I already have done
Things great enough. All Rome hath been my slave;
The senate sat an idle looker-on
And witness of my power; when I have blush'd
More to command, than it to suffer; all
The fathers have sat ready and prepar'd
To give me empire, temples, or their throats,
When I would ask 'em; and, what crowns the top,
Rome, senate, people, all the world have seen
Jove but my equal: Cæsar but my second.
'Tis then your malice, Fates, who, but your own,
Envy and fear, t' have any power long known.   [*Exit*

ACT V. SCENE V

A room in the same.

Enter Terentius *and* Tribunes.

Ter. Stay here: I'll give his lordship you are come.

Enter Minutius, Cotta, *and* Latiaris.

Min. Marcus Terentius, pray you tell my lord
Here's Cotta and Latiaris.
Ter.   Sir, I shall.   [*Exit.*
Cot. My letter is the very same with yours;
Only requires me to be present there
And give my voice to strengthen his design.
Lat. Names he not what it is?
Cot.   No, nor to you.
Lat. 'Tis strange and singular doubtful!
Cot.   So it is?
It may be all is left to lord Sejanus.

Enter Natta *and* Laco.

Nat. Gentlemen, where's my lord?
Tri.   We wait him here.
Cot. The provost Laco! what's the news?
Lat.   My lord——

Enter Sejanus.

Sej. Now, my right dear, noble, and trusted friends;
How much I am a captive to your kindness!
Most worthy Cotta, Latiaris; Laco,
Your valiant hand; and gentlemen, your loves.
I wish I could divide myself unto you;
Or that it lay within our narrow powers,
To satisfy for so enlarged bounty.
Gracinus, we must pray you, hold your guards
Unquit, when morning comes. Saw you the consul?
Min. Trio will presently be here, my lord.
Cot. They are but giving order for the edict,
To warn the senate.

Sej.   How! the senate?

Lat.   Yes.

This morning, in Apollo's temple.

Cot.   We

Are charg'd by letter to be there, my lord.

Sej. By letter? pray you let's see!

Lat.   Knows not his lordship!

Cot. It seems so!

Sej.   A senate warn'd? without my knowledge?

And on this sudden? senators by letters

Required to be there! who brought these?

Cot.   Macro.

Sej. Mine enemy! And when?

Cot.   This midnight.

Sej.   Time,

With ev'ry other circumstance, doth give

It hath some strains of engine in't!—How now!

Enter Satrius.

Sat. My lord, Sertorius Macro is without,

Alone, and prays t' have private conference

In business of high nature with your lordship,

He says to me, and which regards you much.

Sej. Let him come here.

Sat.   Better, my lord, withdraw,

You will betray what store and strength of friends

Are now about you; which he comes to spy.

Sej. Is he not arm'd?

Sat.   We'll search him.

Sej.   No, but take,

And lead him to some room, where you, conceal'd,

May keep a guard upon us. [*Exit* Sat.] Noble Laco,

You are our trust: and, till our own cohorts

Can be brought up, your strengths must be our guard.

                          [*He salutes them humbly.*

Now, good Minutius, honour'd Latiaris,

Most worthy, and my most unwearied friends:

I return instantly.   [*Exit.*

Lat.   Most worthy lord!

Cot. His lordship is turn'd instant kind, methinks,
I have not observ'd it in him, heretofore.

1 Tri. 'Tis true, and it becomes him nobly.

Min.   I
Am rapt withal.

2 Tri.   By Mars, he has my lives,
Were they a million, for this only grace.

Laco. Aye, and to name a man!

Lat.   As he did me!

Min. And me.

Lat.   Who would not spend his life and fortunes,
To purchase but the look of such a lord?

Laco. He that would nor be lord's fool, nor the world's.
                                                    [*Aside.*

ACT V. SCENE VI

Another room in the same.

Enter Sejanus, Macro, *and* Satrius.

Sej. Macro! most welcome, as most coveted friend!
Let me enjoy my longings. When arriv'd you?

Mac. About the noon of night.

Sej.   Satrius, give leave. [*Exit Sat.*

Mac. I have been, since I came, with both the consuls,
On a particular design from Cæsar.

Sej. How fares it with our great and royal master?

Mac. Right plentifully well; as with a prince
That still holds out the great proportion
Of his large favours, where his judgement hath
Made once divine election: like the god
That wants not, nor is wearied to bestow
Where merit meets his bounty as it doth
In you, already the most happy, and ere
The sun shall climb the south, most high Sejanus.
Let not my lord be amus'd. For, to this end
Was I by Cæsar sent for, to the isle,
With special caution to conceal my journey;
And thence had my dispatch as privately

Again to Rome; charg'd to come here by night,
And only to the consuls make narration
Of his great purpose: that the benefit
Might come more full and striking, by how much
It was less look'd for, or aspir'd by you,
Or least informed to the common thought.

Sej. What may this be? part of myself, dear Macro!
If good, speak out: and share with your Sejanus.

Mac. If bad, I should for ever loath myself,
To be the messenger to so good a lord.
I do exceed m' instructions, to acquaint
Your lordship with thus much; but 'tis my venture
On your retentive wisdom: and because
I would no jealous scruple should molest
Or rack your peace of thought. For, I assure
My noble lord, no senator yet knows
The business meant: though all, by several letters,
Are warned to be there, and give their voices,
Only to add unto the state and grace
Of what is purpos'd.

Sej. You take pleasure, Macro,
Like a coy wench, in torturing your lover.
What can be worth this suffering?

Mac. That which follows,
The tribunitial dignity and power:
Both which Sejanus is to have this day
Conferr'd upon him, and by public senate.

Sej. Fortune, be mine again; thou hast satisfied
For thy suspected loyalty.

Mac. My lord,
I have no longer time, the day approacheth,
And I must back to Cæsar.

Sej. Where's Caligula?

Mac. That I forgot to tell your lordship. Why,
He lingers yonder, about Capreæ,
Disgrac'd; Tiberius hath not seen him yet:
He needs would thrust himself to go with me,
Against my wish or will, but I have quitted
His forward trouble with as tardy note

As my neglect or silence could afford him.
Your lordship cannot now command me aught,
Because I take no knowledge that I saw you,
But I shall boast to live to serve your lordship:
And so take leave.
    Sej.   Honest, and worthy Macro,
Your love and friendship. [*Exit* Macro.] Who's there?
    Satrius,
Attend my honourable friend forth. O!
How vain and vile a passion is this fear!
What base, uncomely things it makes men do.
Suspect their noblest friends, as I did this,
Flatter poor enemies, entreat their servants,
Stoop, court, and catch at the benevolence
Of creatures, unto whom, within this hour,
I would not have vouchsaf'd a quarter-look,
Or piece of face? By you, that fools call gods,
Hang all the sky with your prodigious signs,
Fill earth with monsters, drop the scorpion down
Out of the zodiac, or the fiercer lion.
Shake off the loosen'd globe from her long hinge,
Roll all the world in darkness, and let loose
Th' enraged winds to turn up groves and towns;
When I do fear again, let me be struck
With forked fire, and unpitied die:
Who fears, is worthy of calamity.   [*Exit.*

ACT V. SCENE VII

Another room in the same.

Enter Terentius, Minutius, Laco, Cotta, Latiaris *and* Pomponius, Regulus, Trio *and others, all from different sides.*

    Pom. Is not my lord here?
    Ter.   Sir, he will be straight.
    Cot. What news, Fulcinius Trio?
    Trio.   Good, good tidings.
(But keep it to yourself.) My lord Sejanus

Is to receive this day, in open senate,
The tribunitial dignity.

 Cot.   Is't true?

 Trio. No words; not to your thought: but, sir, believe it.

 Lat. What says the consul?

 Cot.   Speak it not again,
He tells me, that today my lord Sejanus——

 Trio. I must entreat you, Cotta, on your honour
Not to reveal it.

 Cot.   On my life, sir.

 Lat.   Say.

 Cot. Is to receive the tribunitial power.
But, as you are an honourable man,
Let me conjure you, not to utter it:
For it is trusted to me, with that bond.

 Lat. I am Harpocrates.

 Ter.   Can you assure it?

 Pom. The consul told me, but keep it close.

 Min. Lord Latiaris, what's the news?

 Lat.   I'll tell you,
But you must swear to keep it secret——

Enter Sejanus.

 Sej. I knew the fates had on their distaff left
More of our thread, than so.

 Reg.   Hail, great Sejanus!

 Trio. Hail, the most honour'd!

 Cot.   Happy!

 Lat.   High Sejanus!

 Sej. Do you bring prodigies too?

 Trio.   May all presage
Turn to those fair effects, whereof we bring
Your lordship news.

 Reg.   May't please my lord withdraw.

 Sej. Yes; I will speak with you, anon.

[To some that stand by.

 Ter.   My lord,
What is your pleasure for the tribunes?

Sej.   **Why,**
Let 'em be thank'd, and sent away.
    Min.   **My lord——**
    Laco. Will't please your lordship to command me——
    Sej.   **No.**
You are troublesome.
    Min.   The mood is chang'd.
    1 Tri.   **Not speak?**
    2 Tri. Nor look?
    Laco.   He is wise, will make him friends
Of such who never love but for their ends.   *[Exeunt.*

ACT V. SCENE VIII

A space before the Temple of Apollo.

Enter ARRUNTIUS *and* LEPIDUS, *divers other Senators passing by them.*

    Arr. Aye, go, make haste; take heed you be not last
To tender your 'All hail!' in the wide hall
Of huge Sejanus: run, a lictor's pace;
Stay not to put your robes on; but away
With the pale troubled ensigns of great friendship
Stamp'd i' your face! Now, Marcus Lepidus,
You still believe your former augury?
Sejanus must go downward? you perceive
His wane approaching fast?
    Lep.   Believe me, Lucius,
I wonder at this rising!
    Arr.   Aye, and that we
Must give our suffrage to it? you will say,
It is to make his fall more steep and grievous?
It may be so. But think it, they that can
With idle wishes 'say to bring back time:
In cases desperate, all hope is crime.
See, see! what troops of his officious friends
Flock to salute my lord! and start before
My great proud lord! to get a lord-like nod!

Attend my lord unto the senate-house!
Bring back my lord! like servile ushers, make
Way for my lord! proclaim his idol lordship,
More than ten criers or six noise of trumpets!
Make legs, kiss hands, and take a scatter'd hair
From my lord's eminent shoulder! See, Sanquinius!
With his slow belly, and his dropsy! look,
What toiling haste he makes! yet, here's another,
Retarded with the gout, will be afore him!
Get thee Liburnian porters, thou gross fool,
To bear thy obsequious fatness, like thy peers.
They are met! The gout returns, and his great carriage.

Lictors, Consuls, Sejanus, etc. pass over the stage.

Lict. Give way, make place; room for the consul.
San.   Hail,
Hail, great Sejanus!
Hat.   Hail, my honour'd lord!
Arr. We shall be mark'd anon, for our not Hail.
Lep. That is already done.
Arr.   It is a note
Of upstart greatness, to observe and watch
For these poor trifles, which the noble mind
Neglects and scorns.
Lep.   Aye, and they think themselves
Deeply dishonour'd, where they are omitted,
As if they were necessities that help'd
To the perfection of their dignities:
And hate the men that but refrain 'em.
Arr.   O!
There is a farther cause of hate. Their breasts
Are guilty that we know their obscure springs
And base beginnings: thence the anger grows.
On. Follow.   *[Exeunt.*

Enter Macro and Laco.

Mac. When all are entered, shut the temple doors;
And bring your guards up to the gate.
Laco.   I will.

Mac. If you shall hear commotion in the senate,
Present yourself: and charge on any man
Shall offer to come forth.

Laco.   I am instructed.   [*Exeunt.*

ACT V. SCENE IX

The Senate.

In the Temple of Apollo.

Enter Haterius, Trio, Sanquinius, Cotta, Regulus, Sejanus,
Pomponius, Latiaris, Lepidus, Arruntius, Præcones,
Lictores, *and other* Senators.

Hat. How well his lordship looks to-day!
Trio.   As if
He had been born, or made for this hour's state.
Cot. Your fellow consul's come about, methinks?
Trio. Aye, he is wise.
San.   Sejanus trusts him well.
Trio. Sejanus is a noble, bounteous lord.
Hat. He is so, and most valiant.
Lat.   And most wise.
1 Sen. He's everything.
Lat.   Worthy of all, and more
Than bounty can bestow.
Trio.   This dignity
Will make him worthy.
Pom.   Above Cæsar.
San.   Tut,
Cæsar is but the rector of an isle,
He of the empire.
Trio.   Now he will have power
More to reward than ever.
Cot.   Let us look
We be not slack in giving him our voices.
Lat. Not I.
San.   Nor I.

197

Cot.   The readier we seem
To propagate his honours, will more bind
His thought to ours.

Hat.   I think right with your lordship.
It is the way to have us hold our places.

San. Aye, and get more.

Lat.   More office, and more titles.

Pom. I will not lose the part, I hope to share
In these his fortunes, for my patrimony.

Lat. See how Arruntius sits, and Lepidus.

Trio. Let 'em alone, they will be mark'd anon.

1 Sen. I'll do with others.

2 Sen.   So will I.

3 Sen.   And I.
Men grow not in the state, but as they are planted
Warm in his favours.

Cot.   Noble Sejanus!

Hat. Honour'd Sejanus!

Lat.   Worthy, and great Sejanus!

Arr. Gods! how the sponges open, and take in;
And shut again! look, look! is not he bless'd
That gets a seat in eye-reach of him? more,
That comes in ear, or tongue-reach? O, but most,
Can claw his subtle elbow, or with a buzz
Fly-blow his ears.

Præ.   Proclaim the senate's peace;
And give last summons by the edict. Silence:
In the name of Cæsar and the senate: Silence.

'Memmius Regulus, and Fulcinius Trio, consuls, these present kalends of June, with the first light, shall hold a senate, in the temple of Apollo Palatine, all that are fathers, and are registered fathers, that have right of entering the senate, we warn or command you be frequently present, take knowledge the business is the commonwealth's: whosoever is absent, his fine or mulct will be taken, his excuse will not be taken.'

Trio. Note who are absent, and record their names.

Reg. Fathers conscript. May what I am to utter,
Turn good and happy, for the commonwealth.

SEJANUS

And thou Apollo, in whose holy house
We here are met, inspire us all with truth,
And liberty of censure to our thought.
The majesty of great Tiberius Cæsar
Propounds to this grave senate the bestowing
Upon the man he loves, honour'd Sejanus,
The tribunitial dignity and power;
Here are his letters, signed with his signet:
What pleaseth now the Fathers to be done?

   Sen. Read, read 'em, open, publicly, read 'em.

   Cot. Cæsar hath honour'd his own greatness much,
In thinking of this act.

   Trio.   It was a thought
Happy, and worthy Cæsar.

   Lat.   And the lord
As worthy it, on whom it is directed!

   Hat. Most worthy!

   San.   Rome did never boast the virtue
That could give envy bounds, but his: Sejanus——

   1 Sen. Honour'd, and noble!

   2 Sen.   Good and great Sejanus!

   Arr. O, most tame slavery and fierce flattery!

   Præ.   Silence!

'TIBERIUS CÆSAR
To the Senate
Greeting.

'If you, conscript fathers, with your children, be in health,
it is abundantly well: we with our friends here, are so. The
care of the commonwealth, howsoever we are remov'd in
person, cannot be absent to our thought; although, often-
times, even to princes most present, the truth of their own
affairs is hid: than which nothing falls out more miserable
to a state, or makes the art of governing more difficult. But
since it hath been our easeful happiness to enjoy both the
aids and industry of so vigilant a senate, we profess to have
been the more indulgent to our pleasures, not as being
careless of our office, but rather secure of the necessity.
Neither do these common rumours of many and infamous

libels published against our retirement, at all afflict us;
being born more out of men's ignorance than their malice:
and will, neglected, find their own grave quickly; whereas
too sensibly acknowledg'd, it would make their obloquy
ours. Nor do we desire their authors, though found, be
censur'd, since in a free state (as ours) all men ought to
enjoy their minds and tongues free.'

Arr. The lapwing, the lapwing.

'Yet, in things which shall worthily and more near con-
cern the majesty of a prince, we shall fear to be so un-
naturally cruel to our own fame, as to neglect them. True
it is, conscript fathers, that we have raised Sejanus from
obscure and almost unknown gentry

Sen.   How! how!

'to the highest, and most conspicuous point of greatness,
and, we hope, deservingly; yet not without danger: it
being a most bold hazard in that sovereign, who, by his
particular love to one, dares adventure the hatred of all his
other subjects.'

Arr. This touches, the blood turns.

'But we affy in your loves and understandings, and do no
way suspect the merit of our Sejanus to make our favours
offensive to any.'

Sen. O! good, good.

'Though we could have wished his zeal had run a calmer
course against Agrippina and our nephews, howsoever the
openness of their actions declared them delinquents; and
that he would have remembered no innocence is so safe,
but it rejoiceth to stand in the sight of mercy: the use of
which in us he hath so quite taken away toward them by
his loyal fury as now our clemency would be thought but
wearied cruelty, if we should offer to exercise it.'

Arr. I thank him, there I look'd for't. A good fox!

'Some there be that would interpret this his public severity
to be particular ambition; and that, under a pretext of
service to us, he doth but remove his own lets: alleging
the strengths he hath made to himself, by the prætorian
soldiers, by his faction in court and senate, by the offices
he holds himself, and confers on others, his popularity and

dependents, his urging, and almost driving, us to this our
unwilling retirement, and lastly his aspiring to be our son-
in-law.'

  Sen. This's strange!

  Arr. I shall anon believe your vultures, Marcus.

'Your wisdoms, conscript fathers, are able to examine and
censure these suggestions. But, were they left to our absolv-
ing voice, we durst pronounce them, as we think them,
most malicious.'

  Sen. O, he has restor'd all, list.

'Yet are they offer'd to be averr'd, and on the lives of the
informers. What we should say, or rather what we should
not say, lords of the senate, if this be true, our gods and
goddesses confound us if we know! Only we must think
we have plac'd our benefits ill: and conclude, that in our
choice, either we were wanting to the gods, or the gods
to us.'   [*The* Senators *shift their places.*

  Arr. The place grows hot, they shift.

'We have not been covetous, honourable fathers, to change;
neither is it now any new lust that alters our affection, or
old loathing: but those needful jealousies of state, that warn
wiser princes hourly to provide their safety; and do teach
them how learned a thing it is to beware of the humblest
enemy; much more of those great ones, whom their own
employ'd favours have made fit for their fears.'

  1 Sen. Away.

  2 Sen.   Sit farther.

  Cot.   Let's remove——

  Arr. Gods! how the leaves drop off, this little wind!

'We therefore desire, that the offices he holds be first
seized by the senate; and himself suspended from all exer-
cise of place or power——'

  Sen. How!

  San.   By your leave.

  Arr.   Come, porpoise, where's Haterius?
His gout keeps him most miserably constant.
Your dancing shows a tempest.

  Sej.   Read no more.

  Reg. Lords of the senate hold your seats: read on.

SEJANUS

Sej. These letters, they are forg'd.

Reg.   A guard, sit still.

Laco enters with the guards.

Arr. There's change.

Reg.   Bid silence, and read forward.

Præ. Silence——'and himself suspended from all exercise of place or power, but till due and mature trial be made of his innocency, which yet we can faintly apprehend the necessity to doubt. If, conscript fathers, to your more searching wisdoms, there shall appear farther cause, or of farther proceeding, either to seizure of lands, goods, or more—it is not our power that shall limit your authority, or our favour that must corrupt your justice: either were dishonourable in you, and both uncharitable to ourself. We would willingly be present with your counsels in this business, but the danger of so potent a faction, if it should prove so, forbids our attempting it: except one of the consuls would be entreated for our safety to undertake the guard of us home, then we should most readily adventure. In the meantime, it shall not be fit for us to importune so judicious a senate, who know how much they hurt the innocent that spare the guilty: and how grateful a sacrifice to the gods is the life of an ingrateful person. We reflect not in this on Sejanus (notwithstanding, if you keep an eye upon him—and there is Latiaris, a senator, and Pinnarius Natta, two of his most trusted ministers, and so profess'd, whom we desire not to have apprended) but as the necessity of the cause exacts it.'

Reg. A guard on Latiaris.

Arr.   O, the spy!
The reverend spy is caught, who pities him?
Reward, sir, for your service: now, you ha' done
Your property, you see what use is made!

                          [*Exeunt* Latiaris *and* Natta *guarded.*
Hang up the instrument.

Sej.   Give leave.

Laco.   Stand, stand,

He comes upon his death, that doth advance
An inch toward my point.

 Sej.   Have we no friends here?

 Arr.   Hush'd.
Where now are all the hails and acclamations?

Enter Macro.

 Mac. Hail to the consuls, and this noble senate.

 Sej. Is Macro here? O, thou art lost! Sejanus. [*Aside.*

 Mac. Sit still, and unaffrighted, reverend fathers,
Macro, by Cæsar's grace, the new-made provost,
And now possess'd of the prætorian bands,
An honour late belong'd to that proud man,
Bids you be safe: and to your constant doom
Of his deservings, offers you the surety
Of all the soldiers, tribunes, and centurions
Receiv'd in our command.

 Reg.   Sejanus, Sejanus,
Stand forth, Sejanus.

 Sej.   Am I call'd?

 Mac.   Aye, thou,
Thou insolent monster, art bid stand.

 Sej.   Why, Macro.
It hath been otherwise between you and I;
This court, that knows us both, hath seen a difference,
And can, if it be pleas'd to speak, confirm
Whose insolence is most.

 Mac.   Come down, Typhœus,
If mine be most, lo, thus I make it more;
Kick up thy heels in air, tear off thy robe,
Play with thy beard and nostrils. Thus 'tis fit,
(And no man take compassion of thy state)
To use th' ungrateful viper, tread his brains
Into the earth.

 Reg.   Forbear.

 Mac.   If I could lose
All my humanity now, 'twere well to torture
So meriting a traitor. Wherefore, fathers,
Sit you amaz'd and silent? and not censure

This wretch, who in the hour he first rebell'd
'Gainst Cæsar's bounty did condemn himself?
Phlegra, the field where all the sons of earth
Muster'd against the gods, did ne'er acknowledge
So proud and huge a monster.

  Reg.   Take him hence.
And all the gods guard Cæsar.

  Trio.   Take him hence.

  Hat. Hence.

  Cot.   To the dungeon with him.

  San.   He deserves it.

  Sen. Crown all our doors with bays.

  San.   And let an ox,
With gilded horns and garlands, straight be led
Unto the Capitol.

  Hat.   And sacrific'd
To Jove for Cæsar's safety.

  Trio.   All our gods
Be present still to Cæsar.

  Cot.   Phœbus.

  San.   Mars.

  Hat. Diana.

  San.   Pallas.

  Sen.   Juno, Mercury.
All guard him.

  Mac. Forth, thou prodigy of men.
         [Exit Sejanus *guarded.*

  Cot. Let all the traitor's titles be defac'd.

  Trio. His images and statues be pull'd down.

  Hat. His chariot-wheels be broken.

  Arr.   And the legs
Of the poor horses, that deserved naught,
Let them be broken too.

  Lep.   O, violent change,
And whirl of men's affections!

  Arr.   Like, as both
Their bulks and souls were bound on Fortune's wheel,
And must act only with her motion.

    [Exeunt all but Lepidus, Arruntius *and a few* Senators.

Lep. Who would depend upon the popular air,
Or voice of men, that have today beheld
That which if all the gods had fore-declar'd,
Would not have been believ'd, Sejanus' fall?
He that this morn rose proudly as the sun?
And, breaking through a mist of clients' breath,
Came on as gaz'd at and admir'd as he,
When superstitious Moors salute his light!
That had our servile nobles waiting him
As common grooms; and hanging on his look,
No less than human life on destiny!
That had men's knees as frequent as the gods;
And sacrifices more than Rome had altars:
And this man fall! fall? Aye, without a look,
That durst appear his friend; or lend so much
Of vain relief, to his chang'd state, as pity!

Arr. They that before, like gnats, played in his beams,
And throng'd to circumscribe him, now not seen!
Nor deign to hold a common seat with him!
Others, that waited him unto the senate,
Now inhumanely ravish him to prison,
Whom, but this morn, they follow'd as their lord!
Guard through the streets, bound like a fugitive!
Instead of wreaths, give fetters; strokes, for stoops:
Blind shame for honours; and black taunts for titles!
Who would trust slippery chance?

Lep.   They that would make
Themselves her spoil: and foolishly forget,
When she doth flatter, that she comes to prey.
Fortune, thou hadst no deity if men
Had wisdom: we have placed thee so high,
By fond belief in thy felicity.   [*Shout within.*

Sen. The gods guard Cæsar! All the gods guard Cæsar!

Re-enter Macro, Regulus, *and* Senators.

Mac. Now great Sejanus, you that aw'd the state,
And sought to bring the nobles to your whip,
That would be Cæsar's tutor, and dispose
Of dignities and offices! that had

The public head still bare to your designs,
And made the general voice to echo yours!
That look'd for salutations, twelve score off,
And would have pyramids, yea, temples rear'd
To your huge greatness! now, you lie as flat
As was your pride advanc'd.

   Reg.   Thanks to the gods.

   Sen. And praise to Macro that hath saved Rome,
Liberty, liberty, liberty. Lead on,
And praise to Macro, that hath saved Rome.

                     [*Exeunt all but* Arruntius *and* Lepidus.

   Arr. I prophesy out of this senates' flattery
That this new fellow, Macro, will become
A greater prodigy in Rome than he
That now is fallen.

Enter Terentius.

   Ter.   O you, whose minds are good,
And have not forc'd all mankind from your breasts;
That yet have so much stock of virtue left,
To pity guilty states, when they are wretched:
Lend your soft ears to hear, and eyes to weep
Deeds done by men, beyond the acts of furies.
The eager multitude, (who never yet
Knew why to love, or hate, but only pleas'd
T' express their rage of power) no sooner heard
The murmur of Sejanus in decline,
But with that speed and heat of appetite
With which they greedily devour the way
To some great sports, or a new theatre,
They fill'd the *Capitol*, and Pompey's Cirque;
Where, like so many mastiffs, biting stones,
As if his statues now were sensive grown
Of their wild fury first, they tear them down:
Then fastening ropes, drag them along the streets,
Crying in scorn, This, this was that rich head
Was crown'd with garlands and with odours, this
That was in Rome so reverenced! Now
The furnace and the bellows shall to work,

The great Sejanus crack, and piece by piece,
Drop i' the founder's pit.

   Lep.   O, popular rage!

   Ter. The whilst, the senate at the temple of Concord
Make haste to meet again, and thronging cry,
Let us condemn him, tread him down in water,
While he doth lie upon the bank; away:
Where some more tardy cry unto their bearers,
He will be censur'd ere we come; run, knaves,
And use that furious diligence, for fear
Their bondmen should inform against their slackness,
And bring their quaking flesh unto the hook:
The rout they follow with confused voice,
Crying, they are glad, say they could ne'er abide him;
Enquire, what man he was? what kind of face?
What beard he had? what nose? what lips? protest
They ever did presage he would come to this:
They never thought him wise nor valiant: ask
After his garments, when he dies? what death?
And not a beast of all the herd demands,
What was his crime? or, who were his accusers?
Under what proof, or testimony, he fell?
There came, says one, a huge, long, worded letter
From Capreæ against him. Did there so?
O, they are satisfied, no more.

   Lep.   Alas!
They follow fortune, and hate men condemn'd,
Guilty or not.

   Arr.   But had Sejanus thriv'd
In his design, and prosperously oppress'd
The old Tiberius, then, in that same minute,
These very rascals that now rage like furies,
Would have proclaim'd Sejanus emperor.

   Lep. But what hath follow'd?

   Ter.   Sentence, by the senate
To lose his head: which was no sooner off,
But that and the unfortunate trunk were seiz'd
By the rude multitude; who not content
With what the forward justice of the state

Officiously had done, with violent rage
Have rent it limb from limb. A thousand heads,
A thousand hands, ten thousand tongues and voices,
Employ'd at once in several acts of malice!
Old men not staid with age, virgins with shame,
Late wives with loss of husbands, mothers of children,
Losing all grief in joy of his sad fall,
Run quite transported with their cruelty!
These mounting at his head, these at his face,
These digging out his eyes, those with his brain,
Sprinkling themselves, their houses, and their friends;
Others are met, have ravish'd thence an arm,
And deal small pieces of the flesh for favours;
These with a thigh; this hath cut off his hands;
And this his feet; these fingers, and these toes;
That hath his liver; he his heart: there wants
Nothing but room for wrath, and place for hatred!
What cannot oft be done, is now o'erdone.
The whole, and all of what was great Sejanus,
And next to Cæsar did possess the world,
Now torn and scatter'd, as he needs no grave,
Each little dust covers a little part:
So lies he nowhere, and yet often buried!

Enter Nuntius.

Arr. More of Sejanus?
Nun. Yes.
Lep. What can be added?
We know him dead.
Nun. Then there begin your pity.
There is enough behind to melt even Rome
And Cæsar into tears: since never slave
Could yet so highly offend, but tyranny
In torturing him, would make him worth lamenting.
A son and daughter to the dead Sejanus
(Of whom there is not now so much remaining
As would give fastening to the hangman's hook)
Have they drawn forth for farther sacrifice;
Whose tenderness of knowledge, unripe years,

And childish silly innocence was such,
As scarce would lend them feeling of their danger:
The girl so simple, as she often ask'd
Where they would lead her? for what cause they dragg'd
    her?
Cry'd, she would do no more. That she could take
Warning with beating. And because our laws
Admit no virgin immature to die,
The wittily and strangely cruel Macro,
Deliver'd her to be deflowr'd and spoil'd
By the rude lust of the licentious hangman,
Then, to be strangled with her harmless brother.
    Lep. O, act most worthy hell, and lasting night,
To hide it from the world!
    Nun.   Their bodies thrown
Into the Gemonies (I know not how,
Or by what accident return'd), the mother,
Th' expulsed Apicata, finds them there;
Whom when she saw lie spread on the degrees,
After a world of fury on herself,
Tearing her hair, defacing of her face,
Beating her breasts and womb, kneeling amaz'd,
Crying to heaven, then to them; at last,
Her drowned voice gat up above her woes:
And with such black, and bitter execrations
As might affright the gods, and force the sun
Run backward to the east, nay, make the old
Deformed Chaos rise again, t' o'erwhelm
Them, us, and all the world, she fills the air;
Upbraids the heavens with their partial dooms,
Defies their tyrannous powers, and demands
What she, and those poor innocents have transgress'd,
That they must suffer such a share in vengeance,
Whilst Livia, Lygdus, and Eudemus live,
Who, as she says and firmly vows to prove it
To Cæsar and the senate, poison'd Drusus?
    Lep. Confederates with her husband?
    Nun.   Aye.
    Lep.   Strange act!

Arr. And strangely open'd: what says now my monster,
The multitude? they reel now? do they not?

Nun. Their gall is gone, and now they 'gin to weep
The mischief they have done.

Arr.   I thank 'em, rogues!

Nun. Part are so stupid, or so flexible,
As they believe him innocent; all grieve:
And some, whose hands yet reek with his warm blood,
And grip the part which they did tear of him,
Wish him collected and created new.

Lep. How Fortune plies her sports, when she begins
To practise 'em! pursues, continues, adds!
Confounds, with varying her impassion'd moods!

Arr. Dost thou hope, Fortune, to redeem thy crimes,
To make amends for thy ill-placed favours,
With these strange punishments? Forbear, you things,
That stand upon the pinnacles of state,
To boast your slippery height; when you do fall,
You pash yourselves in pieces, ne'er to rise:
And he that lends you pity, is not wise.

Ter. Let this example move the insolent man
Not to grow proud and careless of the gods:
It is an odious wisdom to blaspheme,
Much more to slighten or deny their powers.
For whom the morning saw so great and high,
Thus low and little, 'fore the even doth lie.   [*Exeunt.*

THE END

VOLPONE

or

THE FOX

BEN: IONSON

his

VOLPONE

Or

THE FOXE.

—— *Simul & iucunda, & idonea dicere vitæ.*

Printed for *Thomas Thorppe.*
1607.

BEN: IONSON

his

VOLPONE

Printed for Thomas Thorppe.

The Persons of the Play

VOLPONE, *a Magnifico.*
MOSCA, *his Parasite.*
VOLTORE, *an Advocate.*
CORBACCIO, *an old Gentleman.*
CORVINO, *a Merchant.*
AVOCATORI, *four Magistrates.*
NOTARIO, *the Register.*
NANO, *a Dwarf.*
CASTRONE, *an Eunuch.*
SIR POLITIC WOULD-BE, *a Knight.*

MOB.

PEREGRINE, *a Gentleman traveller.*
BONARIO, *a young Gentleman, son to* Corbaccio.
LADY WOULD-BE, *the Knight's wife.*
CELIA, *the Merchant's wife.*
COMMANDADORI, *Officers.*
MERCATORI, *three Merchants.*
ANDROGYNO, *a Hermaphrodite.*
SERVITORE, *a Servant.*

WOMEN.

THE SCENE

VENICE

215

VOLPONE

or

THE FOX

THE ARGUMENT

V OLPONE, childless, rich, feigns sick, despairs,
O ffers his state to hopes of several heirs,
L ies languishing; his parasite receives
P resents of all, assures, deludes: Then weaves
O ther cross plots, which ope' themselves, are told.
N ew tricks for safety are sought; they thrive: When bold,
E ach tempts th' other again, and all are sold

PROLOGUE

Now, luck yet sends us, and a little wit
Will serve to make our play hit;
(According to the palates of the season)
Here is rhyme, not empty of reason:
This we were bid to credit, from our poet,
Whose true scope, if you would know it,
In all his poems, still hath been this measure,
To mix profit with your pleasure;
And not as some, whose throats their envy failing,
Cry hoarsely, All he writes is railing:
And, when his plays come forth, think they can flout them,
With saying, he was a year about them.
To these there needs no lie, but this his creature,
Which was, two months since, no feature;
And, though he dares give them five lives to mend it,
'Tis known, five weeks fully penn'd it:

From his own hand, without a coadjutor,
Novice, journey-man, or tutor.
Yet, thus much I can give you, as a token
Of his plays' worth, no eggs are broken;
Nor quaking custards with fierce teeth affrighted,
Wherewith your rout are so delighted;
Nor hales he in a gull, old ends reciting,
To stop gaps in his loose writing;
With such a deal of monstrous and forc'd action:
As might make Bet'lem a faction:
Nor made he his play for jests stolen from each table,
But makes jests to fit his fable.
And so presents quick comedy refined,
As best critics have designed,
The laws of time, place, persons he observeth,
From no needful rule he swerveth.
All gall and copperas from his ink he draineth,
Only a little salt remaineth;
Wherewith he'll rub your cheeks, till red with laughter,
They shall look fresh, a week after.

ACT I. SCENE I

A room in Volpone's *house.*

Enter Volpone *and* Mosca.

Volp. Good morning to the day; and next my gold:
Open the shrine, that I may see my saint.

     [Mosca *draws aside the curtain, revealing piles of*
     gold, plate, jewels, etc.

Hail the world's soul, and mine. More glad than is
The teeming earth to see the long'd-for sun
Peep through the horns of the celestial Ram,
Am I, to view thy splendour darkening his:
That lying here, amongst my other hoards,
Show'st like a flame, by night; or like the day
Struck out of chaos when all darkness fled
Unto the centre. O, thou son of Sol,
But brighter than thy father, let me kiss,
With adoration, thee, and every relic
Of sacred treasure in this blessed room.
Well did wise poets, by thy glorious name,
Title that age, which they would have the best;
Thou being the best of things: and far transcending
All styles of joy in children, parents, friends,
Or any other waking dream on earth.
Thy looks, when they to Venus did ascribe,
They should have given her twenty thousand Cupids;
Such are thy beauties, and our loves! Dear saint,
Riches, the dumb god, that giv'st all men tongues:
That canst do nought, and yet mak'st men do all things;
The price of souls; even hell, with thee to boot,
Is made worth heaven! Thou art virtue, fame,
Honour, and all things else! Who can get thee,
He shall be noble, valiant, honest, wise——

   Mos. And what he will, sir. Riches are in fortune
A greater good than wisdom is in nature.

   Volp. True, my beloved Mosca. Yet, I glory
More in the cunning purchase of my wealth,
Than in the glad possession; since I gain

No common way: I use no trade, no venture;
I wound no earth with ploughshares; fat no beasts
To feed the shambles; have no mills for iron,
Oil, corn, or men, to grind 'em into powder;
I blow no subtle glass; expose no ships
To threat'nings of the furrow-faced sea;
I turn no monies in the public bank;
Nor usure private——

    Mos.   No, sir, nor devour
Soft prodigals. You shall ha' some will swallow
A melting heir, as glibly as your Dutch
Will pills of butter, and ne'er purge for't;
Tear forth the fathers of poor families
Out of their beds, and coffin them alive
In some kind clasping prison, where their bones
May be forthcoming when the flesh is rotten:
But your sweet nature doth abhor these courses;
You loathe the widow's or the orphan's tears
Should wash your pavements, or their piteous cries
Ring in your roofs, and beat the air for vengeance.--

    Volp. Right, Mosca, I do loathe it.

    Mos.   And besides, sir,
You are not like the thresher, that doth stand
With a hugh flail, watching a heap of corn,
And, hungry, dares not taste the smallest grain,
But feeds on mallows, and such bitter herbs;
Nor like the merchant who hath fill'd his vaults
With Romagnia, and rich Candian wines,
Yet drinks the lees of Lombard's vinegar:
You will not lie in straw, whilst moths and worms
Feed on your sumptuous hangings and soft beds.
You know the use of riches, and dare give now,
From that bright heap to me, your poor observer,
Or to your dwarf, or your hermaphrodite,
Your eunuch, or what other houshold-trifle
Your pleasure allows maint'nance.——

    Volp.   Hold thee, Mosca. [*Gives him money.*
Take of my hand; thou strik'st on truth, in all:
And they are envious, term thee parasite.

Call forth my dwarf, my eunuch, and my fool,
And let 'em make me sport.   [*Exit* Mosca.
                   What should I do,
But cocker up my genius, and live free
To all delights my fortune calls me to?
I have no wife, no parent, child, ally
To give my substance to; but whom I make,
Must be my heir: and this makes men observe me.
This draws new clients, daily, to my house,
Women and men, of every sex and age,
That bring me presents, send me plate, coin, jewels,
With hope that when I die (which they expect
Each greedy minute) it shall then return
Tenfold upon them; whilst some, covetous
Above the rest, seek to engross me whole,
And counter-work the one unto the other,
Contend in gifts, as they would seem in love:
All which I suffer, playing with their hopes,
And am content to coin 'em into profit,
And look upon their kindness, and take more,
And look on that; still bearing them in hand,
Letting the cherry knock against their lips,
And draw it by their mouths, and back again.
How now!

    Enter Nano, Androgyno, Castrone, *and* Mosca.

  Nan. Now, room for fresh gamesters who do will you
    to know,
They do bring you neither play, nor university show;
And therefore do intreat you, that whatsoever they
    rehearse,
May not fare a whit the worse, for the false pace of the
    verse.
If you wonder at this, you will wonder more ere we pass,
For know, here is enclos'd the soul of Pythagoras,
That juggler divine, as hereafter shall follow:
Which soul, fast and loose, sir, came first from Apollo,
And was breath'd into Æthalides, Mercurius his son,
Where it had the gift to remember all that ever was done.

From thence it fled forth, and made quick transmigration
To goldy-lock Euphorbus who was kill'd in good fashion,
At the siege of old Troy, by the cuckold of Sparta.
Hermotimus was next (I find it in my charta)
To whom it did pass, where no sooner it was missing,
But with one Pyrrhus of Delos it learn'd to go a fishing:
And thence did it enter the sophist of Greece.
From Pythagore she went into a beautiful piece,
Hight Aspasia the meretrix; and the next toss of her
Was again of a whore, she became a philosopher,
Crates the cynic: as itself doth relate it
Since, kings, knights, and beggars, knaves, lords and fools
     gat it,
Besides ox and ass, camel, mule, goat, and brock,
In all which it hath spoke, as in the cobbler's cock.
But I come not here to discourse of that matter,
Or his one, two, or three, or his great oath, By Quater,
His musics, his trigon, his golden thigh,
Or his telling how elements shift: but I
Would ask, how of late thou hast suffered translation,
And shifted thy coat, in these days of reformation?
     And. Like one of the reformed, a fool as you see,
Counting all old doctrine heresy.
     Nan. But not on thine own forbid meats hast thou ven-
     tur'd?
     And. On fish, when first a Carthusian I enter'd.
     Nan. Why, then thy dogmatical silence hath left thee?
     And. Of that an obstreperous lawyer bereft me.
     Nan. O wonderful change! when sir lawyer forsook
     thee,
For Pythagore's sake, what body then took thee?
     And. A good dull mule.
     Nan.   And how! by that means,
Thou wert brought to allow of the eating of beans?
     And. Yes.
     Nan.   But, from the mule, into whom did'st thou pass?
     And. Into a very strange beast, by some writers called
     an ass;
By others, a precise, pure, illuminate brother,

Of those devour flesh, and sometimes one another:
And will drop you forth a libel, or a sanctified lie,
Betwixt every spoonful of a nativity-pie.

Nan. Now quit thee, for heaven, of that profane nation;
And gently, report thy next transmigration.

And. To the same that I am.

Nan.   A creature of delight?
And (what is more than a fool) an hermaphrodite?
Now 'pray thee, sweet soul, in all thy variation,
Which body would'st thou choose to take up thy station?

And. Troth this I am in, even here would I tarry.

Nan. 'Cause here the delight of each sex thou canst vary?

And. Alas, those pleasures be stale and forsaken,
No, 'tis your Fool, wherewith I am so taken,
The only one creature that I can call blessed:
For all other forms I have proved most distressed.

Nan. Spoke true, as thou wert in Pythagoras still.
This learned opinion we celebrate will,
Fellow eunuch (as behoves us) with all our wit and art,
To dignify that, whereof ourselves are so great, and special
    a part.

Volp. Now very, very pretty: Mosca, this
Was thy invention?

Mos.   If it please my patron,
Not else.

Volp. It doth, good Mosca.

Mos.   Then it was, sir.

Nano *and* Castrone *sing*

> Fools, they are the only nation
> Worth men's envy or admiration;
> Free from care or sorrow-taking,
> Selves and others merry-making:
> All they speak or do is sterling.
> Your fool, he is your great man's darling,
> And your ladies' sport and pleasure;
> Tongue and bauble are his treasure.
> E'en his face begetteth laughter,

And he speaks truth free from slaughter;
He's the grace of every feast,
And sometimes the chiefest guest:
Hath his trencher, and his stool,
When wit waits upon the fool.
    O, who would not be
        He, he, he?

                                  [*Knocking without.*

Volp. Who's that? away, look, Mosca.

                            [*Exeunt* Nano *and* Castrone.

                    Fool, begone. [*Exit* Androgyno.

Mos. 'Tis signior Voltore the advocate,
I know him by his knock.

Volp.   Fetch me my gown,
My furs and night-caps; say my couch is changing:
And let him entertain himself awhile,
Without i' th' gallery.

                                [*Exit* Mosca.

                  Now, now, my clients
Begin their visitation! vulture, kite,
Raven, and gorcrow, all my birds of prey,
That think me turning carcase, now they come:
I am not for 'em yet.

Re-enter Mosca *with the gown.*

                How now? the news?

Mos. A piece of plate, sir.

Volp.   Of what bigness?

Mos.   Huge,
Massy and antique, with your name inscrib'd,
And arms engraven.

Volp.   Good! and not a fox
Stretch'd on the earth, with fine delusive sleights,
Mocking a gaping crow? ha, Mosca?

Mos.   Sharp, sir.

Volp. Give me my furs. Why dost thou laugh so, man?

Mos. I cannot choose, sir, when I apprehend
What thoughts he has without now, as he walks:
That this might be the last gift he should give;
That this would fetch you; if you died to-day,

223

And gave him all, what he should be to-morrow;
What large return would come of all his ventures;
How he should worshipped be, and reverenc'd;
Ride with his furs and foot-cloths; waited on
By herds of fools and clients; have clear way
Made for his mule, as letter'd as himself;
Be call'd the great and learned advocate:
And then concludes, there's nought impossible.

   Volp. Yes, to be learned, Mosca.

   Mos.   O, no; rich
Implies it. Hood an ass with reverend purple,
So you can hide his two ambitious ears,
And he shall pass for a cathedral doctor.

   Volp. My caps, my caps, good Mosca, fetch him in.

   Mos. Stay, sir, your ointment for your eyes.

   Volp.   That's true;
Dispatch, dispatch: I long to have possession
Of my new present.

   Mos.   That, and thousands more,
I hope to see you lord of.

   Volp.   Thanks, kind Mosca.

   Mos. And that, when I am lost in blended dust,
And hundred such as I am, in succession——

   Volp. Nay, that were too much, Mosca.

   Mos.   You shall live,
Still, to delude these harpies.

   Volp.   Loving Mosca,
'Tis well, my pillow now, and let him enter.   [*Exit* Mosca.
Now, my feigned cough, my physic and my gout,
My apoplexy, palsy, and catarrhs,
Help, with your forced functions, this my posture,
Wherein, this three year, I have milk'd their hopes.
He comes, I hear him, uh, uh, uh, uh, oh!

Re-enter Mosca *with* Voltore.

   Mos. You still are what you were, sir. Only you,
Of all the rest, are he commands his love:
And you do wisely to preserve it thus,
With early visitation, and kind notes

Of your good meaning to him, which, I know,
Cannot but come most grateful. Patron, sir.
Here's signior Voltore is come——

Volp. What say you?

Mos. Sir, signior Voltore is come, this morning,
To visit you.

Volp. I thank him.

Mos. And hath brought
A piece of antique plate, bought of St. Mark,
With which he here presents you.

Volp. He is welcome.
Pray him to come more often.

Mos. Yes.

Volt. What says he?

Mos. He thanks you, and desires you see him often.

Volp. Mosca.

Mos. My patron?

Volp. Bring him near, where is he?
I long to feel his hand.

Mos. The plate is here, sir.

Volt. How fare you, sir?

Volp. I thank you, signior Voltore.
Where is the plate? mine eyes are bad.

Volt. I'm sorry,
To see you still thus weak.

Mos. That he is not weaker. [*Aside.*

Volp. You are too munificent.

Volt. No, sir, would to heaven
I could as well give health to you, as that plate.

Volp. You give, sir, what you can. I thank you. Your
love
Hath taste in this, and shall not be unanswer'd.
I pray you see me often.

Volt. Yes, I shall, sir.

Volp. Be not far from me.

Mos. Do you observe that, sir?

Volp. Harken unto me, still: It will concern you.

Mos. You are a happy man, sir, you know your good.

Volp. I cannot now last long——

Mos.   You are his heir, sir.

Volt. Am I?

Volp.   I feel me going, uh, uh, uh, uh.
I am sailing to my port, uh, uh, uh, uh!
And I am glad, I am so near my haven.

  Mos. Alas, kind gentleman, well, we must all go——

  Volt. But, Mosca——

  Mos.   Age will conquer.

  Volt. 'Pray thee hear me.
Am I inscrib'd his heir, for certain?

  Mos.   Are you?
I do beseech you, sir, you will vouchsafe
To write me i' your family. All my hopes
Depend upon your worship. I am lost
Except the rising sun do shine on me.

  Volt. It shall both shine and warm thee, Mosca.

  Mos.   Sir,
I am a man that have not done your love
All the worst offices: here I wear your keys,
See all your coffers and your caskets lock'd,
Keep the poor inventory of your jewels,
Your plate, and monies, am your steward, sir
Husband your goods here.

  Volt.   But am I sole heir?

  Mos. Without a partner, sir, confirm'd this morning;
The wax is warm yet, and the ink scarce dry
Upon the parchment.

  Volt.   Happy, happy, me!
By what good chance, sweet Mosca?

  Mos.   Your desert, sir;
I know no second cause.

  Volt.   Thy modesty
Is loth to know it; well, we shall requite it.

  Mos. He ever lik'd your course, sir, that first took him.
I oft have heard him say how he admir'd
Men of your large profession, that could speak
To every cause, and things mere contraries,
Till they were hoarse again, yet all be law;
That with most quick agility could turn,

226

And return; make knots, and undo them;
Give forked counsel; take provoking gold
On either hand, and put it up: these men,
He knew, would thrive with their humility
And, for his part, he thought he should be blest
To have his heir of such a suffering spirit,
So wise, so grave, of so perplex'd a tongue,
And loud withal that would not wag, nor scarce
Lie still without a fee; when every word
Your worship but lets fall, is a *cecchine*!

                                [Knocking without.

Who's that? one knocks; I would not have you seen, sir,
And yet—pretend you came, and went in haste;
I'll fashion an excuse. And, gentle sir,
When you do come to swim in golden lard,
Up to the arms in honey, that your chin
Is borne up stiff with fatness of the flood,
Think on your vassal; but remember me:
I ha' not been your worst of clients.

   Volt.   Mosca——

   Mos. When will you have your inventory brought, sir?
Or see a copy of the will? Anon!
I'll bring 'em to you, sir. Away, begone
Put business i' your face.   *[Exit* Voltore.

   Volp.   Excellent, Mosca!
Come hither, let me kiss thee.

   Mos.   Keep you still, sir.
Here is Corbaccio.

   Volp.   Set the plate away,
The vulture's gone, and the old raven's come.

   Mos. Betake you to your silence and your sleep:
Stand there, and multiply. Now shall we see
A wretch, who is indeed more impotent
Than this can feign to be; yet hopes to hop
Over his grave.

             Enter Corbaccio.

         Signior Corbaccio!
You're very welcome, sir.

Corb. How does your patron?

Mos. Troth, as he did, sir, no amends.

Corb. What? mends he?

Mos. No, sir: he is rather worse.

Corb. That's well.
Where is he?

Mos. Upon his couch, sir, newly fall'n asleep.

Corb. Does he sleep well?

Mos. No wink, sir, all this night,
Nor yesterday, but slumbers.

Corb. Good! He should take
Some counsel of physicians: I have brought him
An opiate here, from mine own doctors——

Mos. He will not hear of drugs.

Corb. Why? I myself
Stood by, while 't was made; saw all th' ingredients:
And know it cannot but most gently work,
My life for his, 'tis but to make him sleep.

Volp. Aye, his last sleep, if he would take it. *[Aside.*

Mos. Sir,
He has no faith in physic.

Corb. Say you? say you?

Mos. He has no faith in physic: he does think
Most of your doctors are the greater danger,
And worse disease, t' escape. I often have
Heard him protest that your physician
Should never be his heir.

Corb. Not I his heir?

Mos. Not your physician, sir.

Corb. O, no, no, no,
I do not mean it.

Mos. No, sir, nor their fees
He cannot brook: he says they flay a man
Before they kill him.

Corb. Right, I do conceive you.

Mos. And then they do it by experiment:
For which the law not only doth absolve 'em,
But gives them great reward: and he is loth
To hire his death so.

228

Corb. It is true, they kill
With as much licence as a judge.

Mos. Nay, more;
For he but kills, sir, where the law condemns,
And these can kill him too.

Corb. Aye, or me:
Or any man. How does his apoplex?
Is that strong on him still?

Mos. Most violent.
His speech is broken, and his eyes are set,
His face drawn longer than 't was wont——

Corb. How? how?
Stronger, than he was wont?

Mos. No, sir: his face
Drawn longer than 't was wont.

Corb. O, good.

Mos. His mouth
Is ever gaping, and his eyelids hang.

Corb. Good.

Mos. A freezing numbness stiffens all his joints,
And makes the colour of his flesh like lead.

Corb. 'Tis good.

Mos. His pulse beats slow and dull.

Corb. Good symptoms, still.

Mos. And, from his brain——

Corb. Ha? how? not from his brain?

Mos. Yes, sir, and from his brain——

Corb. I conceive you, good.

Mos. Flows a cold sweat, with a continual rheum,
Forth the resolved corners of his eyes.

Corb. Is 't possible? yet I am better, ha!
How does he with the swimming of his head?

Mos. O, sir, 'tis past the scotomy; he now
Hath lost his feeling, and hath left to snort:
You hardly can perceive him that he breathes.

Corb. Excellent, excellent, sure I shall outlast him:
This makes me young again, a score of years.

Mos. I was a-coming for you, sir.

Corb. Has he made his will?

What has he given me?

 Mos.   No, sir.

 Corb.   Nothing? ha?

 Mos. He has not made his will, sir.

 Corb.   Oh, oh, oh.

What then did Voltore the lawyer, here?

 Mos. He smelt a carcass, sir, when he but heard
My master was about his testament;
(As I did urge him to it, for your good——)

 Corb. He came unto him, did he? I thought so.

 Mos. Yes, and presented him this piece of plate.

 Corb. To be his heir?

 Mos.   I do not know, sir.

 Corb.   True,
I know it too.

 Mos.   By your own scale, sir.   [*Aside.*

 Corb.   Well,
I shall prevent him yet. See, Mosca, look,
Here, I have brought a bag of bright *cecchines*,
Will quite weigh down his plate.

 Mos.   Yea, marry, sir!
This is true physic, this your sacred medicine,
No talk of opiates to this great elixir.

 Corb. 'Tis *aurum palpabile*, if not *potabile*.

 Mos. It shall be minister'd to him in his bowl?

 Corb. Aye, do, do, do.

 Mos.   Most blessed cordial!
This will recover him.

 Corb. Yes, do, do, do.

 Mos. I think it were not best, sir.

 Corb.   What?

 Mos. To recover him.

 Corb. O, no, no, no; by no means.

 Mos.   Why, sir, this
Will work some strange effect, if he but feel it.

 Corb. 'Tis true, therefore forbear, I'll take my venture;
Give me 't again.

 Mos.   At no hand, pardon me;
You shall not do yourself that wrong, sir. I

Will so advise you, you shall have it all.

Corb. How?

Mos.   All, sir, 'tis your right, your own; no man
Can claim a part: 'tis yours, without a rival,
Decree'd by destiny.

Corb.   How? how, good Mosca?

Mos. I'll tell you, sir. This fit he shall recover——

Corb. I do conceive you.

Mos.   And, on first advantage
Of his gain'd sense, will I re-importune him
Unto the making of his testament:
And show him this.

Corb.   Good, good.

Mos.   'Tis better yet,
If you will hear, sir.

Corb.   Yes, with all my heart.

Mos. Now, would I counsel you, make home with speed;
There, frame a Will: whereto you shall inscribe
My master your sole heir.

Corb.   And disinherit
My son?

Mos. O, sir, the better: for that colour
Shall make it much more taking.

Corb.   O, but colour?

Mos. This Will, sir, you shall send it unto me.
Now, when I come to enforce, as I will do,
Your cares, your watchings, and your many prayers,
Your more than many gifts, your this day's present,
And last, produce your Will; where, without thought,
Or least regard unto your proper issue,
A son so brave and highly meriting,
The stream of your diverted love hath thrown you
Upon my master, and made him your heir:
He cannot be so stupid, or stone dead,
But, out of conscience, and mere gratitude——

Corb. He must pronounce me, his?

Mos.   'Tis true.

Corb.   This plot
Did I think on before.

Mos.   I do believe it.

Corb. Do you not believe it?

Mos.   Yes, sir.

Corb.   Mine own project.

Mos. Which when he hath done, sir——

Corb.   Publish'd me his heir?

Mos. And you so certain to survive him——

Corb.   Aye.

Mos. Being so lusty a man——

Corb.   'Tis true.

Mos.   Yes, sir——

Corb. I thought on that too. See how he should be
The very organ to express my thoughts!

Mos. You have not only done yourself a good——

Corb. But multiplied it on my son?

Mos.   'Tis right, sir.

Corb. Still my invention.

Mos.   'Las, sir, heaven knows,
It hath been all my study, all my care,
(I e'en grow grey withal), how to work things——

Corb. I do conceive, sweet Mosca.

Mos.   You are he
For whom I labour here.

Corb.   Aye, do, do, do:
I'll straight about it.

Mos.   Rook go with you, raven.   [*Aside.*

Corb. I know thee honest.

Mos.   You do lie, sir——

Corb.   And——

Mos. Your knowledge is no better than your ears, sir.

Corb. I do not doubt to be a father to thee.

Mos. Nor I, to gull my brother of his blessing.

Corb. I may ha' my youth restor'd to me, why not

Mos. Your worship is a precious ass——

Corb.   What say'st thou?

Mos. I do desire your worship to make haste, sir.

Corb. 'Tis done, 'tis done, I go.   [*Exit.*

Volp.   O, I shall burst;
Let out my sides, let out my sides——

Mos.   Contain
Your flux of laughter, sir: you know this hope
Is such a bait, it covers any hook.

Volp. O, but thy working, and thy placing it!
I cannot hold; good rascal, let me kiss thee:
I never knew thee in so rare a humour.

Mos. Alas, sir, I but do as I am taught;
Follow your grave instructions; give 'em words;
Pour oil into their ears: and send them hence.

Volp. 'Tis true, 'tis true. What a rare punishment
Is avarice, to itself?

Mos.   Aye, with our help, sir.

Volp. So many cares, so many maladies,
So many fears attending on old age,
Yea, death so often call'd on, as no wish
Can be more frequent with 'em, their limbs faint,
Their senses dull, their seeing, hearing, going,
All dead before them; yea, their very teeth,
Their instruments of eating, failing them:
Yet this is reckon'd life! Nay, here was one,
Is now gone home, that wishes to live longer!
Feels not his gout nor palsy, feigns himself
Younger, by scores of years, flatters his age,
With confident belying it, hopes he may
With charms like Æson, have his youth restor'd:
And with these thoughts so battens, as if fate
Would be as easily cheated on, as he,
And all turns air! [*Another knocks.*] Who's that, there,
    now? a third?

Mos. Close, to your couch again: I hear his voice.
It is Corvino, our spruce merchant.

Volp.   Dead.

Mos. Another bout, sir, with your eyes. Who's there?

Enter Corvino.

Signior Corvino! come most wish'd for! O,
How happy were you, if you knew it, now!

Corv. Why? what? wherein?

Mos.   The tardy hour is come, sir.

Corv. He is not dead?

Mos.   Not dead, sir, but as good;

He knows no man.

Corv.   How shall I do, then?

Mos.   Why, sir?

Corv. I have brought him, here, a pearl.

Mos.   Perhaps he has

So much remembrance left as to know you, sir;

He still calls on you, nothing but your name

Is in his mouth: Is your pearl orient, sir?

Corv. Venice was never owner of the like.

Volp. Signior Corvino.

Mos.   Hark.

Volp.   Signior Corvino.

Mos. He calls you, step and give it him. He's here, sir.

And he has brought you a rich pearl.

Corv.   How do you, sir?

Tell him it doubles the twelve carat.

Mos.   Sir,

He cannot understand, his hearing's gone;

And yet it comforts him to see you——

Corv.   Say,

I have a diamond for him, too.

Mos.   Best show 't, sir,

Put it into his hand; 'tis only there

He apprehends: he has his feeling, yet.

See, how he grasps it!

Corv.   'Las, good gentleman!

How pitiful the sight is!

Mos.   Tut, forget, sir.

The weeping of an heir should still be laughter

Under a visor.

Corv. Why? am I his heir?

Mos. Sir, I am sworn I may not show the will,

Till he be dead: But, here has been Corbaccio,

Here has been Voltore, here were others too,

I cannot number 'em, they were so many,

All gaping here for legacies; but I,

Taking the vantage of his naming you,
'Signior Corvino, Signior Corvino', took
Paper and pen, and ink, and there I ask'd him,
Whom he would have his heir? 'Corvino'. Who
Should be executor? 'Corvino'. And,
To any question he was silent too,
I still interpreted the nods he made
(Through weakness) for consent: and sent home th' others,
Nothing bequeath'd them, but to cry and curse.

    Corv. O, my dear Mosca. [*They embrace.*] Does he not
      perceive us?

    Mos. No more than a blind harper. He knows no man,
No face of friend, nor name of any servant,
Who 't was that fed him last, or gave him drink:
Not those he hath begotten or brought up
Can he remember.

    Corv.   Has he children?

    Mos.   Bastards.
Some dozen or more, that he begot on beggars,
Gipsies, and Jews, and black-moors, when he was drunk.
Knew you not that, sir? 'Tis the common fable,
The dwarf, the fool, the eunuch, are all his;
H' is the true father of his family,
In all, save me: but he has given 'em nothing.

    Corv. That's well, that's well. Art sure he does not hear
    us?

    Mos. Sure, sir? why, look you, credit your own sense.
The pox approach, and add to your diseases,
If it would send you hence the sooner, sir.
For your incontinence, it hath deserv'd it
Throughly, and throughly, and the plague to boot.
(You may come near, sir) would you would once close
Those filthy eyes of yours, that flow with slime,
Like two frog-pits; and those same hanging cheeks,
Cover'd with hide, instead of skin: (nay, help, sir)
That look like frozen dish-clouts set on end.

    Corv. Or like an old smok'd wall, on which the rain
Ran down in streaks.

    Mos.   Excellent, sir, speak out;

You may be louder yet: a culverin
Discharged in his ear would hardly bore it.

Corv. His nose is like a common sewer, still running.

Mos. 'Tis good! and what his mouth?

Corv.   A very draught.

Mos. O, stop it up——

Corv.   By no means.

Mos.   'Pray you let me.
Faith, I could stifle him, rarely, with a pillow,
As well as any woman, that should keep him.

Corv. Do as you will, but I'll be gone.

Mos.   Be so;
It is your presence makes him last so long.

Corv. I pray you, use no violence.

Mos.   No, sir? why?
Why should you be thus scrupulous? 'pray you, sir.

Corv. Nay, at your discretion.

Mos.   Well, good sir, begone.

Corv. I will not trouble him now, to take my pearl?

Mos. Puh, nor your diamond. What a needless care
Is this afflicts you? Is not all, here, yours?
Am not I here? whom you have made? your creature?
That owe my being to you?

Corv.   Grateful Mosca.
Thou art my friend, my fellow, my companion,
My partner, and shalt share in all my fortunes.

Mos. Excepting one.

Corv.   What's that?

Mos.   Your gallant wife, sir. [*Exit* Corvino.
Now is he gone: we had no other means
To shoot him hence, but this.

Volp.   My divine Mosca!
Thou hast to-day outgone thyself. [*Another knocks.*]
       Who's there?
I will be troubled with no more. Prepare
Me music, dances, banquets, all delights;
The Turk is not more sensual in his pleasures,
Than will Volpone.   [*Exit* Mosca.
       Let me see, a pearl?

A diamond? plate? chequins? Good morning's purchase;
Why, this is better than rob churches, yet:
Or fat, by eating, once a month, a man.

Re-enter Mosca.

Who is 't?
    Mos.   The most beauteous lady Would-be, sir,
Wife to the English knight, Sir Politic Would-be,
(This is the style, sir, is directed me)
Hath sent to know, how you have slept tonight,
And if you would be visited.
    Volp.   Not now.
Some three hours hence——
    Mos.   I told the squire so much.
    Volp. When I am high with mirth and wine: then, then.
'Fore heaven, I wonder at the desperate valour
Of the bold English that they dare let loose
Their wives to all encounters!
    Mos.   Sir, this knight
Had not his name for nothing, he is politic
And knows, howe'er his wife affect strange airs,
She hath not yet the face to be dishonest.
But, had she signior Corvino's wife's face——
    Volp. Has she so rare a face?
    Mos.   O, sir, the wonder,
The blazing star of Italy! a wench
O' the first year! a beauty ripe as harvest!
Whose skin is whiter than a swan, all over!
Than silver, snow, or lilies! a soft lip,
Would tempt you to eternity of kissing!
And flesh that melteth in the touch to blood!
Bright as your gold! and lovely as your gold!
    Volp. Why had not I known this, before?
    Mos.   Alas, sir.
Myself but yesterday discover'd it.
    Volp. How might I see her?
    Mos.   O, not possible;
She's kept as warily as is your gold:
Never does come abroad, never takes air

But at a window. All her looks are sweet
As the first grapes or cherries: and are watch'd
As near as they are.

 Volp.   I must see her——
 Mos.   Sir,
There is a guard of ten spies thick upon her;
All his whole household: each of which is set
Upon his fellow, and have all their charge,
When he goes out, when he comes in, examin'd.
 Volp. I will go see her, though but at her window.
 Mos. In some disguise, then.
 Volp.   That is true. I must
Maintain mine own shape still the same: we'll think.

              [Exeunt.

ACT II. SCENE I

St. Mark's Place: a retired corner before Corvino's *house.*

Enter Politic Would-be *and* Peregrine.

 Pol. Sir, to a wise man, all the world's his soil.
It is not Italy nor France nor Europe
That must bound me, if my fates call me forth.
Yet, I protest, it is no salt desire
Of seeing countries, shifting a religion.
Nor any disaffection to the state
Where I was bred, and unto which I owe
My dearest plots, hath brought me out; much less
That idle, antique, stale, grey-headed project
Of knowing men's minds and manners, with Ulysses:
But a peculiar humour of my wife's
Laid for this height of Venice, to observe,
To quote, to learn the language, and so forth——
I hope you travel, sir, with licence?
 Per.   Yes.
 Pol. I dare the safelier converse—How long, sir,
Since you left England?
 Per.   Seven weeks.

Pol. So lately!
You ha' not been with my lord ambassador?

Per. Not yet, sir.

Pol. 'Pray you, what news, sir, vents our
climate?
I heard, last night, a most strange thing reported
By some of my lord's followers, and I long
To hear how 't will be seconded!

Per. What was 't, sir?

Pol. Marry, sir, of a raven, that should build
In a ship royal of the king's.

Per. This fellow
Does he gull me, trow? or is gull'd? [*Aside.*] Your name,
sir?

Pol. My name is Politic Would-be.

Per. O, that speaks him. [*Aside.*
A knight, sir?

Pol. A poor knight, sir.

Per. Your lady
Lies here in Venice for intelligence
Of tires, and fashions, and behaviour,
Among the courtezans? the fine Lady Would-be?

Pol. Yes, sir, the spider and the bee oft-times
Suck from one flower.

Per. Good Sir Politic!
I cry you mercy; I have heard much of you:
'Tis true, sir, of your raven.

Pol. On your knowledge?

Per. Yes, and your lions whelping in the Tower.

Pol. Another whelp!

Per. Another, sir.

Pol. Now, heaven!
What prodigies be these? The fires at Berwick!
And the new star! these things concurring, strange,
And full of omen! Saw you those meteors?

Per. I did, sir.

Pol. Fearful! Pray you, sir, confirm me,
Were there three porpoises seen above the bridge,
As they give out?

Per.   Six, and a sturgeon, sir.

Pol. I am astonish'd!

Per.   Nay, sir, be not so;
I'll tell you a greater prodigy than these——

Pol. What should these things portend!

Per.   The very day
(Let me be sure) that I put forth from London
There was a whale discover'd, in the river,
As high as Woolwich, that had waited there,
Few know how many months, for the subversion
Of the Stode fleet.

Pol.   Is't possible? Believe it
'Twas either sent from Spain, or the Archdukes!
Spinola's whale, upon my life, my credit!
Will they not leave these projects? Worthy sir,
Some other news.

Per.   Faith, Stone, the fool, is dead;
And they do lack a tavern fool, extremely.

Pol. Is Mass Stone dead!

Per.   He's dead, sir, why? I hope
You thought him not immortal? O, this knight,
Were he well known, would be a precious thing
To fit our English stage: He that should write
But such a fellow, should be thought to feign
Extremely, if not maliciously.   [*Aside.*

Pol.   Stone dead!

Per. Dead. Lord! how deeply, sir, you apprehend it?
He was no kinsman to you?

Pol.   That I know of.
Well! that same fellow was an unknown fool.

Per. And yet you knew him, it seems?

Pol.   I did so, sir,
I knew him one of the most dangerous heads
Living within the state, and so I held him.

Per. Indeed, sir?

Pol.   While he liv'd, in action.
He has receiv'd weekly intelligence,
Upon my knowledge, out of the Low Countries,
For all parts of the world in cabbages;

And those dispens'd again to ambassadors,
In oranges, musk-melons, apricots,
Lemons, pome-citrons, and such-like: sometimes.
In Colchester oysters, and your Selsey cockles.

Per. You make me wonder!

Pol.   Sir, upon my knowledge.
Nay, I have observ'd him at your public ordinary
Take his advertisement from a traveller,
A conceal'd statesman, in a trencher of meat:
And, instantly, before the meal was done,
Convey an answer in a toothpick.

Per.   Strange!
How could this be, sir?

Pol.   Why, the meat was cut
So like his character, and so laid, as he
Must easily read the cypher.

Per.   I have heard,
He could not read, sir.

Pol.   So, 'twas given out,
In policy, by those that did employ him:
But he could read, and had your languages,
And to 't, as sound a noddle——

Per.   I have heard, sir,
That your baboons were spies; and that they were
A kind of subtle nation, near to China.

Pol. Aye, aye, your Mamuluchi. Faith, they had
Their hand in a French plot or two; but they
Were so extremely given to women, as
They made discovery of all: yet I
Had my advises here, on Wednesday last,
From one of their own coat, they were return'd,
Made their relations as the fashion is,
And now stand fair for fresh employment.

Per.   'Heart!
This Sir Pol will be ignorant of nothing.   [*Aside.*
It seems, sir, you know all?

Pol.   Not all, sir. But
I have some general notions; I do love
To note and to observe: though I live out,

241

Free from the active torrent, yet I'd mark
The currents, and the passages of things,
For mine own private use; and know the ebbs
And flows of state.
    Per.   Believe it, sir, I hold
Myself in no small tie unto my fortunes,
For casting me thus luckily upon you;
Whose knowledge, if your bounty equal it
May do me great assistance, in instruction
For my behaviour, and my bearing, which
Is yet rude and raw——
    Pol.   Why? came you forth
Empty of rules for travel?
    Per.   Faith, I had
Some common ones, from out that vulgar grammar,
Which he, that cried Italian to me, taught me.
    Pol. Why, this it is that spoils all our brave bloods;
Trusting our hopeful gentry unto pedants:
Fellows of outside, and mere bark. You seem
To be a gentleman of ingenuous race——
I not profess it, but my fate hath been
To be where I have been consulted with,
In this high kind, touching some great man's sons,
Persons of blood and honour——
    Per.   Who be these, sir?

Enter Mosca *and* Nano *disguised, followed by persons
with materials for erecting a stage.*

    Mos. Under that windore, there 't must be. The same.
    Pol. Fellows, to mount a bank! Did your instructor
In the dear tongues, never discourse to you
Of the Italian mountebanks?
    Per.   Yes, sir.
    Pol.   Why,
Here shall you see one.
    Per.   They are quacksalvers,
Fellows that live by venting oils and drugs?
    Pol. Was that the character he gave you of them?

Per. As I remember.

Pol.   Pity his ignorance.

They are the only-knowing men of Europe!
Great general scholars, excellent physicians,
Most admir'd statesmen, profess'd favourites,
And cabinet counsellors to the greatest princes!
The only languag'd men of all the world!

Per. And, I have heard, they are most lewd impostors;
Made all of terms and shreds; no less beliers
Of great men's favours, than their own vile med'cines;
Which they will utter upon monstrous oaths:
Selling that drug for twopence, ere they part,
Which they have valu'd at twelve crowns, before.

Pol. Sir, calumnies are answer'd best with silence:
Yourself shall judge. Who is it mounts, my friends?

Mos. Scoto of Mantus, sir.

Pol.   Is't he? nay then
I'll proudly promise, sir, you shall behold
Another man than has been phant'sied to you.
I wonder, yet, that he should mount his bank
Here in this nook, that has been wont t' appear
In face of the Piazza! Here he comes.

Enter Volpone, *disguised as a mountebank doctor, and
followed by a mob of people.*

Volp.   Mount, zany. [*To* Nano.

Mob. Follow, follow, follow, follow, follow.

Pol. See how the people follow him! He's a man
May write ten thousand crowns, in bank here.

                      [Volpone *mounts the stage.*
                      Note,
Mark but his gesture: I do use to observe
The state he keeps in getting up!

Per.   'Tis worth it, sir.

Volp. 'Most noble gentlemen and my worthy patrons, it
may seem strange that I, your Scoto Mantuano who was
ever wont to fix my bank in face of the public Piazza, near
the shelter of the Portico, to the Procuratia, should now,
after eight month's absence from this illustrious city of

Venice, humbly retire myself, into an obscure nook of the Piazza.'

Pol. Did not I now object the same?

Per.   Peace, sir.

Volp. 'Let me tell you: I am not, as your Lombard proverb saith, cold on my feet; or content to part with my commodities at a cheaper rate than I accustomed: look not for it. Nor that the calumnious reports of that impudent detractor, and shame to our profession (Alessandro Buttone, I mean), who gave out in public I was condemn'd a sforzato to the galleys, for poisoning the Cardinal Bembo's cook, hath at all attached, much less dejected me. No, no, worthy gentlemen; to tell you true, I cannot endure to see the rabble of these ground *ciarlitani*, that spread their cloaks on the pavement as if they meant to do feats of activity and then come in, lamely, with their mouldy tales out of Boccaccio, like stale Tabarine, the fabulist: some of them discoursing their travels, and of their tedious captivity in the Turk's galleys, when indeed, were the truth known, they were the Christian's galleys, where very temperately they ate bread, and drank water, as a wholesome penance, enjoin'd them by their confessors, for base pilferies.'

Pol. Note but his bearing, and contempt of these.

Volp. 'These turdy - facy - nasty - paty - lousy - fartical rogues, with one poor groat's-worth of unprepar'd antimony, finely wrapt up in several *scartoccios*, are able, very well, to kill their twenty a week, and play; yet these meagre starv'd spirits, who have half stopp'd the organs of their minds with earthy oppilations, want not their favourers among your shrivell'd, salad-eating artisans: who are over-joy'd that they may have their half-pe'rth of physic, though it purge 'em into another world, 't makes no matter.'

Pol. Excellent! ha' you heard better language, sir?

Volp. 'Well, let 'em go. And gentlemen, honourable gentlemen, know that for this time, our bank, being thus remov'd from the clamours of the *canaglia*, shall be the scene of pleasure and delight: for I have nothing to sell, little or nothing to sell.'

Pol. I told you, sir, his end.

Per.   You did so, sir.

Volp. 'I protest, I, and my six servants, are not able to make of this precious liquor, so fast as it is fetch'd away from my lodging by gentlemen of your city; strangers of the *terra-firma*; worshipful merchants; aye, and senators too: who, ever since my arrival, have detained me to their uses, by their splendidous liberalities. And worthily. For what avails your rich man to have his magazines stuff'd with *moscadelli*, or of the purest grape, when his physicians prescribe him, on pain of death, to drink nothing but water cocted with aniseeds? O, health! health! the blessing of the rich! the riches of the poor! who can buy thee at too dear a rate, since there is no enjoying this world without thee? Be not then so sparing of your purses, honourable gentlemen, as to abridge the natural course of life——'

Per. You see his end?

Pol.   Aye, is't not good?

Volp. 'For when a humid flux, or catarrh, by the mutability of air, falls from your head into an arm or shoulder, or any other part; take you a ducat, or your *cecchine* of gold, and apply to the place affected: see what good effect it can work. No, no, 'tis blessed *unguento*, this rare extraction, that hath only power to disperse all malignant humours that proceed, either of hot, cold, moist, or windy causes——'

Per. I would he had put in dry too.

Pol.   Pray you, observe.

Volp. 'To fortify the most indigest and crude stomach, aye, were it of one that through extreme weakness vomited blood, applying only a warm napkin to the place, after the unction, and fricace; for the vertigine in the head, putting but a drop into your nostrils, likewise behind the ears; a most sovereign and approved remedy: the *malcaducco*, cramps, convulsions, paralyses, epilepsies, *tremor-cordia*, retired-nerves, ill vapours of the spleen, stoppings of the liver, the stone, the strangury, *hernia ventosa, iliaca passio*; stops a dysenteria, immediately; easeth the torsion of the small guts; and cures *melancholia hypocondriaca*, being taken and applied according to my printed receipt.

[*Pointing to his bill and his glass.*] For this is the physician,
this the medicine; this counsels, this cures; this gives the
direction, this works the effect: And, in sum, both together
may be term'd an abstract of the theoric and practic in the
Æsculapian art. 'Twill cost you eight crowns. And, Zan
Fritada, 'pray thee sing a verse, extempore, in honour of it.'

Pol. How do you like him, sir?

Per.   Most strangely, I!

Pol. Is not his language rare?

Per.   But alchemy,
I never heard the like: or Broughton's books.

Nano sings.

> Had old Hippocrates, or Galen,
> That to their books put med'cines all in
> But known this secret, they had never
> (Of which they will be guilty ever)
> Been murderers of so much paper,
> Or wasted many a hurtless taper:
> No Indian drug had ere been famed,
> Tobacco, sassafras not named;
> Ne yet, of guacum one small stick, sir,
> Nor Raymund Lully's great elixir.
> Ne, had been known the Danish Gonswart,
> Or Paracelsus, with his long sword.

Per. All this, yet, will not do, eight crowns is high.

Volp. 'No more.—Gentlemen, if I had but time to dis-
course to you the miraculous effects of this my oil, sur-
named Oglio del Scoto; with the countless catalogue of
those I have cured of th' aforesaid and many more diseases;
the patents and privileges of all the princes and common-
wealths of Christendom; or but the depositions of those
that appear'd on my part, before the signiory of the Sanità
and most learned College of Physicians; where I was
authorized, upon notice taken of the admirable virtues of
my medicaments, and mine own excellency in matter of
rare and unknown secrets, not only to disperse them pub-
licly in this famous city but in all the territories that

happily joy under the government of the most pious and magnificent states of Italy. But may some other gallant fellow say, O, there be divers that make profession to have as good and as experimented receipts as yours: Indeed, very many have essay'd, like apes in imitation of that which is really and essentially in me, to make of this oil, bestow'd great cost in furnaces, stills, alembecks, continual fires, and preparation of the ingredients (as indeed there goes to it six hundred several simples, besides some quantity of human fat, for the conglutination, which we buy of the anatomists), but, when these practitioners come to the last decoction, blow, blow, puff, puff, and all flies *in fumo*: ha, ha, ha! Poor wretches! I rather pity their folly and indiscretion than their loss of time and money: for those may be recovered by industry: but to be a fool born is a disease incurable. For myself, I always from my youth have endeavoured to get the rarest secrets, and book them; either in exchange, or for money: I spared nor cost nor labour, where anything was worthy to be learned. And gentlemen, honourable gentlemen, I will undertake, by virtue of chemical art, out of the honourable hat that covers your head, to extract the four elements; that is to say, the fire, air, water, and earth, and return you your felt without burn or stain. For, whil'st others have been at the balloo, I have been at my book: and am now past the craggy paths of study and come to the flowery plains of honour and reputation.'

Pol. I do assure you, sir, that is his aim.

Volp. 'But to our price.'

Per.   And that withal, Sir Pol.

Volp. 'You all know, honourable gentlemen, I never valued this *ampulla*, or vial, at less than eight crowns, but for this time I am content to be depriv'd of it for six; six crowns is the price; and less in courtesy I know you cannot offer me: take it or leave it howsoever, both it and I am at your service. I ask you not as the value of the thing, for then I should demand of you a thousand crowns, so the Cardinals Montalto, Fernese, the great Duke of Tuscany, my gossip, with divers other princes have given me; but I despise money: Only to show my affection to you, honour-

able gentlemen, and your illustrious state here, I have neg-
lected the messages of these princes, mine own offices,
fram'd my journey hither, only to present you with the
fruits of my travels. Tune your voices once more to the
touch of your instruments, and give the honourable assem-
bly some delightful recreation.'

Per. What monstrous, and most painful circumstance
Is here, to get some three or four gazettes!
Some threepence, i' th' whole, for that 'twill come to.

Nano *sings.*

> You that would last long, list to my song,
> Make no more coil, but buy of this oil.
> Would you be ever fair? and young?
> Stout of teeth? and strong of tongue?
> Tart of palate? quick of ear?
> Sharp of sight? of nostril clear?
> Moist of hand? and light of foot?
> (Or I will come nearer to 't)
> Would you live free from all diseases?
> Do the act your mistress pleases;
> Yet fright all aches from your bones?
> Here's a med'cine for the nones.

Volp. 'Well, I am in a humour at this time to make a
present of the small quantity my coffer contains: to the
rich in courtesy and to the poor for God's sake. Where-
fore, now mark; I ask'd you six crowns; and six crowns, at
other times, you have paid me; you shall not give me six
crowns, nor five, nor four, nor three, nor two, nor one; nor
half a ducat; no, nor a *moccinigo*: sixpence it will cost you,
or six hundred pound—expect no lower price, for by the
banner of my front, I will not bate a *bagatine*, that I will
have, only, a pledge of your loves, to carry something
from amongst you, to show I am not contemn'd by you.
Therefore, now, toss your handkerchiefs, cheerfully, cheer-
fully; and be advertised, that the first heroic spirit that
deigns to grace me with a handkerchief, I will give it a
little remembrance of something, beside, shall please it
better, than if I had presented it with a double pistolet.'

Per. Will you be that heroic spark, Sir Pol?

[*Celia at the window throws down her handkerchief.*
O, see! the window has prevented you.

Volp. Lady, I kiss your bounty: and, for this timely grace, you have done your poor Scoto of Mantua, I will return you, over and above my oil, a secret of that high and inestimable nature, shall make you for ever enamour'd on that minute wherein your eye first descended on so mean (yet not altogether to be despis'd) an object. Here is a powder, conceal'd in this paper, of which, if I should speak to the worth, nine thousand volumes were but as one page, that page as a line, that line as a word: so short is this pilgrimage of man (which some call life) to the expressing of it. Would I reflect on the price? why, the whole world were but as an empire, that empire as a province, that province as a bank, that bank as a private purse to the purchase of it. I will only tell you; It is the powder, that made Venus a goddess (given her by Apollo), that kept her perpetually young, clear'd her wrinkles, firm'd her gums, fill'd her skin, colour'd her hair; from her, deriv'd to Helen, and at the sack of Troy unfortunately lost: till now, in this our age, it was as happily recover'd, by a studious antiquary out of some ruins of Asia, who sent a moiety of it to the court of France (but much sophisticated) wherewith the ladies there now colour their hair. The rest, at this present, remains with me; extracted to a quintessence: so that, wherever it but touches, in youth it perpetually preserves, in age restores the complexion; seats your teeth, did they dance like virginal jacks, firm as a wall; makes them white as ivory, that were black as——

Enter Corvino.

Corv. Spite o' the devil and my shame! come down, here;
Come down: no house but mine to make your scene?
Signior Flaminio, will you down, sir? down?
What, is my wife your Franciscina, sir?
No windores on the whole Piazza, here,
To make your properties, but mine? but mine?

[*Beats away* Volpone, *etc.*

249

Heart! ere tomorrow, I shall be new christen'd,
And call'd the Pantalone di Besogniosi,
About the town.

Per.   What should this mean, Sir Pol?

Pol. Some trick of state, believe it. I will home.

Per. It may be some design on you.

Pol.   I know not.
I'll stand upon my guard.

Per.   It is your best, sir.

Pol. This three weeks, all my advices, all my letters,
They have been intercepted.

Per.   Indeed, sir?
Best have a care.

Pol.   Nay, so I will.

Per.   This knight,
I may not lose him, for my mirth, till night.   *[Exeunt.*

ACT II. SCENE II

A room in Volpone's *house.*

Enter Volpone *and* Mosca.

Volp. O, I am wounded.

Mos.   Where, sir?

Volp.   Not without;
Those blows were nothing: I could bear them ever.
But angry Cupid, bolting from her eyes,
Hath shot himself into me, like a flame;
Where now he flings about his burning heat,
As in a furnace, an ambitious fire,
Whose vent is stopp'd. The fight is all within me.
I cannot live, except thou help me, Mosca;
My liver melts, and I, without the hope
Of some soft air, from her refreshing breath,
Am but a heap of cinders.

Mos.   'Las, good sir!
Would you had never seen her.

Volp.   Nay, would thou
Had'st never told me of her.

Mos.   Sir, 'tis true;
I do confess, I was unfortunate,
And you unhappy: but I am bound in conscience
No less than duty, to effect my best
To your release of torment, and I will, sir.

Volp. Dear Mosca, shall I hope?

Mos.   Sir, more than dear,
I will not bid you to despair of aught,
Within a human compass.

Volp.   O, there spoke
My better angel. Mosca, take my keys,
Gold, plate, and jewels, all's at thy devotion;
Employ them how thou wilt; nay, coin me, too:
So thou, in this, but crown my longings, Mosca!

Mos. Use but your patience.

Volp.   So I have.

Mos.   I doubt not
To bring success to your desires.

Volp.   Nay, then,
I not repent me of my late disguise.

Mos. If you can horn him, sir, you need not.

Volp.   True:
Besides, I never meant him for my heir.
Is not the colour o' my beard and eye-brows,
To make me known?

Mos.   No jot.

Volp.   I did it well.

Mos. So well, would I could follow you in mine,
With half the happiness; and yet I would
Escape your epilogue.   [*Aside.*

Volp.   But, were they gull'd
With a belief that I was Scoto?

Mos.   Sir,
Scoto himself could hardly have distinguish'd!
I have not time to flatter you now, we'll part:
And, as I prosper, so applaud my art.   [*Exeunt.*

ACT II. SCENE III

Enter Corvino, *sword in hand, dragging in* Celia.

  Corv. Death of mine honour, with the city's fool?
A juggling, tooth-drawing, prating mountebank?
And at a public window? where, whil'st he,
With his strain'd action, and his dole of faces,
To his drug-lecture draws your itching ears,
A crew of old, un-married, noted lechers,
Stood leering up, like satyrs: and you smile,
Most graciously! and fan your favours forth,
To give your hot spectators satisfaction!
What, was your mountebank their call? their whistle?
Or, were you enamour'd on his copper rings?
His saffron jewel, with the toad-stone in't?
Or his embroider'd suit with the cope-stitch,
Made of a hearse cloth? or his old tilt-feather?
Or his starch'd beard? well! you shall have him, yes.
He shall come home, and minister unto you
The fricace, for the mother. Or, let me see,
I think you'd rather mount? would you not mount?
Why, if you'll mount, you may; yes truly, you may:
And so you may be seen, down to th' foot.
Get you a cittern, Lady Vanity,
And be a dealer with the virtuous man;
Make one: I'll but protest myself a cuckold,
And save your dowry. I am a Dutchman, I!
For, if you thought me an Italian,
You would be damn'd, ere you did this, you whore:
Thou'dst tremble to imagine that the murder
Of father, mother, brother, all thy race,
Should follow, as the subject of my justice!
  Cel. Good sir, have patience!
  Corv.   What could'st thou propose
Less to thyself, than in this heat of wrath,
And stung with my dishonour, I should strike
This steel into thee with as many stabs
As thou wert gaz'd upon with goatish eyes?

Cel. Alas, sir! be appeas'd. I could not think
My being at the window should more, now,
Move your impatience, than at other times.

Corv. No? not to seek and entertain a parley
With a known knave? before a multitude?
You were an actor, with your handkerchief!
Which he, most sweetly, kissed in the receipt,
And might, no doubt, return it, with a letter,
And point the place where you might meet: your sister's,
Your mother's, or your aunt's might serve the turn.

Cel. Why, dear sir, when do I make these excuses?
Or ever stir abroad, but to the church?
And that so seldom——

Corv.   Well, it shall be less;
And thy restraint before was liberty
To what I now decree: and therefore mark me.
First, I will have this bawdy light damm'd up;
And till't be done, some two or three yards off,
I'll chalk a line: o'er which, if thou but chance
To set thy desp'rate foot; more hell, more horror,
More wild, remorseless rage shall seize on thee,
Than on a conjurer that had heedless left
His circle's safety ere his devil was laid.
Then, here's a lock, which I will hang upon thee;
And, now I think on't, I will keep thee backwards;
Thy lodging shall be backwards; thy walks backwards;
Thy prospect—all be backwards; and no pleasure
That thou shalt know, but backwards: Nay, since you force
My honest nature, know it is your own
Being too open, makes me use you thus.
Since you will not contain your subtle nostrils
In a sweet room, but, they must snuff the air
Of rank and sweaty passengers——[*Knock within.*]
                         One knocks.
Away, and be not seen, pain of thy life;
Not look toward the window: if thou dost——
Nay stay, hear this—let me not prosper, whore,
But I will make thee an anatomy,

Dissect thee mine own self, and read a lecture
Upon thee, to the city and in public.
Away.   [*Exit* Celia.
          Who's there.

Enter Servant.

 Ser.   'Tis signior Mosca, sir.
 Corv. Let him come in, his master's dead: There's yet
Some good to help the bad.

Enter Mosca.

         My Mosca, welcome,
I guess your news.
 Mos.   I fear you cannot, sir.
 Corv. Is't not his death?
 Mos.   Rather the contrary.
 Corv. Not his recovery?
 Mos.   Yes, sir.
 Corv.   I am curs'd,
I am bewitch'd, my crosses meet to vex me.
How? how? how? how?
 Mos.   Why, sir, with Scoto's oil!
Corbaccio and Voltore brought of it,
Whil'st I was busy in an inner room——
 Corv. Death! that damn'd mountebank! but, for the
   law
Now I could kill the rascal: 't cannot be
His oil should have that virtue. Ha' not I
Known him a common rogue, come fiddling in
To th' *osteria*, with a tumbling whore,
And, when he ha' done all his forc'd tricks, been glad
Of a poor spoonful of dead wine, with flies in 't?
It cannot be. All his ingredients
Are a sheep's gall, a roasted bitch's marrow,
Some few sod earwigs, pounded caterpillars,
A little capon's grease, and fasting spittle:
I know 'em, to a dram.
 Mos.   I know not, sir,
But some on 't, there, they pour'd into his ears,

Some in his nostrils, and recover'd him;
Applying but the fricace.
   Corv.   Pox o' that fricace.
   Mos. And since, to seem the more officious,
And flatt'ring of his health, there, they have had
At extreme fees, the College of Physicians
Consulting on him, how they might restore him;
Where one would have a cataplasm of spices,
Another, a flay'd ape clapp'd to his breast,
A third would ha' it a dog, a fourth an oil,
With wild cat's skins: at last, they all resolv'd
That to preserve him, was no other means
But some young woman must be straight sought out,
Lusty and full of juice, to sleep by him;
And, to this service most unhappily
And most unwillingly, am I now employ'd,
Which, here, I thought to pre-acquaint you with,
For your advice, since it concerns you most,
Because, I would not do that thing might cross
Your ends, on whom I have my whole dependence, sir:
Yet, if I do it not, they may delate
My slackness to my patron, work me out
Of his opinion; and there all your hopes,
Ventures, or whatsoever, are all frustrate.
I do but tell you, sir. Besides, they are all
Now striving, who shall first present him. Therefore——
I could entreat you, briefly conclude somewhat:
Prevent 'em if you can.
   Corv.   Death to my hopes!
This is my villanous fortune! Best to hire
Some common courtesan?
   Mos.   Aye, I thought on that, sir.
But they are all so subtle, full of art,
And age again doting and flexible,
So as—I cannot tell—we may perchance
Light on a quean may cheat us all.
   Corv.   'Tis true.
   Mos. No, no: it must be one that has no tricks, sir,
Some simple thing, a creature, made unto it;

Some wench you may command. Ha' you no kinswoman?
Gods so—Think, think, think, think, think, think, think,
    sir.
One o' the doctors offer'd there his daughter.

    Corv. How!

    Mos.   Yes, signior Lupo, the physician,

    Corv. His daughter?

    Mos.   And a virgin, sir. Why? Alas
He knows the state of 's body what it is;
That nought can warm his blood, sir, but a fever;
Nor any incantation raise his spirit:
A long forgetfulness hath seiz'd that part.
Besides, sir, who shall know it? some one, or two——

    Corv. I pray thee give me leave. [*Walks aside.*] If any
    man
But I had had this luck—The thing, in 'tself,
I know, is nothing—Wherefore should not I
As well command my blood and my affections,
As this dull doctor? In the point of honour,
The cases are all one, of wife, and daughter.

    Mos. I hear him coming.   [*Aside.*

    Corv.   She shall do 't: 'Tis done.
Slight, if this doctor, who is not engag'd,
Unless 't be for his counsel, which is nothing,
Offer his daughter, what should I, that am
So deeply in? I will prevent him: wretch!
Covetous wretch! Mosca, I have determin'd.

    Mos. How, sir?

    Corv.   We'll make all sure. The party you wot of,
Shall be mine own wife, Mosca.

    Mos.   Sir. The thing,
But that I would not seem to counsel you,
I should have motion'd to you, at the first:
And, make your count, you have cut all their throats.
Why! 'tis directly taking a possession!
And, in his next fit, we may let him go.
'Tis but to pull the pillow from his head,
And he is throttled: 't had been done, before.
But for your scrupulous doubts.

Corv.   Aye, a plague on 't,
My conscience fools my wit. Well, I'll be brief,
And so be thou, lest they should be before us;
Go home, prepare him, tell him with what zeal
And willingness I do it: swear it was
On the first hearing, as thou may'st do truly,
Mine own free motion.

Mos.   Sir, I warrant you,
I'll so possess him with it, that the rest
Of his starv'd clients shall be banish'd all,
And only you receiv'd. But come not, sir,
Until I send, for I have something else
To ripen for your good, you must not know 't.

Corv. But do not you forget to send, now.

Mos.   Fear not. [*Exit.*

Re-enter Celia.

Corv. Where are you, wife? my Celia? wife? what,
   blubbering?
Come dry those tears. I think you thought'st me in earnest?
Ha? By this light, I talked so but to try thee.
Methink the lightness of the occasion
Should ha' confirm'd thee. Come, I am not jealous.

Cel. No?

Corv.   Faith, I am not, aye, nor never was:
It is a poor unprofitable humour.
Do not I know, if women have a will,
They'll do 'gainst all the watches o' the world,
And that the fiercest spies are tamed with gold?
Tut, I am confident in thee; thou shalt see 't:
And see, I'll give thee cause, too, to believe it.
Come, kiss me. Go, and make thee ready straight,
In all thy best attire, thy choicest jewels,
Put 'em all on, and, with 'em, thy best looks:
We are invited to a solemn feast
At old Volpone's, where it shall appear
How far I am free from jealousy or fear.   [*Exeunt.*

ACT III. SCENE I

A street.

Enter Mosca.

Mos. I fear I shall begin to grow in love
With my dear self, and my most prosp'rous parts,
They do so spring and burgeon; I can feel
A whimsy i' my blood: I know not how,
Success hath made me wanton. I could skip
Out of my skin now, like a subtle snake,
I am so limber. O! your parasite
Is a most precious thing, dropp'd from above,
Not bred 'mongst clods and clot-poles, here on earth.
I muse, the mystery was not made a science,
It is so liberally profess'd! almost
All the wise world is little else, in nature,
But parasites or sub-parasites. And yet
I mean not those that have your bare town-art,
To know who's fit to feed 'em; have no house,
No family, no care, and therefore mould
Tales for men's ears, to bait that sense; or get
Kitchen-invention and some stale receipts
To please the belly and the groin; nor those,
With their curt dog-tricks, that can fawn and fleer,
Make their revenue out of legs and faces,
Echo my Lord, and lick away a moth:
But your fine elegant rascal, that can rise
And stoop, almost together, like an arrow;
Shoot through the air, as nimbly as a star;
Turn short as doth a swallow; and be here,
And there, and here, and yonder, all at once;
Present to any humour all occasion;
And change a visor swifter than a thought!
This is the creature, had the art born with him;
Toils not to learn it, but doth practise it
Out of most excellent nature: and such sparks,
Are the true parasites, others but their zanies.

Enter Bonario.

Who's this? Bonario? old Corbaccio's son?
The person I was bound to seek. Fair sir,
You are happ'ly met.

   Bon.   That cannot be, by thee.

   Mos. Why, sir?

   Bon.   Nay, 'pray thee know thy way, and leave me:
I would be loath to interchange discourse
With such a mate as thou art.

   Mos.   Courteous sir,
Scorn not my poverty.

   Bon.   Not I, by heaven:
But thou shalt give me leave to hate thy baseness.

   Mos. Baseness?

   Bon.   Aye, answer me, is not thy sloth
Sufficient argument? thy flattery?
Thy means of feeding?

   Mos.   Heaven be good to me.
These imputations are too common, sir,
And eas'ly stuck on virtue, when she's poor;
You are unequal to me, and howe'er
Your sentence may be righteous, yet you are not,
That ere you know me, thus proceed in censure:
St. Mark bear witness 'gainst you, 'tis inhuman.

   Bon. What? does he weep? the sign is soft and good!
I do repent me that I was so harsh.   [*Aside.*

   Mos. 'Tis true that, sway'd by strong necessity,
I am enforc'd to eat my careful bread
With too much obsequy; 'tis true, beside,
That I am fain to spin mine own poor raiment
Out of my mere observance, being not born
To a free fortune: but that I have done
Base offices, in rending friends asunder,
Dividing families, betraying counsels,
Whispering false lies, or mining men with praises,
Train'd their credulity with perjuries,
Corrupted chastity or am in love
With mine own tender ease, but would not rather

Prove the most rugged and laborious course
That might redeem my present estimation;
Let me here perish, in all hope of goodness.

Bon. This cannot be a personated passion!   [*Aside.*
I was to blame, so to mistake thy nature;
'Pray thee forgive me: and speak out thy business.

Mos. Sir, it concerns you; and though I may seem,
At first, to make a main offence in manners,
And in my gratitude unto my master,
Yet for the pure love which I bear all right,
And hatred of the wrong, I must reveal it.
This very hour, your father is in purpose
To disinherit you——

Bon.   How!

Mos.   And thrust you forth,
As a mere stranger to his blood; 'tis true, sir:
The work no way engageth me, but, as
I claim an interest in the general state
Of goodness and true virtue, which I hear
T' abound in you: and for which mere respect,
Without a second aim, sir, I have done it.

Bon. This tale hath lost thee much of the late trust
Thou hadst with me; it is impossible:
I know not how to lend it any thought
My father should be so unnatural.

Mos. It is a confidence that well becomes
Your piety; and form'd, no doubt, it is,
From your own simple innocence: which makes
Your wrong more monstrous and abhor'd. But, sir,
I now will tell you more. This very minute,
It is, or will be doing: And, if you
Shall be but pleas'd to go with me, I'll bring you,
I dare not say where you shall see, but where
Your ear shall be a witness of the deed;
Hear yourself written bastard: and profess'd
The common issue of the earth.

Bon.   I'm 'maz'd!

Mos. Sir, if I do it not, draw your just sword,
And score your vengeance on my front and face;

Mark me your villain: You have too much wrong,
And I do suffer for you, sir. My heart
Weeps blood in anguish——
    Bon.   Lead. I follow thee.   [*Exeunt.*

ACT III. SCENE II

A room in Volpone's house.

Enter Volpone.

Volp. Mosca stays long, methinks. Bring forth your
    sports
And help to make the wretched time more sweet.
             Enter Nano, Androgyno, *and* Castrone.
  Nan. Dwarf, fool, and eunuch, well met here we be.
A question it were now, whether of us three,
Being all the known delicates of a rich man,
In pleasing him, claim the precedency can?
  Cas. I claim for myself.
  And.   And, so doth the fool.
  Nan. 'Tis foolish indeed: let me set you both to school.
First, for your dwarf, he's little, and witty
And everything, as it is little, is pretty;
Else, why do men say to a creature of my shape,
So soon as they see him, it's a pretty little ape?
And, why a pretty ape? but for pleasing imitation
Of greater men's action, in a ridiculous fashion.
Beside, this feat body of mine doth not crave
Half the meat, drink, and cloth, one of your bulks will
    have.
Admit, your fool's face be the mother of laughter,
Yet, for his brain, it must always come after:
And, though that do feed him, it's a pitiful case,
His body is beholding to such a bad face.   [*One knocks.*
  Volp. Who's there? my couch, away, look, Nano, see:
                      [*Exeunt And. and Cas.*
Give me my caps first—go, enquire.   [*Exit Nano.*
                        Now, Cupid
Send it be Mosca, and with fair return.

Nan. [*Within.*] It is the beauteous madam——
Volp.   Would-be—is it?
Nan. The same.
Volp.   Now, torment on me; squire her in:
For she will enter, or dwell here for ever.
Nay, quickly, that my fit were past. I fear
A second hell too, that my loathing this
Will quite expel my appetite to the other:
Would she were taking now her tedious leave.
Lord, how it threats me, what I am to suffer!

Re-enter Nano *with* Lady Politic Would-be.

Lady P. I thank you, good sir. 'Pray you signify
Unto your patron I am here. This band
Shows not my neck enough. I trouble you, sir,
Let me request you, bid one of my women
Come hither to me. In good faith, I am dress'd
Most favourably, to-day, it is no matter,
'Tis well enough.

Enter waiting-woman.

                    Look, see these petulant things!
How they have done this!
Volp.   I do feel the fever
Entering in at mine ears; O for a charm
To fright it hence.   [*Aside.*
Lady P.   Come nearer: is this curl
In his right place? or this? why is this higher
Than all the rest? you ha' not wash'd your eyes, yet?
Or do they not stand even i' your head?
Where's your fellow? call her.   [*Exit woman.*
Nan.   Now St. Mark
Deliver us: anon, she'll beat her women,
Because her nose is red.

Re-enter with second woman.

Lady P.   I pray you, view
This tire, forsooth: are all things apt, or no?

262

Wom. One hair a little here sticks out, forsooth.

Lady P. Does't so, forsooth? and where was your dear
          sight
When it did so, forsooth? what now? bird-ey'd?
And you, too? 'pray you both approach, and mend it.
Now, by that light I muse yo' are not asham'd!
I, that have preach'd these things so oft unto you,
Read you the principles, argu'd all the grounds,
Disputed every fitness, every grace,
Call'd you to counsel of so frequent dressings——

Nan. More carefully, than of your fame or honour.

             [*Aside.*

Lady P. Made you acquainted what an ample dowry
The knowledge of these things would be unto you,
Able, alone, to get you noble husbands
At your return: and you thus to neglect it?
Besides, you seeing what a curious nation
Th' Italians are, what will they say of me?
The English lady cannot dress herself;
Here's fine imputation to our country!
Well, go your ways, and stay i' the next room.
This fucus was too coarse too, it's no matter.
Good sir, you'll give 'em entertainment?

        [*Exeunt* Nano *and women.*

Volp. The storm comes toward me.

Lady P.   How does my Volpone?

Volp. Troubled with noise, I cannot sleep; I dreamt
That a strange fury entered now my house,
And, with the dreadful tempest of her breath,
Did cleave my roof asunder.

Lady P.   Believe me, and I
Had the most fearful dream, could I remember 't——

Volp. Out on my fate; I ha' given her the occasion
How to torment me: she will tell me hers. [*Aside.*

Lady P. Methought the golden mediocrity,
Polite, and delicate——

Volp.   O, if you do love me,
No more; I sweat and suffer at the mention
Of any dream: feel how I tremble yet.

263

Lady P. Alas, good soul! the passion of the heart.
Seed-pearl were good now, boil'd with syrup of apples,
Tincture of gold and coral, citron-pills,
Your elicampane root, myrobalanes——
　　Volp. Ah me, I have ta'en a grasshopper by the wing.
　　　　　　　　　　　　　　　　　　　　　[*Aside.*
　　Lady P. Burnt silk and amber, you have muscadel
Good i' the house——
　　Volp.　　　　　　You will not drink, and part?
　　Lady P. No, fear not that. I doubt we shall not get
Some English saffron, half a dram would serve,
Your sixteen cloves, a little musk, dried mints,
Bugloss and barley-meal——
　　Volp.　　　　　　She's in again,
Before I feign'd diseases, now I have one. [*Aside.*
　　Lady P. And these appli'd with a right scarlet cloth——
　　Volp. Another flood of words! A very torrent! [*Aside.*
　　Lady P. Shall I, sir, make you a poultice?
　　Volp.　　　　　　　　　　No, no, no;
I am very well: you need prescribe no more.
　　Lady P. I have a little studied physic; but now
I am all for music: save, i' the forenoons,
An hour or two for painting. I would have
A lady, indeed, t' have all letters and arts,
Be able to discourse, to write, to paint,
But principal as Plato holds, your music
(And so does wise Pythagoras, I take it)
Is your true rapture; when there is consent
In face, in voice, and clothes: and is, indeed,
Our sex's chiefest ornament.
　　Volp.　　　　　　　The poet,
As old in time as Plato, and as knowing,
Says that your highest female grace is silence.
　　Lady P. Which o' your poets? Petrarch? or 'Tasso? or
Dante?
Guarini? Ariosto? Aretine?
Cieco di Hadria? I have read them all.
　　Volp. Is everything a cause to my destruction? [*Aside.*
　　Lady P. I think I ha' two or three of 'em about me.

Volp. The sun, the sea will sooner both stand still,
Than her eternal tongue! nothing can 'scape it.   *[Aside.*
  Lady P. Here's Pastor Fido——
  Volp.   Profess obstinate silence,
That's now my safest.   *[Aside.*
  Lady P.   All our English writers,
I mean such as are happy in the Italian,
Will deign to steal out of this author, mainly;
Almost as much as from Montagnie:
He has so modern and facile a vein,
Fitting the time, and catching the court-ear.
Your Petrarch is more passionate, yet he,
In days of sonneting, trusted 'em with much:
Dante is hard, and few can understand him.
But for a desperate wit, there's Aretine!
Only his pictures are a little obscene——
You mark me not?
  Volp.   Alas, my mind's perturb'd.
  Lady P. Why, in such cases, we must cure ourselves,
Make use of our philosophy——
  Volp.   Oh me.
  Lady P. And, as we find our passions do rebel,
Encounter 'em with reason; or divert 'em
By giving scope unto some other humour
Of lesser danger: as, in politic bodies,
There's nothing more doth overwhelm the judgement,
And clouds the understanding, than too much
Settling and fixing and, as 't were, subsiding
Upon one object. For the incorporating
Of these same outward things into that part
Which we call mental leaves some certain fæces,
That stop the organs, and, as Plato says,
Assassinates our knowledge.
  Volp.   Now the spirit
Of patience help me.   *[Aside.*
  Lady P.   Come, in faith, I must
Visit you more a days; and make you well:
Laugh, and be lusty.
  Volp.   My good angel save me.   *[Aside.*

Lady P. There was but one sole man in all the world,
With whom I e'er could sympathize; and he
Would lie you often, three, four hours together,
To hear me speak: and be sometime so rapt,
As he would answer me quite from the purpose,
Like you, and you are like him, just. I'll discourse
(And 't be but only, sir, to bring you asleep)
How we did spend our time and loves together,
For some six years.
    Volp.   Oh, oh, oh, oh, oh, oh.
    Lady P. For we were *coetanei*, and brought up——
    Volp. Some power, some fate, some fortune rescue me.
                                  [*Aside.*

Enter Mosca.

    Mos. God save you, Madam.
    Lady P.   Good sir.
    Volp.   Alas my mind's perturb'd.
Welcome to my redemption.
    Mos.   Why, sir?
    Volp.   Oh,
Rid me of this my torture quickly there;
My madam with the everlasting voice:
The bells, in time of pestilence, ne'er made
Like noise, or were in that perpetual motion;
The cock-pit comes not near it. All my house,
But now, steam'd like a bath with her thick breath.
A lawyer could not have been heard; nor scarce
Another woman, such a hail of words
She has let fall. For hell's sake, rid her hence.
    Mos. Has she presented?
    Volp.   O, I do not care,
I'll take her absence upon any price,
With any loss.
    Mos.   Madam——
    Lady P.   I ha' brought your patron
A toy, a cap here, of mine own work——
    Mos.   'Tis well.
I had forgot to tell you, I saw your knight,

Where you'd little think it——
   Lady P.   Where?
   Mos.   Marry,
Where yet, if you make haste, you may apprehend him,
Rowing upon the water in a gondola,
With the most cunning courtesan of Venice.
   Lady P. Is't true?
   Mos.   Pursue 'em, and believe your eyes:
Leave me to make your gift.   [*Exit* Lady P. *hastily.*
                    I knew 't would take.
For lightly they that use themselves most licence
Are still most jealous.
   Volp.   Mosca, hearty thanks,
For thy quick fiction and delivery of me.
Now to my hopes, what say'st thou?

             Re-enter Lady P.

   Lady P.   But do you hear, sir?——
   Volp. Again; I fear a paroxysm.
   Lady P.   Which way
Row'd they together?
   Mos.   Toward the Rialto.
   Lady P. I pray you lend me your dwarf.
   Mos.   I pray you, take him. [*Exit* Lady P.
Your hopes, sir, are like happy blossoms, fair,
And promise timely fruit, if you will stay
But the maturing; keep you at your couch,
Corbaccio will arrive straight, with the will:
When he is gone I'll tell you more.   [*Exit.*
   Volp.   My blood,
My spirits are return'd; I am alive——
And like your wanton gamester, at primero,
Whose thought had whisper'd to him not go less,
Methinks I lie and draw—for an encounter.

ACT III. SCENE III

The passage leading to Volpone's chamber.

Enter Mosca *and* Bonario.

Mos. Sir, here concealed, you may hear all. But 'pray
you
Have patience, sir; the same's your father, knocks:
I am compell'd to leave you.
    Bon.   Do so. Yet
Cannot my thought imagine this a truth.

ACT III. SCENE IV

Another part of the passage.

Enter Mosca *and* Corvino *with* Celia.

Mos. Death on me! you are come too soon, what meant
you?
Did not I say I would send?
    Corv.   Yes, but I feared
You might forget it, and then they prevent us.
    Mos. Prevent? did e'er man haste so, for his horns?
A courtier would not ply it so, for a place.   [*Aside.*
Well, now there's no helping it, stay here;
I'll presently return.   [*Exit.*
    Corv.   Where are you, Celia?
You know not wherefore I have brought you hither?
    Cel. Not well, except you told me.
    Corv.   Now, I will:
Hark hither.   [*Exeunt.*

ACT III. SCENE V

A closet opening into a gallery.

Enter Mosca *and* Bonario.

Mos. Sir, your father hath sent word,
It will be half an hour ere he come;

And therefore, if you please to walk the while,
Into that gallery—at the upper end,
There are some books to entertain the time:
And I'll take care no man shall come unto you, sir.

Bon. Yes, I will stay there. I do doubt this fellow.
  [*Aside, and exit.*

Mos. There, he is far enough; he can hear nothing:
And, for his father, I can keep him off. [*Exit.*

ACT III. SCENE VI

Volpone's *chamber.* Volpone *on his couch,* Mosca *sitting by him.*

Enter Corvino, *forcing in* Celia.

Corv. Nay, now, there is no starting back; and therefore
Resolve upon it: I have so decree'd.
It must be done. Nor would I move 't afore,
Because I would avoid all shifts and tricks
That might deny me.

Cel.   Sir, let me beseech you,
Affect not these strange trials; if you doubt
My chastity, why, lock me up for ever:
Make me the heir of darkness. Let me live
Where I may please your fears, if not your trust.

Corv. Believe it, I have no such humour, I.
All that I speak, I mean; yet I am not mad:
Not horn-mad, see you? Go too, show yourself
Obedient, and a wife.

Cel.   O heaven!

Corv.   I say it,
Do so.

Cel. Was this the train?

Corv.   I have told you reasons;
What the physicians have set down; how much
It may concern me; what my engagements are;
My means; and the necessity of those means
For my recovery: wherefore, if you be
Loyal and mine, be won, respect my venture.

269

Cel. Before your honour?

Corv.   Honour? tut, a breath;
There's no such thing in nature: a mere term
Invented to awe fools. What, is my gold
The worse for touching? clothes, for being look'd on?
Why, this's no more. An old, decrepit wretch,
That has no sense, no sinew; takes his meat
With other's fingers; only knows to gape,
When you do scald his gums; a voice; a shadow;
And what can this man hurt you?

Cel.   Lord! what spirit
Is this hath entered him?   [*Aside.*

Corv.   And for your fame,
That's such a jig; as if I would go tell it,
Cry it, on the piazza! who shall know it,
But he that cannot speak it; and this fellow,
Whose lips are i' my pocket? save yourself,
If you'll proclaim 't, you may. I know no other
Should come to know it.

Cel.   Are heaven and saints then nothing?
Will they be blind, or stupid?

Corv.   How?

Cel.   Good sir,
Be jealous still, emulate them; and think
What hate they burn with toward every sin.

Corv. I grant you: if I thought it were a sin,
I would not urge you. Should I offer this
To some young Frenchman, or hot Tuscan blood,
That had read Aretine, conn'd all his prints,
Knew every quirk within lust's labyrinth,
And were profess'd critic in lechery;
And I would look upon him and applaud him.
This were a sin: but here, 'tis contrary,
A pious work, mere charity for physic,
An honest polity to assure mine own.

Cel. O heaven! canst thou suffer such a change?

Volp. Thou art mine honour, Mosca, and my pride,
My joy, my tickling, my delight! go, bring 'em.

Mos. Please you draw near, sir.

Corv.   Come on, what——
You will not be rebellious? by that light——

Mos. Sir, signior Corvino here is come to see you.

Volp. Oh!

Mos.   And hearing of the consultation had,
So lately, for your health, is come to offer,
Or rather, sir, to prostitute——

Corv.   Thanks, sweet Mosca.

Mos. Freely, unask'd, or unintreated——

Corv.   Well.

Mos. As the true fervent instance of his love
His own most fair and proper wife; the beauty,
Only of price in Venice——

Corv.   'Tis well urg'd.

Mos. To be your comfortress, and to preserve you.

Volp. Alas, I am past already! 'pray you, thank him
For his good care and promptness, but for that,
'Tis a vain labour, e'en to fight 'gainst heaven;
Applying fire to a stone: uh, uh, uh, uh.
Making a dead leaf grow again. I take
His wishes gently, though; and you may tell him
What I have done for him: marry, my state is hopeless!
Will him to pray for me; and t' use his fortune,
With reverence, when he comes to 't.

Mos.   Do you hear, sir?
Go to him with your wife.

Corv.   Heart of my father!
Wilt thou persist thus? come, I pray thee, come.
Thou seest 'tis nothing, Celia. By this hand,
I shall grow violent. Come, do 't, I say.

Cel. Sir, kill me, rather: I will take down poison,
Eat burning coals, do anything——

Corv.   Be damn'd.
Heart, I will drag thee hence home by the hair;
Cry thee a strumpet through the streets; rip up
Thy mouth unto thine ears; and slit thy nose,
Like a raw rochet——Do not tempt me, come.
Yield, I am loth——Death! I will buy some slave,
Whom I will kill, and bind thee to him, alive;

And at my window hang you forth: devising
Some monstrous crime, which I, in capital letters,
Will eat into thy flesh, with *aqua fortis*
And burning corsives, on this stubborn breast.
Now, by the blood thou hast incens'd, I'll do't.

   Cel. Sir, what you please, you may, I am your martyr.

   Corv. Be not thus obstinate, I ha' not deserved it:
Think who it is entreats you. 'Pray thee, sweet;
Good 'faith, thou shalt have jewels, gowns, attires,
What thou wilt think and ask. Do but go kiss him.
Or touch him but. For my sake. At my suit
This once. No? not? I shall remember this.
Will you disgrace me thus? do you thirst my undoing?

   Mos. Nay, gentle lady, be advis'd.

   Corv.   No, no.
She has watch'd her time. God's precious, this is scurvy;
'Tis very scurvy: and you are——

   Mos.   Nay, good sir.

   Corv. An arrant locust, by heaven, a locust. Whore,
Crocodile, that hast thy tears prepar'd,
Expecting how thou'lt bid 'em flow.

   Mos.   Nay, 'pray you, sir,
She will consider.

   Cel.   Would my life would serve
To satisfy.

   Corv.   'Sdeath! if she would but speak to him,
And save my reputation, 'twere somewhat;
But, spitefully to affect my utter ruin.

   Mos. Aye, now you have put your fortune in her hands.
Why i' faith, it is her modesty, I must quit her;
If you were absent, she would be more coming;
I know it: and dare undertake for her.
What woman can before her husband? 'pray you,
Let us depart, and leave her here.

   Corv.   Sweet Celia,
Thou may'st redeem all, yet; I'll say no more:
If not, esteem yourself as lost. Nay, stay there.

                  [*Exit with* Mosca, *shutting the door*

   Cel. O God, and his good angels! whither, whither

Is shame fled human breasts? that with such ease,
Men dare put off your honours, and their own?
Is that, which ever was a cause of life,
Now plac'd beneath the basest circumstance?
And modesty an exile made, for money?

Volp. Aye, in Corvino and such earth-fed minds,

[*He leaps off from his couch.*

That never tasted the true heav'n of love.
Assure thee, Celia, he that would sell thee,
Only for hope of gain, and that uncertain,
He would have sold his part of paradise
For ready money, had he met a cope-man.
Why art thou 'maz'd to see me thus reviv'd?
Rather applaud thy beauty's miracle;
'Tis thy great work: that hath, not now alone,
But sundry times, rais'd me in several shapes,
And, but this morning, like a mountebank,
To see thee at thy window. Aye, before
I would have left my practice for thy love,
In varying figures, I would have contended
With the blue Proteus, or the horned flood.
Now art thou welcome.

    Cel.   **Sir!**

    Volp.   Nay, fly me not.
Nor let thy false imagination
That I was bedrid, make thee think I am so:
Thou shalt not find it. I am now as fresh,
As hot, as high, and in as jovial plight,
As when, in that so celebrated scene,
At recitation of our comedy
For entertainment of the great Valois
I acted young Antinous; and attracted
The eyes and ears of all the ladies present,
T' admire each graceful gesture, note and footing. [*Sings.*

    Come, my Celia, let us prove,
    While we can, the sports of love;
    Time will not be ours for ever,
    He, at length, our good will sever;
    Spend not then his gifts in vain.

Suns that set may rise again:
But if once we lose this light,
'Tis with us perpetual night.
Why should we defer our joys?
Fame and rumour are but toys.
Cannot we delude the eyes
Of a few poor household spies?
Or his easier ears beguile,
Thus removed by our wile?
'Tis no sin love's fruits to steal;
But the sweet thefts to reveal:
To be taken, to be seen,
These have crimes accounted been.

Cel. Some serene blast me, or dire lightning strike
This my offending face.

   Volp.   Why droops my Celia?
Thou hast in place of a base husband, found
A worthy lover: use thy fortune well,
With secrecy and pleasure. See, behold,
What thou art queen of; not in expectation,
As I feed others: but possess'd and crown'd.
See, here, a rope of pearl; and each more orient
Than that the brave Egyptian queen carous'd:
Dissolve, and drink 'em. See, a carbuncle,
May put out both the eyes of our St. Mark;
A diamond would have bought Lollia Paulina
When she came in like star-light, hid with jewels,
That were the spoils of provinces; take these,
And wear, and lose 'em: yet remains an ear-ring
To purchase them again, and this whole state.
A gem but worth a private patrimony
Is nothing: we will eat such at a meal.
The heads of parrots, tongues of nightingales,
The brains of peacocks and of ostriches
Shall be our food: and, could we get the phœnix,
Though nature lost her kind, she were our dish.

   Cel. Good sir, these things might move a mind affected
With such delights; but I, whose innocence
Is all I can think wealthy, or worth th' enjoying,

And which once lost, I have nought to loose beyond it,
Cannot be taken with these sensual baits:
If you have conscience——

Volp.   'Tis the beggar's virtue,
If thou hast wisdom, hear me, Celia.
Thy baths shall be the juice of July-flowers,
Spirit of roses and of violets,
The milk of unicorns and panther's breath,
Gather'd in bags and mix'd with Cretan wines.
Our drink shall be prepared gold and amber;
Which we will take, until my roof whirl round
With the *vertigo*: and my dwarf shall dance,
My eunuch sing, my fool make up the antic
Whil'st we, in changed shapes, act Ovid's tales,
Thou, like Europa now, and I like Jove,
Then I like Mars and thou like Erycine,
So, of the rest, till we have quite run through
And wearied all the fables of the gods.
Then will I have thee in more modern forms,
Attired like some sprightly dame of France,
Brave Tuscan lady, or proud Spanish beauty;
Sometimes unto the Persian Sophie's wife;
Or the Grand Signior's mistress; and for change,
To one of our most artful courtesans,
Or some quick Negro, or cold Russian;
And I will meet thee in as many shapes:
Where we may so transfuse our wandering souls
Out at our lips, and score up sums of pleasures,   [*Sings.*
       That the curious shall not know,
         How to tell them as they flow;
       And the envious, when they find
         What their number is, be pin'd.
  Cel. If you have ears that will be pierc'd; or eyes
That can be open'd; a heart that may be touch'd:
Or any part that yet sounds man about you:
If you have touch of holy saints or heaven,
Do me the grace to let me 'scape. If not,
Be bountiful and kill me. You do know,
I am a creature, hither ill betray'd.

By one whose shame I would forget it were.
If you will deign me neither of these graces,
Yet feed your wrath, sir, rather than your lust;
(It is a vice comes nearer manliness)
And punish that unhappy crime of nature,
Which you miscall my beauty: flay my face
Or poison it with ointments for seducing
Your blood to this rebellion. Rub these hands
With what may cause an eating leprosy,
E'en to my bones and marrow: anything,
That may disfavour me, save in my honour.
And I will kneel to you, pray for you, pay down
A thousand hourly vows, sir, for your health,
Report, and think you virtuous——

    Volp.   Think me cold,
Frozen, and impotent, and so report me?
That I had Nestor's hernia, thou wouldst think.
I do degenerate and abuse my nation,
To play with opportunity thus long:
I should have done the act, and then have parley'd.
Yield, or I'll force thee.

    Cel.   O! just God.

    Volp.   In vain——

       [Bonario *leaps out from where* Mosca *had plac'd him.*

    Bon. Forbear, foul ravisher, libidinous swine,
Free the forc'd lady, or thou diest, impostor.
But that I am loth to snatch thy punishment
Out of the hand of justice, thou shouldst yet
Be made the timely sacrifice of vengeance
Before this altar, and this dross, thy idol.
Lady, let's quit the place, it is the den
Of villainy; fear nought, you have a guard:
And he, ere long, shall meet his just reward.

       [*Exeunt* Bonario *and* Celia.

    Volp. Fall on me, roof, and bury me in ruin,
Become my grave, that wert my shelter. O!
I am unmask'd, unspirited, undone,
Betray'd to beggary, to infamy——

Enter Mosca, *wounded.*

Mos. Where shall I run, most wretched shame of men,
To beat out my unlucky brains?
   Volp.   Here, here.
What! dost thou bleed?
   Mos.   O, that his well-driv'n sword
Had been so courteous to have cleft me down
Unto the navel; ere I liv'd to see
My life, my hopes, my spirits, my patron, all
Thus desperately engaged, by my error.
   Volp. Woe on thy fortune.
   Mos.   And my follies, sir.
   Volp. Th' hast made me miserable.
   Mos.   And myself, sir.
Who would have thought he would have harken'd so?
   Volp. What shall we do?
   Mos.   I know not, if my heart
Could expiate the mischance, I'd pluck it out.
Will you be pleas'd to hang me? or cut my throat?
And I'll requite you, sir. Let's die like Romans
Since we have liv'd like Grecians.   [*They knock without.*
   Volp.   Hark, who's there?
I hear some footing; officers, the *Saffi,*
Come to apprehend us! I do feel the brand
Hissing already at my forehead: now
Mine ears are boring.
   Mos.   To your couch, sir, you
Make that place good, however. Guilty men
Suspect what they deserve still.

Enter Corbaccio.

                    Signior Corbaccio!
   Corb. Why! how now? Mosca!
   Mos.   O, undone, amaz'd, sir.
Your son, I know not by what accident,
Acquainted with your purpose to my patron
Touching your will, and making him your heir,
Entered our house with violence, his sword drawn,

Sought for you, call'd you wretch, unnatural,
Vow'd he would kill you.

    Corb.   Me?

    Mos.   Yes, and my patron.

    Corb. This act shall disinherit him indeed:
Here is the will.

    Mos.   'Tis well, sir.

    Corb.   Right and well.
Be you as careful now, for me.

Enter Voltore, *behind.*

    Mos.   My life, sir,
Is not more tender'd, I am only yours.

    Corb. How does he? will he die shortly, think'st thou?

    Mos.   I fear,
He'll out-last May.

    Corb.   To-day?

    Mos.   No, last-out May, sir.

    Corb. Couldst thou not gi' him a dram?

    Mos.   O, by no means, sir.

    Corb. Nay, I'll not bid you.

    Volt.   This is a knave, I see.

    Mos. How, signior Voltore! did he hear me?   [*Aside.*

    Volt.   Parasite.

    Mos. Who's that? O, sir, most timely welcome——

    Volt.   Scarce,
To the discovery of your tricks, I fear.
You are his, only? and mine, also? are you not?

    Mos. Who? I, sir?

    Volt.   You, sir. What device is this
About a will?

    Mos.   A plot for you, sir.

    Volt.   Come,
Put not your foists upon me, I shall scent 'em.

    Mos. Did you not hear it?

    Volt.   Yes, I hear Corbaccio
Hath made your patron there, his heir.

    Mos.   'Tis true,

By my device, drawn to it by my plot,
With hope——
   Volt.   Your patron should reciprocate?
And you have promis'd?
   Mos.   For your good, I did, sir.
Nay more, I told his son, brought, hid him here,
Where he might hear his father pass the deed;
Being persuaded to it by this thought, sir,
That the unnaturalness, first, of the act,
And then, his father's oft disclaiming in him,
(Which I did mean t' help on) would sure enrage him
To do some violence upon his parent.
On which the law should take sufficient hold,
And you be stated in a double hope:
Truth be my comfort, and my conscience,
My only aim was to dig you a fortune
Out of these two old rotten sepulchres——
   Volt. I cry thee mercy, Mosca.
   Mos.   Worth your patience,
And your great merit, sir. And, see the change!
   Volt. Why? what success?
   Mos.   Most hapless! you must help, sir.
Whilst we expected the old raven, in comes
Corvino's wife, sent hither by her husband——
   Volt. What, with a present?
   Mos.   No, sir, on visitation:
(I'll tell you how, anon) and, staying long,
The youth, he grows impatient, rushes forth,
Seizeth the lady, wounds me, makes her swear
(Or he would murder her, that was his vow)
T' affirm my patron to have done her rape:
Which how unlike it is, you see! and, hence,
With that pretext, he's gone t' accuse his father;
Defame my patron; defeat you——
   Volt.   Where's her husband?
Let him be sent for, straight.
   Mos.   Sir, I'll go fetch him.
   Volt. Bring him to the *Scrutineo*.
   Mos.   Sir, I will.

Volt. This must be stopp'd.

Mos.   O, you do nobly, sir.
Alas, 'twas labour'd all, sir, for your good;
Nor was there want of counsel in the plot:
But fortune can, at any time, o'erthrow
The projects of a hundred learned clerks, sir.

Corb. What's that?

Volt.   Wilt please you, sir, to go along?
                                        [*Exit* Corbaccio *and* Voltore.

Mos. Patron, go in, and pray for our success.

Volp. Need makes devotion: heaven your labour bless.
                                                                [*Exeunt.*

ACT IV. SCENE I

A street.

Enter Sir Politic Would-be *and* Peregrine.

Pol. I told you, sir, it was a plot: you see
What observation is. You mention'd me
For some instructions: I will tell you, sir,
(Since we are met here in this height of Venice)
Some few particulars I have set down,
Only for this meridian; fit to be known
Of your crude traveller, and they are these.
I will not touch, sir, at your phrase or clothes,
For they are old.

Per.   Sir, I have better.

Pol.   Pardon,
I meant, as they are themes.

Per.   O, sir, proceed:
I'll slander you no more of wit, good sir.

Pol. First, for your garb, it must be grave and serious;
Very reserv'd, and lock'd; not tell a secret
On any terms, not to your father; scarce
A fable, but with caution; make sure choice
Both of your company and discourse; beware
You never speak a truth——

Per.   How!

Pol.   Not to strangers,
For those be they you must converse with most;
Others I would not know, sir, but at distance,
So as I still might be a saver in 'em:
You shall have tricks, else, past upon you hourly.
And then, for your religion, profess none;
But wonder at the diversity of all;
And, for your part, protest, were there no other
But simply the laws o' th' land, you could content you:
Nic. Machiavel, and monsieur Bodin, both
Were of this mind. Then must you learn the use
And handling of your silver fork at meals;
The metal of your glass (these are main matters
With your Italian): and to know the hour
When you must eat your melons and your figs.
    Per. Is that a point of state, too?
    Pol.   Here it is.
For your Venetian, if he see a man
Preposterous in the least, he has him straight;
He has: he strips him. I'll acquaint you, sir,
I now have liv'd here, 'tis some fourteen months;
Within the first week of my landing here
All took me for a citizen of Venice:
I knew the forms so well——
    Per.   And nothing else.   [*Aside.*
    Pol. I had read Contarene, took me a house,
Dealt with my Jews to furnish it with movables——
Well, if I could but find one man, one man,
To mine own heart, whom I durst trust, I would——
    Per. What? what, sir?
    Pol.   Make him rich; make him a fortune:
He should not think again. I would command it.
    Per. As how?
    Pol.   With certain projects that I have,
Which I may not discover.
    Per.   If I had
But one to wager with, I would lay odds now,
He tells me instantly.   [*Aside.*
    Pol.   One is (and that

281

I care not greatly who knows) to serve the state
Of Venice with red herrings for three years,
And at a certain rate, from Rotterdam,
Where I have correspondence. There's a letter,
Sent me from one o' the States, and to that purpose;
He cannot write his name, but that's his mark.

   Per. He is a chandler?

   Pol.   No, a cheesemonger.
There are some other too, with whom I treat
About the same negotiation;
And I will undertake it: For, 'tis thus
I'll do 't with ease, I have cast it all. Your hoy
Carries but three men in her, and a boy;
And she shall make me three returns a year:
So, if there come but one of three, I save;
If two, I can defalk. But this is now,
If my main project fail.

   Per.   Then you have others?

   Pol. I should be loth to draw the subtle air
Of such a place, without my thousand aims.
I'll not dissemble, sir, where'er I come,
I love to be considerative; and, 'tis true,
I have at my free hours thought upon
Some certain goods unto the state of Venice,
Which I do call my cautions: and, sir, which
I mean in hope of pension, to propound
To the Great Council, then unto the Forty,
So to the Ten. My means are made already——

   Per. By whom?

   Pol.   Sir, one that though his place be obscure,
Yet he can sway, and they will hear him. He's
A *commandadore*.

   Per.   What, a common sergeant?

   Pol. Sir, such as they are, put it in their mouths
What they should say, sometimes: as well as greater.
I think I have my notes to show you——

   Per.   Good, sir.

   Pol. But you shall swear unto me, on your gentry,
Not to anticipate——

Per.   I, sir?

Pol.   Nor reveal
A circumstance—My paper is not with me.

Per. O, but you can remember, sir.

Pol.   My first is
Concerning tinder-boxes. You must know,
No family is here without its box.
Now sir, it being so portable a thing,
Put case that you or I were ill affected
Unto the state; sir, with it in our pockets,
Might not I go into the Arsenal?
Or you? come out again and none the wiser?

Per. Except yourself, sir.

Pol.   Go too, then. I, therefore,
Advertise to the state how fit it were
That none, but such as were known patriots,
Sound lovers of their country, should be suffer'd
T' enjoy them in their houses: and even those,
Seal'd at some office, and at such a bigness
As might not lurk in pockets.

Per.   Admirable!

Pol. My next is, how t' inquire and be resolv'd
By present demonstration, whether a ship,
Newly arrived from Syria, or from
Any suspected part of all the Levant
Be guilty of the plague: And, where they use
To lie out forty, fifty days, sometimes,
About the Lazaretto for their trial;
I'll save that charge and loss unto the merchant,
And, in an hour, clear the doubt.

Per.   Indeed, sir?

Pol. Or——I will lose my labour.

Per.   'My faith, that's much.

Pol. Nay, sir, conceive me. 'Twill cost me in onions,
Some thirty livres——

Per.   Which is one pound sterling.

Pol. Beside my waterworks: for this I do, sir.
First, I bring in your ship 'twixt two brick walls;
(But those the state shall venture) on the one

524   283   K

I strain me a fair tarpaulin; and in that
I stick my onions, cut in halves: the other
Is full of loop-holes, out at which I thrust
The noses of my bellows; and those bellows
I keep, with waterworks, in perpetual motion,
Which is the easiest matter of a hundred.
Now, sir, your onion, which doth naturally
Attract th' infection; and your bellows, blowing
The air upon him, will show instantly
By his chang'd colour, if there be contagion,
Or else remain as fair as at the first.
Now 'tis known, 'tis nothing.

  Per.   You are right, sir.

 Pol. I would I had my note.

 Per.   'Faith, so would I:
But you ha' done well for once, sir.

 Pol.   Were I false,
Or would be made so, I could show you reasons,
How I could sell this state now to the Turk;
Spite of their galleys, or their——

 Per.   Pray you, Sir Pol.

 Pol. I have 'em not about me.

 Per.   That I fear'd.
They are there, sir?

 Pol.   No, this is my diary,
Wherein I note my actions of the day.

 Per. 'Pray you let's see, sir. What is here? *notandum,*
                [*Reads.*
'A rat had gnawn my spur leathers; notwithstanding,
I put on new, and did go forth: but first
I threw three beans over the threshold. *Item,*
I went and bought two toothpicks, whereof one
I burst immediately, in a discourse
With a Dutch merchant, 'bout *ragion del stato.*
From him I went, and paid a *moccinigo,*
For piecing my silk stockings; by the way
I cheapen'd sprats: and at St. Mark's, I urin'd.'
'Faith, these are politic notes!

 Pol.   Sir, I do slip

284

No action of my life, thus, but I quote it.
　Per. Believe me it is wise!
　Pol. 　　　　　　　Nay, sir, read forth.

Enter Lady Politic Would-be, Nano, *and two waiting-
women.*

　Lady P. Where should this loose knight be, trow? sure,
　　he's hous'd.
　Nan. Why, then he's fast.
　Lady P. 　　　　　Aye, he plays both, with me:
I pray you, stay. This heat will do more harm
To my complexion than his heart is worth.
I do not care to hinder, but to take him.
How it comes off! 　　　　　　*[Rubbing her cheeks.*
　Wom. 　　　My master's yonder.
　Lady P. 　　　　　　　　Where?
　Wom. With a young gentleman.
　Lady P. 　　　　　　　That same's the party!
In man's apparel. 'Pray you, sir, jog my knight:
I will be tender to his reputation,
How ever he demerit.
　Pol. 　　　My lady!
　Per. 　　　　　　Where?
　Pol. 'Tis she indeed, sir, you shall know her. She is,
Were she not mine, a lady of that merit,
For fashion, and behaviour; and for beauty
I durst compare——
　Per. 　　　　It seems you are not jealous,
That dare commend her.
　Pol. 　　　　　　Nay, and for discourse——
　Per. Being your wife, she cannot miss that.
　Pol. 　　　　　　　　　Madam,
Here is a gentleman, 'pray you use him fairly,
He seems a youth, but he is——
　Lady P. 　　　　None?
　Pol. 　　　　　　　Yes, one
Has put his face as soon into the world——
　Lady P. You mean, as early? but to-day?
　Pol. 　　　　　　　　　How's this!

Lady P. Why in this habit, sir, you apprehend me.
Well, master Would-be, this doth not become you;
I had thought the odour, sir, of your good name
Had been more precious to you; that you would not
Have done this dire massacre on your honour;
One of your gravity and rank besides!
But knights, I see, care little for the oath
They make to ladies; chiefly, their own ladies.
　　Pol. Now, by my spurs, the symbol of my knighthood!
　　Per. Lord! how his brain is humbled for an oath. [*Aside.*
　　Pol. I reach you not.
　　Lady P.　　　　　Right, sir, your policy
May bear it through thus. Sir, a word with you. [*To* Per.
I would be loth to contest publicly
With any gentlewoman; or to seem
Froward, or violent, as the courtier says,
It comes too near rusticity in a lady,
Which I would shun by all means: and, however
I may deserve from master Would-be, yet
T' have one fair gentlewoman thus be made
Th' unkind instrument to wrong another,
And one she knows not, aye, and to persever:
In my poor judgement, is not warranted
From being a solecism in our sex,
If not in manners.
　　Per.　　　　How is this!
　　Pol.　　　　　　　Sweet madam,
Come nearer to your aim.
　　Lady P.　　　　Marry, and will, sir.
Since you provoke me with your impudence,
And laughter of your light land-siren here,
Your Sporus, your hermaphrodite——
　　Per.　　　　　　What's here?
Poetic fury and historic storms!
　　Pol. The gentleman, believe it, is of worth,
And of our nation.
　　Lady P.　　　Aye, your Whitefriars nation?
Come, I blush for you, master Would-be, aye;
And am asham'd you should ha' no more forehead

286

Than thus to be the patron or St. George
To a lewd harlot, a base fricatrice,
A female devil in a male outside.

Pol.   Nay,
And you be such a one! I must bid adieu
To your delights. The case appears too liquid.   [*Exit.*

  Lady P. Aye, you may carry 't clear with your state-
face!
But for your carnival concupiscence,
Who here is fled for liberty of conscience,
From furious persecution of the marshal,
Her will I disc'ple.

  Per.   This is fine, i' faith!
And do you use this often? is this part
Of your wit's exercise, 'gainst you have occasion?
Madam——

  Lady P.   Go to, sir.

  Per.   Do you hear me, lady?
Why, if your knight have set you to beg shirts,
Or to invite me home, you might have done it
A nearer way, by far.

  Lady P.   This cannot work you
Out of my snare.

  Per.   Why, am I in it then?
Indeed, your husband told me, you were fair,
And so you are; only your nose inclines
That side, that's next the sun to the queen-apple.

  Lady P. This cannot be endur'd by any patience.

Enter Mosca.

  Mos. What's the matter, madam?

  Lady P.   If the Senate
Right not my quest in this; I will protest 'em,
To all the world, no aristocracy.

  Mos. What is the injury, lady?

  Lady P.   Why, the callet
You told me of, here I have ta'en disguis'd.

  Mos. Who? this? what means your ladyship? the creature

I mention'd to you is apprehended now,
Before the Senate, you shall see her——
 Lady P.   Where?
 Mos. I'll bring you to her. This young gentleman
I saw him land this morning at the port.
 Lady P. Is't possible! how has my judgement wander'd!
Sir, I must, blushing, say to you, I have err'd:
And plead your pardon.
 Per.   What! more changes, yet?
 Lady P. I hope, yo' ha' not the malice to remember
A gentlewoman's passion. If you stay,
In Venice here, please you to use me, sir——
 Mos. Will you go, madam?
 Lady P.   'Pray you, sir, use me. In faith,
The more you see me, the more I shall conceive,
You have forgot our quarrel. [*Exeunt all but* Peregrine.
 Per.   This is rare!
Sir Politic Would-be? no, Sir Politic bawd!
To bring me thus acquainted with his wife!
Well, wise Sir Pol.: since you have practis'd, thus,
Upon my freshman-ship, I'll try your salt-head,
What proof it is against a counter-plot.   [*Exit.*

ACT IV. SCENE II

The Senate House.

Enter Voltore, Corbaccio, Corvino, *and* Mosca.

 Volt. Well, now you know the carriage of the business,
Your constancy is all that is requir'd
Unto the safety of it.
 Mos.   Is the lie
Safely convey'd amongst us? is that sure?
Knows every man his burden?
 Corv.   Yes.
 Mos.   Then shrink not.
 Corv. But, knows the Advocate the truth?

Mos.   O, sir,
By no means. I devis'd a formal tale
That salv'd your reputation. But be valiant, sir.

   Corv. I fear no one but him; that, this his pleading
Should make him stand for a co-heir——

   Mos.   Co-halter.
Hang him: we will but use his tongue, his noise,
As we do croakers, here.

   Corv.   Aye, what shall he do?

   Mos. When we ha' done, you mean?

   Corv.   Yes.

   Mos.   Why, we'll think,
Sell him for *mummia*, he's half dust already.
Do not you smile [*To* Voltore] to see this buffalo,
How he doth sport it with his head?—I should
If all were well and past. Sir [*To* Corbaccio], only you
Are he that shall enjoy the crop of all
And these not know for whom they toil.

   Corb.   Aye, peace.

   Mos. [*To* Corvino, *then to* Voltore *again.*] But you shall
eat it. Much! Worshipful sir,
Mercury sit upon your thundering tongue,
Or the French Hercules, and make your language
As conquering as his club, to beat along,
As with a tempest, flat, our adversaries:
But much more yours, sir.

   Volt.   Here they come, ha' done.

   Mos. I have another witness, if you need, sir,
I can produce.

   Volt. Who is it?

   Mos.   Sir, I have her.

Enter Avocatori, Bonario, Celia, Notario, Commandadori,
and other Officers of Justice.

   1 Avoc. The like of this the Senate never heard of.

   2 Avoc. 'Twill come most strange to them when we
report it.

   4 Avoc. The gentlewoman has been ever held

Of unreproved name.

 3 Avoc.   So, the young man.

 4 Avoc. The more unnatural part that of his father.

 2 Avoc. More of the husband.

 1 Avoc.   I not know to give
His act a name, it is so monstrous!

 4 Avoc. But the impostor, he is a thing created
T' exceed example!

 1 Avoc.   And all after-times!

 2 Avoc. I never heard a true voluptuary
Describ'd, but him.

 3 Avoc.   Appear yet those were cited?

 Not. All but the old magnifico, Volpone.

 1 Avoc. Why is not he here?

 Mos.   Please your fatherhoods,
Here is his advocate. Himself's so weak,
So feeble——

 4 Avoc. What are you?

 Bon.   His parasite,
His knave, his pandar: I beseech the court
He may be forc'd to come, that your grave eyes
May bear strong witness of his strange impostures.

 Volt. Upon my faith and credit with your virtues,
He is not able to endure the air.

 2 Avoc. Bring him, however.

 3 Avoc.   We will see him.

 4 Avoc.   Fetch him.

 Volt. Your fatherhoods' fit pleasures be obey'd,
           [*Exeunt* Officers.
But sure, the sight will rather move your pities,
Than indignation; may it please the court,
In the meantime, he may be heard in me:
I know this place most void of prejudice,
And therefore crave it, since we have no reason
To fear our truth should hurt our cause.

 3 Avoc.   Speak free.

 Volt. Then know, most honour'd fathers, I must now
Discover to your strangely abused ears,
The most prodigious and most frontless piece

Of solid impudence and treachery
That ever vicious nature yet brought forth
To shame the state of Venice. This lewd woman
That wants no artificial looks or tears,
To help the visor she has now put on,
Hath long been known a close adulteress
To that lascivious youth there; not suspected,
I say, but known; and taken in the act
With him; and by this man, the easy husband,
Pardon'd: whose timeless bounty makes him now
Stand here, the most unhappy innocent person
That ever man's own goodness made accus'd.
For these, not knowing how to owe a gift
Of that dear grace but with their shame; being plac'd
So above all powers of their gratitude,
Began to hate the benefit: and, in place
Of thanks, devise t' extirp the memory
Of such an act. Wherein, I pray your fatherhoods,
To observe the malice, yea, the rage of creatures
Discover'd in their evils; and what heart
Such take, even from their crimes. But that, anon,
Will more appear. This gentleman, the father,
Hearing of this foul fact, with many others,
Which daily struck at his too tender ears,
And griev'd in nothing more than that he could not
Preserve himself a parent (his son's ills
Growing to that strange flood) at last decreed
To disinherit him.

 1 Avoc. These be strange turns!

 2 Avoc. The young man's fame was ever fair, and
honest.

 Volt. So much more full of danger is his vice,
That can beguile so under shade of virtue.
But as I said, my honour'd sires, his father,
Having this settled purpose, by what means
To him betray'd we know not, and this day
Appointed for the deed; that parricide
(I cannot style him better), by confederacy
Preparing this his paramour to be there,

Entered Volpone's house, who was the man
Your fatherhoods must understand, design'd
For the inheritance, there sought his father:
But with what purpose sought he him, my lords?
I tremble to pronounce it, that a son
Unto a father, and to such a father
Should have so foul, felonious intent—
It was to murder him. When, being prevented
By his more happy absence, what then did he?
Not check his wicked thoughts; no, now new deeds:
(Mischief doth ever end where it begins)
An act of horror, fathers! he dragg'd forth
The aged gentleman that had there lain, bed-rid,
Three years and more, out of his innocent couch,
Naked upon the floor there left him; wounded
His servant in the face; and with this strumpet,
The stale to his forg'd practice, who was glad
To be so active (I shall here desire
Your fatherhoods to note but my collections,
As most remarkable,) thought at once to stop
His father's ends; discredit his free choice
In the old gentleman; redeem themselves
By laying infamy upon this man,
To whom, with blushing, they should owe their lives.

1 Avoc. What proofs have you of this?

Bon.   Most honour'd fathers
I humbly crave there be no credit given
To this man's mercenary tongue.

2 Avoc.   Forbear.

Bon. His soul moves in his fee.

3 Avoc.   O, sir.

Bon.   This fellow,
For six sols more, would plead against his Maker.

1 Avoc. You do forget yourself.

Volt.   Nay, nay, grave fathers.
Let him have scope: can any man imagine
That he will spare his accuser that would not
Have spar'd his parent?

1 Avoc.   Well, produce your proofs.

Cel. I would I could forget I were a creature.

Volt. Signior Corbaccio.   [*Corbaccio comes forward.*

4 Avoc.   What is he?

Volt. The father.

2 Avoc.   Has he had an oath?

Not.   Yes.

Corb.   What must I do now?

Not. Your testimony's crav'd.

Corb.   Speak to the knave?
I'll ha' my mouth first stopp'd with earth; my heart
Abhors his knowledge: I disclaim in him.

1 Avoc. But for what cause?

Corb.   The mere portent of nature.
He is an utter stranger to my loins.

Bon. Have they made you to this!

Corb.   I will not hear thee,
Monster of men, swine, goat, wolf, parricide,
Speak not, thou viper.

Bon.   Sir, I will sit down,
And rather wish my innocence should suffer,
Than I resist the authority of a father.

Volt. Signior Corvino.   [*Corvino comes forward.*

2 Avoc.   This is strange!

1 Avoc.   Who's this?

Not. The husband.

4 Avoc.   Is he sworn?

Not.   He is.

3 Avoc.   Speak then.

Corv. This woman, please your fatherhoods, is a whore,
Of most hot exercise, more than a partridge,
Upon record——

1 Avoc.   No more.

Corv.   Neighs like a jennet.

Not. Preserve the honour of the court.

Corv.   I shall,
And modesty of your most reverend ears.
And yet I hope that I may say these eyes
Have seen her glued unto that piece of cedar;
That fine well-timber'd gallant: and that here

293

The letters may be read, thorough the horn,
That make the story perfect.

   Mos.   Excellent, sir!

   Corv. There is no shame in this now, is there?

   Mos.   None.

   Corv. Or if I said, I hop'd that she were onward
To her damnation, if there be a hell
Greater than whore and woman; a good Catholic
May make the doubt.

   3 Avoc.   His grief hath made him frantic.

   1 Avoc. Remove him hence.

   2 Avoc.   Look to the woman. [*Celia swoons*

   Corv.   Rare!
Prettily feign'd again!

   4 Avoc.   Stand from about her.

   1 Avoc. Give her the air.

   3 Avoc.   What can you say?

   Mos.   My wound.
May't please your wisdoms, speak for me, receiv'd
In aid of my good patron, when he missed
His sought-for father, when that well-taught dame
Had her cue given her, to cry out a rape.

   Bon. O, most laid impudence! Fathers——

   3 Avoc.   Sir, be silent,
You had your hearing free, so must they theirs.

   2 Avoc. I do begin to doubt th' imposture here.

   4 Avoc. This woman has too many moods.

   Volt.   Grave fathers,
She is a creature of a most profess'd
And prostituted lewdness.

   Corv.   Most impetuous
Unsatisfied, **grave** fathers!

   Volt.   May her feignings
Not take your wisdoms: but this day she baited
A stranger, a grave knight, with her loose eyes,
And more lascivious kisses. This man saw 'em
Together on the water in a gondola.

   Mos. Here is the lady herself, that saw 'em too,
Without; who then had in the open streets

Pursu'd them, but for saving her knight's honour.

   1 Avoc. Produce that lady.   [*Exit* Mosca.

   2 Avoc.   Let her come.

   4 Avoc.   These things,

They strike with wonder!

   3 Avoc.   I am turn'd a stone!

Re-enter Mosca *with* Lady Politic Would-be.

   Mos. Be resolute, madam.

   Lady P.   Aye, this same is she.

Out, thou chameleon harlot; now thine eyes

Vie tears with the hyena: dar'st thou look

Upon my wronged face? I cry your pardons.

I fear I have forgettingly transgress'd

Against the dignity of the court——

   2 Avoc.   No, madam.

   Lady P. And been exorbitant——

   4 Avoc.   You have not, lady.

These proofs are strong.

   Lady P.   Surely, I had no purpose

To scandalize your honours, or my sex's.

   3 Avoc. We do believe it.

   Lady P.   Surely, you may believe it.

   2 Avoc. Madam, we do.

   Lady P.   Indeed, you may; my breeding

Is not so coarse——

   4 Avoc.   We know it.

   Lady P.   To offend

With pertinacy——

   3 Avoc.   Lady.

   Lady P.   Such a presence:

No, surely.

   1 Avoc. We well think it.

   Lady P.   You may think it.

   1 Avoc. Let her o'ercome. What witnesses have you,

To make good your report?

   Bon.   Our consciences.

   Cel. And heaven, that never fails the innocent.

   4 Avoc. These are no testimonies.

    Bon.   Not in your courts,
Where multitude and clamour overcomes.
    1 Avoc. Nay, then you do wax insolent.
                        [*Volpone is brought in on a couch.*
    Volt.   Here, here,
The testimony comes that will convince,
And put to utter dumbness their bold tongues.
See here, grave fathers, here's the ravisher,
The rider on men's wives, the great impostor,
The grand voluptuary! do you not think,
These limbs should affect venery? or these eyes
Covet a concubine? 'pray you mark these hands.
Are they not fit to stroke a lady's breasts?
Perhaps he doth dissemble?
    Bon.   So he does.
    Volt. Would you ha' him tortur'd?
    Bon.   I would have him prov'd.
    Volt. Best try him then, with goads or burning irons;
Put him to the strappado: I have heard
The rack hath cur'd the gout; faith, give it him,
And help him of a malady, be courteous.
I'll undertake, before these honour'd fathers,
He shall have yet as many left diseases,
As she has known adulterers, or thou strumpets.
O, my most equal hearers, if these deeds,
Acts, of this bold and most exorbitant strain,
May pass with sufferance, what one citizen
But owes the forfeit of his life, yea, fame,
To him that dares traduce him? which of you
Are safe, my honour'd fathers? I would ask,
With leave of your grave fatherhoods, if their plot
Have any face or colour like to truth?
Or if, unto the dullest nostril here,
It smell not rank and most abhorred slander?
I crave your care of this good gentleman,
Whose life is much endanger'd by their fable;
And as for them, I will conclude with this,
That vicious persons, when they are hot and flesh'd
In impious acts, their constancy abounds:

Damn'd deeds are done with greatest confidence.

  1 Avoc. Take 'em to custody, and sever them.

  2 Avoc. 'Tis pity two such prodigies should live.

  1 Avoc. Let the old gentleman be return'd with care:
I am sorry, our credulity wrong'd him.

                             [*Volpone is carried out.*

  4 Avoc. These are two creatures!

  3 Avoc.   I have an earthquake in me!

  2 Avoc. Their shame, even in their cradles, fled their
    faces.

  4 Avoc. You have done a worthy service to the state, sir,
In their discovery.

  1 Avoc.   You shall hear, ere night,
What punishment the court decrees upon 'em.

[*Exeunt* Avocs., Not., *and* Officers *with* Bonario *and* Celia.

  Volt. We thank your fatherhoods. How like you it?

  Mos.   Rare.
I'd ha' your tongue, sir, tipp'd with gold, for this;
I'd ha' you be the heir to the whole city;
The earth I'd have want men, ere you want living:
They are bound to erect your statue in St. Mark's.
Signior Corvino, I would have you go
And show yourself, that you have conquer'd.

  Corv.   Yes.

  Mos. It was much better that you should profess
Yourself a cuckold, thus, than that the other
Should have been prov'd.

  Corv.   Nay, I consider'd that:
Now, it is her fault.

  Mos.   Then it had been yours.

  Corv. True, I do doubt this advocate, still.

  Mos.   I' faith,
You need not. I dare ease you of that care.

  Corv. I trust thee, Mosca.   [*Exit.*

  Mos.   As your own soul, sir.

  Corb.   Mosca.

  Mos. Now for your business, sir.

  Corb.   How? ha' you business?

  Mos. Yes, yours, sir.

Corb.   O, none else?

Mos.   None else, not I.

Corb. Be careful then.

Mos.   Rest you, with both your eyes, sir.

Corb. Dispatch it.

Mos.   Instantly.

Corb.   And look, that all,
Whatever be put in, jewels, plate, moneys,
Household stuff, bedding, curtains.

Mos.   Curtain rings, sir,
Only, the advocate's fee must be deducted.

Corb. I'll pay him now: you'll be too prodigal.

Mos. Sir, I must tender it.

Corb.   Two *ceccines* is well?

Mos. No, six, sir.

Corb.   'Tis too much.

Mos.   He talk'd a great while,
You must consider that, sir.

Corb.   Well, there's three——

Mos. I'll give it him.

Corb.   Do so, and there's for thee.   [*Exit.*

Mos. Bountiful bones! What horrid strange offence
Did he commit 'gainst nature, in his youth
Worthy this age? [*Aside.*] You see, sir, how I work
Unto your ends; take you no notice.

Volt.   No,
I'll leave you.   [*Exit.*

Mos.   All is yours; the devil and all:
Good advocate. Madam, I'll bring you home:

Lady P. No, I'll go see your patron.

Mos.   That you shall not:
I'll tell you why. My purpose is to urge
My patron to reform his will; and, for
The zeal you have shown to-day, whereas before
You were but third or fourth, you shall be now
Put in the first: which would appear as begged,
If you were present. Therefore——

Lady P.   You shall sway me. [*Exeunt.*

ACT V. SCENE I

A room in Volpone's *house.*

Enter Volpone.

Volp. Well, I am here; and all this brunt is past:
I ne'er was in dislike with my disguise,
Till this fled moment; here 'twas good, in private,
But, in your public, *cave*, whil'st I breathe.
'Fore God, my left leg 'gan to have the cramp;
And I apprehended straight some power had struck me
With a dead palsy: well, I must be merry,
And shake it off. A many of these fears
Would put me into some villainous disease,
Should they come thick upon me: I'll prevent 'em.
Give me a bowl of lusty wine, to fright
This humour from my heart; [*He drinks.*] Hum, hum,
   hum;
'Tis almost gone already: I shall conquer.
Any device now, of rare, ingenious knavery,
That would possess me with a violent laughter,
Would make me up, again! [*Drinks again.*] So, so, so, so.
This heat is life; 'tis blood by this time: Mosca!

Enter Mosca.

Mos. How now, sir? does the day look clear again?
Are we recover'd? and wrought out of error,
Into our way? to see our path before us?
Is our trade free once more?
Volp.   Exquisite Mosca!
Mos. Was it not carry'd learnedly?
Volp.   And stoutly.
Good wits are greatest in extremities.
Mos. It were a folly beyond thought to trust
Any grand act unto a cowardly spirit:
You are not taken with it enough, methinks?
Volp. O, more than if I had enjoy'd the wench:
The pleasure of all womankind's not like it.

299

Mos. Why, now you speak, sir. We must here be fix'd;
Here we must rest; this is our masterpiece:
We cannot think to go beyond this.

   Volp.   True,
Thou hast play'd thy prize, my precious Mosca.

   Mos.   Nay, sir,
To gull the court——

   Volp.   And quite divert the torrent
Upon the innocent.

   Mos.   Yes, and to make
So rare a music out of discords——

   Volp.   Right.
That yet to me's the strangest! How th' hast borne it!
That these, being so divided 'mongst themselves,
Should not scent somewhat, or in me or thee,
Or doubt their own side.

   Mos. True, they will not see 't.
Too much light blinds 'em, I think. Each of 'em
Is so possess'd and stuff'd with his own hopes,
That anything unto the contrary,
Never so true, or never so apparent,
Never so palpable, they will resist it——

   Volp. Like a temptation of the devil.

   Mos.   Right, sir.
Merchants may talk of trade, and your great signiors
Of land that yields well; but if Italy
Have any glebe more fruitful than these fellows,
I am deceiv'd. Did not your advocate rare?

   Volp. O—'My most honour'd fathers, my grave fathers,
Under correction of your fatherhoods,
What face of truth is here? If these strange deeds
May pass, most honour'd fathers'—I had much ado
To forbear laughing.

   Mos.   'T seem'd to me you sweat, sir.

   Volp. In troth, I did a little.

   Mos.   But confess, sir,
Were you not daunted?

   Volp.   In good faith, I was
A little in a mist; but not dejected:

Never, but still myself.

    Mos.   I think it, sir.
Now, so truth help me, I must needs say this, sir.
And, out of conscience, for your advocate:
He has taken pains, in faith, sir, and deserv'd,
In my poor judgement, I speak it under favour,
Not to contrary you, sir, very richly—
Well—to be cozen'd.

    Volp.   'Troth, and I think so too,
By that I heard him in the latter end.

    Mos. O, but before, sir; had you heard him first
Draw it to certain heads, then aggravate,
Then use his vehement figures—I look'd still
When he would shift a shirt; and doing this
Out of pure love, no hope of gain——

    Volp.   'Tis right.
I cannot answer him, Mosca, as I would,
Not yet; but for thy sake, at thy entreaty,
I will begin, ev'n now, to vex 'em all:
This very instant.

    Mos.   Good, sir.

    Volp.   Call the dwarf
And eunuch forth.

    Mos.   Castrone, Nano.

          Enter Castrone *and* Nano.

    Nan.   Here.

    Volp. Shall we have a jig, now?

    Mos.   What you please, sir.

    Volp.   Go,
Straight, give out about the streets, you two,
That I am dead; do it with constancy,
Sadly, do you hear? impute it to the grief
Of this late slander.   [*Exeunt* Cas. *and* Nan.

    Mos.   What do you mean, sir?

    Volp.   O,
I shall have instantly, my vulture, crow,
Raven, come flying hither on the news,
To peck for carrion, my she-wolf, and all

301

Greedy, and full of expectation——

Mos. And then to have it ravish'd from their mouths?

Volp. 'Tis true, I will ha' thee put on a gown,
And take upon thee, as thou wert mine heir;
Show 'em a will: open that chest, and reach
Forth one of those that has the blanks. I'll straight
Put in thy name.

Mos.   It will be rare, sir.

Volp.   Aye,
When they e'en gape, and find themselves deluded——

Mos. Yes.

Volp.   And thou use them scurvily. Dispatch,
Get on thy gown.

Mos.   But what sir, if they ask
After the body?

Volp.   Say it was corrupted.

Mos. I'll say it stunk, sir; and was fain t' have it
Coffin'd up instantly, and sent away.

Volp. Anything, what thou wilt. Hold, here's my will.
Get thee a cap, a count-book, pen and ink,
Papers afore thee; sit as thou wert taking
An inventory of parcels: I'll get up,
Behind the curtain, on a stool, and hearken;
Sometime peep over; see how they do look;
With what degrees their blood doth leave their faces!
O, 'twill afford me a rare meal of laughter.

Mos. Your advocate will turn stark dull upon it.

Volp. It will take off his oratory's edge.

Mos. But your *clarissimo*, old round-back, he
Will crump you like a hog-louse with the touch.

Volp. And what Corvino?

Mos.   O, sir, look for him,
To-morrow morning, with a rope and dagger,
To visit all the streets; he must run mad.
My lady too, that came into the court,
To bear false witness for your worship——

Volp.   Yes,
And kiss'd me 'fore the fathers, when my face
Flow'd all with oils.

Mos.   And sweat, sir. Why, your gold
Is such another med'cine, it dries up
All those offensive savours! It transforms
The most deformed, and restores 'em lovely,
As 't were the strange poetical girdle. Jove
Could not invent t' himself a shroud more subtle
To pass Acrisius' guards. It is the thing
Makes all the world her grace, her youth, her beauty.

  Volp. I think she loves me.

  Mos.   Who? the lady, sir?
She's jealous of you.

  Volp.   Do'st thou say so? [*Knocking without.*

  Mos.   Hark,
There's some already.

  Volp.   Look.

  Mos.   It is the vulture:
He has the quickest scent.

  Volp.   I'll to my place,
Thou to thy posture.

  Mos.   I am set.

  Volp.   But, Mosca,
Play the artificer now, torture 'em, rarely.

                  Enter Voltore.

  Volt. How now, my Mosca?

  Mos.   Turkey carpets, nine——

  Volt. Taking an inventory? that is well.

  Mos. Two suits of bedding, tissue——

  Volt.   Where's the will?
Let me read that the while.

     Enter servants with Corbaccio *in a chair.*

  Corb.   So, set me down:
And get you home.

  Volt.   Is he come, now, to trouble us?

  Mos. Of cloth of gold, two more——

  Corb.   Is it done, Mosca?

  Mos. Of several velvets, eight——

  Volt.   I like his care.

  Corb. Dost thou not hear?

Enter Corvino.

Corv.   Ha? is the hour come, Mosca?

Volp. [*Peeps from behind a traverse.*] Aye, now they
  muster.

Corv.   What does the advocate here?
Or this Corbaccio?

Corb.   What do these here?

Enter Lady Politic Would-be.

Lady P.   Mosca?
Is his thread spun?

Mos.   Eight chests of linen——

Volp.   O,
My fine dame Would-be, too!

Corv.   Mosca, the will,
That I may show it these, and rid 'em hence.

Mos. Six chests of diaper, four of damask—**There**.
      [*Gives them the Will carelessly over his shoulder.*

Corb. Is that the will?

Mos.   Down-beds, and bolsters——

Volp.   Rare!
Be busy still. Now, they begin to flutter:
They never think of me. Look, see, see, see!
How their swift eyes run over the long deed,
Unto the name, and to the legacies,
What is bequeath'd them, there——

Mos.   Ten suits of hangings——

Volp. Aye, i' their garters, Mosca. Now their hopes
Are at the gasp.

Volt.   Mosca the heir!

Corb.   What's that?

Volp. My advocate is dumb, look to my merchant,
He has heard of some strange storm, a ship is lost,
He faints: my lady will swoon. Old glazen-eyes,
He hath not reach'd his despair, yet.

Corb.   All these
Are out of hope, I am sure the man.

Corv.   But, Mosca——

Mos. Two cabinets——

Corv. Is this in earnest?

Mos. One

Of ebony.——

Corv. Or do you but delude me?

Mos. The other, mother of pearl—I am very busy.
Good faith, it is a fortune thrown upon me—
Item, one salt of agate—not my seeking.

Lady P. Do you hear, sir?

Mos. A perfum'd box—'pray you forbear,
You see I am troubled—made of an onyx—

Lady P. How!

Mos. To-morrow or next day, I shall be at leisure
To talk with you all.

Corv. Is this my large hope's issue?

Lady P. Sir, I must have a fairer answer.

Mos. Madam!
Marry, and shall: pray you, fairly quit my house.
Nay, raise no tempest with your looks; but hark you:
Remember what your ladyship offered me,
To put you in an heir; go to, think on 't.
And what you said e'en your best madams did
For maintenance, and why not you? enough.
Go home, and use the poor Sir Pol, your knight, well;
For fear I tell some riddles: go, be melancholy.

Volp. O, my fine devil!

Corv. Mosca, pray you a word.

Mos. Lord! will not you take your dispatch hence, yet?

[*Exit* Lady P.

Methinks of all, you should have been th' example.
Why should you stay here? with what thought? what
promise?
Hear you, do not you know, I know you an ass?
And that you would most fain have been a wittol,
If fortune would have let you? that you are
A declar'd cuckold, on good terms? this pearl,
You'll say, was yours? right: this diamond?
I'll not deny 't, but thank you. Much here else?
It may be so. Why, think that these good works
May help to hide your bad: I'll not betray you,

Although you be but extraordinary,
And have it only in title, it sufficeth.
Go home, be melancholy too, or mad.   [*Exit* Corvino.

Volp. Rare, Mosca! how his villainy becomes him!
Volt. Certain he doth delude all these for me.
Corb. Mosca, the heir?
Volp.   O, his four eyes have found it!
Corb. I am cozen'd, cheated, by a parasite slave;
Harlot, th' hast gull'd me.
Mos.   Yes, sir. Stop your mouth,
Or I shall draw the only tooth is left.
Are not you he, that filthy covetous wretch
With the three legs, that here, in hope of prey,
Have, any time this three year, snuff'd about,
With your most grovelling nose; and would have hir'd
Me to the poisoning of my patron? sir?
Are not you he, that have, to-day, in court,
Profess'd the disinheriting of your son?
Perjur'd yourself? Go home, and die, and stink;
If you but croak a syllable, all comes out:
Away and call your porters! Go, go, stink.

[*Exit* Corbaccio.

Volp. Excellent varlet!
Volt.   Now, my faithful Mosca,
I find thy constancy.
Mos.   Sir?
Volt.   Sincere.
Mos.   A table
Of porphyry—I mar'l you'll be thus troublesome.
Volt. Nay, leave off now, they are gone.
Mos.   Why? who are you?
What? who did send for you? O cry you mercy,
Reverend sir! good faith, I am griev'd for you,
That any chance of mine should thus defeat
Your (I must needs say) most deserving travails:
But I protest, sir, it was cast upon me,
And I could almost wish to be without it,
But that the will of th' dead must be observ'd.
Marry, my joy is that you need it not,

You have a gift, sir (thank your education),
Will never let you want, while there are men
And malice to breed causes. Would I had
But half the like for all my fortune, sir.
If I have any suits (as I do hope,
Things being so easy and direct, I shall not)
I will make bold with your obstreperous aid,
Conceive me for your fee, sir. In meantime,
You, that have so much law, I know ha' the conscience
Not to be covetous of what is mine.
Good sir, I thank you for my plate: 'twill help
To set up a young man. Good faith, you look
As you were costive; best go home and purge, sir.
                                        [*Exit* Voltore.

Volp. [*Comes from behind curtain.*] Bid him eat lettuce
    well: my witty mischief,
Let me embrace thee. O, that I could now
Transform thee to a Venus——Mosca, go
Straight, take my habit of *clarissimo*;
And walk the streets; be seen, torment 'em more:
We must pursue, as well as plot. Who would
Have lost this feast?
    Mos.   I doubt it will lose them.
    Volp. O, my recovery shall recover all.
That I could now but think on some disguise,
To meet 'em in: and ask 'em questions.
How I would vex 'em still at every turn!
    Mos. Sir, I can fit you.
    Volp.   Canst thou?
    Mos.   Yes, I know
One o' the *commandadori*, sir, so like you,
Him will I straight make drunk, and bring you his habit.
    Volp. A rare disguise, and answering thy brain!
O, I will be a sharp disease unto 'em.
    Mos. Sir, you must look for curses——
    Volp.   Till they burst;
The Fox fares ever best when he is curs'd.   [*Exeunt.*

ACT V. SCENE II

A Hall in Sir Politic's *house.*

Enter Peregrine *disguised, and three merchants.*

Per. Am I enough disguis'd?
1 Mer.   I warrant you.
Per. All my ambition is to fright him only.
2 Mer. If you could ship him away, 'twere excellent.
3 Mer. To Zant or to Aleppo?
Per.   Yes, and ha' his
Adventures put i' the Book of Voyages,
And his gull'd story registered for truth?
Well, gentlemen, when I am in a while,
And that you think us warm in our discourse,
Know your approaches.
1 Mer.   Trust it to our care. [*Exeunt merchants.*

Enter waiting-woman.

Per. Save you, fair lady. Is Sir Pol within?
Wom. I do not know, sir.
Per.   'Pray you, say unto him,
Here is a merchant, upon earnest business,
Desires to speak with him.
Wom.   I will see, sir.   [*Exit.*
Per.   'Pray you.
I see the family is all female here.

Re-enter woman.

Wom. He says, sir, he has weighty affairs of state,
That now require him whole. Some other time
You may possess him.
Per.   'Pray you, say again,
If those require him whole, these will exact him
Whereof I bring him tidings. [*Exit woman.*] What might
be
His grave affair of state now? how to make
Bolognian sausages here in Venice, sparing
One o' th' ingredients.

Re-enter woman.

Wom.   Sir, he says he knows
By your word 'tidings' that you are no statesman,
And therefore wills you stay.

Per.   Sweet, 'pray you return him,
I have not read so many proclamations,
And studied them for words, as he has done,
But—Here he deigns to come.   [*Exit woman.*

Enter Sir Politic.

Pol.   Sir, I must crave
Your courteous pardon. There hath chanc'd to-day
Unkind disaster 'twixt my lady and me:
And I was penning my apology,
To give her satisfaction, as you came now.

Per. Sir, I am griev'd I bring you worse disaster;
The gentleman you met at th' port to-day,
That told you he was newly arriv'd——

Pol.   Aye, was
A fugitive punk?

Per.   No, sir, a spy set on you:
And he has made relation to the Senate,
That you profest to him to have a plot
To sell the state of Venice to the Turk.

Pol. O me!

Per.   For which, warrants are sign'd by this time,
To apprehend you, and to search your study,
For papers——

Pol.   Alas, sir. I have none, but notes,
Drawn out of play-books——

Per.   All the better, sir.

Pol. And some essays. What shall I do?

Per.   Sir, best
Convey yourself into a sugar-chest,
Or, if you could lie round, a frail were rare:
And I could send you aboard.

Pol.   Sir, I but talk'd so
For discourse sake, merely.   [*They knock without.*

Per.   Hark, they are there.

Pol. I am a wretch, a wretch.

Per.   What will you do, sir?
Ha' you ne'er a currant-butt to leap into?
They'll put you to the rack, you must be sudden.

Pol. Sir, I have an ingine——

3 Mer. [*Without*].   Sir Politic Would-be?

2 Mer. [*Without*]. Where is he?

Pol.   That I have thought upon, before time.

Per. What is it?

Pol.   I shall ne'er endure the torture.
Marry, it is, sir, of a tortoise-shell,
Fitted for these extremities: pray you, sir, help me.
Here, I have a place, sir, to put back my legs;
Please you to lay it on, sir, with this cap
And my black gloves. I'll lie, sir, like a tortoise,
Till they are gone.

Per.   And call you this an ingine?

Pol. Mine own device—good sir, bid my wife's women
                            [*Exit Per.*
To burn my papers.   [*They rush in.*

1 Mer.   Where's he hid?

3 Mer.   We must
And will sure find him.

2 Mer.   Which is his study?

Re-enter Peregrine.

1 Mer.   What
Are you, sir?

Per.   I am a merchant, that came here
To look upon this tortoise.

3 Mer.   How?

1 Mer.   St. Mark!
What beast is this?

Per.   It is a fish.

2 Mer.   Come out here.

Per. Nay, you may strike him, sir, and tread upon him:
He'll bear a cart.

1 Mer.   What, to run over him?

Per.   Yes.

3 Mer. Let's jump upon him.

2 Mer.   Can he not go?

Per.   He creeps, sir.

1 Mer. Let's see him creep.

Per.   No, good sir, you will hurt him.

2 Mer. Heart, I'll see him creep; or prick his guts.

3 Mer. Come out here.

Per.   Pray you, sir—Creep a little. [*Aside to* Sir Pol.

1 Mer.   Forth.

2 Mer. Yet farther.

Per.   Good sir, creep.

2 Mer.   We'll see his legs.

3 Mer. Gods so, he has garters!

1 Mer.   Aye, and gloves.

[*They pull off the shell and discover him*

2 Mer.   Is this
Your fearful tortoise?

Per.   Now, Sir Pol, we are even;
For your next project I shall be prepar'd:
I am sorry for the funeral of your notes, sir.

1 Mer. 'Twere a rare motion to be seen in Fleet-street!

2 Mer. Aye, i' the term.

1 Mer.   Or Smithfield, in the fair.

3 Mer. Methinks 'tis but a melancholy sight!

Per. Farewell, most politic tortoise.

[*Exeunt* Per. *and merchants.*

Re-enter waiting-woman.

Pol.   Where's my lady?
Knows she of this?

Wom.   I know not, sir.

Pol.   Enquire.
O, I shall be the fable of all feasts,
The freight of the *gazetti*: ship-boy's tale;
And, which is worst, even talk for ordinaries.

Wom. My lady's come most melancholy home,
And says, sir, she will straight to sea, for physic.

Pol. And I, to shun this place and clime for ever;
Creeping with house on back: and think it well
To shrink my poor head in my politic shell.   [*Exeunt.*

ACT V. SCENE III

A room in Volpone's *house.*

Enter Volpone *and* Mosca. *The first in the habit of a* commandadore: *the other, of a* clarissimo.

  Volp. Am I then like him?
  Mos.   O, sir, you are he:
No man can sever you.
  Volp.   Good.
  Mos.   But what am I?
  Volp. 'Fore heav'n, a brave *clarissimo*, thou becom'st it!
Pity thou wert not born one.
  Mos.   If I hold
My made one, 'twill be well.   *[Aside.*
  Volp.   I'll go and see
What news first at the court.   *[Exit.*
  Mos.   Do so. My Fox
Is out of his hole and ere he shall re-enter,
I'll make him languish in his borrow'd case,
Except he come to composition with me:
Androgyno, Castrone, Nano.

Enter Androgyno, Nano, *and* Castrone.

  All.   Here.
  Mos. Go recreate yourselves abroad; go, sport: *[Exeunt.*
So, now I have the keys, and am possessed.
Since he will needs be dead afore his time,
I'll bury him, or gain by him. I am his heir:
And so will keep me, till he share at least.
To cozen him of all were but a cheat
Well plac'd; no man would construe it a sin:
Let his sport pay for 't, this is call'd the Fox-trap.   *[Exit.*

ACT V. SCENE IV

A street.

Enter Corbaccio *and* Corvino.

Corb. They say the court is set.
  Corv.   We must maintain
Our first tale good, for both our reputations.
  Corb. Why? mine's no tale: my son would there have
    kill'd me.
  Corv. That's true, I had forgot: mine is, I'm sure.
But for your will, sir.
  Corb.   I'll come upon him
For that, hereafter, now his patron's dead.

Enter Volpone.

  Volp. Signior Corvino! and Corbaccio! sir,
Much joy unto you.
  Corv.   Of what?
  Volp.   The sudden good
Dropp'd down upon you——
  Corb.   Where?
  Volp.   (And none knows how),
From old Volpone, sir.
  Corb.   Out, arrant knave.
  Volp. Let not your too much wealth, sir, make you
    furious.
  Corb. Away, thou varlet.
  Volp.   Why, sir?
  Corb.   Do'st thou mock me?
  Volp. You mock the world, sir, did you not change wills?
  Corb. Out, harlot.
  Volp.   O! belike you are the man,
Signior Corvino? 'faith, you carry it well;
You grow not mad withal: O love your spirit.
You are not over-leaven'd with your fortune.
You should ha' some would swell now, like a wine-fat,
With such an autumn——Did he gi' you all, sir?

Corv. Avoid, you rascal.

Volp.   Troth, your wife has shown
Herself a very woman: but you are well,
You need not care, you have a good estate,
To bear it out, sir, better by this chance.
Except Corbaccio have a share?

Corb.   Hence, varlet.

Volp. You will not be a'known sir: why, 'tis wise.
Thus do all gamesters, at all games, dissemble.
No man will seem to win. [*Exeunt* Corvino *and* Corbaccio.
                                Here comes my vulture,
Heaving his beak up i' the air, and snuffing.

Enter Voltore.

Volt. Outstript thus, by a parasite? a slave?
Would run on errands? and make legs for crumbs?
Well, what I'll do——

Volp.   The court stays for your worship.
I e'en rejoice, sir, at your worship's happiness,
And that it fell into so learned hands,
That understand the fingering.——

Volt.   What do you mean?

Volp. I mean to be a suitor to your worship,
For the small tenement, out of reparations;
That, at the end of your long row of houses,
By the Piscaria: it was, in Volpone's time,
Your predecessor, ere he grew diseas'd,
A handsome, pretty, custom'd bawdy-house,
As any was in Venice (none disprais'd),
But fell with him; his body, and that house
Decay'd together.

Volt.   Come, sir, leave your prating.

Volp. Why, if your worship give me but your hand
That I may ha' the refusal, I have done.
'Tis a mere toy to you, sir; candle rents:
As your learn'd worship knows——

Volt.   What do I know?

Volp. Marry, no end of your wealth, sir, God decrease it!

Volt. Mistaking knave! what, mock'st thou my misfor-
tune?   [*Exit.*

Volp. His blessing on your heart, sir, would 'twere more.
Now to my first again; at the next corner.   [*Exit.*

ACT V. SCENE V

Another part of the street.

Enter Corbaccio *and* Corvino. Mosca *passes over the stage,
before them.*

Corb. See, in our habit! see the impudent varlet!

Corv. That I could shoot mine eyes at him, like gun-
stones.

Enter Volpone.

Volp. But is this true, sir, of the parasite?

Corb. Again t' afflict us? monster!

Volp.   In good faith, sir,
I am heartily griev'd a beard of your grave length
Should be so over-reach'd. I never brook'd
That parasite's hair, methought his nose should cozen:
There still was somewhat in his look did promise
The bane of a *clarissimo.*

Corb.   Knave——

Volp.   Methinks
Yet you that are so traded i' the world,
A witty merchant, the fine bird, Corvino,
That have such moral emblems on your name,
Should not have sung your shame, and dropp'd your
    cheese,
To let the Fox laugh at your emptiness.

Corv. Sirrah, you think the privilege of the place,
And your red saucy cap, that seems to me
Nail'd to your jolt-head, with those two *cecchines*,
Can warrant your abuses; come you, hither:
You shall perceive, sir, I dare beat you. Approach.

Volp. No haste, sir, I do know your valour well:
Since you durst publish what you are, sir.

Corv.   Tarry,
I'd speak with you.

    Volp.   Sir, sir, another time——

    Corv. Nay, now.

    Volp.   O god, sir! I were a wise man,
Would stand the fury of a distracted cuckold.

    Corb. What! come again?

    Volp. Upon 'em. [*Mosca walks by.*] Mosca; save me.

    Corb. The air's infected where he breathes.

    Corv.   Let's fly him. [*Exeunt* Corv. *and* Corb

    Volp. Excellent basilisk! turn upon the vulture.

                  Enter Voltore.

    Volt. Well, flesh-fly, it is summer with you, now;
Your winter will come on.

    Mos.   Good advocate;
'Pray thee, not rail, nor threaten out of place, thus;
Thou'lt make a solecism, as madam says.
Get you a biggin more: your brain breaks loose.   [*Exit.*

    Volt. Well, sir.

    Volp.   Would you ha' me beat the insolent slave?
Throw dirt upon his first good clothes?

    Volt.   This same
Is doubtless some familiar!

    Volp.   Sir, the court
In troth stays for you. I am mad, a mule,
That never read Justinian, should get up
And ride an advocate. Had you no quirk
To avoid gullage, sir, by such a creature?
I hope you do but jest; he has not done't:
This's but confederacy to blind the rest.
You are the heir?

    Volt.   A strange, officious,
Troublesome knave! thou dost torment me.

    Volp.   I know——
It cannot be, sir, that you should be cozen'd;
'Tis not within the wit of man to do it:
You are so wise, so prudent, and 'tis fit
That wealth and wisdom still should go together. [*Exeunt.*

ACT V. SCENE VI

The Senate House.

Enter Avocatori, Notario, Commandadori, Bonario, Celia,
Corbaccio, Corvino, *etc.*

1 Avoc. Are all the parties here?
Not.   All but the advocate.
2 Avoc. And here he comes.

Enter Voltore *and* Volpone.

1 Avoc.   Then bring 'em forth to sentence.
Volt. O my most honour'd fathers, let your mercy
Once win upon your justice, to forgive—
I am distracted——
Volp.   What will he do, now?   *[Aside.*
Volt.   O,
I know not which t' address myself to first,
Whether your fatherhoods, or these innocents——
Corv. Will he betray himself?   *[Aside.*
Volt.   Whom, equally,
I have abus'd, out of most covetous ends——
Corv. The man is mad!
Corb.   What's that?
Corv.   He is possess'd.
Volt. For which, now struck in conscience, here I
prostrate
Myself at your offended feet, for pardon.
1, 2 Avoc. Arise.
Cel.   O heav'n, how just thou art!
Volp.   I am caught
I' mine own noose——   *[Aside.*
Corv.   Be constant, sir, nought now
Can help, but impudence.
1 Avoc.   Speak forward.
Com.   Silence.
Volt. It is not passion in me, reverend fathers,
But only conscience, conscience, my good sires,
That makes me now tell truth. That parasite,
That knave hath been the instrument of all.

317

2 Avoc. Where is that knave? fetch him.

Volp.   I go.   [*Exit.*

Corv.   Grave fathers,

This man's distracted; he confess'd it, now:

For hoping to be old Volpone's heir,

Who now is dead——

    3 Avoc.   How?

    2 Avoc.   Is Volpone dead?

Corv. Dead since, grave fathers——

Bon.   O, sure vengeance!

1 Avoc.   Stay,

Then he was no deceiver?

Volt.   O no, none:

The parasite, grave fathers.

Corv.   He does speak

Out of mere envy 'cause the servant's made

The thing he gap't for; please your fatherhoods,

This is the truth: though I'll not justify

The other, but he may be some-deal faulty.

Volt. Aye, to your hopes, as well as mine, Corvino:

But I'll use modesty. Pleaseth your wisdoms

To view these certain notes, and but confer them;

As I hope favour, they shall speak clear truth.

Corv. The devil has entered him!

Bon.   Or bides in you.

4 Avoc. We have done ill, by a public officer

To send for him, if he be heir.

2 Avoc.   For whom?

4 Avoc. Him that they call the parasite.

3 Avoc.   'Tis true;

He is a man of great estate, now left.

4 Avoc. Go you, and learn his name; and say the court

Entreats his presence here, but to the clearing

Of some few doubts.   [*Exit* Notario.

2 Avoc.   This same's a labyrinth!

1 Avoc. Stand you unto your first report?

Corv.   My state,

My life, my fame——

Bon.   Where is't?

Corv.   Are at the stake.

1 Avoc. Is yours so too?

Corb.   The advocate's a knave:
And has a forked tongue——

2 Avoc.   Speak to the point.

Corb. So is the parasite, too.

1 Avoc.   This is confusion.

Volt. I do beseech your fatherhoods, read but those——
                                 [*Gives them papers.*

Corv. And credit nothing the false spirit hath writ:
It cannot be but he is possess'd, grave fathers.

ACT V. SCENE VII

A street.

Enter Volpone.

Volp. To make a snare for mine own neck! and run
My head into it wilfully! with laughter!
When I had newly scap'd, was free and clear!
Out of mere wantonness! O, the dull devil
Was in this brain of mine when I devis'd it;
And Mosca gave it second: he must now
Help to sear up this vein, or we bleed dead.

Enter Nano, Androgymo, *and* Castrone.

How now! who let you loose? whither go you now?
What? to buy gingerbread? or to drown kitlings?

Nan. Sir, master Mosca call'd us out of doors,
And bid us all go play, and took the keys.

And.   Yes.

Volp. Did master Mosca take the keys? why, so!
I am farther in. These are my fine conceits!
I must be merry with a mischief to me!
What a vile wretch was I, that could not bear
My fortune soberly? I must ha' my crotchets
And my conundrums! well, go you and seek him:
His meaning may be truer than my fear.
Bid him he straight come to me to the court;

319

Thither will I, and, if 't be possible,
Unscrew my advocate, upon new hopes:
When I provok'd him, then I lost myself.   *[Exeunt.*

ACT V. SCENE VIII

The Senate House.

Avocatori, Bonario, Celia, Corbaccio, Corvino,
    Commandadori, Saffi, *etc., as before.*

1 Avoc. These things can ne'er be reconcil'd. He, here,
Professeth that the gentleman was wrong'd,
And that the gentlewoman was brought thither,
Forc'd by her husband, and there left.
Volt.   Most true.
Cel. How ready is heav'n to those that pray.
1 Avoc.   But that
Volpone would have ravish'd her, he holds
Utterly false; knowing his impotence.
Corv. Grave fathers, he is possess'd; again, I say,
Possess'd: nay, if there be possession and
Obsession, he has both.
3 Avoc.   Here comes our officer.

Enter Volpone.

Volp. The parasite will straight be here, grave fathers.
4 Avoc. You might invent some other name, sir varlet.
3 Avoc. Did not the notary meet him?
Volp.   Not that I know.
4 Avoc. His coming will clear all.
2 Avoc.   Yet it is misty.
Volt. May 't please your fatherhoods——
Volp. [*Whispers to* Voltore.]   Sir, the parasite
Will'd me to tell you that his master lives;
That you are still the man; your hopes the same;
And this was only a jest——
Volt.   How?

Volp.　　　　　　　　Sir, to try
If you were firm, and how you stood affected.

Volt. Art' sure he lives?

Volp.　　　　　　　　Do I live, sir?

Volt.　　　　　　　　O, me!
I was too violent.

Volp.　　　　　　Sir, you may redeem it:
They said you were possess'd; fall down, and seem so:
I'll help to make it good. [*Voltore falls.*] God bless the
　　man!
—Stop your wind hard, and swell—see, see, see, see!
He vomits crooked pins! his eyes are set,
Like a dead hare's hung in a poulter's shop!
His mouth's running away! do you see, signior?
Now 'tis in his belly.

Corv.　　　　　　Aye, the devil!　　　　　[*Aside.*

Volp. Now in his throat.

Corv.　　　　　　Aye, I perceive it plain.

Volp. 'Twill out, 'twill out; stand clear. See where it
　　flies!
In shape of a blue toad, with a bat's wings!
Do not you see it, sir?

Corb.　　　　　　What? I think I do.

Corv. 'Tis too manifest.

Volp.　　　　　Look! he comes t' himself!

Volt. Where am I?

Volp.　　　　　Take good heart, the worst is past, sir.
You are dispossess'd.

1 Avoc.　　　　What accident is this?

2 Avoc. Sudden, and full of wonder.

3 Avoc.　　　　　If he were
Possess'd, as it appears, all this is nothing.

Corv. He has been often subject to these fits.

1 Avoc. Show him that writing; do you know it, sir?

Volp. Deny it, sir, forswear it, know it not.

Volt. Yes, I do know it well, it is my hand:
But all that it contains is false.

Bon.　　　　　　O practice!

2 Avoc. What maze is this!

1 Avoc.   Is he not guilty, then,
Whom you there name the parasite?
Volt.   Grave fathers,
No more than his good patron, old Volpone.
4 Avoc. Why, he is dead?
Volt.   O no, my honour'd fathers.
He lives——
1 Avoc. How! lives?
Volt.   Lives.
2 Avoc.   This is subtler yet!
3 Avoc. You said he was dead.
Volt.   Never.
3 Avoc.   You said so.
Corv.   I heard so.
4 Avoc. Here comes the gentleman, make him way.

Enter Mosca.

3 Avoc.   A stool.
4 Avoc. A proper man! and were Volpone dead,
A fit match for my daughter.   [*Aside.*
3 Avoc.   Give him way.
Volp. Mosca, I was a'most lost, the advocate
Had betray'd all; but now it is recover'd:
All's o' the hinge again—say I am living.   [*Aside to* Mos.
Mos. What busy knave is this! most reverend fathers,
I sooner had attended your grave pleasures,
But that my order for the funeral
Of my dear patron did require me——
Volp.   Mosca!
Mos. Whom I intend to bury like a gentleman.
Volp. Aye, quick, and cozen me of all.
2 Avoc.   Still stranger!
More intricate!
1 Avoc.   And come about again!
4 Avoc. It is a match, my daughter is bestow'd. [*Aside.*
Mos. Will you gi' me half?   [*Aside to* Volpone.
Volp.   First, I'll be hang'd.
Mos.   I know.
Your voice is good, cry not so loud.

1 Avoc.   **Demand**
The advocate. Sir, did not you affirm
Volpone was alive?

Volp.   Yes, and he is;
This gent'man told me so.—Thou shalt have half. [*To* Mos.

   Mos. Whose drunkard is this same? speak some that
      know him:
I never saw his face.—I cannot now
Afford it you so cheap.   [*To* Volp.

   Volp.   No?

   1 Avoc.   What say you?

   Volt. The officer told me.

   Volp.   I did, grave fathers,
And will maintain he lives with mine own life.
And that this creature told me. I was born
With all good stars my enemies.

   Mos.   Most grave fathers,
If such an insolence as this must pass
Upon me, I am silent: 'twas not this
For which you sent, I hope.

   2 Avoc.   Take him away.

   Volp. Mosca.

   3 Avoc.   Let him be whipp'd.

   Volp.   Wilt thou betray me?
Cozen me?

   3 Avoc. And taught to bear himself
Toward a person of his rank.

   4 Avoc.   Away.

                      [*The officers seize* Volpone.

   Mos. I humbly thank your fatherhoods.

   Volp.   Soft, soft: whipp'd?
And lose all that I have? if I confess,
It cannot be much more.

   4 Avoc.   Sir, are you married?

   Volp. They'll be allied, anon; I must be resolute:
The Fox shall here uncase.   [*He puts off his disguise.*

   Mos.   Patron.

   Volp.   Nay, now,
My ruins shall not come alone; your match

I'll hinder sure: my substance shall not glue you,
Nor screw you into a family.

   Mos.   Why, patron!

   Volp. I am Volpone, and this is my knave;
                           [Pointing to Mosca.
This [*To* Volt.], his own knave; this [*To* Corb.], avarice's
   fool;
This [*To* Corv.], a chimera of wittol, fool, and knave;
And, reverend fathers, since we all can hope
Nought but a sentence, let's not now despair it.
You hear me brief.

   Corv.   May it please your fatherhoods——

   Com.   Silence.

   1 Avoc. The knot is now undone by miracle!

   2 Avoc. Nothing can be more clear.

   3 Avoc.   Or can more prove
These innocent.

   1 Avoc.   Give 'em their liberty.

   Bon. Heaven could not long let such gross crimes be
   hid.

   2 Avoc. If this be held the highway to get riches,
May I be poor.

   3 Avoc. This 's not the gain, but torment.

   1 Avoc. These possess wealth as sick men possess fevers,
Which trulier may be said to possess them.

   2 Avoc. Disrobe that parasite.

   Corv., Mos.   Most honour'd fathers.

   1 Avoc. Can you plead ought to stay the course of
   justice?
If you can, speak.

   Corv., Volt. We beg favour.

   Cel.   And mercy.

   1 Avoc. You hurt your innocence, suing for **the guilty**.
Stand forth; and first the parasite. You appear
T' have been the chiefest minister, if not plotter,
In all these lewd impostures; and now, lastly,
Have with your impudence abus'd the court,
And habit of a gentleman of Venice,
Being a fellow of no birth or blood:

For which, our sentence is, first thou be whipp'd;
Then live perpetual prisoner in our galleys.

   Volp. I thank you for him.

   Mos.   Bane to thy wolvish nature.

   1 Avoc. Deliver him to the *Saffi.*   [*Mosca is carried out.*

                          Thou, Volpone,
By blood and rank a gentleman, canst not fall
Under like censure; but our judgement on thee
Is that thy substance all be straight confiscate
To the hospital of the *Incurabili:*
And since the most was gotten by imposture,
By feigning lame, gout, palsy, and such diseases,
Thou art to lie in prison, cramp'd with irons,
Till thou be'st sick and lame indeed. Remove him.

                        [*He is taken from the Bar.*

   Volp. This is call'd mortifying of a Fox.

   1 Avoc. Thou, Voltore, to take away the scandal
Thou hast giv'n all worthy men of thy profession,
Art banish'd from their fellowship, and our state.
Corbaccio, bring him near. We here possess
Thy son of all thy state; and confine thee
To the monastery of San Spirito:
Where, since thou knew'st not how to live well here,
Thou shalt be learn'd to die well.

   Corb.   Ha! what said he?

   Com. You shall know anon, sir.

   1 Avoc.   Thou, Corvino, shalt
Be straight embark'd from thine own house, and row'd
Round about Venice through the grand canal,
Wearing a cap with fair long ass's ears,
Instead of horns: and so to mount, a paper
Pinn'd on thy breast, to the *berlina*——

   Corv.   Yes,
And have mine eyes beat out with stinking fish,
Bruis'd fruit, and rotten eggs—'Tis well. I am glad
I shall not see my shame yet.

   1 Avoc.   And to expiate
Thy wrongs done to thy wife, thou art to send her
Home to her father, with her dowry trebled:

And these are all your judgements.

   All.   Honour'd fathers.

1 Avoc. Which may not be revok'd. Now you begin,
When crimes are done and past, and to be punish'd,
To think what your crimes are: away with them.
Let all that see these vices thus rewarded,
Take heart, and love to study 'em. Mischiefs feed
Like beasts, till they be fat, and then they bleed.   *[Exeunt.*

        Volpone *comes forward.*

The seasoning of a play is the applause.
Now, though the Fox be punish'd by the laws,
He yet doth hope there is no suffering due,
For any fact which he hath done 'gainst you;
If there be, censure him: here he doubtful stands.
If not. fare jovially, and clap your hands.

                            [Exit.

THE END

THE ALCHEMIST

THE
ALCHEMIST.

VVritten
by
BEN. IONSON.

———Neque, me vt miretur turba, laboro:
Contentus paucis lectoribus.

LONDON,
Printed by *Thomas Snodham*, for *Walter Burre*,
and are to be sold by *Iohn Stepneth*, at the
West-end of Paules.
1612.

THE

TO THE LADY, MOST DESERVING HER NAME AND BLOOD:
Mary,
LADY WROTH.

MADAM,

IN the age of sacrifices, the truth of religion was not in the greatness and fat of the offerings, but in the devotion and zeal of the sacrificers: Else what could a handful of gums have done in the sight of a hecatomb? or how might I appear at this altar, except with those affections that no less love the light and witness, than they have the conscience of your virtue? If what I offer bear an acceptable odour and hold the first strength, it is your value of it which remembers where, when, and to whom it was kindled. Otherwise, as the times are, there comes rarely forth that thing, so full of authority or example, but by assiduity and custom, grows less and looses. This, yet, safe in your judgement (which is a SIDNEY's) is forbidden to speak more; lest it talk or look like one of the ambitious faces of the time: who, the more they paint, are the less themselves

Your Ladyship's
true honourer,
BEN. JONSON.

To the Reader

If thou beest more, thou art an Understander, and then I trust thee. If thou art one that tak'st up, and but a Pretender, beware at what hands thou receiv'st thy commodity; for thou wert never more fair in the way to be coz'ned than in this age in Poetry, especially in the Plays: wherein, now the concupiscence of dances and antics so reigneth, as to run away from nature, and be afraid of her, is the only point of art that tickles the spectators. But how out of purpose, and place, do I name art? when the professors are grown so obstinate contemners of it, and presumers on their own naturals, as they are deriders of all diligence that way, and, by simple mocking at the terms, when they understand not the things, think to get off wittily with their ignorance. Nay, they are esteem'd the more learned and sufficient for this, by the many, through their excellent vice of judgement. For they commend writers as they do fencers or wrestlers; who, if they come in robustuously, and put for it with a great deal of violence, are receiv'd for the braver fellows: when many times their own rudeness is the cause of their disgrace, and a little touch of their adversary gives all that boisterous force the foil. I deny not but that these men, who always seek to do more than enough, may sometime happen on something that is good and great; but very seldom: And when it comes it doth not recompense the rest of their ill. It sticks out perhaps, and is more eminent, because all is sordid and vile about it: as lights are more discern'd in a thick darkness than a faint shadow. I speak not this out of a hope to do good on any man against his will; for I know if it were put to the question of theirs and mine, the worse would find more suffrages: because the most favour common errors. But I give thee this warning, that there is a great difference between those that, to gain the opinion of copy, utter all they can, however unfitly; and those that use election, and a mean. For it is only the disease of the unskilful to think rude things greater than polish'd: or scatter'd more numerous than compos'd.

The Persons of the Play

SUBTLE, *the alchemist.*
FACE, *the house-keeper.*
DOL COMMON, *their colleague.*
DAPPER, *a clerk.*
DRUGGER, *a tobaccoman.*
LOVEWIT, *master of the house.*

EPICURE MAMMON, *a knight.*
SURLY, *a gamester.*
TRIBULATION, *a pastor of Amsterdam.*
ANANIAS, *a deacon there.*
KASTRIL, *the angry boy.*

DAME PLIANT, *his sister: a widow.*

NEIGHBOURS.

OFFICERS.

MUTES.

THE SCENE

LONDON

THE ARGUMENT

T HE sickness hot, a master quit, for fear,
H is house in town: and left one servant there.
E ase him corrupted, and gave means to know
A cheater, and his punk; who, now brought low,
L eaving their narrow practice, were become
C oz'ners at large: and, only wanting some
H ouse to set up, with him they here contract,
E ach for a share, and all begin to act.
M uch company they draw, and much abuse,
I n casting figures, telling fortunes, news,
S elling flies, flat bawdry with the stone:
T ill it, and they, and all in fume are gone.

PROLOGUE

FORTUNE, that favours fools, these two short hours
    We wish away; both for your sakes and ours,
Judging spectators: and desire in place,
    To th' author justice, to ourselves but grace.
Our scene is London 'cause we would make known
    No country's mirth is better than our own.
No clime breeds better matter; for your whore,
    Bawd, squire, impostor, many persons more,
Whose manners, now call'd humours, feed the stage:
    And which have still been subject for the rage
Or spleen of comic writers. Though this pen
    Did never aim to grieve, but better men;
How e'er the age he lives in, doth endure
    The vices that she breeds, above their cure.
But when the wholesome remedies are sweet,
    And, in their working, gain and profit meet,
He hopes to find no spirit so much diseas'd,
    But will, with such fair correctives, be pleas'd.
For here, he doth not fear who can apply.
    If there be any, that will sit so nigh
Unto the stream to look what it doth run,
    They shall find things, they'd think, or wish, were done,
They are so natural follies, but so shown
    As even the doers may see, and yet not own.

ACT I. SCENE I

A room in Lovewit's *house.*

Enter Face, *in a captain's uniform, with his sword drawn, and* Subtle, *with a vial, quarrelling, and followed by* Dol Common.

Face. Believe't, I will.
Subt.   Thy worst. I fart at thee.
Dol. Ha' you your wits? Why, gentlemen! for love——
Face. Sirrah, I'll strip you——
Subt.   What to do? lick figs
Out at my——
Face.   Rogue, rogue, out of all your sleights.
Dol. Nay, look ye! Sovereign, general, are you madmen?
Subt. O, let the wild sheep loose. I'll gum your silks
With good strong water, an' you come.
Dol.   Will you have
The neighbours hear you? Will you betray all? Hark,
I hear somebody.
Face.   Sirrah——
Subt.   I shall mar
All that the tailor has made, if you approach.
Face. You most notorious whelp, you insolent slave,
Dare you do this?
Subt.   Yes faith, yes faith.
Face.   Why! who
Am I, my mongrel? Who am I?
Subt.   I'll tell you.
Since you know not yourself——
Face.   Speak lower, rogue.
Subt. Yes. You were once (time's not long past) the good,
Honest, plain, livery-three-pound-thrum; that kept
Your master's worship's house, here, in the Friars
For the vacations——
Face.   Will you be so loud?
Subt. Since, by my means, translated suburb-captain.

Face. By your means, doctor dog?

Subt.   Within man's memory
All this, I speak of.

Face.   Why, I pray you, have I
Been countenanc'd by you? or you by me?
Do but collect, sir, where I met you first.

Subt. I do not hear well.

Face.   Not of this, I think it.
But I shall put you in mind, sir;—at Pie Corner,
Taking your meal of steam in from cooks' stalls,
Where, like the father of hunger, you did walk
Piteously costive, with your pinch'd-horn-nose
And your complexion of the Roman wash,
Stuck full of black and melancholic worms,
Like powder-corns shot at th' artillery yard.

Subt. I wish you could advance your voice a little.

Face. When you went pinn'd up in the several rags
You had rak'd and pick'd from dunghills, before day,
Your feet in mouldy slippers, for your kibes,
A felt of rug and a thin threaden cloak,
That scarce would cover your no buttocks——

Subt.   So, sir!

Face. When all your alchemy and your algebra,
Your minerals, vegetals, and animals,
Your conjuring, cozening, and your dozen of trades,
Could not relieve your corpse with so much linen
Would make you tinder but to see a fire;
I ga' you count'nance, credit for your coals,
Your stills, your glasses, your materials,
Built you a furnace, drew you customers,
Advanc'd all your black arts; lent you, beside,
A house to practise in——

Subt.   Your master's house?

Face. Where you have studied the more thriving skill
Of bawdry since.

Subt.   Yes, in your master's house.
You, and the rats here, kept possession.
Make it not strange. I know yo' were one could keep
The Buttery-hatch still lock'd, and save the chippings,

Sell the dole beer to aqua-vitæ men,
The which, together with your Christmas vails,
At post-and-pair, your letting out of counters,
Made you a pretty stock, some twenty marks,
And gave you credit, to converse with cobwebs,
Here, since your mistress' death hath broke up house.

   Face. You might talk softlier, rascal.

   Subt.   No, you scarab,
I'll thunder you in pieces. I will teach you
How to beware to tempt a Fury again
That carries tempest in his hand and voice.

   Face. The place has made you valiant.

   Subt.   No, your clothes.
Thou vermin, have I ta'en thee out of dung,
So poor, so wretched, when no living thing
Would keep thee company but a spider, or worse?
Rais'd thee from brooms and dust and watering plots?
Sublim'd thee, and exalted thee, and fix'd thee
I' the third region call'd our state of grace?
Wrought thee to spirit, to quintessence, with pains
Would twice have won me the Philosopher's work?
Put thee in words and fashion? made thee fit
For more than ordinary fellowships?
Giv'n thee thy oaths, thy quarrelling dimensions?
Thy rules to cheat at horse-race, cock-pit, cards,
Dice, or what ever gallant tincture else?
Made thee a second in mine own great art?
And have I this for thank? Do you rebel?
Do you fly out i' the projection?
Would you be gone now?

   Dol.   Gentlemen, what mean you?
Will you mar all?

   Subt.   Slave, thou hadst had no name——

   Dol. Will you undo yourselves with civil war?

   Subt. Never been known, past *equi clibanum*,
The heat of horse-dung, underground, in cellars,
Or an ale-house, darker than deaf John's; been lost
To all mankind but laundresses and tapsters,
Had not I been.

Dol.   Do you know who hears you, sovereign?

Face. Sirrah——

Dol. Nay, general, I thought you were civil——

Face. I shall turn desperate, if you grow thus loud.

Subt. And hang thyself, I care not.

Face.   Hang thee, collier,
And all thy pots and pans, in picture, I will,
Since thou hast mov'd me.——

Dol.   O, this'll o'erthrow all. [*Aside.*

Face. Write thee up bawd, in Paul's; have all thy tricks
Of cozening with a hollow cole, dust, scrapings,
Searching for things lost, with a sieve and shears,
Erecting figures in your rows of houses,
And taking in of shadows with a glass,
Told in red letters: and a face cut for thee,
Worse than Gamaliel Ratsey's.

Dol.   Are you sound?
Ha' you your senses, masters?

Face.   I will have
A book, but barely reckoning thy impostures,
Shall prove a true Philosopher's Stone to printers.

Subt. Away, you trencher rascal.

Face.   Out, you dog-leech,
The vomit of all prisons——

Dol.   Will you be
Your own destructions, gentlemen?

Face.   Still spew'd out
For lying too heavy o' the basket.

Subt.   Cheater!

Face. Bawd!

Subt.   Cow-herd!

Face.   Conjurer!

Subt.   Cut-purse!

Face.   Witch!

Dol.   O me!
We are ruin'd! lost! Ha' you no more regard
To your reputations? Where's your judgement? 'Slight,
Have yet some care of me, o' your republic——

Face. Away, this brach! I'll bring thee, rogue, within

339

The statute of sorcery, *tricesimo tertio*,
Of Harry the Eighth: aye, and perhaps thy neck
Within a noose, for laundering gold, and barbing it.

   Dol. [*Snatches* Face's *sword.*] You'll bring your head
     within a cockscomb, will you?
And you, sir, with your menstrue [*Dashes* Subtle's *vial out
     of his hand*]—gather it up.
'Sdeath, you abominable pair of stinkards,
Leave off your barking, and grow one again,
Or, by the light that shines, I'll cut your throats.
I'll not be made a prey unto the marshal
For ne'er a snarling dog-bolt o' you both.
Ha' you together cozen'd all this while,
And all the world, and shall it now be said
Yo' have made most courteous shift to cozen yourselves?
You will accuse him? You will bring him in   [*To* Face.
Within the statute? Who shall take your word?
A whoreson, upstart, apocryphal captain,
Whom not a puritan in Blackfriars will trust
So much as for a feather! And you, too,   [*To* Subtle.
Will give the cause, forsooth? You will insult,
And claim a primacy in the divisions?
You must be chief? as if you only had
The powder to project with? and the work
Were not begun out of equality?
The venture tripartite? All things in common?
Without priority? 'Sdeath, you perpetual curs,
Fall to your couples again, and cozen kindly,
And heartily, and lovingly, as you should,
And lose not the beginning of a term,
Or, by this hand, I shall grow factious too,
And take my part, and quit you.

   Face.   'Tis his fault,
He ever murmurs and objects his pains,
And says the weight of all lies upon him.

   Subt. Why, so it does.

   Dol.   How does it? Do not we
Sustain our parts?

   Subt.   Yes, but they are not equal.

Dol. Why, if your part exceed to-day, I hope
Ours may to-morrow match it.

Subt.   Aye, they may.

Dol. May, murmuring mastiff? Aye, and do. Death on
me!
Help me to throttle him.   [*Seizes* Subtle *by the throat.*

Subt.   Dorothy, mistress Dorothy,
'Ods precious, I'll do anything. What do you mean?

Dol. Because o' your fermentation and cibation?

Subt. Not I, by heaven——

Dol.   Your Sol and Luna—help me. [*To* Face.

Subt. Would I were hang'd then. I'll conform myself.

Dol. Will you, sir? Do so then, and quickly: swear.

Subt. What should I swear?

Dol.   To leave your faction, sir.
And labour, kindly, in the common work.

Subt. Let me not breathe, if I meant ought beside.
I only us'd those speeches as a spur
To him.

Dol. I hope we need no spurs, sir. Do we?

Face. 'Slid, prove to-day who shall shark best.

Subt.   Agreed.

Dol. Yes, and work close, and friendly.

Subt.   'Slight, the knot
Shall grow the stronger, for this breach with me.

Dol. Why, so, my good baboons! Shall we go make
A sort of sober, scurvy, precise neighbours,
That scarce have smil'd twice, sin' the king came in,
A feast of laughter at our follies? Rascals
Would run themselves from breath, to see me ride,
Or you t' have but a hole to thrust your heads in,
For which you should pay ear-rent? No, agree.
And may Don Provost ride a feasting long,
In his old velvet jerkin and stain'd scarfs,
My noble sovereign, and worthy general,
Ere we contribute a new crewel garter
To his most worsted worship.

Subt.   Royal Dol!
Spoken like Claridiana and thyself!

Face. For which, at supper, thou shalt sit in triumph,
And not be styl'd Dol Common, but Dol Proper,
Dol Singular: the longest cut, at night,
Shall draw thee for his Dol Particular. [*Bell rings without.*

Subt. Who's that? one rings. To the window, Dol: [*Exit
Dol.*] Pray heav'n,
The master do not trouble us this quarter.

Face. O, fear not him. While there dies one a week
O' the plague, he's safe from thinking toward London.
Beside, he's busy at his hop-yards now:
I had a letter from him. If he do,
He'll send such word, for airing o' the house,
As you shall have sufficient time to quit it:
Though we break up a fortnight 'tis no matter.

Re-enter Dol.

Subt. Who is it, Dol?

Dol.   A fine young quodling.

Face.   O,
My lawyer's clerk, I lighted on, last night,
In Holborn at the Dagger. He would have
(I told you of him) a familiar
To rifle with at horses, and win cups.

Dol. O, let him in.

Subt.   Stay. Who shall do't?

Face.   Get you
Your robes on. I will meet him, as going out.

Dol. And what shall I do?

Face.   Not be seen, away.
Seem you very reserv'd.   [*Exit Dol.*

Subt. Enough.   [*Exit.*

Face.   God b' w' you, sir.
I pray you, let him know that I was here.
His name is Dapper. I would gladly have stay'd, but——

Dap. [*Without.*] Captain, I am here.

Face.   Who's that? He's come, I think, doctor.

Enter Dapper.

Good faith, sir, I was going away.

Dap.   In truth,
I am very sorry, captain.

Face.   But I thought
Sure I should meet you.

Dap.   Aye, I am very glad.
I had a scurvy writ or two to make,
And I had lent my watch last night to one
That dines to-day at the sheriffs: and so was robb'd
Of my pass-time.

Re-enter Subtle in his velvet cap and gown.

                    Is this the cunning man?

Face. This is his worship.

Dap.   Is he a doctor?

Face.   Yes.

Dap. And ha' you broke with him, captain?

Face.   Aye.

Dap.   And how?

Face. Faith, he does make the matter, sir, so dainty,
I know not what to say——

Dap.   Not so, good captain.

Face. Would I were fairly rid on it, believe me.

Dap. Nay, now you grieve me, sir. Why should you
    wish so?
I dare assure you, I'll not be ungrateful.

Face. I cannot think you will, sir. But the law
Is such a thing——And then, he says, Read's matter
Falling so lately——

Dap.   Read? He was an ass,
And dealt, sir, with a fool.

Face.   It was a clerk, sir.

Dap. A clerk?

Face.   Nay, hear me, sir, you know the law
Better, I think——

Dap.   I should, sir, and the danger.
You know I show'd the statute to you?

Face.   You did so.

Dap. And will I tell, then? By this hand of flesh,

343

Would it might never write good court-hand more,
If I discover. What do you think of me,
That I am a chiaus?

 Face.   What's that?

 Dap.   The Turk was here——
As one would say, do you think I am a Turk?

 Face. I'll tell the doctor so.

 Dap.   Do, good sweet captain.

 Face. Come, noble doctor, 'pray thee, let's prevail;
This is the gentleman, and he is no chiaus.

 Subt. Captain, I have return'd you all my answer.
I would do much, sir, for your love—but this
I neither may, nor can.

 Face.   Tut, do not say so.
You deal now with a noble fellow, doctor,
One that will thank you richly; and he's no chiaus:
Let that, sir, move you.

 Subt.   Pray you, forbear——

 Face.   He has
Four angels, here——

 Subt.   You do me wrong, good sir.

 Face. Doctor, wherein? To tempt you with these spirits?

 Subt. To tempt my arm and love, sir, to my peril.
'Fore heav'n, I scarce can think you are my friend,
That so would draw me to apparent danger.

 Face. I draw you? A horse draw you, and a halter,—
You, and your flies together——

 Dap.   Nay, good captain.

 Face. That know no difference of men.

 Subt.   Good words, sir.

 Face. Good deeds, sir doctor dogs-meat. 'Slight I bring
you
No cheating Clim o' the Cloughs, or Claribels,
That look as big as five-and-fifty, and flush,
And spit out secrets like hot custard——

 Dap.   Captain!

 Face. Nor any melancholic underscribe,
Shall tell the vicar; but a special gentle,
That is the heir to forty marks a year,

Consorts with the small poets of the time,
Is the sole hope of his old grandmother,
That knows the law, and writes you six fair hands,
Is a fine clerk, and has his cyphering perfect,
Will take his oath, o' the Greek Xenophon
If need be, in his pocket: and can court
His mistress out of Ovid.

 Dap.   Nay, dear captain.

 Face. Did you not tell me so?

 Dap.   Yes, but I'd ha' you
Use master doctor with some more respect.

 Face. Hang him, proud stag, with his broad velvet head.
But for your sake, I'd choke ere I would change
An article of breath with such a puck-fist——
Come, let's be gone.

 Subt.   Pray you, let me speak with you.

 Dap. His worship calls you, captain.

 Face.   I am sorry
I e'er embark'd myself in such a business.

 Dap. Nay, good sir. He did call you.

 Face.   Will he take, then?

 Subt. First, hear me——

 Face.   Not a syllable, 'less you take.

 Subt. Pray ye, sir——

 Face.   Upon no terms, but an *assumpsit*.

 Subt. Your humour must be law. [*He takes the money.*

 Face.   Why now, sir, talk.
Now, I dare hear you with mine honour. Speak.
So may this gentleman too.

 Subt.   Why, sir——

 Face.   No whispering.

 Subt. 'Fore heav'n, you do not apprehend the loss
You do yourself in this.

 Face.   Wherein? For what?

 Subt. Marry, to be so importunate for one,
That, when he has it, will undo you all;
He'll win up all the money i' the town.

 Face. How!

 Subt.   Yes. And blow up gamester after gamester,

As they do crackers in a puppet-play.
If I do give him a familiar,
Give you to him all you play for; never set him:
For he will have it.

    Face.   Y' are mistaken, doctor.
Why, he does ask one but for cups and horses,
A rifling fly: none o' your great familiars.

    Dap. Yes, captain, I would have it for all games.

    Subt. I told you so.

    Face. [*To* Dapper.] 'Slight, that's a new business!
I understood you, a tame bird, to fly
Twice in a term, or so; on Friday-nights
When you had left the offices: for a nag
Of forty or fifty shillings.

    Dap.   Aye, 'tis true, sir,
But I do think, now, I shall leave the law,
And therefore——

    Face.   Why, this changes quite the case!
Do' you think that I dare move him?

    Dap.   If you please, sir,
All's one to him, I see.

    Face.   What! for that money?
I cannot with my conscience. Nor should you
Make the request, methinks.

    Dap.   No, sir, I mean
To add consideration.

    Face.   Why, then, sir,
I'll try. Say, that it were for all games, doctor?

    Subt. I say, then, not a mouth shall eat for him
At any ordinary but o' the score
That is a gaming mouth, conceive me.

    Face.   Indeed!

    Subt. He'll draw you all the treasure of the realm,
If it be set him.

    Face.   Speak you this from art?

    Subt. Aye, sir, and reason too: the ground of art.
He's o' the only best complexion
The queen of Faery loves.

    Face.   What! is he?

Subt.   Peace.

He'll overhear you. Sir, should she but see him——

    Face.   **What?**

    Subt. Do not you tell him.

    Face.   Will he win at cards too?

    Subt. The spirits of dead Holland, living Isaac,

You'd swear, were in him: such a vigorous luck

As cannot be resisted. 'Slight, he'll put

Six o' your gallants to a cloak, indeed.

    Face. A strange success, that some man shall be born
to!

    Subt. He hears you, man——

    Dap.   Sir, I'll not be ingrateful.

    Face. Faith. I have a confidence in his good nature:

You hear, he says he will not be ingrateful.

    Subt. Why, as you please, my venture follows yours.

    Face. Troth, do it, doctor. Think him trusty, and make
him.

He may make us both happy in an hour:

Win some five thousand pound, and send us two on 't.

    Dap. Believe it, and I will, sir.

    Face.   And you shall, sir.

You have heard all?

    Dap. No, what was't? [*Face takes him aside.*] Nothing,

I, sir.

    Face. Nothing?

    Dap.   A little, sir.

    Face.   Well, a rare star

Reign'd at your birth.

    Dap.   At mine, sir? no.

    Face.   The doctor

Swears that you are——

    Subt.   Nay, captain, you'll tell all now.

    Face. Allied to the queen of Faery.

    Dap.   Who? that I am?

Believe it, no such matter——

    Face.   Yes, and that

You were born with a caul o' your head.

    Dap.   Who says so?

524

M

Face.   **Come.**
You know it well enough, though you dissemble it.

Dap. I' fac, I do not. You are mistaken.

Face.   **How!**
Swear by your fac? and in a thing so known
Unto the doctor? How shall we, sir, trust you
I' the other matter? Can we ever think,
When you have won five or six thousand pound,
You'll send us shares in 't, by this rate?

Dap.   By Jove, sir,
I'll win ten thousand pound, and send you half.
I' fac's no oath.

Subt.   No, no, he did but jest.

Face. Go to. Go thank the doctor. He's your friend
To take it so.

Dap.   I thank his worship.

Face.   **So?**
Another angel.

Dap.   Must I?

Face.   Must you? 'Slight,
What else is thanks? will you be trivial? Doctor,
                  [*Dapper gives him the money.*
When must he come for his familiar?

Dap. Shall I not ha' it with me?

Subt.   O, good sir!
There must a world of ceremonies pass,
You must be bath'd and fumigated, first;
Besides, the Queen of Faery does not rise
Till it be noon.

Face.   Not if she danc'd to-night.

Subt. And she must bless it.

Face.   Did you never see
Her royal grace yet?

Dap.   Whom?

Face.   Your aunt of Faery?

Subt. Not since she kiss'd him in the cradle, captain.
I can resolve you that.

Face.   Well, see her grace
Whate'er it cost you, for a thing that I know!

It will be somewhat hard to compass: but.
However, see her. You are made, believe it,
If you can see her. Her grace is a lone woman,
And very rich, and if she take a fancy
She will do strange things. See her, at any hand.
'Slid, she may hap to leave you all she has!
It is the doctor's fear.

    Dap.   How will't be done, then?

    Face. Let me alone, take you no thought. Do you
But say to me, 'Captain, I'll see her grace'.

    Dap. Captain, I'll see her grace.

    Face.   Enough. [*Knocking without.*

    Subt.   Who's there?

Anon. Conduct him forth, by the back way, [*Aside to* Face.
Sir, against one o'clock, prepare yourself.
Till when you must be fasting; only take
Three drops of vinegar in at your nose;
Two at your mouth; and one at either ear;
Then bathe your fingers' ends, and wash your eyes;
To sharpen your five senses, and, cry *hum*,
Thrice; and then *buz* as often; and then come.   [*Exit.*

    Face. Can you remember this?

    Dap.   I warrant you.

    Face. Well, then, away. 'Tis but your bestowing
Some twenty nobles 'mong her grace's servants;
And put on a clean shirt: You do not know
What grace her grace may do you in clean linen.

                        [*Exeunt* Face *and* Dapper.

    Subt. [*Within.*] Come in! Good wives, I pray you for-
      bear me, now.
Troth I can do you no good till afternoon.

      Re-enters, followed by Drugger.

What is your name, say you, Abel Drugger?

    Dru.   Yes, sir.

    Subt. A seller of tobacco?

    Dru.   Yes, sir.

    Subt.   'Umph.
Free of the grocers?

Dru.   Aye, and't please you.

Subt.   Well——

Your business, Abel?

Dru.   This, and't please your worship;
I am a young beginner, and am building
Of a new shop, and't like your worship; just
At corner of a street: (Here's the plot on't.)
And I would know, by art, sir, of your worship,
Which way I should make my door, by necromancy,
And where my shelves. And which should be for boxes,
And which for pots. I would be glad to thrive, sir.
And I was wish'd to your worship by a gentleman,
One Captain Face, that says you know men's planets,
And their good angels, and their bad.

Subt.   I do,
If I do see 'em——   [*Re-enter Face.*
Face.   What! my honest Abel?
Thou art well met, here!

Dru.   Troth, sir, I was speaking,
Just as your worship came here, of your worship.
I pray you, speak for me to master doctor.

Face. He shall do anything. Doctor, do you hear?
This is my friend, Abel, an honest fellow,
He lets me have good tobacco, and he does not
Sophisticate it with sack-lees or oil,
Nor washes it in muscadel and grains,
Nor buries it in gravel, under ground,
Wrapp'd up in greasy leather, or piss'd clouts:
But keeps it in fine lilly-pots, that, open'd,
Smell like conserve of roses, or French beans.
He has his maple block, his silver tongs,
Winchester pipes, and fire of juniper.
A neat spruce-honest fellow, and no goldsmith.

Subt. He's a fortunate fellow, that I am sure on——
Face. Already, sir, ha' you found it? Lo' thee, Abel!
Subt. And in right way toward riches——
Face.   Sir.
Subt.   This summer.
He will be of the clothing of his company:

And next spring, call'd to the scarlet. Spend what he can.

   Face. What, and so little beard?

   Subt.   Sir, you must think,
He may have a receipt to make hair come.
But he'll be wise, preserve his youth, and fine for't:
His fortune looks for him another way.

   Face. 'Slid, Doctor! How canst thou know this so soon?
I am amus'd at that!

   Subt.   By a rule, captain,
In metoposcopy which I do work by,
A certain star i' the forehead, which you see not.
Your chestnut or your olive-colour'd face
Does never fail: and your long ear doth promise.
I knew't by certain spots, too, in his teeth,
And on the nail of his Mercurial finger.

   Face. Which finger's that?

   Subt.   His little finger. Look.
You were born upon a Wednesday?

   Dru.   Yes, indeed, sir.

   Subt. The thumb, in chiromancy, we give Venus;
The forefinger to Jove; the midst to Saturn;
The ring to Sol; the least to Mercury,
Who was the lord, sir, of his horoscope.
His house of life being Libra, which foreshow'd
He should be a merchant, and should trade with balance.

   Face. Why, this is strange! Is't not, honest Nab?

   Subt. There is a ship now, coming from Ormus,
That shall yield him such a commodity
Of drugs—This is the west, and this the south?

   Dru. Yes, sir.

   Subt.   And those are your two sides?

   Dru.   Aye, sir.

   Subt. Make me your door then, south; your broad side,
   west:
And, on the eastside of your shop, aloft,
Write *Mathlai*, *Tarmiel* and *Baraborat*;
Upon the north part, *Rael*, *Velel*, *Thiel*.
They are the names of those Mercurial spirits
That do fright flies from boxes.

Dru.　　　　　　　　　Yes, sir.

Subt.　　　　　　　　　　　　And

Beneath your threshold, bury me a loadstone

To draw in gallants that wear spurs. The rest,

They'll seem to follow.

Face.　　　　　　　That's a secret, Nab!

Subt. And, on your stall, a puppet, with a vice,

And a court-fucus to call city-dames.

You shall deal much with minerals.

Dru.　　　　　　　　　　Sir, I have

At home, already——

Subt.　　　　　　I know you have arsenic,

Vitriol, sal-tartar, argaile, alkali,

Cinoper: I know all. This fellow, captain,

Will come in time to be a great distiller,

And give a 'say (I will not say directly,

But very fair) at the Philosopher's Stone.

Face. Why, how now, Abel! Is this true?

Dru.　　　　　　　　　Good Captain, *[Aside to* Face.

What must I give?

Face.　　　　　Nay, I'll not counsel thee.

Thou hear'st what wealth (he says, Spend what thou canst)

Th'art like to come too.

Dru.　　　　　I would gi' him a crown.

Face. A crown! and toward such a fortune? Heart,

Thou shalt rather gi' him thy shop. No gold about thee?

Dru. Yes, I have a portague, I ha' kept this half year.

Face. Out on thee, Nab! 'Slight, there was such an

offer——

'Shalt keep 't no longer, I'll gi' it him for thee?

Doctor, Nab prays your worship to drink this: and swears

He will appear more grateful, as your skill

Does raise him in the world.

Dru.　　　　　　I would entreat

Another favour of his worship.

Face.　　　　　　　What is 't, Nab?

Dru. But to look over, sir, my almanac,

And cross out my ill-days, that I may neither

Bargain nor trust upon them.

Face. That he shall, Nab.
Leave it, it shall be done, 'gainst afternoon.
  Subt. And a direction for his shelves.
  Face. Now, Nab?
Art thou well pleas'd, Nab?
  Dru. Thank, sir, both your worships. [*Exit* Drugger.
  Face. Away.
Why, now, you smoky persecutor of nature!
Now, do you see, that something's to be done,
Beside your beech-coal, and your corsive waters,
Your crosslets, crucibles, and cucurbites?
You must have stuff brought home to you to work on?
And yet you think, I am at no expense,
In searching out these veins, then following 'em,
Then trying 'em out. 'Fore God, my intelligence
Costs me more money than my share oft comes to,
In these rare works.
  Subt. You are pleasant, sir.

Re-enter Dol.

How now?
What says my dainty Dolkin?
  Dol. Yonder fish-wife
Will not away. And there's your giantess,
The bawd of Lambeth.
  Subt. Heart, I cannot speak with 'em.
  Dol. Not afore night, I have told 'em, in a voice
Thorough the trunk, like one of your familiars.
But I have spied Sir Epicure Mammon——
  Subt. Where?
  Dol. Coming along at far end of the lane,
Slow of his feet but earnest of his tongue,
To one that's with him.
  Subt. Face, go you, and shift. [*Exit* Face.
Dol, you must presently make ready, too——
  Dol. Why, what's the matter?
  Subt. O, I did look for him
With the sun's rising: Marvel he could sleep!
This is the day I am to perfect for him

The magisterium, our great work, the Stone;
And yield it, made, into his hands: of which
He has, this month, talk'd as he were possess'd.
And now he's dealing pieces on't away.
Methinks I see him entering ordinaries,
Dispensing for the pox; and plaguy houses,
Reaching his dose; walking Moorfields for lepers;
And offering citizen's wives pomander-bracelets
As his preservative, made of the elixir;
Searching the spittle to make old bawds young;
And the highways for beggars to make rich:
I see no end of his labours. He will make
Nature asham'd of her long sleep: when Art,
Who's but a step-dame, shall do more than she,
In her best love to mankind, ever could.
If his dream last, he'll turn the age to gold.   [*Exeunt.*

ACT II. SCENE I

An outer room in Lovewit's *house.*

Enter Sir Epicure Mammon *and* Surly.

Mam. Come on, sir. Now you set your foot on shore
In *Novo Orbe*; here's the rich Peru:
And there within, sir, are the golden mines,
Great Solomon's Ophir! He was sailing to't,
Three years, but was reach'd it in ten months.
This is the day wherein, to all my friends,
I will pronounce the happy word, Be rich.
This day, you shall be *spectatissimi.*
You shall no more deal with the hollow dye
Or the frail card. No more be at charge of keeping
The livery-punk for the young heir, that must
Seal, at all hours, in his shirt. No more,
If he deny, ha' him beaten to't, as he is
That brings him the commodity. No more
Shall thirst of satin, or the covetous hunger
Of velvet entrails, for a rude-spun cloak,

To be displayed at Madam Augusta's, make
The sons of Sword and Hazard fall before
The golden calf, and on their knees, whole nights,
Commit idolatry with wine and trumpets:
Or go a feasting after drum and ensign.
No more of this. You shall start up young Viceroys,
And have your punk and punketees, my Surly.
And unto thee I speak it first, 'Be rich'.
Where is my Subtle, there? Within, ho?

    Face. [*Within.*]   Sir,
He'll come to you, by and by.

    Mam.   That's his fire-drake,
His Lungs, his Zephyrus, he that puffs his coals
Till he firk nature up in her own centre.
You are not faithful, sir. This night I'll change
All that is metal in my house to gold.
And early in the morning will I send
To all the plumbers and the pewterers,
And buy their tin and lead up: and to Lothbury,
For all the copper.

    Sur.   What, and turn that too?

    Mam. Yes, and I'll purchase Devonshire and Cornwall
And make them perfect Indies! You admire now?

    Sur.   No faith.

    Mam. But when you see th' effects of the great med'cine!
Of which one part projected on a hundred
Of Mercury or Venus or the moon,
Shall turn it to as many of the sun;
Nay, to a thousand, so *ad infinitum*:
You will believe me.

    Sur.   Yes, when I see 't, I will.
But, if my eyes do cozen me so, and I
Giving 'em no occasion, sure I'll have
A whore, shall piss 'em out next day.

    Mam.   Ha! Why?
Do you think I fable with you? I assure you,
He that has once the flower of the sun,
The perfect ruby which we call elixir,
Not only can do that, but by its virtue,

Can confer honour, love, respect, long life,
Give safety, valour: yea, and victory,
To whom he will. In eight and twenty days,
I'll make an old man of fourscore, a child.

Sur. No doubt, he's that already.

Mam.   Nay, I mean
Restore his years, renew him, like an eagle,
To the fifth age; make him get sons and daughters,
Young giants; as our philosophers have done,
The ancient patriarchs afore the flood,
But taking, once a week, on a knife's point,
The quantity of a grain of mustard of it:
Become stout Marses and beget young Cupids.

Sur. The decay'd vestals of Pict-hatch would thank you,
That keep the fire alive there.

Mam.   'Tis the secret
Of nature, naturiz'd 'gainst all infections,
Cures all diseases coming of all causes,
A month's grief in a day; a year's, in twelve:
And, of what age soever, in a month.
Past all the doses of your drugging doctors.
I'll undertake, withal, to fright the plague
Out o' the kingdom in three months.

Sur.   And I'll
Be bound, the players shall sing your praises, then,
Without their poets.

Mam.   Sir, I'll do 't. Meantime,
I'll give away so much unto my man;
Shall serve th' whole city with preservative,
Weekly, each house his dose, and at the rate——

Sur. As he that built the water-work does with water?

Mam. You are incredulous.

Sur.   Faith, I have a humour.
I would not willingly be gull'd. Your Stone
Cannot transmute me.

Mam.   Pertinax, my Surly.
Will you believe antiquity? records?
I'll show you a book, where Moses and his sister,
And Solomon have written of the art;

Aye, and a treatise penn'd by Adam.

 Sur.   How!

 Mam. O' the Philosopher's Stone, and in High Dutch.

 Sur. Did Adam write, sir, in High Dutch?

 Mam.   He did:

Which proves it was the primitive tongue.

 Sur.   What paper?

 Mam. On cedar board.

 Sur.   O that, indeed, they say,

Will last 'gainst worms.

 Mam.   'Tis like your Irish wood,

'Gainst cobwebs. I have a piece of Jason's fleece, too,

Which was no other than a book of alchemy

Writ in large sheepskin, a good fat ram-vellum.

Such was Pythagoras' thigh, Pandora's tub;

And all that fable of Medea's charms,

The manner of our work: the bulls, our furnace,

Still breathing fire; our argent-vive, the dragon:

The dragon's teeth, mercury sublimate,

That keeps the whiteness, hardness, and the biting;

And they are gather'd into Jason's helm,

Th' alembic, and then sow'd in Mars his field,

And thence sublim'd so often, till they are fix'd.

Both this, th' Hesperian garden, Cadmus' story,

Jove's shower, the boon of Midas, Argus' eyes,

Boccace his Demogorgon, thousands more,

All abstract riddles of our Stone. How now?

Enter Face as a servant.

Do we succeed? Is our day come? and holds it?

 Face. The evening will set red upon you, sir;

You have colour for it, crimson: the red ferment

Has done his office. Three hours hence, prepare you

To see projection.

 Mam.   Pertinax, my Surly

Again I say to thee aloud: Be rich.

This day thou shalt have ingots: and, to-morrow,

Give lords th' affront. Is it, my Zephyrus, right?

Blushes the bolt's-head?

Face.   Like a wench with child, sir,
That were but now discover'd to her master.

Mam. Excellent witty Lungs! My only care is,
Where to get stuff enough now, to project on,
This town will not half serve me.

Face.   No, sir? Buy
The covering off o' churches.

Mam.   That's true.

Face.   Yes.
Let 'em stand bare, as do their auditory
Or cap 'em new with shingles.

Mam.   No, good thatch:
Thatch will lie light upo' the rafters, Lungs.
Lungs, I will manumit thee from the furnace;
I will restore thee thy complexion, Puff,
Lost in the embers; and repair this brain,
Hurt wi' the fume o' the metals.

Face.   I have blown, sir,
Hard, for your worship; thrown by many a coal,
When 'twas not beech; weigh'd those I put in, just
To keep your heat still even; these bleared-eyes
Have wak'd to read your several colours, sir,
Of the pale citron, the green lion, the crow,
The peacock's tail, the plumed swan.

Mam.   And, lastly,
Thou hast descried the flower, the *sanguis agni?*

Face. Yes, sir.

Mam. Where's master?

Face.   At's prayers, sir, he,
Good man, he's doing his devotions,
For the success.

Mam.   Lungs, I will set a period
To all thy labours: Thou shalt be the master
Of my seraglio.

Face.   Good, sir.

Mam.   But do you hear?
I'll geld you, Lungs.

Face.   Yes, sir.

Mam.   For I do mean

To have a list of wives and concubines,
Equal with Solomon, who had the Stone
Alike with me: and I will make me a back
With the elixir, that shall be as tough
As Hercules to encounter fifty a night.
Th'art sure, thou saw'st it blood?

Face.   Both blood and spirit, sir.

Mam. I will have all my beds blown up, not stuff'd;
Down is too hard. And then, mine oval room
Fill'd with such pictures as Tiberius took
From Elephantis: and dull Aretine
But coldly imitated. Then, my glasses,
Cut in more subtle angles, to disperse
And multiply the figures, as I walk
Naked between my *succubæ*. My mists
I'll have of perfume, vapour'd 'bout the room,
To lose ourselves in; and my baths, like pits
To fall into: from whence we will come forth,
And roll us dry in gossamer and roses.
(Is it arriv'd at ruby?)—Where I spy
A wealthy citizen, or rich lawyer,
Have a sublim'd pure wife, unto that fellow
I'll send a thousand pound to be my cuckold.

Face. And I shall carry it?

Mam.   No. I'll ha' no bawds,
But fathers and mothers. They will do it best.
Best of all others. And my flatterers
Shall be the pure and gravest of divines,
That I can get for money. My mere fools,
Eloquent burgesses, and then my poets,
The same that writ so subtly of the fart,
Whom I will entertain still for that subject.
The few that would give out themselves to be
Court and town-stallions, and, each-where, bely
Ladies, who are known most innocent, for them;
Those will I beg to make me eunuchs of:
And they shall fan me with ten ostrich tails
Apiece, made in a plume to gather wind.
We will be brave, Puff, now we ha' the med'cine.

My meat shall all come in, in Indian shells,
Dishes of agate, set in gold, and studded
With emeralds, sapphires, hyacinths, and rubies.
The tongues of carps, dormice, and camels' heels,
Boil'd i' the spirit of Sol, and dissolv'd pearl,
Apicius' diet, 'gainst the epilepsy,
And I will eat these broths with spoons of amber,
Headed with diamond and carbuncle.
My foot-boy shall eat pheasants, calvered salmons,
Knots, godwits, lampreys: I myself will have
The beards of barbels serv'd, instead of salads;
Oiled mushrooms; and the swelling unctuous paps
Of a fat pregnant sow, newly cut off,
Dress'd with an exquisite and poignant sauce;
For which I'll say unto my cook, 'There's gold,
Go forth and be a knight.'

 Face.   Sir, I'll go look
A little, how it heightens.   [*Exit.*

 Mam.   Do. My shirts
I'll have of taffeta-sarsnet, soft and light
As cobwebs; and for all my other raiment
It shall be such as might provoke the Persian,
Were he to teach the world riot anew.
My gloves of fishes' and birds' skins, perfum'd
With gums of paradise and Eastern air——

 Sur. And do you think to have the Stone with this?

 Mam. No. I do think t' have all this with the Stone.

 Sur. Why, I have heard he must be *homo frugi*,
A pious, holy, and religious man,
One free from mortal sin, and very virgin.

 Mam. That makes it, sir, he is so. But I buy it.
My venture brings it me. He, honest wretch,
A notable, superstitious, good soul,
Has worn his knees bare, and his slippers bald,
With prayer and fasting for it: and, sir, let him
Do it alone for me still. Here he comes.
Not a profane word afore him: 'tis poison.

Enter Subtle.

Good morrow, father.

Subt.   Gentle son, good morrow,
And to your friend there. What is he, is with you?

Mam. An heretic that I did bring along,
In hope, sir, to convert him.

Subt.   Son, I doubt
You're covetous, that thus you meet your time
I' the just point: prevent your day at morning.
This argues something worthy of a fear
Of importune and carnal appetite.
Take heed you do not cause the blessing leave you,
With your ungovern'd haste. I should be sorry,
To see my labours, now e'en at perfection,
Got by long watching and large patience,
Not prosper where my love and zeal hath plac'd 'em.
Which (heaven I call to witness, with yourself,
To whom I have pour'd my thoughts) in all my ends,
Have look'd no way but unto public good,
To pious uses, and dear charity,
Now grown a prodigy with men. Wherein
If you, my son, should now prevaricate,
And, to your own particular lusts, employ
So great and catholic a bliss: be sure
A curse will follow, yea, and overtake
Your subtle and most secret ways.

Mam.   I know, sir,
You shall not need to fear me. I but come
To ha' you confute this gentleman.

Sur.   Who is,
Indeed, sir, somewhat costive of belief
Toward your Stone: would not be gull'd.

Subt.   Well, son,
All that I can convince him in, is this:
The work is done; Bright Sol is in his robe.
We have a med'cine of the triple Soul,
The glorified spirit. Thanks be to heaven,
And make us worthy of it.—Ulen Spiegel.

Face. [*Within.*] Anon, sir.

Subt.   Look well to the register,

And let your heat still lessen by degrees,
To the aludels.

Face. Yes, sir.

Subt. Did you look
O' the bolt's-head yet?

Face. Which, on D, sir?

Subt. Aye.
What's the complexion?

Face. Whitish.

Subt. Infuse vinegar,
To draw his volatile substance and his tincture:
And let the water in glass E be filtered
And put into the gripe's egg. Lute him well;
And leave him clos'd in *balneo.*

Face. I will, sir.

Sur. What a brave language here is! next to canting!

Subt. I have another work; you never saw, son,
That three days since passed the Philosopher's wheel
In the lent heat of Athanor, and 's become
Sulphur o' nature.

Mam. But 'tis for me?

Subt. What need you?
You have enough in that is perfect.

Mam. O, but——

Subt. Why, this is covetise!

Mam. No, I assure you,
I shall employ it all in pious uses,
Founding of colleges and grammar schools,
Marrying young virgins, building hospitals,
And now and then a church.

Re-enter Face.

Subt. How now?

Face. Sir, please you,
Shall I not change the filter?

Subt. Marry, yes.
And bring me the complexion of glass B. [*Exit* Face.

Mam. Ha' you another?

Subt. Yes, son, were I assur'd

Your piety were firm, we would not want
The means to glorify it. But I hope the best:
I mean to tinct C in sand-heat to-morrow,
And give him imbibition.

    Mam.   Of white oil?

    Subt.   No, sir, of red. F is come over the helm too,
I thank my Maker, in St. Mary's bath,
And shows *lac virginis*. Blessed be heaven.
I sent you of his fæces there, calcin'd.
Out of that calx I ha' won the salt of Mercury.

    Mam. By pouring on your rectified water?

    Subt. Yes, and reverberating in Athanor.

Re-enter Face.

How now? What colour says it?

    Face.   The ground black, sir.

    Mam. That's your crow's head?

    Sur. Your cock's-comb's is it not?

    Subt. No, 'tis not perfect. Would it were the crow!
That work wants something.

    Sur.   O, I look'd for this.
[*Aside.*] The hay is a pitching.

    Subt.   Are you sure you loos'd 'em
I' their own menstrue?

    Face. Yes, sir, and then married 'em,
And put 'em in a bolt's-head, nipp'd to digestion,
According as you bade me; when I set
The liquor of Mars to circulation
In the same heat.

    Subt.   The process then, was right.

    Face. Yes, by the token, sir, the retort brake,
And what was sav'd, was put into the pellican,
And sign'd with Hermes' seal.

    Subt.   I think 'twas so.
We should have a new amalgama.

    Sur.   O, this ferret   [*Aside.*
Is rank as any polecat!

    Subt.   But I care not.

Let him e'en die; we have enough beside,
In embryon. H has his white shirt on?

   Face.   Yes, sir

He's ripe for inceration: He stands warm
In his ash-fire. I would not you should let
Any die now, if I might counsel, sir,
For luck's sake to the rest. It is not good.

   Mam. He says right.

   Sur.   Aye, are you bolted?   [*Aside.*

   Face.   Nay, I know 't, sir,

I have seen th' ill fortune. What is some three ounces
Of fresh materials?

   Mam.   Is't no more?

   Face.   No more, sir,

Of gold, t' amalgam, with some six of mercury.

   Mam. Away, here's money. What will serve?

   Face.   Ask him, sir.

   Mam. How much?

   Subt.   Give him nine pound: you may gi' him ten.

   Sur. Yes, twenty and be cozened, do.

   Mam.   There 'tis. [*Gives* Face *the money.*

   Subt. This needs not. But that you will have it so,
To see conclusions of all. For two
Of our inferior works are at fixation.
A third is in ascension. Go your ways.
Ha' you set the oil of luna in *kemia*?

   Face.   Yes, sir.

   Subt. And the Philosopher's vinegar?

   Face.   Aye.   [*Exit.*

   Sur. We shall have a salad.

   Mam.   When do you make projection?

   Subt. Son, be not hasty. I exalt our med'cine,
By hanging him in *balneo vaporoso*;
And giving him solution; then congeal him;
And then dissolve him; then again congeal him;
For look, how oft I iterate the work,
So many times I add unto his virtue.
As, if at first one ounce convert a hundred,
After his second loose, he'll turn a thousand;

His third solution, ten; his fourth, a hundred.
After his fifth, a thousand thousand ounces
Of any imperfect metal, into pure
Silver or gold, in all examinations,
As good as any of the natural mine.
Get you your stuff here, against afternoon,
Your brass, your pewter, and your andirons.

Mam. Not those of iron?

Subt.   Yes. You may bring them, too.
We'll change all metals.

Sur.   I believe you, in that.

Mam. Then I may send my spits?

Subt.   Yes, and your racks.

Sur. And dripping-pans, and pot-hangers, and hooks?
Shall he not?

Subt.   If he please.

Sur.   To be an ass.

Subt. How, sir!

Mam.   This gent'man, you must bear withal.
I told you he had no faith.

Sur.   And little hope, sir,
But much less charity should I gull myself.

Subt. Why, what have you observ'd sir, in our art,
Seems so impossible?

Sur.   But your whole work, no more.
That you should hatch gold in a furnace, sir,
As they do eggs in Egypt!

Subt.   Sir, do you
Believe that eggs are hatch'd so?

Sur.   If I should?

Subt. Why, I think that the greater miracle.
No egg but differs from a chicken more
Than metals in themselves.

Sur.   That cannot be.
The egg's ordain'd by nature to that end:
And is a chicken *in potentia.*

Subt. The same we say of lead, and other metals
Which would be gold if they had time.

Mam.   And that

365

Our art doth further.

 Subt.   Aye, for 'twere absurd
To think that nature in the earth bred gold
Perfect i' the instant. Something went before.
There must be remote matter.

 Sur.   Aye, what is that?

 Subt. Marry, we say——

 Mam.   Aye, now it heats: stand, father,
Pound him to dust——

 Subt.   It is, of the one part,
A humid exhalation, which we call
Materia liquida, or the unctuous water;
On th' other part, a certain crass and viscous
Portion of earth; both which, concorporate,
Do make the elementary matter of gold:
Which is not yet *propria materia*,
But common to all metals, and all stones.
For, where it is forsaken of that moisture,
And hath more dryness, it becomes a stone;
Where it retains more of the humid fatness,
It turns to sulphur or to quicksilver,
Who are the parents of all other metals.
Nor can this remote matter suddenly
Progress so from extreme unto extreme,
As to grow gold, and leap o'er all the means.
Nature doth first beget th' imperfect; then
Proceeds she to the perfect. Of that airy
And oily water, mercury is engendered;
Sulphur o' the fat and earthy part: the one,
Which is the last, supplying the place of male,
The other of the female, in all metals.
Some do believe hermaphrodeity,
That both do act and suffer. But these two
Make the rest ductile, malleable, extensive.
And even in gold they are; for we do find
Seeds of them by our fire, and gold in them:
And can produce the species of each metal
More perfect thence than nature doth in earth.
Beside, who doth not see, in daily practice,

Art can beget bees, hornets, beetles, wasps,
Out of the carcases and dung of creatures;
Yea, scorpions of an herb, being rightly plac'd:
And these are living creatures, far more perfect
And excellent than metals.

 Mam.   Well said, father!
Nay, if he take you in hand, sir, with an argument,
He'll bray you in a mortar.

 Sur.   'Pray you, sir, stay.
Rather than I'll be bray'd, sir, I'll believe
That alchemy is a pretty kind of game,
Somewhat like tricks o' the cards, to cheat a man
With charming.

 Subt. Sir?

 Sur.   What else are all your terms,
Whereon no one o' your writers 'grees with other?
Of your elixir, your *lac virginis*,
Your Stone, your med'cine, and your chrysosperm,
Your sal, your sulphur and your mercury,
Your oil of height, your tree of life, your blood,
Your merchesite, your tutie, your magnesia,
Your toad, your crow, your dragon, and your panther,
Your sun, your moon, your firmament, your adrop,
Your *lato, azoch, zernich, chibrit, heautarit*,
And then your red man and your white woman.
With all your broths, your menstrues and materials,
Of piss, and eggshells, women's terms, man's blood,
Hair o' the head, burnt clouts, chalk, merds, and clay,
Powder of bones, scalings of iron, glass,
And worlds of other strange ingredients,
Would burst a man to name?

 Subt.   And all these, nam'd
Intending but one thing: which art our writers
Us'd to obscure their art.

 Mam.   Sir, so I told him,
Because the simple idiot should not learn it,
And make it vulgar.

 Subt.   Was not all the knowledge
Of the Egyptians writ in mystic symbols?

Speak not the Scriptures oft in parables?
Are not the choicest fables of the poets,
That were the fountains and first springs of wisdom,
Wrapped in perplexed allegories?

Mam.   I urg'd that,
And clear'd to him that Sisyphus was damn'd
To roll the ceaseless stone, only because
He would have made ours common.

                     [*Dol appears at the door.*
                     Who is this?

    Subt. God's precious—What do you mean? Go in, good lady,
Let me entreat you. [*Dol retires.*] Where's this varlet?

Re-enter Face.

    Face.   Sir?
    Subt. You very knave! do you use me thus?
    Face.   Wherein, sir?
    Subt. Go in and see, you traitor. Go.   [*Exit Face.*
    Mam.   Who is it, sir?
    Subt. Nothing, sir. Nothing.
    Mam.   What's the matter? good sir!
I have not seen you thus distemper'd. Who is't?
    Subt. All arts have still had, sir, their adversaries,
But ours the most ignorant. [*Face returns.*] What now?
    Face. 'Twas not my fault, sir, she would speak with you.
    Subt. Would she, sir? Follow me.   [*Exit.*
    Mam.   Stay, Lungs.
    Face.   I dare not, sir.
    Mam. Stay, man; what is she?
    Face.   A lord's sister, sir.
    Mam. How! 'Pray thee stay?
    Face.   She's mad, sir, and sent hither——
He'll be mad too.
    Mam.   I warrant thee.—Why sent hither?
    Face. Sir, to be cur'd.
    Subt. [*Within.*] Why, rascal!
    Face.   Lo you. Here sir.   [*Exit.*
    Mam. 'Fore God, a Bradamante, a brave piece.

Sur. 'Heart, this is a bawdy-house! I'll be burnt else.

Mam. O, by this light, no. Do not wrong him. He's
Too scrupulous that way. It is his vice.
No, he's a rare physician, do him right.
An excellent Paracelsian! and has done
Strange cures with mineral physic. He deals all
With spirits, he. He will not hear a word
Of Galen, or his tedious recipes.

Re-enter Face.

How now, Lungs!

    Face.   Softly, sir, speak softly, I meant
To ha' told your worship all. This must not hear.

    Mam. No, he will not be gull'd; let him alone.

    Face. You are very right, sir, she is a most rare scholar;
And is gone mad with studying Broughton's works.
If you but name a word touching the Hebrew,
She falls into her fit, and will discourse
So learnedly of genealogies,
As you would run mad, too, to hear her, sir.

    Mam. How might one do t' have conference with her,
      Lungs?

    Face. O, divers have run mad upon the conference.
I do not know, sir: I am sent in haste
To fetch a vial.

    Sur.   Be not gull'd, Sir Mammon.

    Mam. Wherein? 'Pray ye, be patient.

    Sur.   Yes, as you are.
And trust confederate knaves and bawds and whores.

    Mam. You are too foul, believe it. Come here, Ulen.
One word.

    Face.   I dare not, in good faith.

    Mam.   Stay, knave.

    Face. He's extreme angry that you saw her, sir.

    Mam. Drink that. [*Gives him money.*] What is she,
when she's out of her fit?

    Face. O, the most affablest creature, sir! so merry!
So pleasant! she'll mount you up like quicksilver,

Over the helm; and circulate like oil.
A very vegetal: discourse of state,
Of mathematics, bawdry, anything——

   Mam. Is she no way accessible? no means—
No trick to give a man a taste of her—wit—
Or so?

   Subt. [*Within.*] Ulen.

   Face.   I'll come to you again, sir. [*Exit.*

   Mam. Surly, I did not think one o' your breeding
Would traduce personages of worth.

   Sur.   Sir Epicure,
Your friend to use: yet still loth to be gull'd.
I do not like your philosophical bawds.
Their Stone is lechery enough to pay for,
Without this bait.

   Mam.   'Heart, you abuse yourself.
I know the lady, and her friends, and means,
The original of this disaster. Her brother
Has told me all.

   Sur.   And yet you ne'er saw her
Till now?

   Mam. O, yes, but I forgot. I have, believe it,
One of the treacherousest memories, I do think,
Of all mankind.

   Sur. What call you her brother?

   Mam.   My lord——
He wi' not have his name known, now I think on 't.

   Sur. A very treacherous memory!

   Mam.   O' my faith——

   Sur. Tut, if you ha' it not about you, pass it,
Till we meet next.

   Mam.   Nay, by this hand, 'tis true.
He's one I honour, and my noble friend,
And I respect his house.

   Sur.   'Heart! can it be,
That a grave sir, a rich, that has no need,
A wise sir, too, at other times, should thus
With his own oaths and arguments, make hard means
To gull himself? And this be your elixir,

Your *lapsis mineralis* and your lunary,
Give me your honest trick yet at primero
Or gleek; and take your *lutum sapientis*,
Your *menstruum simplex*: I'll have gold before you,
And with less danger of the quicksilver;
Or the hot sulphur.

Re-enter Face.

Face. [*To* Surly.] Here's one from Captain Face, sir.
Desires you meet him i' the Temple church,
Some half hour hence, and upon earnest business.
Sir, [*Whispers to* Mammon.] if you please to quit us now;
and come
Again within two hours: you shall have
My master busy examining o' the works;
And I will steal you in unto the party,
That you may see her converse. [*To* Sur.] Sir, shall I say
You'll meet the captain's worship?
Sur.   Sir, I will.
But by attorney, and to a second purpose. [*Walks aside.*
Now I am sure it is a bawdy-house;
I'll swear it were the marshal here to thank me:
The naming this commander doth confirm it.
Don Face! Why, he's the most authentic dealer
I' these commodities! The superintendent
To all the quainter traffickers in town.
He is their visitor, and does appoint
Who lies with whom; and at what hour; what price;
Which gown; and in what smock; what fall; what tire.
Him will I prove, by a third person, to find
The subtleties of this dark labyrinth:
Which, if I do discover, dear Sir Mammon,
You'll give your poor friend leave, though no philosopher,
To laugh: for you that are, 'tis thought, shall weep.
Face. Sir. He does pray you'll not forget.
Sur.   I will not, sir.
Sir Epicure, I shall leave you.   [*Exit.*
Mam.   I follow you straight.

Face. But do so, good sir, to avoid suspicion.
This gent'man has a parlous head.
 Mam.   But wilt thou, Ulen,
Be constant to thy promise?
 Face.   As my life, sir.
 Mam. And wilt thou insinuate what I am? and praise
me?
And say I am a noble fellow?
 Face.   O, what else, sir?
And, that you'll make her royal with the Stone,
An empress; and yourself King of Bantam.
 Mam. Wilt thou do this?
 Face.   Will I, sir?
 Mam.   Lungs, my Lungs!
I love thee.
 Face.   Send your stuff, sir, that my master
May busy himself about projection.
 Mam. Th' hast witch'd me, rogue: Take, go.
           [*Gives him money.*
 Face.   Your jack, and all, sir.
 Mam. Thou art a villain—I will send my jack;
And the weights too. Slave, I could bite thine ear.
Away, thou dost not care for me.
 Face.   Not I, sir?
 Mam. Come, I was born to make thee, my good weasel;
Set thee on a bench: and ha' thee twirl a chain
With the best lord's vermin of 'em all.
 Face.   Away, sir.
 Mam. A Count, nay, a Count Palatine——
 Face.   Good sir, go.
 Mam. ——Shall not advance thee better: no, nor faster.
             [*Exit.*

Re-enter Subtle *and* Dol.

 Subt. Has he bit? Has he bit?
 Face.   And swallow'd too, my Subtle.
I ha' given him line, and now he plays, i' faith.
 Subt. And shall we twitch him?

THE ALCHEMIST

Face.   Thorough both the gills.
A wench is a rare bait, with which a man
No sooner 's taken, but he straight firks mad.

Subt. Dol, my Lord Whats'hum's sister, you must now
Bear yourself *statelich.*

Dol.   O, let me alone.
I'll not forget my race, I warrant you.
I'll keep my distance, laugh, and talk aloud;
Have all the tricks of a proud scurvy lady
And be as rude as her woman.

Face.   Well said, Sanguine.

Subt. But will he send his andirons?

Face.   His jack too;
And 's iron shoeing-horn: I ha' spoke to him. Well,
I must not loose my wary gamester, yonder.

Subt. O, Monsieur Caution, that will not be gull'd?

Face. Aye, if I can strike a fine hook into him, now,
The Temple church, there I have cast mine angle.
Well, pray for me. I'll about it.   [*Knocking without.*

Subt.   What, more gudgeons!
Dol, scout, scout; stay, Face, you must go to the door:
'Pray God it be my Anabaptist. Who is 't, Dol?

Dol. I know him not. He looks like a gold-end-man.

Subt. God's so! 'tis he, he said he would send. What
    call you him?
The sanctified elder, that should deal
For Mammon's jack and andirons! Let him in.
Stay, help me off, first, with my gown. [*Exit* Face *with
    gown.*] Away,
Madam, to your withdrawing chamber. [*Exit* Dol.] Now,
In a new tune, new gesture, but old language.
This fellow is sent from one negotiates with me
About the Stone too, for the holy brethren
Of Amsterdam, the exil'd saints, that hope
To raise their discipline by it. I must use him
In some strange fashion, now, to make him admire me.

Enter Ananias.

Ana. Where is my drudge?   [*Re-enter* Face.

Face.   Sir.

Subt.   Take away the recipient,
And rectify your menstrue from the *phlegma*.
Then pour it o' the Sol in the *cucurbite*,
And let 'em macerate together.

Face.   Yes, sir.
And save the ground?

Subt.   No. *Terra damnata*
Must not have entrance in the work. Who are you?

Ana. A faithful brother, if it please you.

Subt.   What's that?
A Lullianist? a Ripley? *Filius artis*?
Can you sublime and dulcify? calcine?
Know you the *sapor pontic*? *sapor stiptic*?
Or what is homogene, or heterogene?

Ana. I understand no heathen language, truly.

Subt. Heathen? you Knipper-doling! Is *Ars sacra*,
Or *chrysopœia*, or *spagyrica*,
Or the *pamphysic*, or *panarchic* knowledge,
A heathen language?

Ana.   Heathen Greek, I take it.

Subt. How? heathen Greek?

Ana.   All's heathen but the Hebrew.

Subt. Sirrah my varlet, stand you forth, and speak to
         him
Like a philosopher: Answer i' the language,
Name the vexations, and the martyrizations
Of metals in the work.

Face.   Sir, putrefaction,
Solution, ablution, sublimation,
Cohobation, calcination, ceration, and
Fixation.

Subt. This is heathen Greek to you, now?
And when comes vivification?

Face.   After mortification.

Subt. What's cohobation?

Face.   'Tis the pouring on
Your *aqua regis*, and then drawing him off
To the trine circle of the seven spheres.

374

Subt. What's the proper passion of metals?

Face.   Malleation.

Subt. What's your *ultimum supplicium auri?*

Face.   Antimonium.

Subt. This's heathen Greek to you? And what's your
   Mercury?

Face. A very fugitive, he will be gone, sir.

Subt. How know you him?

Face.   By his viscosity,
His oleosity and his suscitability.

Subt. How do you sublime him?

Face.   With the calce of eggshells,
White marble, talc.

Subt.   Your magisterium now?
What's that?

Face.   Shifting, sir, your elements,
Dry into cold, cold into moist, moist into hot,
Hot into dry.

Subt.   This's heathen Greek to you, still?
Your *Lapis philosophicus?*

Face.   'Tis a stone
And not a stone; a spirit, a soul, and a body:
Which, if you do dissolve, it is dissolv'd,
If you coagulate, it is coagulated,
If you make it to fly, it flyeth.

Subt.   Enough.   [*Exit* Face.
This's heathen Greek to you? What are you, sir?

Ana. Please you, a servant of the exil'd brethren,
That deal with widows' and with orphans' goods;
And make a just account unto the saints:
A deacon.

Subt.   O, you are sent from master Wholesome,
Your teacher?

Ana.   From Tribulation Wholesome,
Our very zealous pastor.

Subt.   Good. I have
Some orphans' goods to come here.

Ana.   Of what kind, sir?

Subt. Pewter and brass, andirons and kitchen ware,

Metals, that we must use our med'cine on:
Wherein the brethren may have a penn'orth
For ready money.

Ana.   Were the orphan's parents
Sincere professors?

Subt.   Why do you ask?

Ana.   Because
We then are to deal justly, and give in truth
Their utmost value.

Subt.   'Slid, you'd cozen, else,
And if their parents were not of the faithful?
I will not trust you, now I think on 't,
Till I ha' talk'd with your pastor. Ha' you brought money
To buy more coals?

Ana.   No, surely.

Subt.   No? How so?

Ana. The brethren bid me say unto you, sir,
Surely, they will not venture any more,
Till they may see projection.

Subt.   How!

Ana.   You have had
For the instruments, as bricks, and loam, and glasses,
Already thirty pound; and, for materials,
They say some ninety more: And, they have heard since,
That one at Heidelberg made it of an egg
And a small paper of pin-dust.

Subt.   What's your name?

Ana. My name is Ananias.

Subt.   Out, the varlet
That cozen'd the apostles! Hence, away,
Flee, Mischief; had your holy consistory
No name to send me of another sound,
Than wicked Ananias? Send your elders
Hither, to make atonement for you quickly.
And gi' me satisfaction; or out goes
The fire: and down th' alembics and the furnace,
Piger Henricus, or what not. Thou wretch,
Both sericon and bufo shall be lost,
Tell 'em. All hope of rooting out the bishops

Or th' antichristian hierarchy shall perish,
If they stay threescore minutes. The Aqueity,
Terreity and Sulphureity
Shall run together again, and all be annull'd.
Thou wicked Ananias.   *[Exit Ananias.*
This will fetch 'em,
And make 'em haste towards their gulling more.
A man must deal like a rough nurse, and fright
Those that are froward to an appetite.

Re-enter Face *with* Drugger.

 Face. He's busy with his spirits, but we'll upon him.
 Subt. How now! What mates? What Bayards ha' we here?
 Face. I told you he would be furious. Sir, here's Nab,
Has brought you another piece of gold to look on:
(We must appease him. Give it me) and prays you,
You would devise (what is it, Nab?)——
 Dru.   A sign, sir.
 Face. Aye, a good lucky one, a thriving sign, doctor.
 Subt. I was devising now.
 Face.   ('Slight, do not say so,
He will repent he ga' you any more.)
What say you to his constellation, doctor?
The Balance?
 Subt.   No, that way is stale and common.
A townsman, born in Taurus, gives the bull;
Or the bull's head: In Aries, the ram——
A poor device. No, I will have his name
Form'd in some mystic character; whose *radii*,
Striking the senses of the passers-by,
Shall, by a virtual influence, breed affections
That may result upon the party owns it:
As thus——
 Face. Nab!
 Subt.   He first shall have a bell, that's Abel;
And, by it, standing one, whose name is Dee,
In a rug gown; there's D. and *Rug*, that's *Drug*:
And, right anenst him, a dog snarling *er*;

377

There's *Drugger*, *Abel Drugger*. That's his sign.
And here's now mystery and hieroglyphic!

Face. Abel, thou art made.

Dru.   Sir, I do thank his worship.

Face. Six o' thy legs more will not do it, Nab.
He has brought you a pipe of tobacco, doctor.

Dru.   Yes, sir:
I have another thing I would impart——

Face. Out with it, Nab.

Dru.   Sir, there is lodg'd, hard by me
A rich young widow——

Face.   Good! a bona roba?

Dru. But nineteen at the most.

Face.   Very good, Abel.

Dru. Marry, she's not in fashion yet; she wears
A hood: but't stands a cop.

Face.   No matter, Abel.

Dru. And I do, now and then, give her a *fucus*——

Face. What! dost thou deal, Nab?

Subt.   I did tell you, captain.

Dru. And physic too sometime, sir: for which she trusts
me
With all her mind. She's come up here, of purpose
To learn the fashion.

Face.   Good (his match too!) On, Nab.

Dru. And she does strangely long to know her fortune.

Face. God's lid, Nab, send her to the doctor, hither.

Dru. Yes, I have spoke to some of his worship already:
But she's afraid it will be blown abroad,
And hurt her marriage.

Face.   Hurt it? 'Tis the way
To heal it, if 'twere hurt; to make it more
Follow'd and sought: Nab, thou shalt tell her this:
She'll be more known, more talk'd of, and your widows
Are ne'er of any price till they be famous;
Their honour is their multitude of suitors:
Send her; it may be thy good fortune. What?
Thou dost not know.

378

Dru. No, sir, she'll never marry
Under a knight. Her brother has made a vow.

Face. What, and dost thou despair, my little Nab,
Knowing what the doctor has set down for thee,
And seeing so many o' the city dub'd?
One glass o' thy water, with a Madam I know,
Will have it done, Nab. What's her brother? a knight?

Dru. No, sir, a gentleman, newly warm in his land, sir,
Scarce cold in his one and twenty; that does govern
His sister here: and is a man himself
Of some three thousand a year, and is come up
To learn to quarrel, and to live by his wits,
And will go down again, and die i' the country.

Face. How! to quarrel?

Dru. Yes, sir, to carry quarrels
As gallants do, and manage 'em by line.

Face. 'Slid, Nab! The doctor is the only man
In Christendom for him. He has made a table
With mathematical demonstrations,
Touching the art of quarrels. He will give him
An instrument to quarrel by. Go, bring 'em both:
Him, and his sister. And, for thee, with her
The doctor happ'ly may persuade. Go to.
'Shalt give his worship a new damask suit
Upon the premises.

Subt. O, good captain.

Face. He shall,
He is the honestest fellow, doctor. Stay not,
No offers, bring the damask, and the parties.

Dru. I'll try my power, sir.

Face. And they will too, Nab.

Subt. 'Tis good tobacco, this! What, is't an ounce?

Face. He'll send you a pound, doctor.

Subt. O, no.

Face. He will do't.
It is the goodest soul. Abel, about it.
Thou shalt know more anon. Away, be gone. [*Exit Abel.*
A miserable rogue, and lives with cheese,
And has the worms. That was the cause indeed

Why he came now. He dealt with me, in private,
To get a med'cine for 'em.

Subt.   And shall, sir. This works.

Face. A wife, a wife, for one of us, my dear Subtle:
We'll e'en draw lots, and he that fails shall have
The more in goods the other has in tail.

Subt. Rather the less. For she may be so light
She may want grains.

Face.   Aye, or be such a burden,
A man would scarce endure her for the whole.

Subt. Faith, best let's see her first, and then determine.

Face. Content. But Dol must ha' no breath on't.

Subt.   Mum.
Away, you to your Surly yonder, catch him.

Face. 'Pray God I ha' not stay'd too long.

Subt.   I fear it.

[*Exeunt.*

ACT III. SCENE I

The lane before Lovewit's *house.*

Enter Tribulation *and* Ananias.

Trib. These chastisements are common to the saints,
And such rebukes we of the separation
Must bear with willing shoulders, as the trials
Sent forth to tempt our frailties.

Ana.   In pure zeal,
I do not like the man: He is a heathen,
And speaks the language of Canaan, truly.

Trib. I think him a profane person, indeed.

Ana.   He bears
The visible mark of the beast in his forehead.
And for his Stone, it is a work of darkness,
And, with philosophy, blinds the eyes of man.

Trib. Good brother, we must bend unto all means
That may give furtherance to the holy cause.

Ana. Which his cannot: the sanctified cause
Should have a sanctified course.

Trib.   Not always necessary.
The children of perdition are oft-times
Made instruments even of the greatest works.
Beside, we should give somewhat to man's nature,
The place he lives in, still about the fire,
The fume of metals that intoxicate
The brain of man and make him prone to passion.
Where have you greater atheists than your cooks?
Or more profane or choleric than your glassmen?
More anti-christian than your bell-founders?
What makes the devil so devillish, I would ask you,
Satan, our common enemy, but his being
Perpetually about the fire, and boiling
Brimstone and arsenic? We must give, I say,
Unto the motives and the stirrers up
Of humours in the blood. It may be so,
When as the work is done, the Stone is made,
This heat of his may turn into a zeal,
And stand up for the beauteous discipline,
Against the menstruous cloth and rag of Rome.
We must await his calling, and the coming
Of the good spirit. You did fault, t' upbraid him
With the brethren's blessing of Heidelberg, weighing
What need we have to hasten on the work,
For the restoring of the silenc'd saints,
Which ne'er will be, but by the Philosopher's Stone.
And so a learned elder, one of Scotland,
Assur'd me; *Aurum potabile* being
The only med'cine for the civil magistrate,
T' incline him to a feeling of the cause:
And must be daily us'd in the disease.
    Ana. I have not edified more, truly, by man;
Not since the beautiful light first shone on me:
And I am sad my zeal hath so offended.
    Trib. Let us call on him then.
    Ana.   The motion's good,
And of the spirit; I will knock first: Peace be within!

                    [*The door is opened, and they enter.*

ACT III. SCENE II

A room in Lovewit's *house.*

Enter Subtle, Tribulation, *and* Ananias.

  Subt. O, are you come? 'Twas time. Your three-score
    minutes
Were at the last thread, you see; and down had gone
Furnus acediæ, Turris circulatorius:
Lembic, bolt's-head, retort, and pellican
Had all been cinders. Wicked Ananias!
Art thou return'd? Nay then, it goes down yet.
  Trib. Sir, be appeased, he is come to humble
Himself in spirit, and to ask your patience,
If too much zeal hath carried him aside
From the due path.
  Subt.   Why, this doth qualify!
  Trib. The brethren had no purpose, verily,
To give you the least grievance: but are ready
To lend their willing hands to any project
The spirit and you direct.
  Subt.   This qualifies more!
  Trib. And, for the orphans' goods, let them be valued
Or what is needful else, to the holy work,
It shall be numbered: here, by me, the Saints
Throw down their purse before you.
  Subt.   This qualifies most!
Why, thus it should be, now you understand.
Have I discours'd so unto you of our Stone?
And of the good that it shall bring your cause?
Show'd you, beside the main of hiring forces
Abroad, drawing the Hollanders, your friends,
From th' Indies to serve you with all their fleet,
That even the med'cinal use shall make you a faction
And party in the realm? As, put the case,
That some great man in state, he have the gout;
Why, you but send three drops of your elixir,
You help him straight: there you have made a friend.
Another has the palsy, or the dropsy,

He takes of your incombustible stuff;
He's young again: there you have made a friend.
A lady that is past the feat of body,
Though not of mind, and hath her face decay'd
Beyond all cure of paintings, you restore
With the oil of talc; there you have made a friend:
And all her friends. A lord that is a leper,
A knight that has the bone-ache, or a squire
That hath both these; you make 'em smooth and sound
With a bare fricace of your med'cine: still
You increase your friends.

    Trib.   Aye, 'tis very pregnant.

    Subt. And then, the turning of this lawyer's pewter
To plate, at Christmas——

    Ana.   Christ-tide, I pray you.

    Subt. Yet, Ananias?

    Ana.   I have done.

    Subt.   Or changing
His parcel gilt to massy gold. You cannot
But raise you friends. Withal to be of power
To pay an army in the field, to buy
The king of France out of his realm, or Spain
Out of his Indies. What can you not do
Against lords spiritual or temporal
That shall oppone you?

    Trib.   Verily, 'tis true.
We may be temporal lords ourselves, I take it.

    Subt. You may be anything, and leave off to make
Long-winded exercises: or suck up
Your *ha* and *hum* in a tune. I not deny
But such as are not graced in a state
May, for their ends, be adverse in religion
And get a tune to call the flock together:
For to say sooth, a tune does much with women
And other phlegmatic people; it is your bell.

    Ana. Bells are profane: a tune may be religious.

    Subt. No warning with you? Then, farewell my
        patience.
'Slight, it shall down: I will not be thus tortur'd.

Trib. I pray you, sir.

    Subt.   All shall perish. I have spoke it.

    Trib. Let me find grace, sir, in your eyes; the man
He stands corrected: neither did his zeal,
But as yourself, allow a tune somewhere.
Which now, being toward the Stone, we shall not need.

    Subt. No, nor your holy vizard, to win widows
To give you legacies; or make zealous wives
To rob their husbands for the common cause:
Nor take the start of bonds broke but one day,
And say 'they were forfeited by providence'.
Nor shall you need, o'er-night, to eat huge meals,
To celebrate your next day's fast the better:
The whilst the brethren and the sisters, humbled,
Abate the stiffness of the flesh. Nor cast
Before your hungry hearers, scrupulous bones,
As whether a Christian may hawk or hunt;
Or whether matrons of the holy assembly
May lay their hair out, or wear doublets,
Or have that idol starch about their linen.

    Ana. It is indeed an idol.

    Trib.   Mind him not, sir.
I do command thee, spirit of zeal, but trouble,
To peace within him. Pray you, sir, go on.

    Subt. Nor shall you need to libel 'gainst the prelates,
And shorten so your ears against the hearing
Of the next wire-drawn grace. Nor, of necessity,
Rail against plays, to please the alderman
Whose daily custard you devour. Nor lie
With zealous rage till you are hoarse. Not one
Of these so singular arts. Nor call yourselves
By names of Tribulation, Persecution,
Restraint, Long-patience, and such like, affected
By the whole family or wood of you,
Only for glory and to catch the ear
Of the disciple.

    Trib.   Truly, sir, they are
Ways that the godly brethren have invented,
For propagation of the glorious cause,

As very notable means, and whereby, also,
Themselves grow soon and profitably famous.

Subt. O, but the Stone, all's idle to it! nothing!
The art of angels, nature's miracle,
The divine secret that doth fly in clouds,
From east to west, and whose tradition
Is not from men, but spirits.

 Ana.   I hate traditions:
I do not trust them——

 Trib.   Peace.

 Ana.   They are popish, all.
I will not peace. I will not——

 Trib.   Ananias!

 Ana. Please the profane, to grieve the godly, I may
not.

 Subt. Well, Ananias, thou shalt overcome.

 Trib. It is an ignorant zeal that haunts him, sir.
But truly, else, a very faithful brother,
A botcher: and a man, by revelation,
That hath a competent knowledge of the truth.

 Subt. Has he a competent sum there, i' the bag,
To buy the goods within? I am made guardian,
And must, for charity and conscience' sake,
Now see the most be made for my poor orphan:
Though I desire the brethren, too, good gainers.
There they are within. When you have view'd, and bought
    'em,
And ta'en the inventory of what they are,
They are ready for projection; there's no more
To do: cast on the med'cine, so much silver
As there is tin there, so much gold as brass,
I'll gi' it you in, by weight.

 Trib.   But how long time,
Sir, must the Saints expect yet?

 Subt.   Let me see,
How's the moon, now? Eight, nine, ten days hence
He will be silver potate; then, three days,
Before he citronise: some fifteen days,
The magisterium will be perfected.

Ana. About the second day of the third week,
In the ninth month?

Subt.   Yes, my good Ananias.

Trib. What will the orphan's goods arise to, think you?

Subt. Some hundred marks; as much as fill'd three cars
Unladed now: you'll make six millions of 'em.
But I must ha' more coals laid in.

Trib.   How!

Subt.   Another load,
And then we ha' finish'd. We must now increase
Our fire to *ignis ardens*, we are past
Fimus equinus, balnei, cineris,
And all those lenter heats. If the holy purse
Should, with this draught, fall low, and that the Saints
Do need a present sum, I have a trick
To melt the pewter, you shall buy now, instantly,
And, with a tincture, make you as good Dutch dollars
As any are in Holland.

Trib.   Can you so?

Subt. Aye, and shall bide the third examination.

Ana. It will be joyful tidings to the brethren.

Subt. But you must carry it secret.

Trib.   Aye, but stay,
This act of coining, is it lawful?

Ana.   Lawful?
We know no magistrate. Or, if we did,
This's foreign coin.

Subt.   It is no coining, sir.
It is but casting.

Trib.   Ha? you distinguish well.
Casting of money may be lawful.

Ana.   'Tis, sir.

Trib. Truly, I take it so.

Subt.   There is no scruple,
Sir, to be made of it; believe Ananias:
This case of conscience he is studied in.

Trib. I'll make a question of it to the brethren.

Ana. The brethren shall approve it lawful, doubt not.
Where shall 't be done?   [*Knocking without.*

Subt.   For that we'll talk anon.
There's some to speak with me. Go in, I pray you,
And view the parcels. That's the inventory.
I'll come to you straight.   [*Exeunt* Trib. *and* Ana.
                  Who is it? Face! Appear.

Enter Face, *in his uniform.*

How now? Good prize?
    Face.   Good pox! Yond' caustive cheater
Never came on.
    Subt.   How then?
    Face.   I ha' walk'd the round,
Till now, and no such thing.
    Subt.   And ha' you quit him?
    Face. Quit him? and hell would quit him too, he were
      happy.
'Slight, would you have me stalk like a mill-jade,
All day, for one that will not yield us grains?
I know him of old.
    Subt.   O, but to ha' gull'd him,
Had been a mastery.
    Face.   Let him go, black boy,
And turn thee, that some fresh news may possess thee.
A noble Count, a Don of Spain, my dear
Delicious compeer and my party bawd,
Who is come hither, private, for his conscience,
And brought munition with him, six great slops,
Bigger than three Dutch hoys, beside round trunks,
Furnish'd with pistolets and pieces of eight,
Will straight be here, my rogue, to have thy bath,
That is the colour, and to make his battery
Upon our Dol, our Castle, our Cinque port,
Our Dover pier, our what thou wilt. Where is she?
She must prepare perfumes, delicate linen,
The bath in chief, a banquet, and her wit,
For she must milk his epididymis.
Where is the doxy?
    Subt.   I'll send her to thee:

And but dispatch my brace of little John Leydens,
And come again myself.

Face.   Are they within then?

Subt. Numbering the sum.

Face.   How much?

Subt.   A hundred marks, boy. [*Exit.*

Face. Why, this's a lucky day! Ten pounds of Mam-
mon!
Three o' my clerk! A portague o' my grocer!
This o' the brethren! beside reversions,
And states to come i' the widow and my Count!
My share to-day will not be bought for forty——

Enter Dol.

Dol. What?

Face.   Pounds, dainty Dorothy, art thou so near?

Dol. Yes, say, lord general, how fares our camp?

Face. As with the few that had entrench'd themselves
Safe, by their discipline, against a world, Doll,
And laugh'd, within those trenches, and grew fat
With thinking on the booties, Dol, brought in
Daily, by their small parties. This dear hour,
A doughty Don is taken with my Dol;
And thou mayst make his ransom what thou wilt,
My Dousabel. He shall be brought here, fetter'd
With thy fair looks, before he sees thee; and thrown
In a down-bed, as dark as any dungeon;
Where thou shalt keep him waking with thy drum;
Thy drum, my Dol; thy drum; till he be tame
As the poor black-birds were i' the great frost,
Or bees are with a basin: and so hive him
I' the swan-skin coverlid, and cambric sheets,
Till he work honey and wax, my little God's-gift.

Dol. What is he, general?

Face.   An adalantado.
A grandee, girl. Was not my Dapper here, yet?

Dol. No.

Face.   Nor my Drugger?

Dol.   Neither.

Face. A pox on 'em,
They are so long a furnishing! Such stinkards
Would not be seen upon these festival days.

Re-enter Subtle.

How now! Ha' you done?
    Subt. Done. They are gone. The sum
Is here in bank, my Face. I would we knew
Another chapman, now, would buy 'em outright.
    Face. 'Slid, Nab shall do 't, against he ha' the widow,
To furnish household.
    Subt. Excellent well thought on.
Pray God he come.
    Face. I pray he keep away
Till our new business be o'erpast.
    Subt. But, Face,
How cam'st thou by this secret Don?
    Face. A spirit
Brought me th' intelligence in a paper, here,
As I was conjuring yonder in my circle
For Surly: I ha' my flies abroad. Your bath
Is famous, Subtle, by my means. Sweet Dol,
You must go tune your virginal, no losing
O' the least time. And, do you hear? good action.
Firk like a flounder; kiss like a scallop, close:
And tickle him with thy mother-tongue. His great
Verdugo-ship has not a jot of language:
So much the easier to be cozened, my Dolly.
He will come here in a hir'd coach, obscure,
And our own coachman, whom I have sent as guide,
No creature else. [*One knocks.*] Who's that? [*Exit* Dol.
    Subt. It is not he?
    Face. O no, not yet this hour.

Re-enter Dol.

    Subt. Who is 't?
    Dol. Dapper,
Your clerk.
    Face. God's will, then, Queen of Faery,

On with your tire; and, doctor, with your robes.
Let's dispatch him, for God's sake.

Subt.   'Twill be long.

Face. I warrant you, take but the cues I give you,
It shall be brief enough. 'Slight, here are more!
Abel and, I think, the angry boy, the heir
That fain would quarrel.

Subt.   And the widow?

Face.   No,
Not that I see. Away. [*Exit* Subt.] O, sir, you are welcome.

Enter Dapper.

The Doctor is within, a moving for you;
I have had the most ado to win him to it.
He swears you'll be the darling o' the dice:
He never heard her highness dote, till now.
Your aunt has given you the most gracious words
That can be thought on.

Dap.   Shall I see her grace?

Face. See her, and kiss her, too.

              [*Enter* Abel Drugger, *followed by* Kastril!
                       What honest Nab!
Hast brought the damask?

Dru.   No, sir, here's tobacco.

Face. 'Tis well done, Nab: Thou'lt bring the damask
    too?

Dru. Yes, here's the gentleman, captain, Master Kastril.
I have brought to see the doctor.

Face.   Where's the widow?

Dru. Sir, as he likes his sister, he says, shall come.

Face. O, is it so? 'good time. Is your name Kastril, sir?

Kas. Aye, and the best o' the Kastrils, I'd be sorry else,
By fifteen hundred a year. Where is this doctor?
My mad tobacco-boy, here, tells me of one
That can do things. Has he any skill?

Face.   Wherein, sir?

Kas. To carry a business, manage a quarrel fairly,
Upon fit terms.

Face.   It seems sir, you are but young
About the town, that can make that a question!

Kas. Sir, not so young, but I have heard some speech
Of the angry boys. and seen 'em take tobacco;
And in his shop: and I can take it too.
And I would fain be one of 'em, and go down
And practise i' the country.

Face.   Sir, for the duello,
The doctor, I assure you, shall inform you
To the least shadow of a hair: and show you
An instrument he has, of his own making,
Wherewith, no sooner shall you make report
Of any quarrel, but he will take the height on 't
Most instantly; and tell in what degree
Of safety it lies in, or mortality.
And how it may be borne, whether in a right line,
Or a half circle; or may else be cast
Into an angle blunt, if not acute:
All this he will demonstrate. And then, rules
To give and take the lie by.

Kas.   How? to take it?

Face. Yes, in oblique, he'll shew you; or in circle:
But never in diameter. The whole town
Study his theorems, and dispute them ordinarily
At the eating-academies.

Kas.   But does he teach
Living by the wits, too?

Face.   Anything whatever.
You cannot think that subtlety but he reads it.
He made me a captain. I was a stark pimp,
Just o' your standing, 'fore I met with him:
It is not two months since. I'll tell you his method.
First, he will enter you at some ordinary.

Kas. No, I'll not come there. You shall pardon me.

Face.   For why, sir?

Kas. There's gaming there, and tricks.

Face.   Why, would you be
A gallant, and not game?

Kas.   Aye, 'twill spend a man.

Face. Spend you? It will repair you when you are spent.
How do they live by their wits, there, that have vented
Six times your fortunes?

    Kas.   What, three thousand a year!

    Face. Aye, forty thousand.

    Kas.   Are there such?

    Face.   Aye, sir.
And gallants, yet. Here's a young gentleman,
Is born to nothing, forty marks a year,
Which I count nothing. He's to be initiated,
And have a fly o' the doctor. He will win you
By unresistable luck, within this fortnight,
Enough to buy a barony. They will set him
Upmost at the groom-porters, all the Christmas!
And, for the whole year through, at every place
Where there is play, present him with the chair;
The best attendance, the best drink, sometimes
Two glasses of Canary, and pay nothing;
The purest linen and the sharpest knife,
The partridge next his trencher: and, somewhere,
The dainty bed, in private, with the dainty.
You shall ha' your ordinaries bid for him,
As playhouses for a poet; and the master
Pray him aloud to name what dish he affects,
Which must be buttered shrimps: and those that drink
To no mouth else will drink to his, as being
The goodly president mouth of all the board.

    Kas. Do you not gull one?

    Face.   'Od's my life! Do you think it?
You shall have a cast commander, can but get
In credit with a glover or a spurrier,
For some two pair of either's ware aforehand,
Will, by most swift posts, dealing with him,
Arrive at competent means to keep himself,
His punk, and naked boy, in excellent fashion.
And be admir'd for't.

    Kas.   Will the doctor teach this?

    Face. He will do more, sir, when your land is gone,
As men of spirit hate to keep earth long,

392

In a vacation, when small money is stirring,
And ordinaries suspended till the term,
He'll show a perspective, where on one side
You shall behold the faces and the persons
Of all sufficient young heirs in town,
Whose bonds are current for commodity;
On th' other side, the merchants' forms and others,
That, without help of any second broker,
Who would expect a share, will trust such parcels:
In the third square, the very street, and sign
Where the commodity dwells, and does but wait
To be deliver'd, be it pepper, soap,
Hops or tobacco, oatmeal, woad, or cheeses.
All which you may so handle to enjoy
To your own use, and never stand oblig'd.

Kas. I' faith! Is he such a fellow?

    Face.   Why, Nab here knows him.
And then for making matches for rich widows,
Young gentlewomen, heirs, the fortunat'st man!
He's sent to, far and near, all over England,
To have his counsel, and to know their fortunes.

Kas. God's will, my suster shall see him.

    Face.   I'll tell you, sir,
What he did tell me of Nab. It's a strange thing!
By the way you must eat no cheese, Nab, it breeds melancholy:
And that same melancholy breeds worms; but pass it:—
He told me, honest Nab here was ne'er at tavern,
But once in 's life.

    Dru.   Truth, and no more I was not.

    Face. And then he was so sick——

    Dru.   Could he tell you that, too?

    Face. How should I know it?

    Dru.   In troth we had been a shooting,
And had a piece of fat ram-mutton to supper,
That lay so heavy o' my stomach——

    Face.   And he has no head
To bear any wine; for, what with the noise o' the fiddlers
And care of his shop, for he dares keep no servants——

Dru. My head did so ache——

Face. As he was fain to be brought home,
The doctor told me. And then, a good old woman——

Dru. Yes, faith, she dwells in Seacoal-lane—did cure me,
With sodden ale, and pellitory o' the wall:
Cost me but twopence. I had another sickness,
Was worse than that.

Face. Aye, that was with the grief
Thou took'st for being sess'd at eighteen pence,
For the water-work.

Dru. In truth, and it was like
T' have cost me almost my life.

Face. Thy hair went off?

Dru. Yes, sir, 'twas done for spite.

Face. Nay, so says the doctor.

Kas. Pray thee, tobacco-boy, go fetch my suster.
I'll see this learned boy before I go:
And so shall she.

Face. Sir, he is busy now:
But, if you have a sister to fetch hither,
Perhaps, your own pains may command her sooner;
And he, by that time, will be free.

Kas. I go. [*Exit.*

Face. Drugger, she's thine: the damask. [*Exit* Drugger.
Subtle and I
Must wrestle for her [*Aside*]. Come on, master Dapper.
You see how I turn clients here away,
To give your cause dispatch. Ha' you perform'd
The ceremonies were enjoin'd you?

Dap. Yes, o' the vinegar
And the clean shirt.

Face. 'Tis well: that shirt may do you
More worship than you think. Your aunt's a-fire,
But that she will not shew it, t' have a sight on you.
Ha' you provided for her grace's servants?

Dap. Yes, here are six score Edward shillings.

Face. Good.

Dap. And an old Harry's sovereign.

Face. Very good.

Dap. And three James shillings, and an Elizabeth groat,
Just twenty nobles.

  Face.   O, you are too just.
I would you had had the other noble in Maries.

  Dap. I have some Philip-and-Maries.

  Face.   Aye, those same
Are best of all. Where are they? Hark, the doctor.

   Enter Subtle *disguised like a Priest of Faery.*

  Subt. [*In a feigned voice.*] Is yet her grace's cousin come?

  Face.   He is come.

  Subt. And is he fasting?

  Face.   Yes.

  Subt.   And hath cried *hum*?

  Face. Thrice, you must answer.

  Dap.   Thrice.

  Subt.   And as oft *buz*?

  Face. If you have, say.

  Dap.   I have.

  Subt.   Then, to her cuz,
Hoping that he hath vinegared his senses,
As he was bid, the Faery queen dispenses
By me, this robe, the petticoat of Fortune;
Which that he straight put on, she doth importune.
And though to Fortune near be her petticoat,
Yet nearer is her smock, the queen doth note:
And, therefore, even of that a piece she hath sent,
Which, being a child, to wrap him in was rent;
And prays him, for a scarf he now will wear it,
With as much love, as then her grace did tear it,
About his eyes, [*They blindfold him with a rag.*] to show
  he is fortunate,
And, trusting unto her to make his state,
He'll throw away all worldly pelf about him;
Which that he will perform, she doth not doubt him.

  Face. She need not doubt him, sir. Alas, he has nothing
But what he will part withal, as willingly,
Upon her grace's word—throw away your purse—
As she would ask it:—handkerchiefs, and all—

She cannot bid that thing but he'll obey.

> [*He throws away, as they bid him.*

If you have a ring about you, cast it off,
Or a silver seal at your wrist, her grace will send
Her faeries here to search you, therefore deal
Directly with her highness. If they find
That you conceal a mite, you are undone.

 Dap. Truly, there's all.

 Face.   All what?

 Dap.   My money, truly.

 Face. Keep nothing that is transitory about you.
Bid Dol play music. [*Aside to* Subt.] Look the elves are come
To pinch you, if you tell not truth. [Dol. *plays on the cittern within.*] Advise you.   [*They pinch him.*

 Dap. O, I have a paper with a spur-royal in't.

 Face.   *Ti, ti,*
They knew't, they say.

 Subt.   *Ti, ti, ti, ti,* he has more yet.

 Face. Ti, ti-ti-ti. I' the tother pocket? [*Aside to* Subt.

 Subt.   *Titi, titi, titi, titi.*
They must pinch him, or he will never confess, they say.

> [*They pinch him again.*

 Dap. O, O!

 Face. Nay, 'pray you hold. He is her grace's nephew.
Ti, ti, ti? What care you? Good faith, you shall care.
Deal plainly, sir, and shame the faeries. Show
You are an innocent.

 Dap.   By this good light, I ha' nothing.

 Subt. Ti ti, ti ti to ta. He does equivocate, she says:
Ti, ti do ti, ti ti do, ti da. And swears by the light, when he
is blinded.

 Dap. By this good dark, I ha' nothing but a half-crown
Of gold, about my wrist, that my love gave me;
And a leaden heart I wore, since she forsook me.

 Face. I thought 'twas something. And would you incur
Your aunt's displeasure for these trifles? Come,
I had rather you had thrown away twenty half-crowns.

> [*Takes it off.*

You may wear your leaden heart still. How now?

Enter Dol *hastily.*

   Subt. What news, Dol?
   Dol.   Yonder's your knight, Sir Mammon.
   Face. God's lid, we never thought of him till now.
Where is he?
   Dol.   Here, hard by. He's at the door.
   Subt. And you are not ready now? Dol, get his suit.
                            [*Exit* Dol.
He must not be sent back.
   Face.   O, by no means.
What shall we do with this same puffin here,
Now he's o' the spit?
   Subt.   Why, lay him back a while
With some device. [*Re-enter* Dol *with* Face's *clothes.*] Ti,
   ti, ti, ti, ti, ti.
Would her grace speak with me?
I come. Help, Dol!
   Face. [*Speaks through the keyhole, the other knocking.*]
             Who's there? Sir Epicure,
My master's i' the way. Please you to walk
Three or four turns, but till his back be turn'd,
And I am for you. Quickly, Dol!
   Subt.   Her grace
Commends her kindly to you, master Dapper.
   Dap. I long to see her grace.
   Subt.   She now is set
At dinner in her bed; and she has sent you,
From her own private trencher, a dead mouse
And a piece of ginger-bread, to be merry withal
And stay your stomach lest you faint with fasting:
Yet, if you could hold out till she saw you, she says
It would be better for you.
   Face.   Sir, he shall
Hold out, and 'twere this two hours, for her highness;
I can assure you that. We will not lose
All we ha' done——

Subt.　　　　　　　　He must nor see, nor speak
To anybody, till then.

Face.　　　　　　　For that we'll put, sir,
A stay in 's mouth.

Subt.　　　　　Of what?

Face.　　　　　　　　Of gingerbread.
Make you it fit. He that hath pleas'd her grace
Thus far, shall not now crinkle for a little.—
Gape, sir, and let him fit you.

　　　　　[*They thrust a gag of gingerbread in his mouth.*

Subt.　　　　　　　　Where shall we now
Bestow him?

Dol.　　　I' the privy.

Subt.　　　　　Come along, sir,
I now must show you Fortune's privy lodgings.

Face. Are they perfum'd? and his bath ready?

Subt.　　　　　　　　　　　　All.
Only the fumigation's somewhat strong.

Face. [*Speaking through the keyhole.*] Sir Epicure, I am
　　yours, sir, by and by.　　　　　[*Exeunt with* Dapper.

ACT IV. SCENE I

A room in Lovewit's *house.*

Enter Face *and* Mammon.

Face. O, Sir, yo' are come i' the only finest time——

Mam. Where's master?

Face.　　　　　　Now preparing for projection, sir.
Your stuff will be all chang'd shortly.

Mam.　　　　　　　Into gold?

Face. To gold and silver, sir.

Mam.　　　　　Silver I care not for.

Face. Yes, sir, a little to give beggars.

Mam.　　　　　　　Where's the lady?

Face. At hand, here. I ha' told her such brave things o'
　　you,
Touching your bounty and your noble spirit——

Mam. Hast thou?

Face. As she is almost in her fit to see you.
But, good sir, no divinity i' your conference,
For fear of putting her in rage——

Mam. I warrant thee.

Face. Six men will not hold her down. And then,
If the old man should hear or see you——

Mam. Fear not.

Face. The very house, sir, would run mad. You know it
How scrupulous he is, and violent
'Gainst the least act of sin. Physic or mathematics,
Poetry, state, or bawdry, as I told you,
She will endure, and never startle: But
No word of controversy.

Mam. I am school'd, good Ulen.

Face. And you must praise her house, remember that,
And her nobility.

Mam. Let me alone:
No herald, no, nor antiquary, Lungs,
Shall do it better. Go.

Face. Why, this is yet
A kind of modern happiness, to have
Dol Common for a great lady. [*Aside, and exit.*

Mam. Now, Epicure,
Heighten thyself, talk to her, all in gold;
Rain her as many showers, as Jove did drops
Unto his Danäe: Show the god a miser,
Compar'd with Mammon. What? the Stone will do 't.
She shall feel gold, taste gold, hear gold, sleep gold:
Nay we will *concumbere* gold. I will be puissant,
And mighty in my talk to her!

Re-enter Face *with* Dol *richly dressed.*

Here she comes.

Face. To him, Dol, suckle him. This is the noble knight,
I told your ladyship——

Mam. Madam, with your pardon,
I kiss your vesture.

399

Dol.　　　　　Sir, I were uncivil
If I would suffer that; my lip to you, sir.

　　Mam. I hope my lord your brother be in health, lady?

　　Dol. My lord, my brother is, though I no lady, sir.

　　Face. Well said my Guinea bird. 　　　　　[*Aside.*

　　Mam.　　　　　Right noble madam——

　　Face. O, we shall have most fierce idolatry! 　[*Aside.*

　　Mam. 'Tis your prerogative.

　　Dol.　　　　　Rather your courtesy.

　　Mam. Were there nought else t' enlarge your virtues to
　　me,
These answers speak your breeding and your blood.

　　Dol. Blood we boast none, sir, a poor baron's daughter.

　　Mam. Poor! and gat you? Profane not. Had your father
Slept all the happy remnant of his life
After the act, lien but there still, and panted,
He had done enough to make himself, his issue,
And his posterity noble.

　　Dol.　　　　　Sir, although
We may be said to want the gilt and trappings,
The dress of honour; yet we strive to keep
The seeds and the materials.

　　Mam.　　　　　I do see
The old ingredient, virtue, was not lost,
Nor the drug, money, us'd to make your compound.
There is a strange nobility i' your eye,
This lip, that chin! Methinks you do resemble
One o' the Austric princes.

　　Face.　　　　　Very like,
Her father was an Irish costermonger. 　　[*Aside.*

　　Mam. The house of Valois just had such a nose,
And such a forehead yet the Medici
Of Florence boast.

　　Dol.　　　　　Troth, and I have been likened
To all these princes.

　　Face. I'll be sworn I heard it.

　　Mam. I know not how! it is not any one,
But e'en the very choice of all their features.

　　Face. I'll in, and laugh. 　　　　　[*Aside, and exit.*

Mam.   A certain touch, or air,
That sparkles a divinity beyond
An earthly beauty!

Dol.   O, you play the courtier.

Mam. Good lady, gi' me leave——

Dol.   In faith, I may not,
To mock me, sir.

Mam. To burn i' this sweet flame:
The phœnix never knew a nobler death.

Dol. Nay, now you court the courtier: and destroy
What you would build. This art, sir, i' your words,
Calls your whole faith in question.

Mam.   By my soul——

Dol. Nay, oaths are made o' the same air, sir.

Mam.   Nature
Never bestow'd upon mortality
A more unblam'd, a more harmonious feature:
She play'd the step-dame in all faces, else.
Sweet madam, let me be particular——

Dol. Particular, sir? I pray you, know your distance.

Mam. In no ill sense, sweet lady, but to ask
How your fair graces pass the hours? I see
You are lodg'd here, i' the house of a rare man,
An excellent artist: but what's that to you?

Dol. Yes, sir. I study here the mathematics,
And distillation.

Mam.   O, I cry your pardon.
He's a divine instructor! can extract
The souls of all things by his art; call all
The virtues and the miracles of the sun
Into a temperate furnace: teach dull nature
What her own forces are. A man the emperor
Has courted above Kelly, sent his medals
And chains, t' invite him.

Dol.   Aye, and for his physic, sir——

Mam. Above the art of Æsculapius,
That drew the envy of the Thunderer!
I know all this, and more.

Dol.   Troth, I am taken, sir,

Whole, with these studies that contemplate nature.

Mam. It is a noble humour. But this form
Was not intended to so dark a use!
Had you been crooked, foul, of some coarse mould,
A cloister had done well: but such a feature
That might stand up the glory of a kingdom,
To live recluse! is a mere solecism,
Though in a nunnery. It must not be.
I muse my lord your brother will permit it!
You should spend half my land first, were I he.
Does not this diamond better on my finger,
Than i' the quarry?

  Dol.   **Yes.**

  Mam.   Why, you are like it.
You were created, lady, for the light!
Here, you shall wear it; take it, the first pledge
Of what I speak: to bind you to believe me.

  Dol. In chains of adamant?

  Mam.   Yes, the strongest bands.
And take a secret, too. Here, by your side,
Doth stand, this hour, the happiest man in Europe.

  Dol. You are contented, sir?

  Mam.   Nay, in true being:
The envy of princes, and the fear of states.

  Dol. Say you so, Sir Epicure!

  Mam.   Yes, and thou shalt prove it,
Daughter of honour. I have cast mine eye
Upon thy form, and I will rear this beauty
Above all styles.

  Dol.   You mean no treason, sir!

  Mam. No, I will take away that jealousy.
I am the lord of the Philosopher's Stone,
And thou the lady.

  Dol.   How sir! ha' you that?

  Mam. I am the master of the mastery.
This day, the good old wretch, here o' the house,
Has made it for us. Now he's at projection.
Think therefore thy first wish, now; let me hear it:
And it shall rain into thy lap; no shower,

But floods of gold, whole cataracts, a deluge,
To get a nation on thee!

Dol.   You are pleas'd, sir,
To work on the ambition of our sex.

Mam. I am pleas'd the glory of her sex should know
This nook, here, of the Friars, is no climate
For her to live obscurely in, to learn
Physic and surgery, for the constable's wife
Of some odd hundred in Essex: but come forth,
And taste the air of palaces; eat, drink
The toils of emp'rics and their boasted practice;
Tincture of pearl and coral, gold and amber;
Be seen at feasts and triumphs; have it ask'd,
What miracle she is? set all the eyes
Of court a-fire, like a burning-glass,
And work 'em into cinders; when the jewels
Of twenty states adorn thee; and the light
Strikes out the stars; that, when thy name is mention'd,
Queens may look pale: and, we but showing our love,
Nero's Poppæa may be lost in story!
Thus will we have it.

Dol.   I could well consent, sir.
But in a monarchy how will this be?
The prince will soon take notice; and both seize
You and your Stone: it being a wealth unfit
For any private subject.

Mam.   If he knew it.

Dol. Yourself do boast it, sir.

Mam.   To thee, my life.

Dol. O, but beware, sir! You may come to end
The remnant of your days in a loathed prison,
By speaking of it.

Mam.   'Tis no idle fear!
We'll therefore go withal, my girl, and live
In a free state; where we will eat our mullets,
Sous'd in high-country wines, sup pheasant's eggs,
And have our cockles boil'd in silver shells,
Our shrimps to swim again, as when they liv'd,
In a rare butter made of dolphin's milk,

403

Whose cream does look like opals: and with these
Delicate meats, set ourselves high for pleasure,
And take us down again, and then renew
Our youth and strength, with drinking the elixir,
And so enjoy a perpetuity
Of life and lust. And thou shalt ha' thy wardrobe
Richer than Nature's, still, to change thyself,
And vary oftener, for thy pride, than she:
Or Art, her wise, and almost-equal servant.

Re-enter Face.

Face. Sir, you are too loud. I hear you, every word,
Into the laboratory. Some fitter place.
The garden, or great chamber above. How like you her?
   Mam. Excellent! Lungs. There's for thee.
   Face.   But, do you hear?
Good sir, beware, no mention of the rabbins.
   Mam. We think not on 'em.   [*Exeunt* Mam. *and* Dol.
   Face.   O, it is well, sir. Subtle!

Enter Subtle.

Dost thou not laugh?
   Subt.   Yes. Are they gone?
   Face.   All's clear.
   Subt. The widow is come.
   Face.   And your quarrelling disciple?
   Subt. Aye.
   Face.   I must to my captainship again then.
   Subt. Stay, bring 'em in, first.
   Face.   So I meant. What is she?
A bonnibel?
   Subt.   I know not.
   Face.   We'll draw lots,
You'll stand to that?
   Subt.   What else?
   Face.   O, for a suit,
To fall now, like a curtain, flap!
   Subt.   To th' door, man!
   Face. You'll ha' the first kiss, 'cause I am not ready. [*Exit.*
   Subt. Yes, and perhaps hit you through both the nostrils.

Face. [*Within.*] Who would you speak with?

Kas. [*Within.*]   Where's the captain?

Face. [*Within.*]   Gone, sir,

About some business.

Kas. [*Within.*]   Gone?

Face. [*Within.*]   He'll return straight.

But master doctor, his lieutenant, is here.

Enter Kastril, *followed by* Dame Pliant.

Subt. Come near, my worshipful boy, my *terræ fili*,

That is, my boy of land; make thy approaches:

Welcome, I know thy lusts and thy desires

And I will serve and satisfy 'em. Begin,

Charge me from thence, or thence, or in this line;

Here is my centre: Ground thy quarrel.

Kas.   You lie.

Subt. How, child of wrath and anger! the loud lie?

For what, my sudden boy?

Kas.   Nay, that look you to,

I am aforehand.

Subt.   O, this 's no true grammar,

And as ill logic! You must render causes, child,

Your first and second intentions, know your canons

And your divisions, moods, degrees and differences,

Your predicaments, substance and accident,

Series extern and intern, with their causes,

Efficient, material, formal, final,

And ha' your elements perfect——

Kas.   What, is this

The angry tongue he talks in?   [*Aside.*

Subt.   That false precept,

Of being aforehand, has deceiv'd a number;

And made 'em enter quarrels, oftentimes,

Before they were aware: and, afterward,

Against their wills.

Kas.   How must I do then, sir?

Subt. I cry this lady mercy. She should first

Have been saluted. [*Kisses her.*] I do call you lady,

405

Because you are to be one, ere 't be long,
My soft and buxom widow. [*Kisses her.*]
Kas.   Is she, i' faith?
Subt. Yes, or my art is an egregious liar.
Kas. How know you?
Subt.   By inspection on her forehead,
And subtlety of her lip, which must be tasted
Often, to make a judgement. [*He kisses her again.*] 'Slight,
she melts
Like a myrobolane! Here is yet a line
In rivo frontis tells me he is no knight.
Pli. What is he then, sir?
Subt.   Let me see your hand.
O, your *linea fortunæ* makes it plain;
And *stella* here, in *monte Veneris*:
But, most of all, *junctura annularis.*
He is a soldier, or a man of art. lady:
But shall have some great honour, shortly.
Pli.   Brother,
He 's a rare man, believe me!

Re-enter Face, *in his uniform.*

Kas.   Hold your peace.
Here comes the tother rare man. 'Save you, captain.
Face. Good master Kastril. Is this your sister?
Kas.   Aye. sir.
Please you to kiss her, and be proud to know her.
Face. I shall be proud to know you, lady.   [*Kisses her.*
Pli.   Brother,
He calls me lady, too.
Kas.   Aye, peace. I heard it. [*Takes her aside.*
Face. The Count is come.
Subt.   Where is he?
Face.   At the door.
Subt. Why, you must entertain him.
Face.   What'll you do
With these the while?
Subt.   Why, have 'em up and show 'em
Some fustian book or the dark glass.

Face.   'Fore God,
She is a delicate dabchick! I must have her.   [*Exit.*
    Subt. Must you? Aye, if your fortune will, you must.
Come, sir, the captain will come to us presently.
I'll ha' you to my chamber of demonstrations,
Where I'll show you both the grammar and logic,
And rhetoric of quarrelling; my whole method,
Drawn out in tables: and my instrument,
That hath the several scale upon 't, shall make you
Able to quarrel at a straw's breadth by moonlight.
And, lady, I'll have you look in a glass,
Some half an hour, but to clear your eyesight,
Against you see your fortune: which is greater
Than I may judge upon the sudden, trust me.
                    [*Exit, followed by* Kas. *and* Dame P.

Re-enter Face.

    Face. Where are you, doctor?
    Subt. [*Within.*]   I'll come to you presently.
    Face. I will ha' this same widow, now I ha' seen her,
On any composition.

Re-enter Subtle.

    Subt.   What do you say?
    Face. Ha' you dispos'd of them?
    Subt.   I ha' sent 'em up.
    Face. Subtle, in troth, I needs must have this widow.
    Subt. Is that the matter?
    Face.   Nay, but hear me.
    Subt.   Go to,
If you rebel once, Dol shall know it all.
Therefore be quiet, and obey your chance.
    Face. Nay, thou art so violent now—Do but conceive:
Thou art old, and canst not serve—
    Subt.   Who, cannot I?
'Slight, I will serve her with thee, for a——
    Face.   Nay,
But understand: I'll gi' you composition.

Subt. I will not treat with thee: what, sell my fortune?
'Tis better than my birth-right. Do not murmur.
Win her, and carry her. If you grumble, Dol
Knows it directly.

Face.　　　　　　　Well, sir, I am silent.
Will you go help, to fetch in Don, in state?　　　*[Exit.*

Subt. I follow you, sir: we must keep Face in awe,
Or he will overlook us like a tyrant.

Re-enter Face, *introducing* Surly *disguised as a Spaniard.*

Brain of a tailor! Who comes here? Don John!

Sur. Señores, beso las manos, à vuestras mercedes.

Subt. Would you had stoop'd a little, and kiss'd our *anos!*

Face. Peace, Subtle.

Subt.　　　　　　　Stab me; I shall never hold, man.
He looks, in that deep ruff, like a head in a platter,
Serv'd in by a short cloak upon two trestles!

Face. Or, what do you say to a collar of brawn, cut down
Beneath the souse, and wriggled with a knife?

Subt. 'Slud, he does look too fat to be a Spaniard.

Face. Perhaps some Fleming, or some Hollander got him
In D'Alva's time: Count Egmont's bastard.

Subt.　　　　　　　　　　　　　　Don,
Your scurvy, yellow, Madrid face is welcome.

Sur. Gratia.

Subt.　　　　He speaks out of a fortification.
'Pray God he ha' no squibs in those deep sets.

Sur. Por dios, señores, muy linda casa!

Subt. What says he?

Face.　　　　　　　Praises the house, I think,
I know no more but 's action.

Subt.　　　　　　　　Yes, the *casa,*
My precious Diego, will prove fair enough,
To cozen you in. Do you mark? you shall
Be cozened, Diego.

Face.　　　　Cozened, do you see?
My worthy Donzel, cozened.

Sur.　　　　　　　Entiendo.

Subt. Do you intend it? So do we, dear Don.

Have you brought pistolets? or portagues?
My solemn Don? Dost thou feel any?

   Face. [*Feels his pockets.*]   Full.

   Subt. You shall be emptied, Don; pumped and drawn
Dry, as they say.

   Face.   Milked, in troth, sweet Don.

   Subt. See all the monsters; the great lion of all, Don.

   Sur. *Con licencia, se puede ver à esta señora?*

   Subt. What talks he now?

   Face.   O' the senora.

   Subt.   O Don,
That is the lioness which you shall see
Also, my Don.

   Face.   'Slid, Subtle, how shall we do?

   Subt. For what?

   Face.   Why, Dol's employ'd, you know.

   Subt.   That's true!
'Fore heaven, I know not: He must stay, that's all.

   Face. Stay? That he must not by no means.

   Subt.   No, why?

   Face. Unless you'll mar all. 'Slight, he'll suspect it.
And then he will not pay, not half so well.
This is a travell'd punk-master, and does know
All the delays: a notable hot rascal,
And looks already rampant.

   Subt.   'Sdeath, and Mammon
Must not be troubled.

   Face.   Mammon, in no case!

   Subt. What shall we do then?

   Face.   Think: you must be sudden.

   Sur. *Entiendo, que la señora es tan hermosa, que codìcio
tan
À verla, como la bien aventuránza de mi vida.*

   Face. *Mi vida?* 'Slid, Subtle, he puts me in mind o' the
widow.
What dost thou say to draw her to it? ha?
And tell her it is her fortune? All our venture
Now lies upon 't. It is but one man more,
Which on 's chance to have her: and, beside,

There is no maidenhead to be fear'd or lost.
What dost thou think on't, Subtle?

Subt.   Who, I? Why——

Face. The credit of our house too is engag'd.

Subt. You made me an offer for my share erewhile.
What wilt thou gi' me, i' faith?

Face.   O, by that light,
I'll not buy now. You know your doom to me.
E'en take your lot, obey your chance, sir; win her,
And wear her out for me.

Subt.   'Slight. I'll not work her then.

Face. It is the common cause, therefore bethink you.
Dol else must know it, as you said.

Subt.   I care not.

Sur. Señores, por que se tarda tanta?

Subt. Faith, I am not fit, I am old.

Face.   That's now no reason, sir.

Sur. Puede ser, de hazer burla de mi amor?

Face. You hear the Don too? By this air, I call,
And loose the hinges. Dol!

Subt.   A plague of hell——

Face. Will you then do?

Subt.   You are a terrible rogue,
I'll think of this: will you, sir, call the widow?

Face. Yes, and I'll take her too, with all her faults,
Now I do think on't better.

Subt.   With all my heart, sir,
Am I discharg'd o' the lot?

Face.   As you please.

Subt.   Hands. [*They shake hands.*

Face. Remember now, that, upon any change,
You never claim her.

Subt.   Much good joy and health to you, sir.
Marry a whore? Fate, let me wed a witch first.

Sur. Por estas honradas barbas——

Subt.   He swears by his beard.
Dispatch, and call the brother too.   [*Exit* Face.

Sur.   *Tengo dùda, señores,
Que no me hágan alguna traycíon.*

410

Subt. How, issue on? Yes, *præsto, señor*. Please yon
Enthratha the *chambratha*, worthy Don?
Where if it please the Fates in your *bathada*,
You shall be soak'd, and strok'd, and tubb'd, and rubb'd:
And scrubb'd, and fubb'd, dear Don, before you go.
You shall, in faith, my scurvy baboon Don:
Be curried, claw'd, and flaw'd, and taw'd, indeed.
I will the heartlier go about it now,
And make the widow a punk so much the sooner,
To be reveng'd on this impetuous Face:
The quickly doing of it is the grace.

[*Exeunt* Subtle *and* Surly.

ACT IV. SCENE II

Another room in the same.

Enter Face, Kastril, *and* Dame Pliant.

Face. Come, lady: I knew the doctor would not leave,
Till he had found the very nick of her fortune.
Kas. To be a countess, say you? A Spanish countess, sir?
Pli. Why? is that better than an English countess?
Face. Better? 'Slight, make you that a question, lady?
Kas. Nay, she is a fool, Captain, you must pardon her.
Face. Ask from your courtier, to your inns-of-court-
man,
To your mere milliner: they will tell you all,
Your Spanish jennet is the best horse. Your Spanish
Stoup is the best garb. Your Spanish beard
Is the best cut. Your Spanish ruffs are the best
Wear. Your Spanish pavin the best dance.
Your Spanish titillation in a glove
The best perfume. And, for your Spanish pike,
And Spanish blade, let your poor captain speak.
Here comes the doctor.

Enter Subtle *with a paper.*

Subt. My most honour'd lady,
For so I am now to style you, having found

411

By this my scheme, you are to undergo
An honourable fortune, very shortly.
What will you say now, if some——

    Face.   I ha' told her all, sir.
And her right worshipful brother, here, that she shall be
A countess: do not delay 'em, sir. A Spanish countess.

    Subt. Still, my scarce worshipful Captain, you can keep
No secret? Well, since he has told you, madam,
Do you forgive him and I do.

    Kas.   She shall do that, sir.
I'll look to 't, 'tis my charge.

    Subt.   Well then, nought rests
But that she fit her love now to her fortune.

    Pli. Truly, I shall never brook a Spaniard.

    Subt.   No?

    Pli. Never since eighty-eight could I abide 'em,
And that was some three year afore I was born, in truth.

    Subt. Come, you must love him, or be miserable:
Choose which you will.

    Face.   By this good rush, persuade her,
She will cry strawberries else, within this twelve-month.

    Subt. Nay, shads and mackerel, which is worse.

    Face.   Indeed, sir?

    Kas. God's lid, you shall love him, or I'll kick you.

    Pli.   Why?
I'll do as you will ha' me, brother.

    Kas.   Do,
Or by this hand, I'll maul you.

    Face.   Nay, good sir,
Be not so fierce.

    Subt.   No, my enraged child,
She will be rul'd. What, when she comes to taste
The pleasures of a countess! to be courted——

    Face. And kiss'd, and ruffled!

    Subt.   Aye, behind the hangings.

    Face. And then come forth in pomp!

    Subt.   And know her state!

    Face. Of keeping all th' idolaters o' the chamber
Barer to her, than at their prayers!

Subt.   Is serv'd
Upon the knee!

Face.   And has her pages, huishers,
Footmen and coaches——

Subt.   Her six mares——

Face.   Nay, eight!

Subt. To hurry her through London to th' Exchange
Bet'lem, the china-houses——

Face.   Yes, and have
The citizens gape at her, and praise her tires!
And my lord's goose-turd bands, that ride with her!

Kas. Most brave! By this hand, you are not my suster
If you refuse.

Enter Surly.

Pli.   I will not refuse, brother.

*Sur. Que es esto, señores, que non se venga?
Esta tardanza me mata!*

Face.   It is the Count come!
The doctor knew he would be here, by his art.

Subt. En gallanta madama, Don! gallantissima!

*Sur. Por tódos los dioses, la más acabada
Hermosura, que he visto en mi vìda!*

Face. Is't not a gallant language that they speak?

Kas. An admirable language! Is't not French?

Face. No, Spanish, sir.

Kas.   It goes like law-French,
And that, they say, is the courtliest language.

Face.   List, sir.

*Sur. El sol ha perdido su lumbre, con el
Esplandor, que tràe esta dama. Valgame dios!*

Face. He admires your sister.

Kas.   Must not she make curtsy?

Subt. 'Ods will, she must go to him, man; and kiss him!
It is the Spanish fashion, for the women
To make first court.

Face.   'Tis true he tells you, sir:
His art knows all.

413

Sur.   *Porque no se acude?*

Kas. He speaks to her, I think?

Face.   That he does, sir.

Sur. *Por el amor de dios, que es esto, que se tàrda?*

Kas. Nay, see: she will not understand him! Gull!
Noddy.

Pli. What say you, brother?

Kas.   Ass, my suster,
Go kuss him, as the cunning man would ha' you,
I'll thrust a pin i' your buttocks else.

Face.   O, no sir.

Sur. *Señora mia, mi persona esta muy indigna*
Allegar à tànta hermosura.

Face. Does he not use her bravely?

Kas.   Bravely, i' faith!

Face. Nay, he will use her better.

Kas.   Do you think so?

Sur. *Señora, si sera servida, entremos.*

                           [*Exit with* Dame Pliant.

Kas. Where does he carry her?

Face.   Into the garden, sir;
Take you no thought: I must interpret for her.

Subt. Give Dol the word. [*Aside to* Face *who goes out.*]
      Come, my fierce child, advance,
We'll to our quarrelling lesson again.

Kas.   Agreed.
I love a Spanish Boy, with all my heart.

Subt. Nay, and by this means, sir, you shall be brother
To a great Count.

Kas.   Aye, I knew that, at first.
This match will advance the house of the Kastrils.

Subt. 'Pray God, your sister prove but pliant.

Kas.   Why,
Her name is so: by her other husband.

Subt.   How!

Kas. The widow Pliant. Knew you not that?

Subt.   No faith, sir.
Yet, by erection of her figure I guess'd it.
Come, let's go practise.

Kas. Yes, but do you think, doctor,
I e'er shall quarrel well?

  Subt.   I warrant you.   *[Exeunt.*

ACT IV. SCENE III

Another room in the same.

Enter Dol, *in her fit of raving, followed by* Mammon.

Dol. For, after *Alexander's death*——

Mam.   Good lady——

Dol. That Perdiccas, and Antigonus *were slain,*
The two that stood, Seleuc *and* Ptolomee——

Mam. Madam.

Dol.   *Made up the two legs, and the fourth beast.*
That was Gog-north, *and* Egypt-south: *which after*
Was call'd Gog Iron-leg, *and South Iron-leg*——

Mam.   Lady——

Dol. And then Gog-horned. *So was* Egypt, *too.*
Then Egypt clay-leg, *and* Gog clay-leg——

Mam.   Sweet madam——

Dol. And last Gog-dust, *and* Egypt-dust, *which fall*
In the last link of the fourth chain. And these
Be stars in story, which none see, or stop at——

Mam. What shall I do?

Dol.   *For, as he says, except*
We call the rabbins, and the heathen Greeks——

Mam. Dear lady.

Dol.   *To come from* Salem *and from* Athens,
And teach the people of Great Britain——

Enter Face *hastily, in his servant's dress.*

Face.   What's the matter, sir?

Dol. To speak the tongue of Eber *and* Javan——

Mam.   O,
She's in her fit.

Dol.   *We shall know nothing*——

Face.   Death, sir,
We are undone!

Dol.   *Where then a learned linguist*
Shall see the ancient used communion
Of vowels and consonants——
  Face.   My master will hear!
  Dol. A wisdom, which Pythagoras *held most high——*
  Mam. Sweet honourable lady!
  Dol.   *To comprise*
All sounds of voices, in few marks of letters——
  Face. Nay, you must never hope to lay her now.
                         [They speak together.
  Dol. And so we may arrive by Talmud skill,
And profane Greek, to raise the building up
Of Helen's house against the Ismaelite,
King of Thogarma, and his habergeons
Brimstony, blue, and fiery; and the force
Of King Abaddon, and the beast of Cittim,
Which Rabbi David Kimchi, Onkelos,
And Aben Ezra do interpret Rome.
  Face. How did you put her into 't?
  Mam.   Alas, I talk'd
Of a fifth monarchy I would erect,
With the Philosopher's Stone, by chance, and she
Falls on the other four straight.
  Face.   Out of Broughton!
I told you so. 'Slid, stop her mouth.
  Mam.   Is 't best?
  Face. She'll never leave else. If the old man hear her,
We are but fæces, ashes.
  Subt. [Within.]   What's to do there?
  Face. O, we are lost! Now she hears him, she is quiet.

        Enter Subtle. *They disperse.*

  Mam. Where shall I hide me?
  Subt.   How! What sight is here?
Close deeds of darkness, and that shun the light!
Bring him again. Who is he? What, my son!
O, I have lived too long.
  Mam.   Nay good, dear father,
There was no unchaste purpose.

Subt.   Not? and flee me
When I come in?

Mam.   That was my error.

Subt.   Error?
Guilt, guilt, my son! Give it the right name. No marvel,
If I found check in our great work within,
When such affairs as these were managing!

Mam. Why, have you so?

Subt.   It has stood still this half hour:
And all the rest of our less works gone back.
Where is the instrument of wickedness,
My lewd false drudge?

Mam.   Nay, good sir, blame not him.
Believe me, 'twas against his will or knowledge.
I saw her by chance.

Subt.   Will you commit more sin,
T' excuse a varlet?

Mam.   By my hope, 'tis true, sir.

Subt. Nay, then I wonder less, if you, for whom
The blessing was prepar'd, would so tempt heaven
And lose your fortunes.

Mam.   Why, sir?

Subt.   This'll retard
The work a month at least.

Mam.   Why, if it do,
What remedy? but think it not, good father:
Our purposes were honest.

Subt.   As they were,
So the reward will prove. [*A great crack and noise within.*
                        How now! Ah me!
God and all saints be good to us. What's that?

Re-enter Face.

Face. O sir, we are defeated! all the works
Are flown *in fumo*, every glass is burst.
Furnace and all rent down! as if a bolt
Of thunder had been driven through the house.
Retorts, receivers, pellicans, bolt-heads,
All struck in shivers!   [*Subtle falls down as in a swoon.*

417

Help, good sir! Alas,
Coldness and death invades him. Nay, Sir Mammon,
Do the fair offices of a man! You stand
As you were readier to depart than he. [*Knocking within.*
Who's there? My lord her brother is come.

Mam.   Ha, Lungs?

Face. His coach is at the door. Avoid his sight,
For he's as furious as his sister is mad.

Mam. Alas!

Face.   My brain is quite undone with the fume, sir,
I ne'er must hope to be mine own man again.

Mam. Is all lost, Lungs? Will nothing be preserved
Of all our cost?

Face.   Faith, very little, sir.
A peck of coals or so, which is cold comfort, sir.

Mam. O my voluptuous mind! I am justly punish'd.

Face. And so am I, sir.

Mam.   Cast from all my hopes——

Face. Nay, certainties, sir.

Mam.   By mine own base affections.

Subt. [*Seems to come to himself.*] O, the curst fruits of
vice and lust!

Mam.   Good father,
It was my sin. Forgive it.

Subt.   Hangs my roof
Over us still, and will not fall, O justice,
Upon us, for this wicked man!

Face.   Nay, look, sir.
You grieve him, now, with staying in his sight:
Good sir, the nobleman will come in too, and take you,
And that may breed a tragedy.

Mam.   I'll go.

Face. Aye, and repent at home, sir. It may be,
For some good penance, you may ha' it, yet,
A hundred pound to the box at Bet'lem——

Mam.   Yes.

Face. For the restoring such as ha' their wits.

Mam. I'll do 't.

Face.   I'll send one to you to receive it.

Mam.　　　　　　　　　　　　　　　　　　　Do.
Is no projection left?

　　Face.　　　　　All flown, or stinks, sir.

　　Mam. Will nought be sav'd, that's good for med'cine,
　　　thinkst thou?

　　Face. I cannot tell, sir. There will be, perhaps,
Something about the scraping of the shards
Will cure the itch: though not your itch of mind, sir.

　　　　　　　　　　　　　　　　　　　　　　　[Aside.
It shall be sav'd for you, and sent home. Good sir,
This way: for fear the lord should meet you.

　　　　　　　　　　　　　　　　　　[Exit Mammon.
　　Subt.　　　　　　　　　　　　　　　　*Face.*

　　Face. Aye.

　　Subt.　　　Is he gone?

　　Face.　　　　　　　Yes, and as heavily
As all the gold he hop'd for were in his blood.
Let us be light, though.

　　Subt. [*Leaping up.*] Aye, as balls, and bound
And hit our heads against the roof for joy:
There's so much of our care now cast away.

　　Face. Now to our Don.

　　Subt.　　　　　Yes, your young widow, by this time
Is made a countess, Face: Sh' has been in travail
Of a young heir for you.

　　Face.　　　　　Good, sir.

　　Subt.　　　　　　　Off with your case,
And greet her kindly, as a bridegroom should,
After these common hazards.

　　Face.　　　　　　Very well, sir.
Will you go fetch Don Diego off, the while?

　　Subt. And fetch him over too, if you'll be pleas'd, sir:
Would Dol were in her place, to pick his pockets now.

　　Face. Why, you can do it as well, if you would set to 't.
I pray you prove your virtue.

　　Subt.　　　　　For your sake, sir.　*[Exeunt.*

419

ACT IV. SCENE IV

Another room in the same.

Enter Surly *and* Dame Pliant.

Sur. Lady, you see into what hands you are fallen,
'Mongst what a nest of villains! and how near
Your honour was t' have catch'd a certain clap
Through your credulity had I but been
So punctually forward, as place, time,
And other circumstance would ha' made a man:
For you're a handsome woman: would you were wise, too.
I am a gentleman, come here disguis'd,
Only to find the knaveries of this citadel.
And where I might have wrong'd your honour, and have
    not,
I claim some interest in your love. You are,
They say, a widow, rich: and I am a bachelor
Worth nought: Your fortunes may make me a man,
As mine ha' preserv'd you a woman. Think upon it,
And whether I have deserv'd you or no.
    Pli.   I will, sir.
  Sur. And for these household-rogues, let me alone
To treat with them.

Enter Subtle.

  Subt. How doth my noble Diego?
And my dear madam, Countess? Hath the Count
Been courteous, lady? liberal? and open?
Donzel, methinks you look melancholic,
After your *coitum*, and scurvy! Truly,
I do not like the dullness of your eye:
It hath a heavy cast, 'tis upsee Dutch
And says you are a lumpish whore-master.
Be lighter, I will make your pockets so.
                           [*Falls to picking of them.*
  Sur. Will you, Don bawd, and pick-purse? [*Strikes him
  down.*] How now? reel you?

Stand up, sir, you shall find since I am so heavy,
I'll gi' you equal weight.

 Subt.   Help, murder!

 Sur.   No, sir.

There's no such thing intended. A good cart,
And a clean whip shall ease you of that fear.
I am the Spanish Don that should be cozened,
Do you see? cozened? Where's your Captain Face?
That parcel broker and whole-bawd, all rascal.

Enter Face *in his uniform.*

 Face. How, Surly!

 Sur.   O, make your approach, good captain.
I have found from whence your copper rings and spoons
Come now, wherewith you cheat abroad in taverns.
'Twas here you learn'd t' anoint your boot with brimstone,
Then rub men's gold on 't, for a kind of touch,
And say 'twas naught, when you had chang'd the colour,
That you might ha 't for nothing. And this doctor,
Your sooty, smoky-bearded compeer, he
Will close you so much gold in a bolt's-head,
And, on a turn, convey, i' the stead, another
With sublim'd Mercury that shall burst i' the heat,
And fly out all *in fumo*! Then weeps Mammon:
Then swoons his worship. [*Face goes out quietly.*] Or, he
  is the Faustus,
That casteth figures, and can conjure, cures
Plague, piles, and pox, by the Ephemerides,
And holds intelligence with all the bawds
And midwives of three shires? while you send in——
Captain (what, is he gone?), damsels with child,
Wives that are barren, or the waiting-maid
With the green sickness. [*Seizes* Subtle *as he is retiring.*]
       Nay, sir, you must tarry
Though he be scap'd; and answer by the ears, sir.

Re-enter Face *with* Kastril.

 Face. Why, now's the time, if ever you will quarrel

Well, as they say, and be a true-born child.
The doctor and your sister both are abus'd.

   Kas. Where is he? which is he? he is a slave
Whate'er he is, and the son of a whore. Are you
The man, sir, I would know?

   Sur.   I should be loth, sir,
To confess so much.

   Kas.   Then you lie i' your throat.

   Sur.   How?

   Face. [*To Kastril.*] A very errant rogue, sir, and a cheater,
Employ'd here by another conjurer,
That does not love the doctor, and would cross him
If he knew how——

   Sur.   Sir, you are abus'd.

   Kas.   You lie:
And 'tis no matter.

   Face.   Well said, sir. He is
The impudent'st rascal——

   Sur.   You are indeed. Will you hear me, sir?

   Face. By no means: Bid him be gone.

   Kas.   Be gone, sir, quickly.

   Sur. This's strange! Lady, do you inform your brother.

   Face. There is not such a foist in all the town,
The doctor had him, presently: and finds, yet,
The Spanish count will come here. Bear up, Subtle. [*Aside.*

   Subt. Yes, sir, he must appear within this hour.

   Face. And yet this rogue would come in a disguise,
By the temptation of another spirit,
To trouble our art, though he could not hurt it.

   Kas.   Aye,
I know—Away [*to his sister*], you talk like a foolish
    mauther.

   Sur. Sir, all is truth she says.

   Face.   Do not believe him, sir:
He is the lying'st swabber! Come your ways, sir.

   Sur. You are valiant, out of company.

   Kas.   Yes, how then, sir?

Enter Drugger *with a piece of damask.*

Face. Nay, here's an honest fellow too, that knows him,
And all his tricks. Make good what I say, Abel,

           [*Aside to* Drugger.

This cheater would ha' cozen'd thee o' the widow.
He owes this honest Drugger, here, seven pound,
He has had on him, in twopenny'orths of tobacco.

 Dru. Yes, sir. And h' has damn'd himself three terms to
  pay me.

 Face. And what does he owe for lotium?

 Dru.   Thirty shillings, sir:
And for six syringes.

 Sur.   Hydra of villany!

 Face. Nay, sir, you must quarrel him out o' the house.

 Kas.   I will.

Sir, if you get not out o' doors, you lie:
And you are a pimp.

 Sur.   Why, this is madness, sir,
Not valour in you: I must laugh at this.

 Kas. It is my humour: You are a pimp, and a trig,
And an Amadis de Gaul, or a Don Quixote.

 Dru. Or a knight o' the curious coxcomb. Do you see?

Enter Ananias.

 Ana. Peace to the household.

 Kas.   I'll keep peace for no man.

 Ana. Casting of dollars is concluded lawful.

 Kas. Is he the constable?

 Subt.   Peace, Ananias.

 Face.   No, sir.

 Kas. Then you are an otter, and a shad, a whit,
A very tim.

 Sur.   You'll hear me, sir?

 Kas.   I will not.

 Ana. What is the motive?

 Subt.   Zeal in the young gentleman,
Against his Spanish slops——

 Ana.   They are profane,
Lewd, superstitious, and idolatrous breeches.

Sur. New rascals!

Kas.   Will you be gone, sir?

Ana.   Avoid Satan,
Thou art not of the light. That puff of pride
About thy neck betrays thee: 'and is the same
With that which the unclean birds, in seventy-seven,
Were seen to prank it with on divers coasts.
Thou look'st like Antichrist in that lewd hat.

    Sur. I must give way.

    Kas.   Be gone, sir.

    Sur.   But I'll take
A course with you——

    Ana.   Depart, proud Spanish fiend!

    Sur. Captain and doctor——

    Ana.   Child of perdition.

    Kas.   Hence, sir. [*Exit* Surly.
Did I not quarrel bravely?

    Face.   Yes, indeed, sir.

    Kas. Nay, and I give my mind to 't, I shall do 't.

    Face. O, you must follow, sir, and threaten him tame.
He'll turn again else.

    Kas.   I'll re-turn him, then.   [*Exit.*

    Face. Drugger, this rogue prevented us, for thee.
We had determin'd that thou shouldst ha' come,
In a Spanish suit, and ha' carried her so; and he,
A brokerly slave, goes, puts it on himself.
Hast brought the damask?

    Dru.   Yes, sir.

    Face.   Thou must borrow
A Spanish suit. Hast thou no credit with the players?

    Dru. Yes, sir, did you never see me play the Fool?

    Face. I know not, Nab: thou shalt, if I can help it. [*Aside.*
Hieronimo's old cloak, ruff, and hat will serve,
I'll tell thee more when thou bringst 'em.   [*Exit* Drugger.

    Ana.   Sir, I know
The Spaniard hates the brethren and hath spies
Upon their actions: and that this was one
I make no scruple. But the holy synod
Have been in prayer and meditation for it.

And 'tis reveal'd no less to them than me,
That casting of money is most lawful.

    Subt.   True.

But here I cannot do it; if the house
Should chance to be suspected, all would out,
And we be lock'd up in the Tower for ever,
To make gold there for th' state, never come out:
And then you are defeated.

    Ana.   I will tell

This to the elders, and the weaker brethren,
That the whole company of the separation
May join in humble prayer again.

    Subt.   And fasting.

    Ana. Yea, for some fitter place. The peace of mind
Rest with these walls.   [*Exit.*

    Subt.   Thanks, courteous Ananias.

    Face. What did he come for?

    Subt.   About casting dollars,

Presently, out of hand. And so, I told him,
A Spanish minister came here to spy
Against the faithful——

    Face.   I conceive. Come, Subtle.

Thou art so down upon the least disaster!
How wouldst tho' ha' done, if I had not help'd thee out?

    Subt. I thank thee, Face, for the angry boy, i' faith.

    Face. Who would ha' look'd it should ha' been that
rascal,
Surly? He had dy'd his beard and all. Well, sir,
Here's damask come to make you a suit.

    Subt.   Where's Drugger?

    Face. He is gone to borrow me a Spanish habit;
I'll be the Count now.

    Subt.   But where's the widow?

    Face. Within, with my lord's sister: Madam **Dol**
Is entertaining her.

    Subt.   By your favour, **Face,**
Now she is honest, I will stand again.

    Face. You will not offer it?

    Subt.   Why?

Face. Stand to your word,
Or—here comes Dol. She knows——
Subt. You are tyrannous still.

Enter Dol *hastily.*

Face. Strict for my right. How now, Dol? Hast' told
her
The Spanish Count will come?
Dol. Yes, but another is come,
You little look'd for!
Face. Who's that?
Dol. Your master:
The master of the house.
Subt. How, Dol!
Face. She lies.
This is some trick. Come, leave your quiblins, Dorothy.
Dol. Look out, and see. [Face *goes to the window.*
Subt. Art thou in earnest, Dol?
Dol. 'Slight,
Forty o' the neighbours are about him, talking.
Face. 'Tis he, by this good day.
Dol. 'Twill prove ill day
For some on us.
Face. We are undone and taken.
Dol. Lost, I am afraid.
Subt. You said he would not come,
While there died one a week within the liberties.
Face. No: 'twas within the walls.
Subt. Was't so? Cry you mercy:
I thought the liberties. What shall we do now, Face?
Face. Be silent: not a word if he call or knock.
I'll into mine old shape again and meet him,
Of Jeremy the butler. I' the meantime,
Do you two pack up all the goods and purchase,
That we can carry i' the two trunks. I'll keep him
Off for to-day, if I cannot longer: and then
At night, I'll ship you both away to Ratcliff
Where we'll meet tomorrow, and there we'll share.

Let Mammon's brass and pewter keep the cellar:
We'll have another time for that. But, Dol,
Pray thee, go heat a little water, quickly;
Subtle must shave me. All my captain's beard
Must off, to make me appear smooth Jeremy.
You'll do't?

    Subt.   Yes, I'll shave you, as well as I can.

    Face.   And not cut my throat, but trim me?

    Subt.   You shall see, sir.

                                        [Exeunt.

ACT V. SCENE I

Before Lovewit's *door.*

Enter Lovewit *and his* Neighbours.

    Lov.   Has there been such resort, say you?

    Nei. 1.   Daily, sir.

    Nei. 2.   And nightly, too.

    Nei. 3.   Aye, some as brave as lords.

    Nei. 4.   Ladies and gentlewomen.

    Nei. 5.   Citizen's wives.

    Nei. 1.   And knights.

    Nei. 6.   In coaches.

    Nei. 2.   Yes, and oyster-women.

    Nei. 1.   Beside other gallants.

    Nei. 3.   Sailor's wives.

    Nei. 4.   Tobacco-men.

    Nei. 5.   Another Pimlico!

    Lov.   What should my knave advance,
To draw this company? He hung out no banners
Of a strange calf with five legs, to be seen?
Or a huge lobster with six claws?

    Nei. 6.   No, sir.

    Nei. 3.   We had gone in then, sir.

    Lov.   He has no gift
Of teaching i' the nose, that e'er I knew of!
You saw no bills set up, that promis'd cure
Of agues, or the tooth-ache?

Nei. 2.   No such thing, sir.

Lov. Nor heard a drum struck, for baboons, or puppets?

Nei. 5. Neither, sir.

Lov.   What device should he bring forth now!
I love a teeming wit as I love my nourishment.
'Pray God he ha' not kept such open house,
That he hath sold my hangings and my bedding:
I left him nothing else. If he have eat 'em
A plague o' the moth, say I. Sure he has got
Some bawdy pictures, to call all this ging;
The Friar and the Nun; or the new motion
Of the knight's courser covering the parson's mare;
The boy of six year old with the great thing:
Or 't may be, he has the fleas that run at tilt,
Upon a table, or some dog to dance?
When saw you him?

Nei. 1.   Who, sir, Jeremy?

Nei. 2.   Jeremy butler?
We saw him not this month.

Lov.   How!

Nei. 4.   Not these five weeks, sir.

Nei. 1. These six weeks, at the least.

Lov.   You amaze me, neighbours!

Nei. 5. Sure, if your worship know not where he is,
He's slipped away.

Nei. 6.   Pray God, he be not made away!

Lov. Ha? It's not time to question, then.   *[Knocks.*

Nei. 6.   About
Some three week's since, I heard a doleful cry,
As I sat up, a-mending my wife's stockings.

Lov. This's strange! that none will answer! Didst thou
   hear
A cry, sayest thou?

Nei. 6.   Yes, sir, like unto a man
That had been strangled an hour, and could not speak.

Nei. 2. I heard it too, just this day three weeks at two
   o'clock
Next morning.

Lov.   These be miracles, or you make 'em so!

A man an hour strangled, and could not speak,
And both you heard him cry?

    Nei. 3.   Yes, downward, sir.

    Lov. Thou art a wise fellow: Give me thy hand, I pray
    thee.

What trade art thou on?

    Nei. 3.   A smith, and 't please your worship.

    Lov. A smith? Then lend me thy help to get this door
open.

    Nei. 3. That I will presently, sir, but fetch my tools——
                                        [*Exit.*

    Nei. 1. Sir, best to knock again, afore you break it.

          Enter Face *in his butler's livery.*

    Lov. I will.

    Face.   What mean you, sir?

    Nei. 1. 2. 4.   O, here's Jeremy!

    Face. Come sir, come from the door.

    Lov.   Why! what's the matter?

    Face. Yet farther, you are too near, yet.

    Lov.   I' the name of wonder!

What means the fellow?

    Face.   The house, sir, has been visited.

    Lov. What? with the plague? stand thou then farther.

    Face.   No, sir,

I had it not.

    Lov. Who had it then? I left
None else but thee i' the house!

    Face.   Yes, sir. My fellow,
The cat, that kept the buttery, had it on her
A week before I spied it: but I got her
Convey'd away i' the night. And so I shut
The house up for a month——

    Lov.   How!

    Face.   Purposing then, sir,
T' have burnt rose-vinegar, treacle, and tar,
And ha' made it sweet, that you should ne'er ha' known it:
Because I knew the news would but afflict you, sir.

    Lov. Breathe less, and farther off. Why, this is stranger!

The neighbours tell me all, here, that the doors
Have still been open——

Face. How, sir!

Lov. Gallants, men, and women,
And of all sorts, tag-rag, been seen to flock here
In threaves, these ten weeks, as to a second Hogsden
In days of Pimlico and Eye-bright!

Face. Sir,
Their wisdoms will not say so!

Lov. To-day, they speak
Of coaches and gallants; one in a French hood
Went in, they tell me: and another was seen
In a velvet gown at the window! divers more
Pass in and out!

Face. They did pass through the doors then,
Or walls, I assure their eye-sights and their spectacles;
For here, sir, are the keys: and here have been,
In this my pocket, now, above twenty days!
And for before, I kept the fort alone there.
But that 'tis yet not deep i' the afternoon,
I should believe my neighbours had seen double
Through the black-pot, and made these apparitions!
For, on my faith to your worship, for these three weeks
And upwards, the door has not been open'd.

Lov. Strange!

Nei. 1. Good faith, I think I saw a coach!

Nei. 2. And I too,
I'd ha' been sworn!

Lov. Do you but think it now?
And but one coach?

Nei. 4. We cannot tell, sir: Jeremy
Is a very honest fellow.

Face. Did you see me at all?

Nei. 1. No. That we are sure on.

Nei. 2. I'll be sworn o' that.

Lov. Fine rogues, to have your testimonies built on!

Re-enter third Neighbour *with his tools.*

Nei. 3. Is Jeremy come?

430

Nei. 1.   O, yes, you may leave your tools;
We were deceiv'd, he says.

Nei. 2.   He has had the keys,
And the door has been shut these three weeks.

Nei. 3.   Like enough.

Lov. Peace, and get hence, you changelings.

Enter Surly *and* Mammon.

Face.   Surly come!
And Mammon made acquainted? They'll tell all.
How shall I beat them off? What shall I do?
Nothing's more wretched than a guilty conscience. [*Aside.*

Sur. No, sir, he was a great physician. This,
It was no bawdy-house: but a mere chancel.
You knew the lord and his sister.

Mam.   Nay, good Surly——

Sur. The happy word, Be rich——

Mam.   Play not the truant——

Sur. Should be to-day pronounc'd to all your friends.
And where be your andirons now? and your brass pots?
That should ha' been golden flagons and great wedges?

Mam. Let me but breathe. What! They ha' shut their
        doors,
Methinks!

Sur.   Aye, now 'tis holy-day with them.

Mam.   Rogues,
Cozeners, imposters, bawds. [*Mammon and Surly knock.*

Face.   What mean you, sir?

Mam. To enter if we can.

Face.   Another man's house?
Here is the owner, sir. Turn you to him.
And speak your business.

Mam.   Are you, sir, the owner?

Lov. Yes, sir.

Mam.   And are those knaves within, your cheaters?

Lov. What knaves? what cheaters?

Mam.   Subtle, and his Lungs.

Face. The gentleman is distracted, sir! No Lungs

Nor lights ha' been seen here these three weeks, sir,
Within these doors, upon my word!

Sur.   Your word,
Groom arrogant?

Face.   Yes, sir, I am the housekeeper,
And know the keys ha' not been out o' my hands.

Sur. This's a new Face?

Face.   You do mistake the house, sir!
What sign was't at?

Sur.   You rascal! This is one
O' the confederacy. Come, let's get officers,
And force the door.

Lov.   Pray you stay, gentlemen.

Sur. No, sir, we'll come with warrant.

Mam.   Aye, and then
We shall ha' your doors open.

             [*Exeunt* Surly *and* Mammon.

Lov.   What means this?

Face. I cannot tell, sir!

Nei. 1.   These are two o' the gallants
That we do think we saw.

Face.   Two o' the fools?
You talk as idly as they. Good faith, sir,
I think the moon has craz'd 'em all!—O me,

Enter Kastril.

The angry boy come too? He'll make a noise
And ne'er away till he have betray'd us all.   [*Aside.*

Kas. [*Knocking.*] What rogues, bawds, slaves, you'll
     open the door anon.
Punk, cockatrice, my suster. By this light
I'll fetch the marshal to you. You are a whore,
To keep your castle——

Face.   Who would you speak with, sir?

Kas. The bawdy doctor, and the cozening captain,
And Puss my suster.

Lov.   This is something, sure!

Face. Upon my trust, the doors were never open, sir.

Kas. I have heard all their tricks told me twice over,
By the fat knight and the lean gentleman.

Lov. Here comes another.

Enter Ananias *and* Tribulation.

Face.   Ananias too?
And his pastor?

Trib.   The doors are shut against us.

                    [*They beat too, at the door.*

Ana. Come forth, you seed of sulphur, sons of fire,
Your stench, it is broke forth: abomination
Is in the house.

Kas.   Aye, my suster's there.

Ana.   The place,
It is become a cage of unclean birds.

Kas. Yes, I will fetch the scavenger and the constable.

Trib. You shall do well.

Ana.   We'll join to weed them out.

Kas. You will not come then? punk, device, my suster!

Ana. Call her not sister. She is a harlot, verily.

Kas. I'll raise the street.

Lov.   Good gentlemen, a word.

Ana. Satan, avoid, and hinder not our zeal.

                    [*Exeunt* Ananias *and* Tribulation.

Lov. The world's turn'd Bethlem.

Face.   These are all broke loose
Out of St. Katherine's, where they use to keep
The better sort of mad-folks.

Nei. 1.   All these persons
We saw go in and out, here.

Nei. 2.   Yes, indeed, sir.

Nei. 3. These were the parties.

Face.   Peace, you drunkards! Sir,
I wonder at it! Please you to give me leave
To touch the door, I'll try an' the lock be chang'd.

Lov. It 'mazes me!

Face. [*Goes to the door.*] Good faith, sir, I believe,
There's no such thing. 'Tis all *deceptio visus.*
Would I could get him away.   [*Aside.*

433

Dap. [*Within.*]　　　Master Captain, master Doctor.

Lov. Who's that?

Face. Our clerk within, that I forgot! [*Aside.*] I know
　not, sir.

Dap. [*Within.*] For God's sake, when will her Grace be
　at leisure?

Face.　　　Ha!

Illusions, some spirit o' the air:—his gag is melted,
And now he sets out the throat.　　　　　　　[*Aside.*

Dap. [*Within.*]　　　I am almost stifled——

Face. Would you were altogether.　　　　　[*Aside.*

Lov.　　　　　　　'Tis i' the house.

Ha! List.

Face.　　Believe it, sir, i' the air!

Lov.　　　　　　　　Peace, you——

Dap. [*Within.*] Mine aunt's Grace does not use me well.

Subt. [*Within.*]　　　　　　You fool,

Peace, you'll mar all.

Face. [*Through the keyhole.*] Or you will else, you
　rogue!

Lov. O, is it so? Then you converse with spirits!

Come sir. No more o' your tricks, good Jeremy,
The truth, the shortest way.

Face.　　　　　Dismiss this rabble, sir.

What shall I do? I am catch'd.　　　　　　[*Aside.*

Lov.　　　　　Good neighbours,

I thank you all. You may depart. [*Exeunt* neighbours.]
Come, sir,
You know that I am an indulgent master:
And therefore conceal nothing. What's your med'cine,
To draw so many several sorts of wild-fowl?

Face. Sir, you were wont to affect mirth and wit:
But here's no place to talk on't i' the street.
Give me but leave to make the best of my fortune,
And only pardon me th' abuse of your house:
It's all I beg. I'll help you to a widow,
In recompense, that you shall gi' me thanks for,
Will make you seven years younger, and a rich one.
'Tis but your putting on a Spanish cloak;

434

I have her within. You need not fear the house,
It was not visited.
    Lov.   But by me, who came
Sooner than you expected.
    Face.   It is true, sir.
Pray you forgive me.
    Lov. Well: let's see your widow.

                                    [*Exeunt.*

ACT V. SCENE II

A room in Lovewit's *house.*

Enter Subtle, *leading in* Dapper, *who has his eyes bound as
before.*

    Subt. How! Ha' you eaten your gag?
    Dap.   Yes, faith, it crumbled
Away i' my mouth.
    Subt.   You ha' spoil'd all then.
    Dap.   No,
I hope my aunt of Faery will forgive me.
    Subt. Your aunt's a gracious lady: but in troth
You were to blame.
    Dap.   The fume did overcome me,
And I did do 't to stay my stomach. Pray you
To satisfy her Grace.

            Enter Face *in his uniform.*

                    Here comes the captain.
    Face. How now! Is his mouth down?
    Subt.   Aye! he has spoken.
    Face. A pox, I heard him, and you too. He's undone,
        then.
I have been fain to say the house is haunted
With spirits, to keep churl back.
    Subt.   And hast thou done it?
    Face. Sure, for this night.
    Subt.   Why; then, triumph and sing
Of Face so famous, the precious king
Of present wits.

                        435

Face.　　　　Did you not hear the coil
About the door?

Subt.　Yes, and I dwindled with it.

Face.　Show him his aunt, and let him be dispatch'd:
I'll send her to you.　　　　　　　　　　*[Exit* Face.

Subt.　　　　Well sir, your aunt her Grace
Will give you audience presently, on my suit,
And the captain's word that you did not eat your gag
In any contempt of her Highness.

Dap.　　　　　　Not I, in troth, sir.

Enter Dol *like the Queen of Faery.*

Subt. Here she is come. Down o' your knees, and
　wriggle:
She has a stately presence. Good. Yet nearer,
And bid God save you.

Dap.　　　　Madam.

Subt.　　　　　　　And your aunt.

Dap. And my most gracious aunt, God save your Grace.

Dol. Nephew, we thought to have been angry with you:
But that sweet face of yours hath turn'd the tide,
And made it flow with joy, that ebb'd of love.
Arise, and touch our velvet gown.

Subt.　　　　　　The skirts,
And kiss 'em. So.

Dol.　　　Let me now stroke that head,
Much, nephew, shalt thou win; much shalt thou spend;
Much shalt thou give away: much shalt thou lend.

Subt. Aye, much, indeed. *[Aside.]* Why do you not
　thank her Grace?

Dap. I cannot speak for joy.

Subt.　　　　See, the kind wretch!
Your Grace's kinsman right.

Dol.　　　Give me the bird.
Here is your fly in a purse; about your neck, cousin,
Wear it, and feed it, about this day sev'night,
On your right wrist.

Subt.　　　Open a vein with a pin,

436

And let it suck but once a week: till then
You must not look on 't.

Dol.   No. And, kinsman,
Bear yourself worthy of the blood you come on.

Subt. Her Grace would ha' you eat no more Woolsack
pies,
Nor Dagger frume'ty.

Dol.   Nor break his fast,
In Heaven and Hell.

Subt.   She's with you everywhere!
Nor play with costermongers at mum-chance, tray-trip,
God-make-you-rich (when as your aunt has done it:) but
keep
The gallant'st company, and the best games——

Dap.   Yes, sir.

Subt. Gleek and primero, and what you get, be true to
us.

Dap. By this hand, I will.

Subt.   You may bring's a thousand pound,
Before to-morrow night, (if but three thousand,
Be stirring) an' you will.

Dap.   I swear I will then.

Subt. Your fly will learn you all games.

Face. [*Within.*]   Ha' you done there?

Subt. Your Grace will command him no more duties?

Dol.   No.
But come and see me often. I may chance
To leave him three or four hundred chests of treasure,
And some twelve thousand acres of Faeryland:
If he game well and comely, with good gamesters.

Subt. There's a kind aunt! kiss her departing part.
But you must sell your forty mark a year now:

Dap. Aye, sir, I mean.

Subt.   Or, gi' it away: pox on 't.

Dap. I'll gi' it mine aunt. I'll go and fetch the writings.

                                                [*Exit.*

Subt. 'Tis well, away.

Re-enter Face.

Face. Where's Subtle?

Subt. Here. What news?

Face. Drugger is at the door, go take his suit,
And bid him fetch a parson, presently:
Say he shall marry the widow. Thou shalt spend
A hundred pound by the service! [*Exit* Subtle.] Now,
    Queen Dol,
Ha' you pack'd up all?

Dol. Yes.

Face. And how do you like
The lady Pliant?

Dol. A good dull innocent.

Re-enter Subtle.

Subt. Here's your Hieronimo's cloak and hat.

Face. Give me 'em.

Subt. And the ruff too?

Face. Yes, I'll come to you presently. [*Exit.*

Subt. Now, he is gone about his project, Dol,
I told you of, for the widow.

Dol. 'Tis direct
Against our articles.

Subt. Well, we'll fit him, wench.
Hast thou gull'd her of her jewels, or her bracelets?

Dol. No, but I will do't.

Subt. Soon at night, my Dolly,
When we are shipp'd, and all our goods aboard,
Eastward for Ratcliff; we will turn our course
To Brainford westward, if thou sayest the word:
And take our leaves of this o'erweening rascal,
This peremptory Face.

Dol. Content, I am weary of him.

Subt. Tho' hast cause, when the slave will run a wiving,
    Dol,
Against the instrument that was drawn between us.

Dol. I'll pluck his bird as bare as I can.

Subt. Yes, tell her,
She must by any means address some present
To th' cunning man; make him amends, for wronging

His art with her suspicion; send a ring;
Or chain of pearl; she will be tortur'd else
Extremely in her sleep, say: and ha' strange things
Come to her. Wilt thou?

   Dol.   Yes.

   Subt.   My fine flitter-mouse,
My bird o' the night; we'll tickle it at the pigeons
When we have all, and may unlock the trunks,
And say, this's mine, and thine, and thine, and mine——

                                 [They kiss.

Re-enter Face.

   Face. What now, a billing?

   Subt.   Yes, a little exalted
In the good passage of our stock-affairs.

   Face. Drugger has brought his parson; take him in, Subtle,
And send Nab back again, to wash his face.

   Subt. I will: and shave himself?   *[Exit* Subtle.

   Face.   If you can get him.

   Dol. You are hot upon it, Face, whate'er it is!

   Face. A trick, that Dol shall spend ten pound a month by.
Is he gone?

Re-enter Subtle.

   Subt.   The chaplain waits you i' the hall, sir.

   Face. I'll go bestow him.   *[Exit* Face.

   Dol.   He'll now marry her, instantly.

   Subt. He cannot, yet, he is not ready. Dear Dol,
Cozen her of all thou canst. To deceive him
Is no deceit, but justice, that would break
Such an inextricable tie as ours was.

   Dol. Let me alone to fit him.

Re-enter Face.

   Face.   Come, my venturers,
You ha' pack'd up all? Where be the trunks. Bring forth.

   Subt. Here.

   Face.   Let's see 'em. Where's the money?

Subt.   Here,
In this.

Face. Mammon's ten pound: eight score before.
The brethren's money, this. Drugger's, and Dapper's.
What paper's that?

Dol.   The jewel of the waiting maid's,
That stole it from her lady, to know certain——

Face. If she should have precedence of her mistress?

Dol. Yes.

Face.   What box is that?

Subt.   The fish-wife's rings, I think:
And th' ale-wife's single money. Is't not, Dol?

Dol. Yes: and the whistle that the sailor's wife
Brought you, to know, and her husband were with Ward.

Face. We'll wet it to-morrow: and our silver beakers,
And tavern cups. Where be the French petticoats
And girdles and hangers?

Subt.   Here i' the trunk,
And the bolts of lawn.

Face.   Is Drugger's damask there?
And the tobacco?

Subt.   Yes.

Face.   Give me the keys.

Dol. Why you the keys!

Subt.   No matter, Dol: because
We shall not open 'em, before he comes.

Face. 'Tis true, you shall not open them, indeed:
Nor have 'em forth. Do you see? Not forth, Dol.

Dol.   No!

Face. No, my smock-rampant. The right is, my master
Knows all, has pardon'd me, and he will keep 'em.
Doctor, 'tis true you look for all your figures:
I sent for him, indeed. Wherefore, good partners,
Both he and she be satisfied: for here
Determines the *indenture tripartite*,
Twixt Subtle, Dol, and Face. All I can do
Is to help you over the wall, o' the back-side;
Or lend you a sheet to save your velvet gown, Dol.
Here will be officers, presently; bethink you,

Of some course suddenly to 'scape the dock:
For thither you'll come else. [*Some knock.*] Hark you,
    thunder.

    Subt. You are a precious fiend!

    Off. [*Without.*]   Open the door.

    Face. Dol, I am sorry for thee, i' faith. But hear'st thou?
It shall go hard, but I will place thee somewhere:
Thou shalt ha' my letter to Mistress Amo.

    Dol.   Hang you——

    Face. Or madam Cæsarean.

    Dol.   Pox upon you, rogue,
Would I had but time to beat thee.

    Face.   Subtle,
Let's know where you set up next; I'll send you
A customer, now and then, for old acquaintance:
What new course ha' you?

    Subt.   Rogue, I'll hang myself:
That I may walk a greater devil than thou,
And haunt thee i' the flock-bed and the buttery. [*Exeunt.*

ACT V. SCENE III

An outer room in the same.

Enter Lovewit *in Spanish dress, with the* parson.
Loud knocking at the door.

    Lov. What do you mean, my masters?

    Mam. [*Without.*]   Open your door,
Cheaters, bawds, conjurers.

    Off.   Or we'll break it open.

    Lov. What warrant have you?

    Off. [*Without.*]   Warrant enough, sir, doubt not:
If you'll not open it.

    Lov.   Is there an officer, there?

    Off. [*Without.*] Yes, two or three for failing.

    Lov.   Have but patience,
And I will open it straight.

Enter Face *as butler.*

Face. Sir, ha' you done?
Is it a marriage? perfect?
Lov. Yes, my Brain.
Face. Off with your ruff and cloak then; be yourself, sir.
Sur. [*Without.*] Down with the door.
Kas. [*Without.*]   'Slight, ding it open.
Lov. [*Opening the door.*]   Hold.
Hold, gentlemen, what means this violence?

*Mammon, Surly, Kastril, Ananias, Tribulation and Officers
rush in.*

Mam. Where is this collier?
Sur.   And my Captain Face?
Mam. These day-owls.
Sur.   That are birding in men's purses.
Mam. Madam Suppository.
Kas.   Doxey, my suster.
Ana.   Locusts
Of the foul pit!
Trib.   Profane as Bel and the Dragon!
Ana. Worse than the grasshoppers or the lice of Egypt!
Lov. Good gentlemen, hear me. Are you officers,
And cannot stay this violence?
Off.   Keep the peace.
Lov. Gentlemen, what is the matter? Whom do you
    seek?
Mam. The chemical cozener.
Sur.   And the captain pander.
Kas. The nun my suster.
Mam.   Madam Rabbi.
Ana.   Scorpions
And caterpillars.
Lov.   Fewer at once, I pray you.
Off. One after another, gentlemen, I charge you,
By virtue of my staff——
Ana.   They are the vessels
Of pride, lust, and the cart.
Lov.   Good zeal, lie still
A little while.

Trib.   Peace, Deacon Ananias.

Lov. The house is mine here, and the doors are open:
If there be any such persons as you seek for,
Use your authority, search on o' God's name.
I am but newly come to town, and finding
This tumult 'bout my door, to tell you true,
It somewhat 'maz'd me; till my man, here, fearing
My more displeasure, told me he had done
Somewhat an insolent part, let out my house
Belike presuming on my known aversion
From any air o' the town, while there was sickness,
To a doctor and a captain: who, what they are,
Or where they be, he knows not.

Mam.   Are they gone?

Lov. You may go in and search, sir.

   Mammon, Ananias, *and* Tribulation *go in.*

                              Here, I find
The empty walls, worse than I left 'em, smok'd,
A few crack'd pots, and glasses, and a furnace,
The ceiling fill'd with poesies of the candle:
And Madame, with a Dildo, writ o' the walls.
Only one gentlewoman I met here,
That is within, that said she was a widow——

Kas. Aye, that's my suster. I'll go thump her. Where is
   she?   [*Goes in.*

Lov. And should ha' married a Spanish count, but he,
When he came to 't, neglected her so grossly,
That I, a widower, am gone through with her.

Sur. How! Have I lost her then?

Lov.   Were you the Don, sir?
Good faith, now, she does blame you extremely, and says
You swore, and told her, you had ta'en the pains
To dye your beard, and amber o'er your face,
Borrowed a suit and ruff, all for her love;
And then did nothing. What an oversight,
And want of putting forward, sir, was this!
Well fare an old harquebuszier yet,

Could prime his powder, and give fire, and hit,
All in a twinkling.   [*Mammon comes forth.*

Mam.   The whole nest are fled!

Lov. What sort of birds were they?

Mam.   A kind of choughs,
Or thievish daws, sir, that have pick'd my purse
Of eight score and ten pounds, within these five weeks,
Beside my first materials; and my goods
That lie i' the cellar: which I am glad they ha' left,
I may have home yet.

Lov.   Think you so, sir?

Mam.   Aye.

Lov. By order of law, sir, but not otherwise.

Mam. Not mine own stuff?

Lov.   Sir, I can take no knowledge
That they are yours, but by public means.
If you can bring certificate, that you were gull'd of 'em,
Or any formal writ out of a court
That you did cozen yourself, I will not hold them.

Mam. I'll rather lose 'em.

Lov.   That you shall not, sir,
By me, in troth. Upon these terms they are yours.
What should they ha' been, sir, turn'd into gold all?

Mam.   No.
I cannot tell. It may be they should. What then?

Lov. What a great loss in hope have you sustain'd?

Mam. Not I, the commonwealth has.

Face.   Aye, he would ha' built
The city new; and made a ditch about it
Of silver, should have run with cream from Hogsden:
That, every Sunday in Moorfields, the younkers,
And tits, and tom-boys should have fed on, gratis.

Mam. I will go mount a turnip-cart, and preach
The end o' the world, within these two months.—Surly,
What! in a dream?

Sur.   Must I needs cheat myself,
With that same foolish vice of honesty!
Come let us go, and hearken out the rogues.
That Face I'll mark for mine, if e'er I meet him.

444

Face. If I can hear of him, sir, I'll bring you word
Unto your lodging: for in troth, they were strangers
To me, I thought 'em honest as myself, sir.

[*Exeunt* Mam. *and* Surly.

Re-enter Ananias *and* Tribulation.

Trib. 'Tis well, the saints shall not lose all yet. Go
And get some carts——

Lov. For what, my zealous friends?

Ana. To bear away the portion of the righteous,
Out of this den of thieves.

Lov. What is that portion?

Ana. The goods, sometimes the orphans', that the
brethren
Bought with their silver pence.

Lov. What, those i' the cellar,
The knight Sir Mammon claims?

Ana. I do defy
The wicked Mammon, so do all the brethren.
Thou profane man, I ask thee, with what conscience
Thou canst advance that idol against us,
That have the seal? Were not the shillings numbered,
That made the pounds? Were not the pounds told out,
Upon the second day of the fourth week,
In the eighth month, upon the table dormant,
The year of the last patience of the saints,
Six hundred and ten?

Lov. Mine earnest vehement botcher,
And deacon also, I cannot dispute with you,
But, if you get you not away the sooner,
I shall confute you with a cudgel.

Ana. Sir!

Trib. Be patient, Ananias.

Ana. I am strong,
And will stand up, well girt, against an host,
That threaten Gad in exile.

Lov. I shall send you
To Amsterdam, to your cellar.

Ana. I will pray there,

445

Against thy house: may dogs defile thy walls,
And wasps and hornets breed beneath thy roof,
This seat of falsehood and this cave of cozenage.

[*Exeunt* Ana. *and* Trib.

Enter Drugger.

Lov. Another too?
Dru.   Not I, sir, I am no brother.
Lov. [*Beats him.*] Away, you Harry Nicholas, do you
     talk?   [*Exit* Drugger.
Face. No, this was Abel Drugger. Good sir, go.

[*To the* Parson.

And satisfy him; tell him all is done:
He stay'd too long a washing of his face.
The doctor, he shall hear of him at Westchester;
And of the captain, tell him at Yarmouth: or
Some good port-town else, lying for a wind. [*Exit* Parson.
If you get off the angry child, now, sir——

Enter Kastril, *dragging in his sister.*

Kas. Come on, you ewe, you have match'd most sweetly,
     ha' you not?
Did not I say, I would never ha' you tupped
But by a dubb'd boy, to make you a lady-Tom?
'Slight, you are a mammet! O, I could touse you now.
Death, mun' you marry with a pox?
Lov.   You lie, boy;
As sound as you: and I am aforehand with you.
Kas. Anon?
Lov.   Come, will you quarrel? I will feize you, sirrah.
Why do you not buckle to your tools?
Kas.   God's light!
This is a fine old boy, as e'er I saw!
Lov. What, do you change your copy, now? Proceed,
Here stands my dove: stoop at her if you dare.
Kas. 'Slight, I must love him! I cannot choose, i' faith!
And I should be hanged for't. Suster, I protest
I honour thee for this match.
Lov.   O, do you so, sir?

Kas. Yes, and thou canst take tobacco and drink, old boy,
I'll give her five hundred pound more to her marriage
Than her own state.

 Lov.   Fill a pipe full, Jeremy.

 Face. Yes, but go in and take it, sir.

 Lov.   We will.
I will be rul'd by thee in anything, Jeremy.

 Kas. 'Slight, thou art not hide-bound! thou art a jovy
  boy!
Come let's in, I pray thee, and take our whiffs.

 Lov. Whiff in with your sister, brother boy.

        [*Exeunt* Kastril *and* Dame Pliant.

           That master
That had receiv'd such happiness by a servant,
In such a widow, and with so much wealth,
Were very ungrateful if he would not be
A little indulgent to that servant's wit,
And help his fortune, though with some small strain
Of his own candour. [*Advancing.*] Therefore, gentlemen,
And kind spectators, if I have outstripped
An old man's gravity or strict canon, think
What a young wife and a good brain may do:
Stretch age's truth sometimes, and crack it too.
Speak for thyself, knave.

 Face.   So I will, sir. [*Advancing.*] Gentlemen,
My part a little fell in this last scene,
Yet 'twas decorum. And though I am clean
Got off from Subtle, Surly, Mammon, Dol,
Hot Ananias, Dapper, Drugger, all
With whom I traded; yet I put myself
On you that are my country: and this pelf,
Which I have got, if you do quit me, rests
To feast you often, and invite new guests.   [*Exeunt.*

THE END

BARTHOLOMEW FAIR

BARTHOLMEW FAYRE:

A COMEDIE,

ACTED IN THE YEARE, 1614.

By the Lady *ELIZABETHS* SERVANTS.

And then dedicated to King I A M E S, of *most Blessed Memorie*;

By the Author, B E N I A M I N I O H N S O N.

Si foret in terris, rideret Democritus: nam
Spectaret populum ludis attentius ipsis,
Vt sibi præbentem, mimo spectacula plura.
Scriptores autem narrare putaret asello
Fabellam surdo. Hor.lib.2.Epist.1.

LONDON,
Printed by *I. B.* for R O B E R T A L L O T, and are
to be sold at the signe of the *Beare*, in *Pauls*
Church-yard. 1631.

THE
PROLOGUE
TO
THE KING'S
MAJESTY.

Your Majesty is welcome to a Fair;
Such place, such men, such language and such ware,
You must expect: with these, the zealous noise
Of your land's Faction, scandaliz'd at toys,
As Babies, Hobby-horses, Puppet-plays,
And such the rage, whereof the petulant ways
Yourself have known, and have been vex'd with long.
These for your sport, without particular wrong,
Or just complaint of any private man,
(Who of himself, or shall think well or can)
The Maker doth present: and hopes to-night
To give you for a Fairing, true delight.

THE PERSONS
OF THE PLAY

JOHN LITTLEWIT.	*A proctor.*
SOLOMON.	*His man.*
WIN LITTLEWIT.	*His wife.*
DAME PURECRAFT.	*Her mother, a widow.*
ZEAL-OF-THE-LAND BUSY.	*Her suitor, a Banbury man.*
WINWIFE.	*His rival, a gentleman.*
TOM QUARLOUS.	*His companion, a gamester.*
BARTHOLOMEW COKES.	*An esquire of Harrow.*
HUMPHREY WASPE.	*His man.*
ADAM OVERDO.	*A justice of peace.*
DAME OVERDO.	*His wife.*
GRACE WELLBORN.	*His ward.*
LANTHORN LEATHERHEAD.	*A hobby-horse seller.*
JOAN TRASH.	*A ginger-bread woman.*
EZEKIEL EDGWORTH.	*A cutpurse.*
NIGHTINGALE.	*A ballad-singer.*
URSULA.	*A pig-woman.*
MOONCALF.	*Her tapster.*
DAN JORDAN KNOCKEM.	*A horse-courser, and ranger o' Turnbull.*
VAL CUTTING.	*A roarer.*
CAPTAIN WHIT.	*A bawd.*
PUNQUE ALICE.	*Mistress o' the game.*
TROUBLEALL.	*A madman.*
HAGGIS. }	
BRISTLE.	*Watchmen.*
POCHER.	*A beadle.*
FILCHER. }	
SHARKWELL. }	*Doorkeepers.*
COSTARD-MONGER.	WRESTLER.
CORN-CUTTER.	PORTERS.
MOUSETRAP MAN.	PUPPETS.
	CLOTHIER.

THE INDUCTION
ON THE STAGE

Enter Stage-Keeper.

Stage. Gentlemen, have a little patience, they are e'en upon coming, instantly. He that should begin the play, Master Littlewit, the proctor, has a stitch new fallen in his black silk stocking; 'twill be drawn up ere you can tell twenty. He plays one o' the arches, that dwells about the hospital, and he has a very pretty part. But for the whole play, will you ha' the truth on't? (I am looking, lest the poet hear me, or his man, Master Broome, behind the arras.) It is like to be a very conceited scurvy one, in plain English. When 't comes to the Fair, once: you were e'en as good go to Virginia for anything there is of Smithfield. He has not hit the humours, he do's not know 'em; he has not convers'd with the Bartholomew birds, as they say; he has ne'er a sword and buckler man in his Fair, nor a little Davy to take toll o' the bawds there, as in my time, nor a Kindheart, if anybody's teeth should chance to ache in his play. Nor a juggler with a well-educated ape to come over the chain, for the King of England, and back again for the Prince, and sit still on his arse for the Pope and the King of Spain! None o' these fine sights! Nor has he the canvas-cut i' the night, for a hobby-horseman to creep into his she-neighbour and take his leap there! Nothing! No, and some writer that I know had had but the penning o' this matter, he would ha' made you such a jig-a-jog i' the booths, you should ha' thought an earthquake had been i' the Fair! But these master-poets, they will ha' their own absurd courses; they will be inform'd of nothing! He has (sir reverence) kick'd me three or four times about the Tiring-house, I thank him, for but offering to put in with my experience, I'll be judg'd by you, gentlemen now, but for one conceit of mine! would not a fine pump upon the stage ha' done well for a property now? and a punk set under upon

her head, with her stern upward, and ha' been sous'd by my
witty young masters o' the Inns o' Court? what think you
o' this for a show, now? he will not hear o' this! I am an
ass! Aye! and yet I kept the stage in Master Tarleton's
time, I thank my stars. Ho! and that man had liv'd to have
play'd in *Bartholomew Fair*, you should ha' seen him ha'
come in, and ha' been cozened i' the cloth-quarter, so
finely! And Adams, the rogue, ha' leap'd and caper'd upon
him, and ha' dealt his vermin about, as though they had
cost him nothing. And then a substantial watch to ha'
stolen in upon 'em, and taken 'em away, with mistaking
words, as the fashion is in the stage practice.

Enter Book-Holder *and* Scrivener.

Book. How now? what rare discourse are you fallen
upon? ha? ha' you found any familiars here, that you are
so free? what's the business?

Stage. Nothing, but the understanding gentlemen o' the
ground here, ask'd my judgement.

Book. Your judgement, rascal? for what? sweeping the
stage? or gathering up the broken apples for the bears
within? Away, rogue, it's come to a fine degree in these
spectacles when such a youth as you pretend to a judge-
ment. And yet he may, i' the most o' this matter i' faith:
For the author hath writ it just to his meridian, and the
scale of the grounded judgements here, his play-fellows
in wit. Gentlemen; not for want of a prologue but by way
of a new one I am sent out to you here, with a scrivener
and certain articles drawn out in haste between our author
and you; which if you please to hear, and as they appear
reasonable, to approve of; the play will follow presently.
Read, scribe, gi' me the counterpane.

Scriv. Articles of Agreement, indented, between the
spectators or hearers, at the Hope on the Bankside, in the
county of Surrey on the one party; And the author of *Bar-
tholomew Fair* in the said place and county on the other
party: the one and thirtieth day of Oct., 1614, and in the
twelfth year of the reign of our Sovereign Lord, James,
by the grace of God King of England, France, and Ireland;

Defender of the Faith. And of Scotland the seven and fortieth.

Imprimis. It is covenanted and agreed, by and between the parties abovesaid, and the said spectators and hearers as well the curious and envious, as the favouring and judicious, as also the grounded judgements and understandings, do for themselves severally covenant, and agree to remain in the places, their money or friends have put them in, with patience, for the space of two hours and a half, and somewhat more. In which time the author promises to present them by us, with a new sufficient play called *Bartholomew Fair*, merry, and as full of noise as sport: made to delight all, and to offend none, provided they have either the wit or the honesty to think well of themselves.

It is further agreed that every person here, have his or their free-will of censure, to like or dislike at their own charge, the author having now departed with his right: It shall be lawful for any man to judge his six pen'orth, his twelve pen'orth, so to his eighteen pence, two shillings, half a crown, to the value of his place: provided always his place get not above his wit. And if he pay for half a dozen, he may censure for all them too, so that he will undertake that they shall be silent. He shall put in for censures here, as they do for tots at the lottery: marry, if he drop but sixpence at the door, and will censure a crown's worth, it is thought there is no conscience nor justice in that.

It is also agreed that every man here exercise his own judgement, and not censure by contagion or upon trust from another's voice or face that sits by him, be he never so first, in the commission of wit: As also, that he be fix'd and settled in his censure, that what he approves, or not approves, today, he will do the same tomorrow, and if tomorrow, the next day, and so the next week (if need be:) and not to be brought about by any that sits on the bench with him, though they indict, and arraign plays daily. He that will swear, *Ieronimo* or *Andronicus* are the best plays yet, shall pass unexcepted at, here, as a man whose judgement shows it is constant, and hath stood still, these five and twenty or thirty years. Though it be an ignorance, it is a virtuous and staid ignorance; and next to truth, a confirm'd error does well; such a one the author knows where to find him.

It is further covenanted, concluded and agreed, that how great soever the expectation be, no person here is to expect more than he knows, or better ware than a Fair will afford: neither to look back to the sword and bucklerage of Smithfield, but content himself with the present. Instead of a little Davy, to take toll o' the bawds, the author doth promise a strutting horse-courser, with a leer drunkard, two or three to attend him, in as good equipage as you would wish. And then for Kindheart, the tooth-drawer, a fine oily pig-woman with her tapster to bid you welcome, and a consort of roarers for music. A wise justice of peace meditant, instead of a juggler with an ape. A civil cutpurse searchant. A sweet singer of new ballads allurant: and as fresh a hypocrite, as ever was broach'd, rampant. If there be never a servant-monster i' the Fair who can help it, he says; nor a nest of antiques? He is loth to make Nature afraid in his plays, like those that beget tales, tempests, and such like drolleries, to mix his head with other men's heels, let the concupiscence of jigs and dances reign as strong as it will amongst you: yet if the puppets will please anybody, they shall be entreated to come in.

In consideration of which, it is finally agreed, by the aforesaid hearers and spectators, that they neither in themselves conceal, nor suffer by them to be concealed, any state decipherer, or politic picklock of the scene so solemnly ridiculous, as to search out who was meant by the gingerbread woman, who by the hobby-horse-man, who by the costard-monger, nay, who by their wares. Or that will pretend to affirm (on his own inspired ignorance) what Mirror of Magistrates is meant by the justice, what great lady by the pig-woman, what conceal'd statesman by the seller of mousetraps, and so of the rest. But that such person, or persons so found, be left discovered to the mercy of the author as a forfeiture to the stage, and your laughter, aforesaid. As also, such as shall so desperately, or ambitiously, play the fool by his place aforesaid, to challenge the author of scurrility because the language somewhere savours of Smithfield, the booth, and the pig-broth, or of profaneness, because a madman cries, God quit you, or bless you. In witness whereof, as you have preposterously put to your seals already (which is your money) you will now add the other part of suffrage, your hands. The play shall presently begin. And though the Fair be not kept in the same region that some here, perhaps, would have it, yet think that therein the author hath observ'd a special decorum, the place being as dirty as Smithfield, and as stinking every whit.

Howsoever, he prays you to believe, his ware is still the same, else you will make him justly suspect that he that is so loth to look on a baby or a hobby-horse, here, would be glad to take up a commodity of them, at any laughter or loss, in another place.   [Exeunt.

BARTHOLOMEW FAIR

ACT I. SCENE I

A room in Littlewit's *house.*

Enter Littlewit *with a licence in his hand.*

Lit. A pretty conceit, and worth the finding! I ha' such luck to spin out these fine things still, and like a silk-worm, out of myself. Here's Master Bartholomew Cokes, of Harrow o' th' Hill, i' th' county of Middlesex, esquire, takes forth his licence to marry Mistress Grace Wellborn of the said place and county: and when does he take it forth? today! the four and twentieth of August! Bartholomew day! Bartholomew upon Bartholomew! there's the deuce! who would have mark'd such a leap-frog chance now? A very ... less than ames-ace on two dice! well, go thy ways. John Littlewit, proctor John Littlewit: one o' the pretty wits o' Paul's, the Littlewit of London (so thou art call'd) and something beside. When a quirk or a quiblin does 'scape thee, and thou dost not watch and apprehend it, and bring it afore the constable of conceit: (there now, I speak quib too) let 'em carry thee out o' the archdeacon's court into his kitchen, and make a Jack of thee, instead of a John. (There I am again, la!)

Enter Mrs. Littlewit.

Good morrow, Win. Aye, marry, Win! Now you look finely indeed, Win! this cap does convince! you'd not ha' worn it, Win, nor ha' had it velvet, but a rough country beaver, with a copper-band, like the coney-skin woman of Budge-row; sweet Win, let me kiss it! And her fine high shoes, like the Spanish lady! Good Win, go a little, I would fain see thee pace, pretty Win! By this fine cap, I could never leave kissing on't.

Win. Come, indeed la, you are such a fool, still!

Lit. No, but half a one, Win, you are the t' other half:

man and wife make one fool, Win. Good! Is there the proctor, or doctor indeed, i' the diocese, that ever had the fortune to win him such a Win! There I am again! I do feel conceits coming upon me, more than I am able to turn tongue to. A pox o' these pretenders to wit! your Three Cranes, Mitre, and Mermaid men! Not a corn of true salt nor a grain of right mustard amongst them all. They may stand for places or so again the next witfall, and pay two-pence in a quart more for their canary than other men. But gi' me the man can start up a justice of wit out of six shillings beer, and give the law to all the poets and poet-suckers i' town, because they are the players' gossips! 'Slid, other men have wives as fine as the players, and as well dressed. Come hither, Win. [*Kisses her.*

Enter Winwife.

Winw. Why, how now, Master Littlewit! measuring of lips? or moulding of kisses? which is it?

Lit. Troth, I am a little taken with my Win's dressing here! Do'st not fine, Master Winwife? How do you apprehend, sir? She would not ha' worn this habit. I challenge all Cheapside to show such another: Moorfields, Pimlico path, or the Exchange, in a summer evening, with a lace to boot, as this has. Dear Win, let Master Winwife kiss you. He comes a-wooing to our mother, Win, and maybe our father perhaps, Win. There's no harm in him, Win.

Winw. None i' the earth, Master Littlewit. [*Kisses her.*

Lit. I envy no man my delicates, sir.

Winw. Alas, you ha' the garden where they grow still! A wife here with a strawberry breath, cherry-lips, apricot-cheeks, and a soft velvet head, like a melicotton.

Lit. Good, i' faith! now dullness upon me, that I had not that before him, that I should not light on't, as well as he! Velvet head!

Winw. But my taste, Master Littlewit, tends to fruit of a later kind: the sober matron, your wife's mother.

Lit. Aye! we know you are a suitor, sir. Win and I both wish you well: by this licence here, would you had her, that your two names were as fast in it, as here are a couple.

Win would fain have a fine young father i' law, with a feather: that her mother might hood it, and chain it, with Mistress Overdo. But you do not take the right course, Master Winwife.

Winw. No? Master Littlewit, why?

Lit. You are not mad enough.

Winw. How? Is madness a right course?

Lit. I say nothing, but I wink upon Win. You have a friend, one Master Quarlous, comes here sometimes?

Winw. Why? he makes no love to her, does he?

Lit. Not a tokenworth that ever I saw, I assure you, but——

Winw. What?

Lit. He is the more madcap o' the two. You do not apprehend me.

Win. You have a hot coal i' your mouth, now, you cannot hold.

Lit. Let me out with it, dear Win.

Win. I'll tell him myself.

Lit. Do, and take all the thanks, and much good do thy pretty heart, Win.

Win. Sir, my mother has had her nativity-water cast lately by the cunning men in Cow-lane, and they ha' told her her fortune, and do ensure her she shall never have happy hour unless she marry within this sen'night, and when it is, it must be a madman, they say.

Lit. Aye, but it must be a gentleman madman.

Win. Yes, so the t' other man of Moorfields says.

Winw. But does she believe 'em?

Lit. Yes, and has been at Bedlam twice since, every day, to enquire if any gentleman be there, or to come there, mad!

Winw. Why, this is a confederacy, a mere piece of practice upon her, by these impostors.

Lit. I tell her so; or else say I, that they mean some young madcap gentleman (for the devil can equivocate, as well as a shopkeeper); and therefore would I advise you to be a little madder than Master Quarlous hereafter.

Winw. Where is she? stirring yet?

Lit. Stirring! Yes, and studying an old elder, come from Banbury, a suitor that puts in here at mealtide, to praise the painful brethren, or pray that the sweet singers may be restor'd; Says a grace as long as his breath lasts him! Sometime the spirit is so strong with him, it gets quite out of him, and then my mother, or Win, are fain to fetch it again with malmsey, or aqua cœlestis.

Win. Yes indeed, we have such a tedious life with him for his diet, and his clothes too, he breaks his buttons and cracks seams at every saying he sobs out.

Lit. He cannot abide my vocation, he says.

Win. No. he told my mother, a proctor was a claw of the beast, and that she had little less than committed abomination in marrying me so as she has done.

Lit. Every line (he says) that a proctor writes, when it comes to be read in the bishop's court, is a long black hair, kemb'd out of the tail of Antichrist.

Winw. When came this proselyte?

Lit. Some three days since.

Enter Quarlous.

Quar. O sir, ha' you ta'en soil here? it's well, a man may reach you, after three hours running, yet! what an unmerciful companion art thou, to quit thy lodging at such ungentlemanly hours! None but a scattered covey of fiddlers, or one of these rag-rakers in dunghills, or some marrowbone man at most, would have been up, when thou wert gone abroad, by all description. I pray thee what ailest thou; thou canst not sleep? hast thou thorns i' thy eyelids, or thistles i' thy bed?

Winw. I cannot tell: It seems you had neither i' your feet; that took this pain to find me.

Quar. No, and I had, all the lime-hounds o' the City should have drawn after you, by the scent rather. Master John Littlewit! God save you, sir. 'Twas a hot night with some of us, last night, John: shall we pluck a hair o' the same wolf today, Proctor John?

Lit. Do you remember, Master Quarlous, what we discours'd on last night?

Quar. Not I, John: nothing that I either discourse or do: at those times I forfeit all to forgetfulness.

Lit. No? not concerning Win? look you: there she is, and dress'd as I told you she should be: hark you, sir, had you forgot?

Quar. By this head, I'll beware how I keep you company, John, when I am drunk, and you have this dangerous memory! that's certain.

Lit. Why, sir?

Quar. Why? we were all a little stain'd last night, sprinkled with a cup or two, and I agreed with Proctor John here, to come and do somewhat with Win (I know not what 'twas) today; and he puts me in mind on 't, now; he says he was coming to fetch me: before truth, if you have that fearful quality, John, to remember when you are sober, John, what you promise drunk, John, I shall take heed of you, John. For this once, I am content to wink at you, where's your wife? come hither, Win.   [*Kisses her.*

Win. Why, John! do you see this, John? look you! help me, John.

Lit. O Win, fie, what do you mean, Win! Be womanly, Win; make an outcry to your mother, Win? Master Quarlous is an honest gentleman, and our worshipful good friend, Win: and he is Master Winwife's friend, too: And Master Winwife comes a suitor to your mother, Win; as I told you before, Win, and may perhaps be our father, Win: they'll do you no harm, Win, they are both our worshipful good friends. Master Quarlous! you must know Master Quarlous, Win; you must not quarrel with Master Quarlous, Win.

Quar. No, we'll kiss again and fall in.   [*Kisses her again.*

Lit. Yes, do, good Win.

Win. I' faith you are a fool, John.

Lit. A fool-John she calls me, do you mark that, gentlemen? pretty littlewit of velvet! a fool-John!

Quar. She may call you an apple-John if you use this. [*Aside.*]   [*Kisses her again.*

Winw. Pray thee forbear, for my respect somewhat.

Quar. Hoy-day! how respective you are become o' the

sudden! I fear this family will turn you reformed too, pray
you come about again. Because she is in possibility to be
your daughter-in-law, and may ask you blessing hereafter,
when she courts it to Tottenham to eat cream. Well, I will
forbear, sir, but i' faith, would thou wouldst leave thy exer-
cise of widow-hunting once! this drawing after an old
reverend smock by the splay-foot! There cannot be an
ancient tripe or trillibub i' the town, but thou art straight
nosing it, and 'tis a fine occupation thou'lt confine thyself
to, when thou hast got one; scrubbing a piece of buff, as if
thou hadst the perpetuity of Pannier Alley to stink in; or
perhaps worse, currying a carcass that thou hast bound
thyself to alive. I'll be sworn some of them that thou art,
or hast been a suitor to, are so old as no chaste or married
pleasure can ever become 'em: the honest instrument of
procreation has (forty years since) left to belong to 'em,
thou must visit 'em, as thou wouldst do a tomb, with a
torch, or three handfuls of link, flaming hot, and so thou
mayst hap to make 'em feel thee, and after, come to inherit
according to thy inches. A sweet course for a man to waste
the brand of life for, to be still raking himself a fortune in
an old woman's embers; we shall ha' thee, after thou hast
been but a month married to one of 'em, look like the
quartan ague, and the black jaundice met in a face, and
walk as if thou had'st borrow'd legs of a spinner, and
voice of a cricket. I would endure to hear fifteen sermons
a week for her, and such coarse and loud ones as some of
'em must be; I would e'en desire of Fate, I might dwell in
a drum, and take in my sustenance with an old broken
tobacco pipe and a straw. Dost thou ever think to bring
thine ears or stomach to the patience of a dry grace; as long
as thy tablecloth? and dron'd out by thy son here (that
might be thy father) till all the meat o' thy board has for-
got it was that day i' the kitchen? Or to brook the noise
made, in a question of predestination, by the good labourers
and painful eaters, assembled together, put to 'em by the
matron, your spouse; who moderates with a cup of wine,
ever and anon, and a sentence out of Knox between? or the
perpetual spitting before and after a sober drawn exhorta-

tion of six hours, whose better part was the hum-ha-hum? Or to hear prayers groan'd out, over thy iron-chests, as if they were charms to break 'em? And all this for the hope of two apostle-spoons, to suffer! and a cup to eat a cawdle in! For that will be thy legacy. She'll ha' convey'd her state, safe enough from thee, an' she be a right widow.

Winw. Alas, I am quite off that scent now.

Quar. How so?

Winw. Put off by a brother of Banbury, one that, they say, is come here and governs all already.

Quar. What do you call him? I knew divers of those Banburians when I was in Oxford.

Winw. Master Littlewit can tell us.

Lit. Sir! good Win, go in, and if Master Bartholomew Coke's his man come for the licence: (the little old fellow) let him speak with me. [*Exit* Mrs. Littlewit. What say you, gentlemen?

Winw. What call you the reverend elder, you told me of? your Banbury man?

Lit. Rabbi Busy, sir, he is more than an elder, he is a prophet, sir.

Quar. O, I know him! a baker, is he not?

Lit. He was a baker, sir, but he does dream now, and see visions; he has given over his trade.

Quar. I remember that too: out of a scruple he took, that (in spic'd conscience) those cakes he made, were serv'd to bridales, maypoles, morrises, and such profane feasts and meetings; his Christian-name is Zeal-of-the-land.

Lit. Yes, sir, Zeal-of-the-land Busy.

Winw. How, what a name's there!

Lit. O, they have all such names, sir; he was witness for Win here (they will not be call'd godfathers), and nam'd her Win-the-fight, you thought her name had been Wini-fred, did you not?

Winw. I did indeed.

Lit. He would ha' thought himself a stark reprobate, if it had.

Quar. Aye, for there was a blue-starch-woman o' the name, at the same time. A notable hypocritical vermin it is;

I know him. One that stands upon his face more than his faith at all times; ever in seditious motion, and reproving for vain-glory: of a most lunatic conscience and spleen, and affects the violence of singularity in all he does. He has undone a grocer here, in Newgate-market, that broke with him, trusted him with currants, as arrant a zeal as he, that's by the way. By his profession, he will ever be i' the state of innocence though, and childhood; derides all antiquity; defies any other learning than inspiration; and what discretion soever years should afford him, it is all prevented in his original ignorance: ha' not to do with him: for he is a fellow of a most arrogant and invincible dullness, I assure you. Who is this?

Re-enter Mrs. Littlewit *with* Waspe.

Was. By your leave, gentlemen, with all my heart to you: and God you good morrow; Master Littlewit, my business is to you. Is this licence ready?

Lit. Here, I ha' it for you in my hand, Master Humphrey.

Was. That's well, nay, never open or read it to me, it's labour in vain, you know. I am no clerk, I scorn to be sav'd by my book, i' faith I'll hang first; fold it up o' your word and gi' it me; what must you ha' for't?

Lit. We'll talk of that anon, Master Humphrey.

Was. Now, or not at all, good Master Proctor, I am for no anon's, I assure you.

Lit. Sweet Win, bid Solomon send me the little black box within, in my study.

Was. Aye, quickly, good mistress, I pray you: for I have both eggs o' the spit, and iron i' the fire.

[*Exit* Mrs. Littlewit.
Say what you must have, good Master Littlewit.

Lit. Why, you know the price, Master Numps.

Was. I know? I know nothing, I; what tell you me of knowing? now I am in haste, sir, I do not know, and I will not know, and I scorn to know, and yet (now I think on't), I will, and do know, as well as another; you must have a mark for your thing here, and eightpence for the box; I could ha' sav'd twopence i' that, an' I had bought it myself, but here's fourteen shillings for you. Good Lord! how long your little wife stays! pray God, Solomon your clerk be not looking i' the wrong box, Master Proctor.

Lit. Good, i' faith! no, I warrant you, Solomon is wiser than so, sir.

Was. Fie, fie, fie, by your leave, Master Littlewit, this is scurvy, idle, foolish and abominable; with all my heart, I do not like it.

Winw. Do you hear? Jack Littlewit, what business does thy pretty head think this fellow may have, that he keeps such a coil with?

Quar. More than buying of ginger-bread i' the Cloister, here, for that we allow him, or a gilt pouch i' the Fair?

Lit. Master Quarlous, do not mistake him: he is his master's both-hands, I assure you.

Quar. What? to pull on his boots, a-mornings, or his stockings, does he?

Lit. Sir, if you have a mind to mock him, mock him softly, and look t' other way: for if he apprehend you flout him once he will fly at you presently. A terrible testy old fellow; and his name is Waspe too.

Quar. Pretty insect! make much on him.

Was. A plague o' this box, and the pox too, and on him that made it, and her that went for 't, and all that should ha' sought it, sent it, or brought it! do you see, sir?

Lit. Nay, good Master Waspe.

Was. Good Master Hornet, turd i' your teeth, hold you your tongue; do not I know you? your father was a 'pothecary, and sold glisters, more than he gave, I wusse: and turd i' your little wife's teeth too—here she comes——

Re-enter Mrs. Littlewit *with the box.*

'Twill make her spit, as fine as she is, for all her velvet-custard on her head, sir.

Lit. O! be civil, Master Numps.

Was. Why, say I have a humour not to be civil; how then? who shall compel me? you?

Lit. Here is the box, now.

Was. Why a pox o' your box, once again: let your little

wife stale in it, and she will. Sir, I would have you to under-
stand, and these gentlemen too, if they please——

Winw. With all our hearts, sir.

Was. That I have a charge, gentlemen.

Lit. They do apprehend, sir.

Was. Pardon me, sir, neither they nor you can appre-
hend me yet. You are an ass. I have a young master, he is
now upon his making and marring; the whole care of his
well-doing is now mine. His foolish schoolmasters have
done nothing but run up and down the country with him,
to beg puddings and cake-bread of his tenants, and almost
spoiled him; he has learn'd nothing but to sing catches and
repeat 'Rattle bladder rattle', and 'O, Madge'. I dare not let
him walk alone, for fear of learning of vile tunes which he
will sing at supper and in the sermon-times! if he meet but
a carman i' the street, and I find him not talk to keep him
off on him, he will whistle him, and all his tunes over, at
night in his sleep! he has a head full of bees! I am fain now,
for this little time I am absent, to leave him in charge with
a gentlewoman; 'tis true, she is a Justice of Peace his wife,
and a gentlewoman o' the hood, and his natural sister: but
what may happen under a woman's government, there's
the doubt. Gentlemen, you do not know him: he is another
manner of piece than you think for! but nineteen year old,
and yet he is taller than either of you, by the head, God
bless him.

Quar. Well, methinks, this is a fine fellow!

Winw. He has made his master a finer by this descrip-
tion, I should think.

Quar. 'Faith, much about one, it's cross and pile whether
for a new farthing.

Was. I'll tell you, gentlemen——

Lit. Will't please you drink, Master Waspe?

Was. Why, I ha' not talk'd so long to be dry, sir, you see
no dust or cobwebs come out o' my mouth, do you? you'd
ha' me gone, would you?

Lit. No, but you were in haste e'en now, Master Numps.

Was. What an' I were? so I am still, and yet I will stay
too; meddle you with your match, your Win, there; she

has as little wit as her husband, it seems: I have others to talk to.

Lit. She's my match indeed, and as little wit as I, good!

Was. We ha' been but a day and a half in town, gentlemen, 'tis true; and yesterday i' the afternoon, we walk'd London, to show the city to the gentlewoman he shall marry, Mistress Grace; but afore I will endure such another half day with him, I'll be drawn with a good gib-cat through the great pond at home, as his uncle Hodge was! why, we could not meet that heathen thing, all day, but stay'd him; he would name you all the signs over, as he went, aloud: and where he spied a parrot, or a monkey, there he was pitch'd, with all the little long-coats about him, male and female; no getting him away! I thought he would ha' run mad o' the black boy in Bucklersbury that takes the scurvy, roguy tobacco, there.

Lit. You say true, Master Numps; there's such a one indeed.

Was. It's no matter, whether there be, or no, what's that to you?

Quar. He will not allow of John's reading at any hand.

Enter Cokes, Mistress Overdo *and* Grace.

Cok. O, Numps! are you here, Numps? look where I am, Numps, and Mistress Grace too! nay, do not look angry, Numps: my sister is here and all, I do not come without her.

Was. What the mischief do you come with her? or she with you?

Cok. We came all to seek you, Numps.

Was. To seek me? why, did you all think I was lost? or run away with your fourteen shillings worth of small ware, here? or that I had chang'd it i' the Fair, for hobby-horses? 'Sprecious—to seek me!

Mrs. Over. Nay, good Master Numps, do you show discretion, though he be exorbitant, (as Master Overdo says,) and't be but for conservation of the peace.

Was. Marry gip, goody she Justice Mistress Frenchhood! turd i' your teeth; and turd i' your Frenchhoods teeth, too, to do you service, do you see? must you quote your Adam to me! you think you are Madam Regent still, Mistress Overdo; when I am in place? no such matter, I assure you, your reign is out when I am in, dame.

Mrs. Over. I am content to be in abeyance, sir, and be govern'd by you; so should he too, if he did well; but 'twill be expected you should also govern your passions.

Was. Will't so, forsooth? good Lord! how sharp you are! with being at Bedlam yesterday? Whetstone has set an edge upon you, has he?

Mrs. Over. Nay, if you know not what belongs to your dignity, I do yet to mine.

Was. Very well, then.

Cok. Is this the licence, Numps? for love's sake, let me see't. I never saw a licence.

Was. Did you not so? why, you shall not see't, then.

Cok. An' you love me, good Numps.

Was. Sir, I love you, and yet I do not love you, i' these fooleries; set your heart at rest; there's nothing in't but hard words: and what would you see't for?

Cok. I would see the length and the breadth on't, that's all; and I will see't now, so I will.

Was. You sha' not see it here.

Cok. Then I'll see't at home, and I'll look upo' the case here.

Was. Why, do so, a man must give way to him a little in trifles: Gentlemen, these are errors, diseases of youth: which he will mend when he comes to judgement and knowledge of matters. I pray you conceive so, and I thank you. And I pray you pardon him, and I thank you again.

Quar. Well, this dry nurse, I say still, is a delicate man.

Winw. And I am for the cosset, his charge! Did you ever see a fellow's face more accuse him for an ass?

Quar. Accuse him? it confesses him one without accusing. What pity 'tis yonder wench should marry such a Cokes!

Winw. 'Tis true.

Quar. She seems to be discreet, and as sober as she is handsome.

Winw. Aye, and if you mark her, what a restrain'd scorn she casts upon all his behaviour and speeches?

Cok. Well, Numps, I am now for another piece of business more; the Fair, Numps, and then——

Was. Bless me! deliver me, help, hold me! the Fair!

Cok. Nay, never fidge up and down, Numps, and vex itself. I am resolute Bartholomew, in this; I'll make no suit on't to you; 'twas all the end of my journey, indeed, to shew Mistress Grace my Fair! I call't my Fair because of Bartholomew: you know my name is Bartholomew and Bartholomew Fair.

Lit. That was mine afore, gentlemen: this morning, I had that i' faith, upon his licence, believe me, there he comes, after me.

Quar. Come, John, this ambitious wit of yours, I am afraid, will do you no good i' the end.

Lit. No? why, sir?

Quar. You grow so insolent with it, and overdoing, John: that if you look not to it, and tie it up, 'twill bring you to some obscure place in time, and there 'twill leave you.

Winw. Do not trust it too much, John, be more sparing, and use it but now and then; a wit is a dangerous thing in this age; do not over-buy it.

Lit. Think you so, gentlemen? I'll take heed on't, hereafter.

Win. Yes, do, John.

Cok. A pretty little soul, this same Mistress Littlewit! would I might marry her.

Gra. So would I, or anybody else, so I might 'scape you.
[*Aside.*

Cok. Numps, I will see it, Numps, 'tis decreed: never be melancholy for the matter.

Was. Why, see it, sir, see it, do you see it! who hinders you? why do you not go see it? 'Slid, see it.

Cok. The Fair, Numps, the Fair.

Was. Would the Fair, and all the drums and rattles in't, were i' your belly for me: they are already i' your brain: he that had the means to travel your head, now should meet finer sights than any are i' the Fair: and make a finer voyage on't; to see it all hung with cockle-shells, pebbles, fine wheat-straws, and here and there a chicken's feather, and a cobweb.

Quar. Good faith, he looks, methinks, an' you mark him, like one that were made to catch flies, with his Sir Cranion-legs.

Winw. And his Numps to flap 'em away.

Was. God be wi' you, sir, there's your bee in a box, and much good do't you.   [*Gives* Cokes *the box.*

Cok. Why, your friend, and Bartholomew; an' you be so contumacious.

Quar. What mean you, Numps?

Was. I'll not be guilty, I, gentlemen.

Mrs. Over. You will not let him go, brother, and lose him?

Cok. Who can hold that will away? I had rather lose him than the Fair, I wusse.

Was. You do not know the inconvenience, gentlemen, you persuade to: nor what trouble I have with him in these humours. If he go to the Fair he will buy of everything to a baby there; and household-stuff for that too. If a leg or an arm on him did not grow on, he would lose it i' the press. Pray heaven, I bring him off with one stone! And then he is such a ravener after fruit! you will not believe what a coil I had, t' other day, to compound a business between a Cather 'ne-pear-woman and him, about snatching! 'tis intolerable, gentlemen!

Winw. O! but you must not leave him, now, to these hazards, Numps.

Was. Nay, he knows too well I will not leave him, and that makes him presume: well, sir, will you go now? if you have such an itch i' your feet, to foot it to the Fair, why do you stop, am I your tarriers? go, will you go? sir, why do you not go?

Cok. O Numps! have I brought you about? come Mistress Grace, and sister, I am resolute Bat, i' faith, still.

Gra. Truly, I have no such fancy to the Fair nor ambition to see it; there's none goes thither of any quality or fashion.

Cok. O Lord, sir! you shall pardon me, Mistress Grace, we are enough of ourselves to make it a fashion: and for qualities, let Numps alone, he'll find qualities.

[*Exeunt* Cokes, Waspe, Grace *and* Mrs. Overdo.

Quar. What a rogue in apprehension is this! to understand her language no better.

Winw. Aye, and offer to marry her? well, I will leave the chase of my widow, for to-day, and directly to the Fair. These flies cannot, this hot season, but engender us excellent creeping sport.

Quar. A man that has but a spoonful of brain would think so. Farewell, John. [*Exeunt* Quarlous *and* Winwife.

Lit. Win, you see, 'tis in fashion to go to the Fair, Win: we must to the Fair too, you and I, Win. I have an affair i' the Fair, Win, a puppet-play of mine own making, say nothing, that I wrote for the motion-man, which you must see, Win.

Win. I would I might, John, but my mother will never consent to such a profane motion, she will call it.

Lit. Tut, we'll have a device, a dainty one; (Now, Wit, help at a pinch, good Wit come, come, good Wit, and 't be thy will.) I have it, Win, I have it i' faith, and 'tis a fine one. Win, long to eat of a pig, sweet Win, i' the Fair: do you see? i' the heart o' the Fair; not at Pie-Corner. Your mother will do anything, Win, to satisfy your longing, you know, pray thee long, presently, and be sick o' the sudden, good Win. I'll go in and tell her, cut thy lace i' the meantime and play the hypocrite, sweet Win.

Win. No, I'll not make me unready for it. I can be hypocrite enough, though I were never so strait-lac'd.

Lit. You say true, you have been bred i' the family, and brought up to 't. Our mother is a most elect hypocrite and has maintain'd us all this seven year with it, like gentlefolks.

Win. Aye, let her alone, John, she is not a wise wilful widow for nothing, nor a sanctified sister for a song. And let me alone too, I ha' somewhat o' the mother in me, you shall see; fetch her, fetch her. [*Exit* Littlewit. Ah! ah! [*Seems to swoon.*]

Re-enter Littlewit *with* Dame Purecraft.

Pure. Now the blaze of the beauteous discipline fright away this evil from our house! how now, Win-the-fight, child: how do you? Sweet child, speak to me.

Win. Yes, forsooth.

Pure. Look up, sweet Win-the-fight, and suffer not the enemy to enter you at this door, remember that your education has been with the purest, what polluted one was it that nam'd first the unclean beast, pig, to you, child?

Win. Uh, uh.

Lit. Not I, o' my sincerity, mother: she long'd above three hours, ere sh'ould let me know it; who was it, Win?

Win. A profane black thing with a beard, John.

Pure. O! resist it, Win-the-fight, it is the tempter, the wicked tempter, you may know it by the fleshly motion of pig, be strong against it, and its foul temptations, in these assaults, whereby it broacheth flesh and blood, as it were, on the weaker side, and pray against its carnal provocations, good child, sweet child, pray.

Lit. Good mother, I pray you, that she may eat some pig, and her belly full, too; and do not you cast away your own child, and perhaps one of mine, with your tale of the tempter: how do you, Win? Are you not sick?

Win. Yes, a great deal, John. Uh, uh.

Pure. What shall we do? call our zealous brother Busy hither, for his faithful fortification in this charge of the adversary. [*Exit* Littlewit.
Child, my dear child, you shall eat pig, be comforted, my sweet child.

Win. Aye, but i' the Fair, mother.

Pure. I mean i' the Fair, if it can be anyway made or found lawful.

Re-enter Littlewit.

Where is our brother Busy? Will he not come? look up, child.

Lit. Presently, mother, as soon as he has cleans'd his beard. I found him, fast by the teeth, i' the cold turkey-pie, i' the cupboard, with a great white loaf on his left hand, and a glass of malmsey on his right.

Pure. Slander not the brethren, wicked one.

Lit. Here he is now, purified, mother.

Enter Zeal-of-the-land Busy.

Pure. O brother Busy! your help here to edify and raise us up in a scruple; my daughter Win-the-fight is visited with a natural disease of women call'd a longing to eat pig.

Lit. Aye, sir, a Bartholomew pig: and in the Fair.

Pure. And I would be satisfied from you, religiously-wise, whether a widow of the sanctified assembly, or widow's daughter, may commit the act, without offence to the weaker sisters.

Busy. Verily, for the disease of longing, it is a disease, a carnal disease, or appetite, incident to women: and as it is carnal and incident, it is natural, very natural: Now, pig, it is a meat, and a meat that is nourishing, and may be long'd for, and so consequently eaten; it may be eaten; very exceedingly well eaten: but in the Fair, and as a Bartholomew pig, it cannot be eaten, for the very calling it a Bartholomew pig, and to eat it so, is a spice of idolatry, and you make the Fair no better than one of the high places. This I take it, is the state of the question. A high place.

Lit. Aye, but in state of necessity, place should give place, Mr. Busy. (I have a conceit left yet.)

Pure. Good brother Zeal-of-the-land, think to make it as lawful as you can.

Lit. Yes, sir, and as soon as you can: for it must be, sir; you see the danger my little wife is in, sir.

Pure. Truly, I do love my child dearly, and I would not have her miscarry, or hazard her first fruits, if it might be otherwise.

Busy. Surely it may be otherwise, but it is subject to construction, subject, and hath a face of offence, with the weak, a great face, a foul face; but that face may have a veil put over it and be shadowed, as it were; it may be eaten, and in the Fair, I take it, in a booth, the tents of the wicked: the place is not much, not very much; we may be religious in midst of the profane, so it be eaten with a reformed mouth, with sobriety and humbleness; not gorg'd in with gluttony or greediness; there's the fear: for, should she go there, as taking pride in the place, or delight in the unclean dressing, to feed the vanity of the eye, or the lust of the palate, it were not well, it were not fit, it were abominable, and not good.

Lit. Nay, I knew that afore, and told her on't, but courage, Win, we'll be humble enough; we'll seek out the homeliest booth i' the Fair, that's certain; rather than fail, we'll eat it o' the ground.

Pure. Aye, and I'll go with you myself, Win-the-fight, and my brother, Zeal-of-the-land, shall go with us too, for our better consolation.

Win. Uh, uh.

Lit. Aye, and Solomon too, Win, the more the merrier, Win, we'll leave Rabby Busy in a booth. Solomon, my cloak.

Enter Solomon *with the cloak.*

Sol. Here, sir.

Busy. In the way of comfort to the weak, I will go and eat. I will eat exceedingly, and prophesy; there may be a good use made of it, too, now I think on't: by the public eating of swine's flesh, to profess our hate and loathing of Judaism, whereof the brethren stand taxed. I will therefore eat, yea, I will eat exceedingly.

Lit. Good, i' faith, I will eat heartily too, because I will be no Jew, I could never away with that stiffnecked generation: and truly, I hope my little one will be like me, that cries for pig so, i' the mother's belly.

Busy. Very likely, exceeding likely, very exceeding likely.   [*Exeunt.*

ACT II. SCENE I

THE FAIR

A number of booths and stalls are set out.

Lanthorn Leatherhead, Joan Trash *and others are sitting by their wares.*

Enter Justice Overdo, *in disguise.*

Jus. Well, in Justice name, and the King's; and for the Commonwealth! defy all the world, Adam Overdo, for a disguise, and all story; for thou hast fitted thyself, I swear; fain would I meet the Linceus now, that eagle's eye, that piercing Epidaurian serpent (as my Quintus Horace calls him) that could discover a Justice of Peace (and lately of the Quorum) under this covering. They may have seen many a fool in the habit of a Justice; but never till now, a Justice in the habit of a fool. Thus must we do, though, that wake for the public good: and thus hath the wise magistrate done in all ages. There is a doing of right out of wrong, if the way be found. Never shall I enough commend a worthy worshipful man, sometime a capital member of this city, for his high wisdom, in this point, who would take you, now the habit of a porter; now of a carman; now of the dog-killer, in this month of August; and in the winter, of a seller of tinder-boxes; and what would he do in all these shapes? marry, go you into every alehouse, and down into every cellar; measure the length of puddings, take the gauge of black pots and cans, aye, and custards with a stick; and their circumference with a thread; weigh the loaves of bread on his middle-finger; then would he send for 'em home; give the puddings to the poor, the bread to the hungry, the custards to his children; break the pots and burn the cans, himself; he would not trust his corrupt officers; he would do 't himself. Would all men in authority would follow this worthy precedent! For, alas, as we are public persons, what do we know? nay, what can we know? we hear with other men's ears; we see with other men's eyes; a foolish constable, or a sleepy watchman, is all our information, he slanders a gentleman by the virtue of his place, as he calls it, and we by the vice of ours, must believe him. As a while agone, they made me, yea me, to mistake an honest zealous pursivant for a seminary: and a proper young Bachelor of Music for a bawd. This we are subject to, that live in high place, all our intelligence is idle, and most of our intelligencers knaves: and by your leave, ourselves, thought little better if not arrant fools, for believing 'em. I, Adam Overdo, am resolv'd therefore, to spare spy-money hereafter, and make mine own discoveries. Many are the yearly enormities of this Fair in whose courts of Pie-pouldres I have had the honour during the three days sometimes to sit as judge. But this is the special day for detection of those aforesaid enormities. Here is my black book, for the purpose; this the cloud that hides me: under this cover I shall see, and not be seen. On, Junius Brutus. And as I began, so I'll end: in Justice name, and the King's; and for the Commonwealth.

Lea. The Fair's pestilence dead, methinks; people come not abroad, today, what ever the matter is. Do you hear, Sister Trash, Lady o' the Basket? sit farther with your ginger-bread progeny there, and hinder not the prospect of my shop, or I'll ha' it proclaim'd i' the Fair, what stuff they are made on.

Tra. Why, what stuff are they made on, Brother Leatherhead? nothing but what's wholesome, I assure you.

Lea. Yes, stale bread, rotten eggs, musty ginger, and dead honey, you know.

Jus. Aye! have I met with enormity, so soon?   [*Aside.*

Lea. I shall mar your market, old Joan.

Tra. Mar my market, thou too-proud pedlar? do thy worst; I defy thee, aye, and thy stable of hobby-horses. I pay for my ground as well as thou dost, and thou wrong'st me, for all thou art parcel-poet, and an inginer. I'll find a friend shall right me, and make a ballad of thee and thy cattle all over. Are you puffed up with the pride of your wares? your arsedine?

Lea. Go to, old Joan, I'll talk with you anon; and take

you down too, afore Justice Overdo; he is the man must charm you, I'll ha' you i' the Pie-pouldres.

Tra. Charm me? I'll meet thee face to face, afore his worship, when thou dar'st: and though I be a little crooked o' my body, I'll be found as upright in my dealing as any woman in Smithfield, I; charm me!

Jus. I am glad to hear my name is their terror, yet; this is doing of Justice.

Lea. What do you lack? what is't you buy? what do you lack? Rattles, drums, halberts, horses, babies o' the best? Fiddles o' th' finest?

Enter Costard-monger *followed by* Nightingale.

Cos. Buy any pears, pears, fine, very fine pears!

Tra. Buy any ginger-bread, gilt ginger-bread!

Nig. Hey, now the Fair's a filling!   [*Sings.*
            O, for a tune to startle
        The birds o' the booths here billing
            Yearly with old Saint Bartle!
        The drunkards they are wading,
        The punks and chapmen trading;
    Who'd see the Fair without his lading?
Buy any ballads; new ballads?

Enter Ursula *from her booth.*

Urs. Fie upon't: who would wear out their youth and prime thus, in roasting of pigs, that had any cooler vocation? Hell's a kind of cold cellar to't, a very fine vault, o' my conscience! what, Mooncalf?

Moon. [*Within.*] Here, Mistress.

Nig. How now, Ursula? in a heat, in a heat?

Urs. My chair, you false faucet you; and my morning's draught, quickly, a bottle of ale, to quench me, rascal. I am all fire and fat, Nightingale. I shall e'en melt away to the first woman, a rib again, I am afraid. I do water the ground in knots as I go, like a great garden pot, you may follow me by the S.S. I make.

Nig. Alas, good Ursula; was Zekiel here this morning?

Urs. Zekiel? what Zekiel?

Nig. Zekiel Edgworth, the civil cutpurse, you know

479

him well enough; he that talks bawdy to you still: I call him my secretary.

Urs. He promis'd to be here this morning, I remember.

Nig. When he comes, bid him stay: I'll be back again presently.

Urs. Best take your morning's dew in your belly, Nightingale—— [*Mooncalf brings in the chair.*
Come, sir, set it here, did not I bid you should get this chair let out o' the sides for me, that my hips might play? you'll never think of anything, till your dame be rump-gall'd; 'tis well, changeling: because it can take in your grasshopper's thighs, you care for no more. Now you look as you had been i' the corner o' the booth, fleaing your breech with a candle's end, and set fire o' the Fair. Fill, Stote: fill.

Jus. This pig-woman do I know, and I will put her in, for my second enormity; she hath been before me, punk, pinnace and bawd, any time these two and twenty years, upon record i' the Pie-pouldres.

Urs. Fill again, you unlucky vermin.

Moon. 'Pray you be not angry, mistress, I'll ha' it widen'd anon.

Urs. No, no, I shall e'en dwindle away to't, ere the Fair be done, you think, now you ha' heated me? A poor vex'd thing I am, I feel myself dropping already, as fast as I can: two stone a suet a day is my proportion: I can but hold life and soul together, with this (here's to you, Nightingale) and a whiff of tobacco, at most. Where's my pipe now? not fill'd? thou arrant incubee.

Nig. Nay, Ursula, thou'lt gall between the tongue and the teeth, with fretting, now.

Urs. How can I hope that ever he'll discharge his place of trust, tapster, a man of reckoning under me, that remembers nothing I say to him?   [*Exit* Nightingale.
But look to't, sirrah, you were best, threepence a pipefull, I will ha' made, of all my whole half pound of tobacco, and a quarter of a pound of coltsfoot, mix'd with it too, to itch it out. I that have dealt so long in the fire, will not be to seek in smoke, now. Then six and twenty shillings a barrel I will advance o' my beer; and fifty shillings a hundred o'

my bottle-ale, I ha' told you the ways how to raise it.
Froth your cans well i' the filling, at length, rogue, and jog
your bottles o' the buttock, sirrah, then skink out the first
glass ever, and drink with all companies, though you be
sure to be drunk; you'll mis-reckon the better, and be less
asham'd on't. But your true trick, rascal, must be to be
ever busy and mistake away the bottles and cans, in haste
before they be half drunk off, and never hear anybody call
(if they should chance to mark you) till you ha' brought
fresh, and be able to forswear 'em. Give me a drink of ale.

Jus. This is the very womb and bed of enormity! gross
as herself! this must all down for enormity, all, every whit
on't. [*Aside.*]   [*Knocking within.*

Urs. Look, who's there, sirrah? five shillings a pig is my
price, at least; if it be a sow-pig, sixpence more: if she be a
great-bellied wife, and long for't, sixpence more for that.

Jus. O tempora! O mores! I would not ha' lost my dis-
covery of this one grievance, for my place and worship o'
the bench! How is the poor subject abus'd here! well, I
will fall in with her, and with her Mooncalf, and win out
wonders of enormity.——By thy leave, goodly woman, and
the fatness of the Fair: oily as the King's constable's lamp,
and shining as his shooing-horn! hath thy ale virtue, or thy
beer strength? that the tongue of man may be tickled? and
his palate pleas'd in the morning? let thy pretty nephew
here go search and see.

Urs. What new roarer is this?

Moon. O Lord! do you not know him, mistress, 'tis mad
Arthur of Bradley, that makes the orations. Brave master,
old Arthur of Bradley, how do you? welcome to the Fair,
when shall we hear you again to handle your matters? with
your back against a booth, ha? I ha' bin one o' your little
disciples, i' my days!

Jus. Let me drink, boy, with my love, thy Aunt, here;
that I may be eloquent: but of thy best, lest it be bitter in
my mouth, and my words fall foul on the Fair.

Urs. Why dost thou not fetch him drink? and offer him
to sit?

Moon. Is't ale or beer, Master Arthur?

Jus. Thy best, pretty stripling, thy best; the same thy dove drinketh, and thou drawest on holy days.

Urs. Bring him a sixpenny bottle of ale; they say a fool's handsel is lucky.

Jus. Bring both, child. Ale for Arthur and beer for Bradley. Ale for thine Aunt, boy. [*Exit* Mooncalf.
My disguise takes to the very wish and reach of it. I shall, by the benefit of this, discover enough, and more: and yet get off with the reputation of what I would be: a certain middling thing, between a fool and a madman. [*Aside.*

Enter Knockem.

Kno. What! my little lean Ursula! my she-bear! art thou alive, yet, with thy litter of pigs to grunt out another Bartholomew Fair? ha!

Urs. Yes, and to amble afoot, when the Fair is done, to hear you groan out of a cart, up the heavy hill.

Kno. Of Holborn, Ursula, meanst thou so? for what? for what, pretty Urs?

Urs. For cutting half-penny purses: or stealing little penny dogs out o' the Fair.

Kno. O! good words, good words, Urs.

Jus. Another special enormity. A cutpurse of the sword, the boot, and the feather! those are his marks. [*Aside.*

Re-enter Mooncalf *with the ale.*

Urs. You are one of those horse-leeches that gave out I was dead, in Turnbull-street, of a surfeit of bottle-ale and tripes?

Kno. No, 'twas better meat, Urs: cow's udders, cow's udders!

Urs. Well, I shall be meet with your mumbling mouth one day.

Kno. What? thou'lt poison me with a newt in a bottle of ale, wilt thou? or a spider in a tobacco-pipe, Urs. Come, there's no malice in these fat folks, I never fear thee, and I can 'scape thy lean Mooncalf here. Let's drink it out, good Urs, and no vapours! [*Exit* Ursula.

Jus. Dost thou hear, boy? There's for thy ale, and the

remnant for thee. Speak in thy faith of a faucet, now; is this goodly person before us here, this vapours, a knight of the knife?

Moon. What mean you by that, Master Arthur?

Jus. I mean a child of the horn-thumb, a babe of booty, boy; a cutpurse.

Moon. O Lord, sir! far from it. This is Master Dan Knockem: Jordan, the ranger of Turnbull. He is a horse-courser, sir.

Jus. Thy dainty dame, though, call'd him cutpurse.

Moon. Like enough, sir, she'll do forty such things in an hour an you listen to her, for her recreation, if the toy take her i' the greasy kerchief: it makes her fat, you see. She battens with it.

Jus. Here might I ha' been deceiv'd, now: and ha' put a fool's blot upon myself, if I had not play'd an after game o' discretion. [*Aside.*

Ursula *comes in again dropping.*

Kno. Alas, poor Urs, this's an ill season for thee.

Urs. Hang yourself, hackney-man.

Kno. How? how? Urs, vapours! motion breed vapours?

Urs. Vapours? Never tusk nor twirl your dibble, good Jordan; I know what you'll take to a very drop. Though you be captain o' the roarers, and fight well at the case of piss-pots, you shall not fright me with your lion-chap, sir, nor your tusks; you angry? you are hungry: come, a pig's head will stop your mouth, and stay your stomach, at all times.

Kno. Thou art such another mad merry Urs still! Troth, I do make conscience of vexing thee, now i' the dog-days, this hot weather, for fear of foundering thee i' the body; and melting down a pillar of the Fair. Pray thee take thy chair again, and keep state; and let's have a fresh bottle of ale, and a pipe of tobacco; and no vapours. I'll ha' this belly o' thine taken up, and thy grass scour'd, wench; look! here's Ezekiel Edgworth; a fine boy of his inches, as any is i' the Fair! has still money in his purse, and will pay all with a kind heart, and good vapours.

Enter Edgworth.

Edg. That I will, indeed, willingly, Master Knockem! Fetch some ale, and tobacco.   [*Exit* Mooncalf.

Lea. What do you lack, gentlemen? Maid: see a fine hobby-horse for your young master: cost you but a token a week his provender.

Re-enter Nightingale *with* Corncutter *and* Mousetrap Man.

Corn. Ha' you any corns i' your feet, and toes?

Tin. Buy a mousetrap, a mousetrap, or a tormentor for a flea.

Tra. Buy some ginger-bread.

Nig. Ballads, ballads! fine new ballads:

> Hear for your love, and buy for your money.
> A delicate ballad o' the ferret and the coney.
> A preservative again' the punks' evil.
> Another of goose-green starch, and the devil.
> A dozen of divine points, and the godly garters.
> The fairing of good counsel, of an ell and three
>   quarters.
> What is 't you buy?
> The windmill blown down by the witch's fart!
> Or Saint George, that O! did break the dragon's
>   heart!

Re-enter Mooncalf *with ale and tobacco.*

Edg. Master Nightingale, come hither, leave your mart a little.

Nig. O my secretary! what says my secretary?

Jus. Child o' the bottles, what's he? what's he?

Moon. A civil young gentleman, Master Arthur, that keeps company with the roarers, and disburses all, still. He has ever money in his purse; he pays for them; and they roar for him: one does good offices for another. They call him the secretary, but he serves nobody. A great friend of the ballad-man's, they are never asunder.

Jus. What pity 'tis, so civil a young man should haunt this debauch'd company? here's the bane of the youth of our time apparent. A proper penman, I see 't in his countenance, he has a good clerk's look with him, and I warrant him a quick hand.

Moon. A very quick hand, sir. [*Exit.*

Edg. [*This they whisper, that* Overdo *hears it not.*] All the purse and purchase, I give you to-day by conveyance, bring hither to Ursula's presently. Here we will meet at night in her lodge, and share. Look you choose good places for your standing i' the Fair, when you sing, Nightingale.

Urs. Aye, near the fullest passages; and shift 'em often.

Edg. And i' your singing, you must use your hawk's eye nimbly, and fly the purse to a mark, still, where 'tis worn, and o' which side; that you may gi' me the sign with your beak, or hang your head that way i' the tune.

Urs. Enough, talk no more on't; your friendship, masters, is not now to begin. Drink your draught of indenture, your sup of covenant, and away; the Fair fills apace, company begins to come in, and I ha' ne'er a pig ready, yet.

Kno. Well said! fill the cups, and light the tobacco: let's give fire i' th' works, and noble vapours.

Edg. And shall we ha' smocks, Ursula, and good whimsies, ha?

Urs. Come, you are i' your bawdy vein! the best the Fair will afford, Zekiel, if bawd Whit keep his word:

Re-enter Mooncalf.

How do the pigs, Mooncalf?

Moon. Very passionate, mistress, one on 'em has wept out an eye. Master Arthur o' Bradley's melancholy, here; nobody talks to him. Will you any tobacco, Master Arthur?

Jus. No, boy, let my meditations alone.

Moon. He's studying for an oration, now.

Jus. If I can, with this day's travel, and all my policy, but rescue this youth, here, out of the hands of the lewd man and the strange woman, I will sit down at night, and say with my friend Ovid, *Jamque; opus exegi, quod nec Jovis ira, nec ignis, &c.* [*Aside.*

Kno. Here, Zekiel; here's a health to Ursula, and a kind vapour, thou hast money i' thy purse still; and store! how dost thou come by it? Pray thee vapour thy friends some in a courteous vapour.

Edg. Half I have, Master Dan Knockem, is always at your service. [*Pulls out his purse.*

Jus. Ha, sweet nature! what goshawk would prey upon such a lamb? [*Aside.*

Kno. Let's see what 'tis, Zekiel! count it, come, fill him to pledge me.

Enter Winwife and Quarlous.

Winw. We are here before 'em, methinks.

Quar. All the better, we shall see 'em come in now.

Lea. What do you lack, gentlemen, what is't you lack? a fine horse? a lion? a bull? a bear? a dog, or a cat? an excellent fine Bartholomew bird? or an instrument? what is't you lack?

Quar. 'Slid! here's Orpheus among the beasts, with his fiddle, and all!

Tra. Will you buy any comfortable bread, gentlemen?

Quar. And Ceres selling her daughter's picture, in ginger-work!

Winw. That these people should be so ignorant to think us chapmen for 'em! do we look as if we would buy gingerbread? or hobby-horses?

Quar. Why, they know no better ware than they have, nor better customers than come. And our very being here makes us fit to be demanded, as well as others. Would Cokes would come! there were a true customer for 'em.

Kno. How much is't? thirty shillings? who's yonder! Ned Winwife? and Tom Quarlous, I think? yes, gi' me it all, gi' me it all, Master Winwife! Master Quarlous! will you take a pipe of tobacco with us? do not discredit me now, Zekiel.

Winw. Do not see him! he is the roaring horse-courser; pray thee, let's avoid him: turn down this way.

Quar. 'Slud, I'll see him, and roar with him, too, and he roar'd as loud as Neptune, pray thee go with me.

Winw. You may draw me to as likely an inconvenience, when you please, as this.

Quar. Go to then, come along, we ha' nothing to do, man, but to see sights now.

Kno. Welcome Master Quarlous, and Master Winwife! Will you take any froth, and smoke with us?

Quar. Yes, sir, but you'll pardon us, if we knew not of so much familiarity between us afore.

Kno. As what, sir?

Quar. To be so lightly invited to smoke, and froth.

Kno. A good vapour! will you sit down, sir? this is old Ursula's mansion, how like you her bower? here you may ha' your punk, and your pig in state, sir, both piping hot.

Quar. I had rather ha' my punk cold, sir.

Jus. There's for me, punk! and pig!   *[Aside.*

Urs. What, Mooncalf? you rogue.   *[She calls within.*

Moon. By and by, the bottle is almost off, mistress, here, Master Arthur.

Urs. I'll part you and your play-fellow there, i' the guarded coat, an' you sunder not the sooner.

Kno. Master Winwife, you are proud methinks, you do not talk, nor drink, are you proud?

Winw. Not of the company I am in, sir, nor the place, I assure you.

Kno. You do not except at the company do you? are you in vapours, sir?

Moon. Nay, good Master Dan Knockem, respect my mistress's bower, as you call it; for the honour of our booth, none o' your vapours, here.

Ursula *comes out with a fire-brand.*

Urs. Why, you thin lean polecat you, and they have a mind to be i' their vapours, must you hinder 'em? what did you know, vermin, if they would ha' lost a cloak, or such a trifle? must you be drawing the air of pacification, here? while I am tormented, within, i' the fire, you weasel?

Moon. Good mistress, 'twas in the behalf of your booth's credit, that I spoke.

Urs. Why? would my booth ha' broke, if they had fallen out in't? or would their heat ha' fired it? in, you rogue, and wipe the pigs, and mend the fire, that they fall not, or

I'll both baste and roast you, till your eyes drop out, like 'em—Leave the bottle behind you, and be curst a while!

[*Exit* Mooncalf.

Quar. Body o' the Fair! what's this? mother o' the bawds?

Kno. No, she's mother o' the pigs, sir, mother o' the pigs!

Winw. Mother o' the furies, I think, by her firebrand.

Quar. Nay, she is too fat to be a fury, sure, some walking sow of tallow!

Winw. An inspir'd vessel of kitchen-stuff!

She drinks this while.

Quar. She'll make excellent gear for the coach-makers, here in Smithfield, to anoint wheels and axle-trees with.

Urs. Aye, aye, gamesters, mock a plain plump soft wench o' the suburbs, do, because she's juicy and whole-some: you must ha' your thin pinch'd ware, pent up i' the compass of a dog-collar (or 'twill not do), that looks like a long lac'd conger set upright, and a green feather, like fennel i' the jowl on 't.

Kno. Well said, Urs, my good Urs, to 'em, Urs.

Quar. Is she your quagmire, Dan Knockem? is this your bog?

Nig. We shall have a quarrel presently.

Kno. How? Bog? Quagmire? foul vapours! hum'h!

Quar. Yes, he that would venture for't, I assure him, might sink into her, and be drown'd a week, ere any friend he had could find where he were.

Winw. And then he would be a fortnight weighing up again.

Quar. 'Twere like falling into a whole shire of butter: they had need be a team of Dutchmen should draw him out.

Kno. Answer 'em, Urs, where's thy Barthol'mew wit, now? Urs, thy Barthol'mew wit?

Urs. Hang 'em, rotten, roguy cheaters, I hope to see 'em plagu'd one day (pox'd they are already, I am sure) with lean playhouse poultry, that has the bony rump, sticking out like the ace of spades, or the point of a partizan, that every rib of 'em is like the tooth of a saw: and will so grate 'em with their hips and shoulders, as (take 'em altogether) they were as good lie with a hurdle.

Quar. Out upon her, how she drips! she's able to give a man the sweating sickness with looking on her.

Urs. Marry look off, with a patch o' your face; and a dozen i' your breech, though they be o' scarlet, sir, I ha' seen as fine outsides, as either o' yours, bring lousy linings to the brokers, ere now, twice a week.

Quar. Do you think there may be a fine new cucking-stool i' the Fair, to be purchas'd? one large enough, I mean. I know there is a pond of capacity for her.

Urs. For your mother, you rascal; out, you rogue, you hedge bird you pimp, you pannier-man's bastard, you!

Quar. Ha, ha, ha.

Urs. Do you sneer, you dog's-head, you trendle tail! you look as you were begotten a'top of a cart in harvest-time, when the whelp was hot and eager. Go, snuff after your brother's bitch, Mistress Commodity, that's the livery you wear, 'twill be out at the elbows, shortly. It's time you went to't, for the t' other remnant.

Kno. Peace, Urs, peace, Urs, they'll kill the poor whale, and make oil of her. Pray thee go in.

Urs. I'll see 'em pox'd first, and pil'd, and double pil'd.

Winw. Let's away, her language grows greasier than her pigs.

Urs. Does't so, snotty nose? good Lord! are you snivelling? you were engendered on a she-beggar, in a barn, when the bald thrasher, your sire, was scarce warm.

Winw. Pray thee, let's go.

Quar. No, faith: I'll stay the end of her, now: I know she cannot last long; I find by her similes she wanes a pace.

Urs. Does she so? I'll set you gone. Gi' me my pig-pan hither a little. I'll scald you hence, and you will not go.

[*Exit.*

Kno. Gentlemen, these are very strange vapours! and very idle vapours! I assure you.

Quar. You are a very serious ass, we assure you.

Kno. Humh! Ass? and serious? nay, then pardon me my vapour. I have a foolish vapour, gentlemen: any man that does vapour me the ass, Master Quarlous——

Quar. What then, Master Jordan?

Kno. I do vapour him the lie.

Quar. Faith, and to any man that vapours me the lie, I do vapour that. [*Strikes him.*

Kno. Nay, then, vapours upon vapours.

Edg. and Nig. 'Ware the pan, the pan, the pan, she comes with the pan, gentlemen. God bless the woman.

Ursula comes in with the scalding-pan. They fight. She falls with it.

Urs. Oh!

Tra. [*Running in.*] What's the matter?

Jus. Goodly woman! [*Exeunt Quar. and Winw.*

Moon. Mistress!

Urs. Curse of hell, that ever I saw these fiends, oh! I ha' scalded my leg, my leg, my leg, my leg. I ha' lost a limb in the service! run for some cream and salad oil, quickly. Are you under-peering, you baboon? rip off my hose, an' you be men, men, men!

Moon. Run you for some cream, good mother Joan. I'll look to your basket. [*Exit Trash.*

Lea. Best sit up i' your chair, Ursula. Help, gentlemen.

Kno. Be of good cheer, Urs. Thou hast hindered me the currying of a couple of stallions, here, that abus'd the good race-bawd o' Smithfield; 'twas time for 'em to go.

Nig. I' faith, when the pan came, they made you run else. This had been a fine time for purchase, if you had ventur'd. [*Aside to* Edgworth.

Edg. Not a whit, these fellows were too fine to carry money.

Kno. Nightingale, get some help to carry her leg out o' the air; take off her shoes; body o' me, she has the mallanders, the scratches, the crown scab, and the quitter bone, i' the tother leg.

Urs. Oh! the pox, why do you put me in mind o' my

leg, thus, to make it prick and shoot? would you ha' me i' the hospital afore my time?

Kno. Patience, Urs, take a good heart, 'tis but a blister as big as a windgall; I'll take it away with the white of an egg, a little honey, and hog's grease; ha' thy pasterns well roll'd, and thou shalt pass again by tomorrow. I'll tend thy booth, and look to thy affairs, the while: thou shalt sit i' thy chair, and give directions, and shine Ursa major.

[*Exeunt* Knock. *and* Moon. *with* Ursula *in her chair.*

Jus. These are the fruits of bottle-ale and tobacco! the foam of the one, and the fumes of the other! Stay, young man, and despise not the wisdom of these few hairs, that are grown grey in care of thee.

Edg. Nightingale, stay a little. Indeed I'll hear some o' this!

Enter Cokes, Waspe, Mistress Overdo *and* Grace.

Cok. Come, Numps, come, where are you? welcome into the Fair, Mistress Grace.

Edg. 'Slight, he will call company, you shall see, and put us into doings presently.

Jus. Thirst not after that frothy liquor, ale: for who knows, when he openeth the stopple, what may be in the bottle? hath not a snail, a spider, yea, a newt been found there? thirst not after it, youth: thirst not after it.

Cok. This is a brave fellow, Numps, let's hear him.

Was. 'Sblood, how brave is he? in a guarded coat? you were best truck with him, e'en strip, and truck presently, it will become you. Why will you hear him? because he is an ass, and may be a kin to the Cokeses?

Cok. O, good Numps!

Jus. Neither do thou lust after that tawny weed, tobacco.

Cok. Brave words!

Jus. Whose complexion is like the Indian's that vents it!

Cok. Are they not brave words, sister?

Jus. And who can tell, if, before the gathering. and making up thereof, the Alligarta hath not piss'd thereon?

Was. 'Heart, let 'em be brave words, as brave as they will! and they were all the brave words in a country, how

then? will you away yet? ha' you enough on him? Mistress
Grace, come you away, I pray you, be not you accessary.
If you do lose your licence, or somewhat else, sir, with
listening to his fables: say, Numps is a witch, with all my
heart, do say so.

Cok. Avoid i' your satin doublet, Numps.

Jus. The creeping venom of which subtle serpent, as
some late writers affirm; neither the cutting of the perilous
plant, nor the drying of it, nor the lighting, or burning, can
any way persway or assuage.

Cok. Good, i' faith! is 't not, sister?

Jus. Hence it is, that the lungs of the tobacconist are
rotted, the liver spotted, the brain smok'd like the backside
of the pig-woman's booth, here, and the whole body within,
black as her pan you saw e'en now without.

Cok. A fine similitude, that sir! did you see the pan?

Edg. Yes, sir.

Jus. Nay, the hole in the nose here, of some tobacco-
takers, or the third nostril (if I may so call it) which makes
that they can vent the tobacco out, like the ace of clubs, or
rather the flower-de-lys, is caused from the tobacco, the
mere tobacco! when the poor innocent pox, having nothing
to do there, is miserably and most unconscionably slan-
der'd.

Cok. Who would ha' miss'd this, sister?

Mrs. Over. Not anybody, but Numps.

Cok. He does not understand.

Edg. Nor you feel.   [*He picks his purse.*

Cok. What would you have, sister, of a fellow that
knows nothing but a basket-hilt, and an old fox in 't? the
best music i' the Fair will not move a log.

Edg. [*Giving the purse aside to* Nightingale.] In to
Ursula, Nightingale, and carry her comfort: see it told.
This fellow was sent to us by fortune for our first fairing.

                                        [*Exit* Nightingale.

Jus. But what speak I of the diseases of the body, chil-
dren of the Fair?

Cok. That's to us, sister, brave, i' faith!

Jus. Hark, O, you sons and daughters of Smithfield! and

hear what malady it doth the mind: It causeth swearing, it causeth swaggering, it causeth snuffling, and snarling, and now and then a hurt.

Mrs. Over. He hath something of Master Overdo, methinks, brother.

Cok. So me thought, sister, very much of my brother Overdo: and 'tis when he speaks.

Jus. Look into any angle o' the town, the Straits, or the Bermudas, where the quarrelling lesson is read, and how do they entertain the time, but with bottle-ale and tobacco? The lecturer is o' one side, and his pupils o' the other; But the seconds are still bottle-ale and tobacco, for which the lecturer reads, and the novices pay. Thirty pound a week in bottle-ale! forty in tobacco! and ten more in ale again. Then for a suit to drink in, so much, and that being slaver'd so much for another suit, and then a third suit, and a fourth suit! and still the bottle-ale slavereth, and the tobacco stinketh!

Was. Heart of a madman! are you rooted here? will you never away? what can any man find out in this bawling fellow, to grow here for? he is a full handful higher sin' he heard him. Will you fix here, and set up a booth, sir?

Jus. I will conclude briefly——

Was. Hold your peace, you roaring rascal, I'll run my head i' your chaps, else. You were best build a booth, and entertain him, make your will, and you say the word, and him your heir! heart, I never knew one taken with a mouth of a peck, afore. By this light, I'll carry you away o' my back, and you will not come.

[*He gets* Cokes *up on pick-back.*

Cok. Stay, Numps, stay, set me down: I ha' lost my purse, Numps, O my purse! one o' my fine purses is gone.

[*Examines his pockets.*

Mrs. Over. Is't indeed, brother?

Cok. Aye, as I am an honest man, would I were an arrant rogue, else! a plague of all roguy, damn'd cutpurses for me.

Was. Bless 'em with all my heart, with all my heart, do you see! Now, as I am no infidel that I know of, I am glad on't. Aye, I am (here's my witness!) do you see, sir? I did not tell you of his fables. I? no, no, I am a dull malt-horse. aye, I know nothing. Are you not justly serv'd i' your conscience now? speak i' your conscience. Much good do you with all my heart, and his good heart that has it, with all my heart again.

Edg. This fellow is very charitable, would he had a purse too! but I must not be too bold, all at a time.   [*Aside.*

Cok. Nay, Numps, it is not my best purse.

Was. Not your best! death! why should it be your worst? why should it be any, indeed, at all? answer me to that, gi' me a reason from you, why it should be any?

Cok. Nor my gold, Numps; I ha' that yet, look here else, sister.   [*Shows the other purse.*

Was. Why so, there's all the feeling he has!

Mrs. Over. I pray you, have a better care of that, brother.

Cok. Nay, so I will, I warrant you; let him catch this, that catch can. I would fain see him get this, look you here.

Was. So, so, so, so, so, so, so, so! Very good.

Cok. I would ha' him come again, now, and but offer at it. Sister, will you take notice of a good jest? I will put it just where th' other was, and if we ha' good luck, you shall see a delicate fine trap to catch the cutpurse nibbling.

Edg. Faith, and he'll try ere you be out o' the Fair.

[*Aside.*

Cok. Come, Mistress Grace, prithee be not melancholy for my mischance; sorrow wi' not keep it, sweet-heart.

Gra. I do not think on 't, sir.

Cok. 'Twas but a little scurvy white money, hang it: it may hang the cutpurse, one day. I ha' gold left to gi' thee a fairing, yet, as hard as the world goes: nothing angers me, but that nobody here look'd like a cutpurse, unless 'twere Numps.

Was. How? I? I look like a cutpurse? death! your sister's a cutpurse! and your mother and father, and all your kin were cutpurses! And here is a rogue is the bawd o' the cutpurses, whom I will beat to begin with.

They speak all together. Waspe *beats the* Justice.

Jus. Hold thy hand, child of wrath and heir of anger,

494

make it not Childermass day in thy fury, or the feast of French Bartholomew, parent of the massacre.

Cok. Numps, Numps!

Mrs. Over. Good Master Humphrey!

Was. You are the Patrico, are you? The patriarch of the cutpurses? You share, sir, they say; let them share this with you. Are you i' your hot fit of preaching again. I'll cool you.   *[Beats him again.*

Jus. Murther, murther, murther!   *[Exeunt.*

ACT III. SCENE I

THE FAIR

Lanthorn Leatherhead, Joan Trash *and others, sitting by their wares as before.*

Enter Val, Whit, Haggis *and* Bristle.

Whi. Nay, tish all gone, now! dish tish, phen tou vilt not be phitin call, master offisher, phat ish a man te better to lishen out noishes for tee, and tou art in an oder 'orld, being very shuffishient noishes and gallantsh too, one o' their brabblesh would have fed ush all dish fortnight, but tou art so bushy about beggersh still, tou hast no leshure to intend shentlemen, and 't be.

Hag. Why, I told you, Davy Bristle.

Bri. Come, come, you told me a pudding, Toby Haggis; A matter of nothing; I am sure it came to nothing! you said, let's go to Ursula's indeed; but then you met the man with the monsters, and I could not get you from him. An old fool, not leave seeing yet?

Hag. Why, who would ha' thought anybody would ha' quarrell'd so early? or that the ale o' the Fair would ha' been up so soon?

Whi. Phy? phat a clock toest tou tink it ish, man?

Hag. I cannot tell.

Whi. Tou art a vish vatchman, i' te mean teem.

Hag. Why? should the watch go by the clock, or the clock by the watch, I pray?

Bri. One should go by another, if they did well.

Whi. Tou art right now! phen didst tou ever know, or hear of a shuffishient vatchman, but he did tell the clock, phat business soever he had?

Bri. Nay, that's most true, a sufficient watchman knows what a clock it is.

Whi. Shleeping, or vaking! ash well as te clock himshelf, or te jack dat shtrikes him!

Bri. Let's enquire of Master Leatherhead or Joan Trash here. Master Leatherhead, do you hear, Master Leatherhead?

Whi. If it be a Ledderhead, tish a very tick Ledderhead, tat sho mush noish vill not peirsh him.

Lea. I have a little business now, good friends; do not trouble me.

Whi. Phat? because o' ty wrought neet cap, and ty phelvet sherkin, man? phy? I have sheen tee in ty ledder sherkin, ere now, mashter o' de hobby-horses, as bushy and as stately as tou sheem'st to be.

Tra. Why, what an' you have, Captain Whit? he has his choice of jerkins, you may see by that, and his caps too, I assure you, when he pleases to be either sick or employ'd.

Lea. God a mercy, Joan, answer for me.

Whi. Away, be not sheen i' my company, here be shentlemen, and men of vorship.   [*Exeunt* Haggis *and* Bristle.

Enter Quarlous *and* Winwife.

Quar. We had wonderful ill luck to miss this prologue o' the purse, but the best is, we shall have five acts of him ere night: he'll be spectacle enough! I'll answer for 't.

Whi. O Creesh! Duke Quarlous, how dosht tou? tou dosht not know me, I fear? I am te vishesht man, but Justice Overdo, in all Bartholomew Fair now. Gi' me twelvepence from tee, I vill help tee to a vife vorth forty marks for 't, and 't be.

Quar. Away, rogue, pimp, away.

Whi. And she shall show tee as fine cut 'ork for 't in her shmock too, as tou cansht vish i' faith; vilt tou have her, vorshipfull Vinvife? I vill help tee to her, here, be an't be, in te pig-quarter, gi' me ty twelpence from tee.

Winw. Why, there's twelpence; pray thee, wilt thou be gone?

Whi. Tou art a vorthy man, and a vorshipfull man still.

Quar. Get you gone, rascal.

Whi. I do mean it, man. Prinsh Quarlous, if tou hasht need on me, tou shalt find me here, at Ursula's. I vill see phat ale and punk ish i' te pigshty for tee, bless ty good vorship. [*Exit.*

Quar. Look! who comes here! John Littlewit!

Winw. And his wife, and my widow, her mother: the whole family.

Quar. 'Slight, you must gi' em all fairings, now!

Winw. Not I, I'll not see 'em.

Quar. They are going a-feasting. What school-master's that is with 'em?

Winw. That's my rival I believe, the baker!

Enter Rabbi Busy, Dame Purecraft, John Littlewit *and* Mrs. Littlewit.

Busy. So, walk on in the middle way, fore-right, turn neither to the right hand, not to the left: let not your eyes be drawn aside with vanity, nor your ear with noises.

Quar. O, I know him by that start!

Lea. What do you lack? what do you buy, pretty Mistress! a fine hobby-horse, to make your son a tilter? a drum to make him a soldier? a fiddle, to make him a reveller? What is't you lack? Little dogs for your daughters? or babies, male or female?

Busy. Look not toward them, harken not: the place is Smithfield or the field of smiths, the grove of hobby-horses and trinkets, the wares are the wares of devils. And the whole Fair is the shop of Satan! They are hooks and baits, very baits, that are hung out on every side to catch you and to hold you as it were, by the gills; and by the nostrils, as the fisher doth: therefore you must not look nor turn toward them.—The heathen man could stop his

ears with wax, against the harlot o' the sea: do you the like
with your fingers, against the bells of the beast.

Winw. What flashes comes from him!

Quar. O, he has those of his oven! a notable hot baker
'twas, when he plied the peel: he is leading his flock into
the Fair now.

Winw. Rather driving 'em to the pens: for he will let
'em look upon nothing.

Enter Knockem *and* Whit *from* Ursula's *booth.*

Kno. Gentlewomen, the weather's hot! whither walk
you? Have a care o' your fine velvet caps, the Fair is dusty.
Take a sweet delicate booth, with boughs, here, i' the way,
and cool yourselves i' the shade: you and your friends. The
best pig and bottle-ale i' the Fair, sir. Old Ursula is Cook,
there you may read: [Littlewit *is gazing at the sign; which
is the Pigshead with a large writing under it.*] the pig's head
speaks it. Poor soul, she has had a stringhalt, the Mary-
hinchco, but she's prettily amended.

Whi. A delicate show-pig, little mistress, with shweet
sauce, and crackling, like de bay-leaf i' de fire, la! Tou
shalt ha' de clean side o' de table-clot and di glass vash'd
with phatersh of Dame Annessh Cleare.

Lit. This's fine, verily. *Here be the best pigs: and she
does roast 'em as well as ever she did,* the pig's head says.

Kno. Excellent, excellent, mistress, with fire o' juniper
and rosemary branches! The Oracle of the pig's head, that,
sir.

Pure. Son, were you not warn'd of the vanity of the eye?
have you forgot the wholesome admonition so soon?

Lit. Good mother, how shall we find a pig, if we do not
look about for 't? will it run off o' the spit into our mouths,
think you? as in Lubberland? and cry, *we, we?*

Busy. No, but your mother, religiously wise, conceiveth
it may offer itself, by other means, to the sense, as by way
of steam, which I think it doth, here in this place. Huh,
huh [Busy *scents after it like a hound*], yes, it doth. And it
were a sin of obstinacy, great obstinacy, high and horrible

498

obstinacy, to decline or resist the good titillation of the famelic sense, which is the smell. Therefore be bold (huh, huh, huh) follow the scent. Enter the tents of the unclean, for once, and satisfy your wife's frailty. Let your frail wife be satisfied: your zealous mother, and my suffering self, will also be satisfied.

Lit. Come, Win, as good winny here, as go farther and see nothing.

Busy. We 'scape so much of the other vanities, by our early entering.

Pure. It is an edifying consideration.

Win. This is scurvy, that we must come into the Fair, and not look on't.

Lit. Win, have patience, Win, I'll tell you more anon.

[*Exeunt into booth,* Littlewit, Mrs. Lit., Busy *and* Pure.

Kno. Mooncalf, entertain within there, the best pig i' the booth; a porklike pig. These are Banbury-bloods, o' the sincere stud, come a pig-hunting. Whit, wait, Whit, look to your charge.   [*Exit* Whit.

Busy. [*Within.*] A pig prepare, presently, let a pig be prepared to us.

Enter Mooncalf *and* Ursula.

Moon. 'Slight, who be these?

Urs. Is this the good service, Jordan, you'd do me?

Kno. Why, Urs? why, Urs? thou'lt ha' vapours i' thy leg again presently, pray thee go in, 't may turn to the scratches else.

Urs. Hang your vapours, they are stale, and stink like you. Are these the guests o' the game, you promis'd to fill my pit withal, today?

Kno. Aye, what ail they, Urs?

Urs. Ail they? they are all sippers, sippers o' the city, they look as they would not drink off two penn'orth of bottle-ale amongst 'em.

Moon. A body may read that i' their small printed ruffs.

Kno. Away, thou art a fool, Urs, and thy Mooncalf too, i' your ignorant vapours, now? hence! good guests, I say; right hypocrites, good gluttons. In, and set a couple o' pigs

o' the board, and half a dozen of the biggest bottles afore
'em, and call Whit. [*Exit* Mooncalf.] I do not love to hear
innocents abus'd: Fine ambling hypocrites! and a stone-
puritan, with a sorrel head and beard, good mouth'd glut-
tons: two to a pig, away.

Urs. Are you sure they are such?

Kno. O' the right breed, thou shalt try 'em by the teeth,
Urs. Where's this Whit?

Re-enter Whit.

Whi. Behold, man, and see, what a worthy man am ee!
    With the fury of my sword, and the shaking of my
        beard,
    I will make ten thousand men afeard.

Kno. Well said, brave Whit, in, and fear the ale out o'
the bottles, into the bellies of the brethren, and the sisters,
drink to the cause, and pure vapours.

               [*Exeunt* Knockem, Whit, *and* Ursula.

Quar. My roarer is turn'd tapster, methinks. Now were
a fine time for thee, Winwife, to lay aboard thy widow,
thou'lt never be master of a better season, or place; she that
will venture herself into the Fair and a pig-box, will admit
any assault, be assur'd of that.

Winw. I love not enterprises of that suddenness, though.

Quar. I'll warrant thee, then, no wife out o' the widow's
hundred: if I had but as much title to her, as to have
breath'd once on that straight stomacher of hers, I would
now assure myself to carry her, yet, ere she went out of
Smithfield. Or she should carry me, which were the fitter
sight, I confess. But you are a modest undertaker, by cir-
cumstances, and degrees; come, 'tis disease in thee, not
judgement, I should offer at all together. Look, here's the
poor fool again that was stung by the wasp erewhile.

Enter Justice Overdo.

Jus. I will make no more orations, shall draw on these
tragical conclusions. And I begin now to think, that by a
spice of collateral justice, Adam Overdo deserv'd this beat-
ing; for I, the said Adam, was one cause (a by-cause) why

the purse was lost: and my wife's brother's purse too, which they know not of yet. But I shall make very good mirth with it at supper (that will be the sport), and put my little friend, Master Humphrey Waspe's choler quite out of countenance. When, sitting at the upper end o' my table, as I use, and drinking to my brother Cokes and Mrs. Alice Overdo, as I will, my wife, for their good affection to old Bradley, I deliver to 'em it was I that was cudgell'd, and show 'em the marks. To see what bad events may peep out o' the tail of good purposes! the care I had of that civil young man, I took fancy to this morning (and have not left it yet), drew me to that exhortation, which drew the company, indeed which drew the cutpurse; which drew the money; which drew my brother Cokes his loss; which drew on Waspe's anger; which drew on my beating: a pretty gradation! And they shall ha' it i' their dish, i' faith, at night for fruit: I love to be merry at my table. I had thought once, at one special blow he ga' me, to have revealed myself; but then (I thank thee, fortitude) I remembered that a wise man (and who is ever so great a part o' the Commonwealth in himself) for no particular disaster ought to abandon a public good design. The husbandman ought not, for one unthankful year, to forsake the plough; the shepherd ought not, for one scabb'd sheep, to throw by his tar-box; the pilot ought not for one leak i' the poop, to quit the helm; nor the alderman ought not, for one custard more at a meal, to give up his cloak; the constable ought not to break his staff, and forswear the watch, for one roaring night; nor the piper o' the parish (*ut parvis componere magna solebam*) to put up his pipes, for one rainy Sunday. These are certain knocking conclusions; out of which, I am resolv'd, come what come can, come beating, come imprisonment, come infamy, come banishment, nay, come the rack, come the hurdle (welcome all), I will not discover who I am, till my due time; and yet still, all shall be, as I said ever, in justice' name, and the King's, and for the Commonwealth.

Winw. What does he talk to himself, and act so seriously? poor fool!

Quar. No matter what. Here's fresher argument, intend that.

Enter Cokes, Mistress Overdo *and* Grace, *followed by*
Waspe, *loaded with toys.*

Cok. Come, Mistress Grace, come sister, here's more fine sights, yet i' faith. God's lid, where's Numps?

Lea. What do you lack, gentlemen? what is't you buy? fine rattles, drums, babies, little dogs and birds for ladies? What do you lack?

Cok. Good honest Numps, keep afore, I am so afraid thou'lt lose somewhat: my heart was at my mouth when I miss'd thee.

Was. You were best buy a whip i' your hand to drive me.

Cok. Nay, do not mistake, Numps, thou art so apt to mistake: I would but watch the goods. Look you now, the treble fiddle was e'en almost like to be lost.

Was. Pray you take heed you lose not yourself: your best way were e'en get up, and ride for more surety. Buy a token's worth of great pins, to fasten yourself to my shoulder.

Lea. What do you lack, gentlemen? fine purses, pouches, pincases, pipes? What is't you lack? a pair o' smiths to wake you i' the morning? or a fine whistling bird?

Cok. Numps, here be finer things then any we ha' bought, by odds! and more delicate horses, a great deal! good Numps, stay, and come hither.

Was. Will you scourse with him? you are in Smithfield, you may fit yourself with a fine easy-going street-nag, for your saddle again' Michaelmas term, do, has he ne'er a little odd cart for you, to make a caroch on, i' the country, with four pied hobby horses? why the measles should you stand here with your train, cheaping of dogs, birds, and babies? you ha' no children to bestow 'em on? ha' you?

Cok. No, but again' I ha' children, Numps, that's all one.

Was. Do, do, do, do; how many shall you have, think you? an' I were as you, I'd buy for all my tenants, too; they are a kind o' civil savages, that will part with their children for rattles, pipes, and knives. You were best buy a hatchet, or two, and truck with 'em.

Cok. Good Numps, hold that little tongue o' thine, and save it a labour. I am resolute Bat, thou know'st.

Was. A resolute fool you are, I know, and a very sufficient coxcomb; with all my heart; nay, you have it, sir, and you be angry, turd i' your teeth, twice (if I said it not once afore), and much good do you.

Winw. Was there ever such a self-affliction? and so impertinent?

Quar. Alas! his care will go near to crack him, let's in and comfort him.

Was. Would I had been set i' the ground, all but the head on me, and had my brains bowl'd at, or thresh'd out, when first I underwent this plague of a charge!

Quar. How now, Numps! almost tir'd i' your protectorship? overparted? overparted?

Was. Why, I cannot tell, sir, it may be I am, does't grieve you?

Quar. No, I swear does't not, Numps: to satisfy you.

Was. Numps? 'Sblood, you are fine and familiar! how long ha' we been acquainted, I pray you?

Quar. I think it may be remembered, Numps, that? 'twas since morning sure.

Was. Why, I hope I know't well enough, sir, I did not ask to be told.

Quar. No? why then?

Was. It's no matter why, you see with your eyes, now, what I said to you today? you'll believe me another time?

Quar. Are you removing the Fair, Numps?

Was. A pretty question! and a very civil one! yes faith, I ha' my lading, you see; or shall have anon, you may know whose beast I am, by my burden. If the pannier-man's jack were ever better known by his loins of mutton I'll be flayed, and feed dogs for him, when his time comes.

Winw. How melancholy Mistress Grace is yonder! pray thee let's go enter ourselves in Grace with her.

Cok. Those six horses, friend, I'll have——

Was. How!

503

Cok. And the three Jews-trumps; and half a dozen o'
birds, and that drum (I have one drum already); and your
smiths; I like that device o' your smiths, very pretty well,
and four halberts—and (le' me see) that fine painted great
lady, and her three women for state, I'll have.

Was. No, the shop; buy the whole shop, it will be best,
the shop, the shop!

Lea. If his worship please.

Was. Yes, and keep it during the Fair, Bobchin.

Cok. Peace, Numps. Friend, do not meddle with him, an'
you be wise, and would show your head above board: he
will sting through your wrought nightcap, believe me. A
set of these violins I would buy too, for a delicate young
noise I have i' the country, that are every one a size less
than another, just like your fiddles. I would fain have a fine
young masque at my marriage, now I think on't: but I do
want such a number o' things. And Numps will not help
me now, and I dare not speak to him.

Tra. Will your worship buy any gingerbread, very good
bread, comfortable bread?

Cok. Gingerbread! yes, let's see. [*He runs to her shop.*

Was. There's the tother springe?

Lea. Is this well, goody Joan? to interrupt my market?
in the midst? and call away my customers? can you answer
this at the Pie-pouldres?

Tra. Why? if his mastership have a mind to buy, I hope
my ware lies as open as another's; I may show my ware, as
well as you yours.

Cok. Hold your peace; I'll content you both: I'll buy up
his shop, and thy basket.

Was. Will you, i' faith?

Lea. Why should you put him from it, friend?

Was. Cry you mercy! you'ld be sold too, would you?
what's the price on you? Jerkin, and all as you stand? ha'
you any qualities?

Tra. Yes, good-man angry-man, you shall find he has
qualities, if you cheapen him.

Was. God's so, you ha' the selling of him! what are
they? will they be bought for love, or money?

Tra. No indeed, sir.

Was. For what then? victuals?

Tra. He scorns victuals, sir, he has bread and butter at home, thanks be to God! and yet he will do more for a good meal, if the toy take him i' the belly, marry then they must not set him at lower end; if they do, he'll go away, though he fast. But put him a top o' the table where his place is, and he'll do you forty fine things. He has not been sent for, and sought out for nothing, at your great city-suppers, to put down Coriat and Cokely, and bin laugh'd at for his labour; he'll play you all the puppets i' the town over, and the players, every company, and his own company too; he spares nobody!

Cok. I' faith?

Tra. He was the first, sir, that ever baited the fellow i' the bear's skin, an't like your worship: no dog ever came near him, since. And for fine motions!

Cok. Is he good at those too? can he set out a masque, trow?

Tra. O Lord, Master! sought to, far and near, for his inventions: and he engrosses all, he makes all the puppets i' the Fair.

Cok. Dost thou, in troth, old velvet Jerkin? give me thy hand.

Tra. Nay, sir, you shall see him in his velvet jerkin, and a scarf too, at night, when you hear him interpret Master Littlewit's motion.

Cok. Speak no more, but shut up shop presently, friend. I'll buy both it and thee too, to carry down with me, and her hamper, beside. Thy shop shall furnish out the masque, and her's the banquet: I cannot go less, to set out anything with credit. What's the price, at a word, o' thy whole shop, case and all as it stands?

Lea. Sir, it stands me in six and twenty shillings, seven pence ha'penny, besides three shillings for my ground.

Cok. Well, thirty shillings will do all, then! And what comes yours too?

Tra. Four shillings and eleven pence, sir, ground, and all, an't like your worship.

Cok. Yes, it does like my worship very well. Poor woman; that's five shillings more. What a masque shall I furnish out, for forty shillings? (twenty pound Scotch) and a banquet of ginger-bread? there's a stately thing! Numps? sister? and my wedding gloves too? (that I never thought on afore.) All my wedding gloves, ginger-bread? O me! what a device will there be? to make 'em eat their fingers' ends! and delicate brooches for the bride-men! and all! and then I'll ha' this poesie put to 'em: *For the best grace,* meaning Mistress Grace, *my wedding poesy.*

Gra. I am beholden to you, sir, and to your Bartholomew wit.

Was. You do not mean this, do you? is this your first purchase?

Cok. Yes, faith, and I do not think, Numps, but thou'lt say, it was the wisest act that ever I did in my wardship.

Was. Like enough! I shall say anything, I!

Enter Edgworth *and* Nightingale, *followed by* Overdo.

Jus. I cannot beget a project, with all my political brain, yet; my project is how to fetch off this proper young man from his debauch'd company: I have followed him all the Fair over, and still I find him with this songster: And I begin shrewdly to suspect their familiarity; and the young man of a terrible taint, poetry! with which idle disease, if he be infected, there's no hope of him, in a state-course. *Actum est* of him for a commonwealths-man: if he go to't in rhyme, once. [*Aside.*]

Edg. [*To* Nightingale.] Yonder he is buying o' ginger-bread: set in quickly, before he part with too much of his money.

Nig. My masters and friends, and good people, draw near,——

Cok. Ballads! hark, hark! [*He runs to the ballad-man.*] pray thee, fellow, stay a little. Good Numps, look to the goods. What ballads hast thou? let me see, let me see myself.

Was. Why so! he's flown to another lime-bush, there he will flutter as long more; till he ha' ne'er a feather left.

Is there a vexation like this, gentlemen? will you believe me now, hereafter shall I have credit with you?

Quar. Yes faith, shalt thou, Numps, and thou art worthy on't, for thou sweatest for't. I never saw a young pimp errant and his squire better match'd.

Winw. Faith, the sister comes after 'em, well too.

Gra. Nay, if you saw the Justice her husband, my guardian, you were fitted for the mess, he is such a wise one his way——

Winw. I wonder we see him not here.

Gra. O! he is too serious for this place, and yet better sport than the other three, I assure you, gentlemen: where'er he is, though't be o' the bench.

Cok. How dost thou call it! A caveat against cutpurses! a good jest, i' faith, I would fain see that demon, your cutpurse you talk of, that delicate-handed devil; they say he walks hereabout; I would see him walk now. Look you, sister, here, here, [*He shows his purse boastingly.*] let him come, sister, and welcome. Ballad-man, does any cutpurses haunt hereabout? pray thee raise me one or two: begin and show me one.

Nig. Sir, this is a spell against 'em, spick and span new; and 'tis made as 'twere in mine own person, and I sing it in mine own defence. But 'twill cost a penny alone, if you buy it.

Cok. No matter for the price, thou dost not know me, I see, I am an odd Bartholomew.

Jus. Has't a fine picture, brother?

Cok. O sister, do you remember the ballads over the nursery-chimney at home o' my own pasting up; there be brave pictures. Other manner of pictures than these, friend.

Was. Yet these will serve to pick the pictures out o' your pockets, you shall see.

Cok. So I heard 'em say. Pray thee mind him not, fellow: he'll have an oar in everything.

Nig. It was intended, sir, as if a purse should chance to be cut in my presence, now, I may be blameless, though: as by the sequel will more plainly appear.

Cok. We shall find that i' the matter. Pray thee begin.

Nig. To the tune of Paggington's Pound, sir.

Cok. [*Sings.*] Fa, la la la, la la la, fa la la la! Nay, I'll put thee in tune, and all! mine own country dance! Pray thee begin.

Nig. It is a gentle admonition, you must know, sir, both to the purse-cutter, and the purse-bearer.

Cok. Not a word more, out o' the tune, an' thou lov'st me: Fa, la la la, la la la, fa la la la. Come, when?

Nig. [*Sings.*] My masters and friends, and good people
     draw near,
    And look to your purses, for that I do say;

Cok. Ha, ha, this chimes! good counsel at first dash.

Nig.   And though little money, in them you do
     bear,
    It cost more to get, than to lose in a day.

Cok. Good!

Nig.   You oft have been told,
     Both the young and the old;
    And bidden beware of the cutpurse so bold:

Cok. Well said! he were to blame that would not, i' faith.

Nig. Then if you take heed not, free me from the curse,
  Who both give you warning, for, and the cutpurse.
  Youth, youth, thou hadst better been starv'd by thy
   nurse,
  Than live to be hanged for cutting a purse.

Cok. Good i' faith, how say you, Numps? Is there any harm i' this?

Nig. It hath bin upbraided to men of my trade,
  That oft times we are the cause of this crime.

Cok. The more coxcombs they that did.

Nig. Alack and for pity, why should it be said?
  As if they regarded or places or time.
     Examples have been
     Of some that were seen,
  In Westminster Hall, yea the pleaders between,
  Then why should the judges be free from this curse,
  More than my poor self for cutting the purse?

Cok. God a mercy for that! why should they be more free indeed?

Nig. Youth, youth, thou hadst better been starv'd by thy
        nurse,
    Than live to be hanged for cutting a purse.

Cok. That again, good ballad-man, that again. [*He sings
the burden with him.*] O rare! I would fain rub mine elbow
now, but I dare not pull out my hand. On, I pray thee, he
that made this ballad, shall be poet to my masque.

Nig. At Worc'ter 'tis known well, and even i' the jail,
    A knight of good worship did there show his face,
    Against the foul sinners, in zeal for to rail,
    And lost (*ipso facto*) his purse in the place.

Cok. Is it possible?

Nig.   Nay, once from the seat
        Of judgement so great,
    A judge there did lose a fair pouch of velvet.

Cok. I' faith?

Nig. O Lord for thy mercy, how wicked or worse,
    Are those that so venture their necks for a purse!
        Youth, youth, &c.

Cok. Youth, youth, &c? pray thee stay a little, friend, yet,
o' thy conscience, Numps, speak, is there any harm i' this?

Was. To tell you true, 'tis too good for you, 'less you
had grace to follow it.

Jus. It doth discover enormity. I'll mark it more: I ha'
not lik'd a paltry piece of poetry so well a good while.

                                        [*Aside.*

Cok. Youth, youth, &c! where's this youth, now? A
man must call upon him, for his own good, and yet he
will not appear: look here, here's for him; [*He shows his
purse.*] handy-dandy, which hand will he have? On, I pray
thee, with the rest, I do hear of him, but I cannot see him,
this master youth, the cutpurse.

Nig. At plays and at sermons, and at the sessions,
    'Tis daily their practice such booty to make:
    Yea, under the gallows, at executions,
    They stick not the stare-abouts' purses to take.
        Nay, one without grace,
        At a far better place
    At court and in Christmas, before the King's face.

Cok. That was a fine fellow! I would have him, now.

Nig. Alack then for pity, must I bear the curse,
    That only belongs to the cunning cutpurse?

Cok. But where's their cunning, now, when they should use it? they are all chain'd now, I warrant you. [*Sings.*] Youth, youth, thou hadst better.—The rat-catchers charm are all fools and asses to this! A pox on 'em, that they will not come! that a man should have such a desire to a thing, and want it.

Quar. 'Fore God, I'd give half the Fair, and 'twere mine, for a cutpurse for him to save his longing.

Cok. Look you, sister, here, here, where is't now? which pocket is't in? for a wager?   [*He shows his purse again.*

Was. I beseech you leave your wagers, and let him end his matter, an't may be.

Cok. O, are you edified, Numps?

Jus. Indeed he does interrupt him, too much: There Numps spoke to purpose.   [*Aside.*

Cok. Sister, I am an ass, I cannot keep my purse: [*shows it again*] on, on; I pray thee, friend.

Nig. Youth, youth, thou hadst better been starv'd by thy
    nurse,
    Than live to be hanged for cutting a purse.

[*Edgworth gets up to him and tickles him in the ear with
    a straw twice, to draw his hand out of his pocket.*

Winw. Will you see sport? look, there's a fellow gathers up to him, mark.

Quar. Good, i' faith! Oh, he has lighted on the wrong pocket.

Winw. He has it, 'fore God, he is a brave fellow; pity he should be detected.

Nig. But, O, you vile nation of cutpurses all,
    Relent and repent, and amend and be sound,
    And know that you ought not, by honest men's fall,
    Advance your own fortunes, to die above ground,
        And though you go gay,
        In silks as you may,
    It is not the high way to heaven (as they say),
    Repent then, repent you, for better, for worse:

And kiss not the gallows for cutting a purse.
Youth, youth, thou hadst better been starv'd by thy
    nurse,
Than live to be hanged for cutting a purse.

All. An excellent ballad! an excellent ballad!

Edg. Friend, let me ha' the first, le' me ha' the first, I
pray you.   [*Slips purse into* Nightingale's *hand.*

Cok. Pardon me, sir. First come, first serv'd; and I'll buy
the whole bundle too.

Winw. That conveyance was better than all, did you
see 't? he has given the purse to the ballad-singer.

Quar. Has he?

Edg. Sir, I cry you mercy; I'll not hinder the poor man's
profit: pray you, mistake me not.

Cok. Sir, I take you for an honest gentleman, if that be
mistaking; I met you today afore: ha! hum! O God! my
purse is gone, my purse, my purse, my purse!

Was. Come, do not make a stir, and cry yourself an ass,
thro' the Fair afore your time.

Cok. Why, hast thou it, Numps? good Numps, how
came you by it? I marvel!

Was. I pray you seek some other gamester, to play the
fool with: you may lose it time enough, for all your Fair
wit.

Cok. By this good hand, glove and all, I ha' lost it
already, if thou hast it not: feel else. and Mistress Grace's
handkerchief too, out o' the other pocket.

Was. Why, 'tis well; very well, exceeding pretty, and
well.

Edg. Are you sure you ha' lost it, sir?

Cok. O God! yes; as I am an honest man, I had it but
e'en now, at 'youth, youth'.

Nig. I hope you suspect not me, sir.

Edg. Thee? that were a jest indeed! Dost thou think the
gentleman is foolish? where hadst thou hands, I pray thee?
Away, ass, away.   [*Exit* Nightingale.

Jus. I shall be beaten again, if I be spied.

Edg. Sir, I suspect an odd fellow, yonder, is stealing
away.

Mrs. Over. Brother, it is the preaching fellow! you shall suspect him. He was at your other purse, you know! Nay, stay, sir, and view the work you ha' done, an' you be benefic'd at the gallows, and preach there, thank your own handiwork.

Cok. Sir, you shall take no pride in your preferment: you shall be silenc'd quickly.   [*They seize* Overdo.

Jus. What do you mean, sweet buds of gentility?

Cok. To ha' my pennyworths out on you: bud. No less than two purses a day, serve you? I thought you a simple fellow, when my man Numps beat you i' the morning, and pitied you——

Mrs. Over. So did I, I'll be sworn, brother; but now I see he is a lewd and pernicious enormity, as Master Overdo calls him.

Jus. Mine own words turn'd upon me, like swords.

Cok. Cannot a man's purse be at quiet for you, i' the master's pocket, but you must entice it forth and debauch it?   [Overdo *is carried off*.

Was. Sir, sir, keep your debauch, and your fine Bartholomew terms to yourself; and make as much on 'em as you please. But gi' me this from you, i' the mean time: I beseech you, see if I can look to this.

        [Waspe *takes the licence from him*.

Cok. Why, Numps?

Was. Why? because you are an ass, sir, there's a reason the shortest way, and you will needs ha' it; now you ha' got the trick of losing, you'd lose your breech, an't 'twere loose. I know you, sir, come, deliver, you'll go and crack the vermin you breed now, will you? 'tis very fine, will you ha' the truth on't? they are such retchless flies as you are, that blow cutpurses abroad in every corner; your foolish having of money, makes 'em. An' there were no wiser than I, sir, the trade should lie open for you, sir, it should i' faith, sir. I would teach your wit to come to your head, sir, as well as your land to come into your hand, I assure you, sir.

Winw. Alack, good Numps.

Was. Nay, gentlemen, never pity me, I am not worth it:

Lord send me at home once, to Harrow o' the Hill again,
if I travel any more, call me Coriat with all my heart.

[*Exeunt* Waspe, Cokes *and* Mrs. Overdo, *followed by*
Edgworth.

Quar. [*Stops* Edgworth.] Stay, sir, I must have a word
with you in private. Do you hear?

Edg. With me, sir? what's your pleasure, good sir?

Quar. Do not deny it. You are a cutpurse, sir; this gentle-
man here and I saw you, nor do we mean to detect you
(though we can sufficiently inform ourselves toward the
danger of concealing you) but you must do us a piece of
service.

Edg. Good gentlemen, do not undo me; I am a civil
young man and but a beginner, indeed.

Quar. Sir, your beginning shall bring on your ending for
us. We are no catchpoles nor constables. That you are to
undertake, is this; you saw the old fellow, with the black
box, here?

Edg. The little old governor, sir?

Quar. That same: I see you have flown him to a mark
already. I would ha' you get away that box from him, and
bring it us.

Edg. Would you ha' the box and all, sir? or only that
that is in't? I'll get you that, and leave him the box to play
with still (which will be the harder o' the two), because I
would gain your worship's good opinion of me.

Winw. He says well, 'tis the greater mastery, and 'twill
make the more sport when 'tis missed.

Edg. Aye, and 'twill be the longer a missing, to draw on
the sport.

Quar. But look you do it now, sirrah, and keep your
word: or——

Edg. Sir, if ever I break my word with a gentleman, may
I never read word at my need. Where shall I find you?

Quar. Somewhere i' the Fair, hereabouts. Dispatch it
quickly. I would fain see the careful fool deluded! Of all
beasts, I love the serious ass. He that takes pains to be
one, and plays the fool, with the greatest diligence that
can be.

Gra. Then you would not choose, sir, but love my guardian, Justice Overdo, who is answerable to that description in every hair of him.

Quar. So I have heard. But how came you, Mistress Wellborn, to be his ward? or have relation to him, at first?

Gra. Faith, through a common calamity, he bought me, sir; and now he will marry me to his wife's brother, this wise gentleman, that you see, or else I must pay value o' my land.

Quar. 'Slid, is there no device of disparagement? or so? talk with some crafty fellow, some picklock o' the Law! Would I had studied a year longer i' the Inns of Court, and't had been but i' your case.

Winw. Aye, Master Quarlous, are you proffering? [*Aside.*

Gra. You'd bring but little aid, sir.

Winw. I'll look to you i' faith, gamester. [*Aside.*] An unfortunate foolish tribe you are fallen into, lady, I wonder you can endure 'em.

Gra. Sir, they that cannot work their fetters off must wear 'em.

Winw. You see what care they have on you, to leave you thus.

Gra. Faith, the same they have of themselves, sir. I cannot greatly complain, if this were all the plea I had against 'em.

Winw. 'Tis true! but will you please to withdraw with us a little, and make them think they have lost you. I hope our manners ha' been such hitherto, and our language, as will give you no cause to doubt yourself in our company.

Gra. Sir, I will give myself no cause; I am so secure of mine own manners, as I suspect not yours.

Quar. Look where John Littlewit comes.

Winw. Away, I'll not be seen by him.

Quar. No, you were not best, he'd tell his mother, the widow.

Winw. Heart, what do you mean?

Quar. Cry you mercy, is the wind there? must not the widow be nam'd?

Enter Littlewit *and* Mrs. Littlewit.

Lit. Do you hear, Win, Win?

Win. What say you, John?

Lit. While they are paying the reckoning, Win, I'll tell you a thing, Win, we shall never see any sights i' the Fair Win, except you long still, Win, good Win, sweet Win, long to see some hobby-horses, and some drums, and rattles, and dogs, and fine devices, Win. The bull with the five legs, Win; and the great hog: now you ha' begun with pig, you may long for anything, Win, and so for my motion, Win.

Win. But we sha' not eat o' the bull and the hog, John, how shall I long then?

Lit. O yes! Win: you may long to see, as well as to taste, Win: how did the 'pothecary's wife, Win, that long'd to see the anatomy, Win? or the lady, Win, that desir'd to spit i' the great lawyer's mouth, after an eloquent pleading? I assure you they long'd, Win, good Win, go in, and long.

[*Exeunt* Littlewit *and* Mrs. Littlewit.

Tra. I think we are rid of our new customer, brother Leatherhead, we shall hear no more of him.

Lea. All the better, let's pack up all and begone, before he find us.

Tra. Stay a little, yonder comes a company: it may be we may take some more money.

Enter Knockem *and* Busy.

Kno. Sir, I will take your counsel, and cut my hair, and leave vapours: I see that tobacco, and bottle-ale, and pig, and whit, and very Ursula herself, is all vanity.

Busy. Only pig was not comprehended in my admonition, the rest were. For long hair, it is an ensign or pride, a banner, and the world is full of those banners, very full of banners. And, bottle-ale is a drink of Satan's, a diet-drink of Satan's, devised to puff us up, and make us swell in this latter age of vanity, as the smoke of tobacco, to keep us in mist and error: But the fleshly woman (which you call Ursula) is above all to be avoided, having the marks upon her of the three enemies of man; the world, as being in the

Fair; the devil as being in the fire; and the flesh as being herself.

Enter Dame Purecraft.

Pure. Brother Zeal-of-the-land! what shall we do? my daughter Win-the-fight is fallen into her fit of longing again.

Busy. For more pig? there is no more, is there?

Pure. To see some sights, i' the Fair.

Busy. Sister, let her fly the impurity of the place, swiftly, lest she partake of the pitch thereof. Thou art the seat of the beast, O Smithfield, and I will leave thee. Idolatry peepeth out on every side of thee.

Kno. An excellent right hypocrite? now his belly is full, he falls a railing and kicking, the jade. A very good vapour! I'll in, and joy Ursula with telling how her pig works, two and a half he eat to his share. And he has drunk a pailfull. He eats with his eyes, as well as his teeth.   [*Exit.*

Lea. What do you lack, gentlemen? What is't you buy? Rattles, drums, babies.——

Busy. Peace, with thy apocryphal wares, thou profane publican: thy bells, thy dragons and thy Toby's dogs. Thy hobby-horse is an idol, a very idol, a fierce and rank idol: And thou, the Nebuchadnezzar, the proud Nebuchadnezzar of the Fair that set'st it up for children to fall down to and worship.

Lea. Cry you mercy, sir, will you buy a fiddle to fill up your noise?

Re-enter Littlewit *and* Win.

Lit. Look, Win, do, look a God's name and save your longing. Here be fine sights.

Pure. Aye child, so you hate 'em, as our Brother Zeal does, you may look on 'em.

Lea. Or what do you say to a drum, sir?

Busy. It is the broken belly of the beast, and thy bellows there are his lungs, and these pipes are his throat, those feathers are of his tail, and thy rattles, the gnashing of his teeth.

Tra. And what's my ginger-bread? I pray you.

Busy. The provender that pricks him up. Hence with thy basket of popery, thy nest of images: and whole legend of ginger-work.

Lea. Sir, if you be not quiet the quicklier, I'll ha' you clapp'd fairly by the heels, for disturbing the Fair.

Busy. The sin of the Fair provokes me, I cannot be silent.

Pure. Good brother Zeal!

Lea. Sir, I'll make you silent, believe it.

Lit. I'd give a shilling, you could i' faith, friend.

Lea. Sir, give me your shilling. I'll give you my shop if I do not, and I'll leave it in pawn with you i' the mean time.

Lit. A match i' faith, but do it quickly, then.

[*Exit* Leatherhead.

Busy. [*He speaks to the widow.*] Hinder me not, woman. I was mov'd in spirit, to be here this day, in this Fair, this wicked and foul Fair; and fitter may it be called a foul than a Fair: To protest against the abuses of it, the foul abuses of it, in regard of the afflicted saints that are troubled, very much troubled, exceedingly troubled, with the opening of the merchandise of Babylon again and the peeping of popery upon the stalls, here, here, in the high places. See you not Goldylocks, the purple strumpet, there? in her yellow gown and green sleeves? the profane pipes, the tinkling timbrels? A shop of relics!

[*Attempts to seize the toys.*

Lit. Pray you forbear, I am put in trust with 'em.

Busy. And this idolatrous grove of images, this flasket of idols! which I will pull down——

[*Overthrows the ginger-bread.*

Tra. O my ware, my ware, God bless it.

Busy. In my zeal, and glory to be thus exercis'd.

Leatherhead *enters with officers.*

Lea. Here he is, pray you lay hold on his zeal, we cannot sell a whistle for him, his noise is so in tune. Stop his noise, first.

Busy. Thou canst not: 'tis a sanctified noise. I will make a loud and most strong noise, till I have daunted the profane enemy. And for this cause——

Lea. Sir, here's no man afraid of you, or your cause. You shall swear it i' the stocks, sir.

Busy. I will thrust myself into the stocks, upon the pikes of the land.   *[They seize him.*

Lea. Carry him away.

Pure. What do you mean, wicked men?

Busy. Let them alone; I fear them not.

[Exeunt officers, with Busy, *followed by* Dame Purecraft.

Lit. Was not this shilling well ventur'd, Win, for our liberty? Now we may go play, and see over the Fair, where we list ourselves; my mother is gone after him, and let her e'en go, and loose us.

Win. Yes, John, but I know not what to do.

Lit. For what, Win?

Win. For a thing, I am asham'd to tell you, i' faith, and 'tis too far to go home.

Lit. I pray thee be not asham'd, Win. Come, i' faith thou shall not be asham'd, is it anything about the hobby-horse-man? an't be, speak freely.

Win. Hang him, base bobchin, I scorn him; no, I have very great what sha' call 'um, John.

Lit. O! Is that all, Win? we'll go back to Captain Jordan, to the pig-woman, Win, he'll help us, or she with a dripping pan, or an old kettle, or something. The poor greasy soul loves you, Win, and after we'll visit the Fair all over, Win, and see my puppet play, Win, you know it's a fine matter, Win.   *[Exeunt Littlewit with* Win.

Lea. Let's away, I counsell'd you to pack up afore, Joan.

Tra. A pox of his Bedlam purity. He has spoil'd half my ware; but the best is, we lose nothing if we miss our first merchant.

Lea. It shall be hard for him to find, or know us, when we are translated, Joan.   *[Exeunt.*

ACT IV. SCENE I

THE FAIR

Booths, stalls, a pair of stocks, etc.

Enter Cokes, Haggis *and* Bristle *with* Overdo, *followed by*
Troubleall.

Tro. My Masters, I do make no doubt, but you are
officers.

Bri. What then, sir?

Tro. And the King's loving and obedient subjects.

Bri. Obedient, friend? take heed what you speak, I advise
you: Oliver Bristle advises you. His loving subjects, we
grant you: but not his obedient, at this time, by your leave;
we know ourselves a little better than so; we are to com-
mand, sir, and such as you are to be obedient. Here's one of
his obedient subjects going to the stocks, and we'll make
you such another if you talk.

Tro. You are all wise enough i' your places, I know.

Bri. If you know it, sir, why do you bring it in question?

Tro. I question nothing, pardon me. I do only hope you
have warrant, for what you do and so quit you, and so
multiply you. [*He goes away again.*

Hag. What's he? bring him up to the stocks there. Why
bring you him not up?

Tro. [*Comes again.*] If you have Justice Overdo's war-
rant, 'tis well: you are safe; that is the warrant of warrants.
I'll not give this button for any man's warrant else.

Bri. Like enough, sir, but let me tell you, an' you play
away your buttons, thus, you will want 'em ere night, for
any store I see about you: you might keep 'em, and save
pins, I wusse. [*Exit* Troubleall.

Jus. What should he be, that doth so esteem and advance
my warrant? he seems a sober and discreet person! it is a
comfort to a good conscience, to be follow'd with a good
fame, in his sufferings. The world will have a pretty taste
by this, how I can bear adversity: and it will beget a kind of

reverence toward me, hereafter, even from mine enemies,
when they shall see I carry my calamity nobly, and that it
doth neither break me nor bend me. [*Aside.*

Hag. Come, sir, here's a place for you to preach in.
[*They put him in the stocks.*
Will you put in your leg?

Jus. That I will, cheerfully.

Bri. O' my conscience, a seminary! he kisses the stocks.

Cok. Well, my masters, I'll leave him with you; now I
see him bestow'd I'll go look for my goods and Numps.

Hag. You may, sir, I warrant you; where's the other
bawler? fetch him too, you shall find 'em both fast enough.
[*Exit Cokes.*

Jus. In the midst of this tumult I will yet be the author
of mine own rest, and not minding their fury, sit in the
stocks, in that calm as shall be able to trouble a triumph.

Tro. [*Comes again.*] Do you assure me upon your words?
may I undertake for you, if I be ask'd the question; that you
have this warrant.

Hag. What's this fellow, for God's sake?

Tro. Do but show me Adam Overdo, and I am satisfied.
[*Goes out.*

Bri. He is a fellow that is distracted, they say; one
Troubleall: he was an officer in the court of Pie-pouldres
here last year, and put out of his place by Justice Overdo.

Jus. Ha! [*Aside.*

Bri. Upon which he took an idle conceit, and's run
mad upon't. So that ever since, he will do nothing, but by
Justice Overdo's warrant, he will not eat a crust, nor drink
a little, nor make him in his apparel ready. His wife, sir-
reverence, cannot get him make his water, or shift his shirt,
without his warrant.

Jus. If this be true, this is my greatest disaster! how am
I bound to satisfy this poor man, that is of so good a nature
to me, out of his wits! where there is no room left for dis-
sembling. [*Aside.*

Tro. [*Comes in.*] If you cannot show me Adam Overdo,
I am in doubt of you: I am afraid you cannot answer it.
[*Goes again.*

Hag. Before me, neighbour Bristle (and now I think on 't better) Justice Overdo is a very parantory person.

Bri. O! are you advis'd of that? and a severe Justicer, by your leave.

Jus. Do I hear ill o' that side, too?

Bri. He will sit as upright o' the bench, an' you mark him, as a candle i' the socket, and give light to the whole court in every business.

Hag. But he will burn blue and swell like a bile (God bless us) an' he be angry.

Bri. Aye, and he will be angry too, when him list, that's more: and when he is angry, be it right or wrong, he has the law on 's side, ever. I mark that too.

Jus. I will be more tender hereafter. I see compassion may become a Justice, though it be a weakness, I confess; and nearer a vice, than a virtue.   [*Aside.*

Hag. Well, take him out o' the stocks again; we'll go a sure way to work, we'll ha' the ace of hearts of our side, if we can.   [*They take the* Justice *out.*

Enter **Pocher** with Busy, *followed by* Dame Purecraft.

Poch. Come, bring him away to his fellow, there. Master Busy, we shall rule your legs, I hope, though we cannot rule your tongue.

Busy. No, minister of darkness, no, thou canst not rule my tongue, my tongue it is mine own, and with it I will both knock and mock down your Bartholomew-abominations, till you be made a hissing to the neighbour parishes, round about.

Hag. Let him alone, we have devis'd better upon 't.

Pure. And shall he not into the stocks, then?

Bri. No, mistress, we'll have 'em both to Justice Overdo, and let him do over 'em as is fitting. Then I and my gossip Haggis and my beadle Pocher are discharg'd.

Pure. O, I thank you, blessed, honest men!

Bri. Nay, never thank us, but thank this madman that comes here, he put it in our heads.

Re-enter **Troubleall.**

Pure. Is he mad? Now heaven increase his madness, and bless it, and thank it, sir, your poor handmaid thanks you.

Tro. Have you a warrant? an' you have a warrant, show it.

Pure. Yes, I have a warrant out of the word, to give thanks for removing any scorn intended to the brethren.

                          [Exeunt all but Troubleall.

Tro. It is Justice Overdo's warrant, that I look for, if you have not that, keep your word, I'll keep mine. Quit ye, and multiply ye.

Enter Edgworth *and* Nightingale.

Edg. Come away, Nightingale, I pray thee.

Tro. Whither go you? where's your warrant?

Edg. Warrant for what, sir?

Tro. For what you go about, you know how fit it is, an' you have no warrant, bless you, I'll pray for you, that's all I can do.   *[Goes out.*

Edg. What means he?

Nig. A madman that haunts the Fair, do you not know him? it's marvel he has not more followers after his ragged heels.

Edg. Beshrew him, he startled me: I thought he had known of our plot. Guilt's a terrible thing! ha' you prepar'd the costard-monger?

Nig. Yes, and agreed for his basket of pears; he is at the corner here, ready. And your prize, he comes down, sailing that way, all alone; without his protector: he is rid of him, it seems.

Edg. Aye, I know; I should ha' follow'd his Protectorship for a feat I am to do upon him: But this offer'd itself so i' the way, I could not let it scape: here he comes; whistle; be this sport call'd Dorring the Dottrell.

Re-enter Cokes.

Nig. Wh, wh, wh, wh, &c. *[Whistles.]*

Cok. By this light, I cannot find my ginger-bread-wife nor my hobby-horse-man in all the Fair now; to ha' my money again. And I do not know the way out on't, to go home for more, do you hear, friend, you that whistle; what tune is that, you whistle?

Nig. A new tune I am practising, sir.

Cok. Dost thou know where I dwell, I pray thee? nay, on with thy tune, I ha' no such haste for an answer: I'll practise with thee.

Enter Costard-monger *with a basket of pears.*

Cos. Buy any pears, very fine pears, pears fine.

Nightingale *sets his foot afore him, and he falls with his basket.*

Cok. God's so! a muss, a muss, a muss, a muss.

Cos. Good gentleman, my ware, my ware, I am a poor man. Good sir, my ware.

Nig. Let me hold your sword, sir, it troubles you.

Cok. Do, and my cloak an' thou wilt; and my hat, too.

Cokes *falls a scrambling whilst they run away with his things.*

Edg. A delicate great boy! methinks, he out-scrambles 'em all. I cannot persuade myself but he goes to grammar school yet; and plays the truant to-day.

Nig. Would he had another purse to cut, Zekiel.

Edg. Purse? a man might cut out his kidneys, I think, and he never feel 'em, he is so earnest at the sport.

Nig. His soul is half-way out on 's body at the game.

Edg. Away, Nightingale: that way.

[Nightingale *runs off with his sword, cloak and hat.*

Cok. I think I am furnish'd for Catherne pears, for one under-meal: gi' me my cloak.

Cos. Good gentleman, give me my ware.

Cok. Where's the fellow I ga' my cloak to? my cloak? and my hat? ha! God's lid, is he gone? thieves, thieves; help me to cry, gentlemen. [*He runs out.*

Edg. Away, costard-monger, come to us to Ursula's. Talk of him to have a soul? 'heart, if he have any more than a thing given him instead of salt, only to keep him from stinking, I'll be hang'd afore my time, presently: where should it be, trow? in his blood? he has not so much to'ard it in his whole body, as will maintain a good flea; And if he take this course, he will not ha' so much land left, as to rear a calf within this twelvemonth. Was there ever green plover so pull'd? That his little overseer had been here now, and been but tall enough to see him steal pears in exchange for his beaver-hat, and his cloak thus? I must go find him out, next, for his black box and his patent (it seems) he has of his place; which I think the gentleman would have a reversion of that spoke to me for it so earnestly.   [*Exit.*]

Re-enter Cokes.

Cok. Would I might lose my doublet, and hose, too; as I am an honest man, and never stir, if I think there be anything but thieving and coz'ning i' this whole Fair. Bartholomew-fair, quoth he; an' ever any Bartholomew had that luck in 't that I have had, I'll be martyr'd for him, and in Smithfield too. I ha' paid for my pears, a rot on 'em, [*throws away his pears.*] I'll keep 'em no longer; you were choke-pears to me; I had been better ha' gone to mum-chance for you, I wuss. Methinks the Fair should not have us'd me thus, and 'twere but for my name's sake, I would not ha' us'd a dog o' the name, so. O, Numps will triumph, now! [*Troubleall* comes again.] Friend, do you know who I am? or where I lie? I do not myself, I'll be sworn. Do but carry me home, and I'll please thee, I ha' money enough there, I ha' lost myself, and my cloak and my hat; and my fine sword, and my sister, and Numps, and Mistress Grace (a gentlewoman that I should ha' married) and a cutwork handkerchief she ga' me, and two purses to-day. And my bargain o' hobby-horses and ginger-bread, which grieves me worst of all.

Tro. By whose warrant, sir, have you done all this?

Cok. Warrant? thou art a wise fellow, indeed, as if a man need a warrant to lose anything with.

Tro. Yes, Justice Overdo's warrant, a man may get, and lose with, I'll stand to 't.

Cok. Justice Overdo? Dost thou know him? I lie there.

he is my brother-in-law, he married my sister: pray thee show me the way, dost thou know the house?

Tro. Sir, show me your warrant, I know nothing without a warrant, pardon me.

Cok. Why, I warrant thee, come along: thou shalt see, I have wrought pillows there, and cambric sheets, and sweet bags, too. Pray thee guide me to the house.

Tro. Sir, I'll tell you; go you thither yourself, first, alone; tell your worshipful brother your mind: and but bring me three lines of his hand, or his clerk's, with Adam Overdo underneath; here I'll stay you, I'll obey you, and I'll guide you presently.

Cok. 'Slid, this is an ass, I ha' found him, pox upon me, what do I talking to such a dull fool; farewell, you are a very coxcomb, do you hear?

Tro. I think I am, if Justice Overdo sign to it, I am, and so we are all, he'll quit us all, multiply us all. [*Exeunt.*

ACT IV. SCENE II

Another part of the Fair.

Enter Grace, Quarlous *and* Winwife, *their swords drawn.*

Gra. Gentlemen, this is no way that you take: you do but breed one another trouble and offence, and give me no contentment at all. I am no she that affects to be quarrell'd for, or have my name or fortune made the question of men's swords.

Quar. 'S'lood, we love you.

Gra. If you both love me, as you pretend, your own reason will tell you but one can enjoy me; and to that point, there leads a directer line than by my infamy, which must follow if you fight. 'Tis true, I have profess'd it to you ingenuously that, rather than to be yok'd with this bridegroom is appointed me, I would take up any husband, almost upon any trust. Though subtlety would say to me, I know he is a fool, and has an estate, and I might govern him, and enjoy a friend, beside. But these are not my aims.

I must have a husband I must love, or I cannot live with him. I shall ill make one of these politic wives!

Winw. Why, if you can like either of us, lady, say which is he, and the other shall swear instantly to desist.

Quar. Content, I accord to that willingly.

Gra. Sure you think me a woman of extreme levity, gentlemen, or a strange fancy, that, meeting you by chance in such a place as this, both at one instant, and not yet of two hours acquaintance, neither of you deserving afore the other of me, I should so forsake my modesty (though I might affect one more particularly) as to say, this is he, and name him.

Quar. Why, wherefore should you not? What should hinder you?

Gra. If you would not give it to my modesty, allow it yet to my wit; give me so much of woman and cunning as not to betray myself impertinently. How can I judge of you, so far as to a choice, without knowing you more? you are both equal and alike to me, yet: and so indifferently affected by me, as each of you might be the man, if the other were away. For you are reasonable creatures, you have understanding and discourse. And if fate send me an understanding husband, I have no fear at all but mine own manners shall make him a good one.

Quar. Would I were put forth to making for you, then.

Gra. It may be you are, you know not what's toward you: will you consent to a motion of mine, gentlemen?

Winw. Whatever it be, we'll presume reasonableness, coming from you.

Quar. And fitness, too.

Gra. I saw one of you buy a pair of tables, e'en now.

Winw. Yes, here they be, and maiden ones too, unwritten in.

Gra. The fitter for what they may be employed in. You shall write either of you, here, a word, or a name, what you like best; but of two or three syllables at most: and the next person that comes this way (because destiny has a high hand in business of this nature) I'll demand which of the two words he or she doth approve; and according to that sentence, fix my resolution and affection **without** change.

Quar. Agreed, my word is conceived already.

Winw. And mine shall not be long creating after.

Gra. But you shall promise, gentlemen, not to be curious to know which of you it is, is taken; but give me leave to conceal that till you have brought me, either home, or where I may safely tender myself.

Winw. Why, that's but equal.

Quar. We are pleas'd.

Gra. Because I will bind both your endeavours to work together, friendly and jointly, each to the other's fortune, and have myself fitted with some means to make him that is forsaken, a part of amends.

Quar. These conditions are very courteous. Well, my word is out of the *Arcadia*, then: *Argalus*.

Winw. And mine out of the play, *Palemon.* [*They write.*

Troubleall *comes again.*

Tro. Have you any warrant for this, gentlemen?

Quar. & *Winw.* Ha!

Tro. There must be a warrant had, believe it.

Winw. For what?

Tro. For whatsoever it is, anything indeed, no matter what.

Quar. 'Slight, here's a fine ragged prophet, dropp'd down i' the nick!

Tro. Heaven quit you, gentlemen.

Quar. Nay, stay a little. Good lady, put him to the question.

Gra. You are content, then?

Winw. & *Quar.* Yes, yes.

Gra. Sir, here are two names written——

Tro. Is Justice Overdo, one?

Gra. How, sir? I pray you read 'em to yourself, it is for a wager between these gentlemen, and, with a stroke or any difference, mark which you approve best.

Tro. They may be both worshipful names for aught I

know, mistress, but Adam Overdo had been worth three
of 'em, I assure you, in this place; that's in plain English.

Gra. This man amazes me! I pray you, like one of 'em,
sir.

Tro. [*Marks the book.*] I do like him there, that has the
best warrant. Mistress, to save your longing (and multiply
him) it may be this. But I am still for Justice Overdo, that's
my conscience. And quit you.   [*Exit.*

Winw. Is't done, lady?

Gra. Aye, and strangely as ever I saw! What fellow is
this, trow?

Quar. No matter what, a fortune-teller we ha' made him.
Which is't, which is't?

Gra. Nay, did you not promise not to enquire?

Enter Edgworth.

Quar. 'Slid, I forgot that, pray you pardon me. Look,
here's our Mercury come: The licence arrives i' the finest
time, too! 'tis but scraping out Cokes his name, and 'tis
done.

Winw. How now, lime-twig? hast thou touch'd?

Edg. Not yet, sir, except you would go with me, and
see 't, it's not worth speaking on. The act is nothing with-
out a witness. Yonder he is, your man with the box fallen
into the finest company, and so transported with vapours,
they ha' got in a northern clothier, and one Puppy, a
western man, that's come to wrestle before my Lord
Mayor, anon, and Captain Whit, and one Val Cutting, that
helps Captain Jordan to roar, a circling boy, with whom
your Numps is so taken that you may strip him of his
clothes if you will. I'll undertake to geld him for you, if
you had but a surgeon ready to sear him. And Mistress
Justice there, is the goodest woman! she does so love 'em
all over, in terms of Justice, and the style of authority, with
her hood upright—that I beseech you come away, gentle-
men, and see 't.

Quar. 'Slight, I would not lose it for the Fair, what'll you
do, Ned?

Winw. Why, stay here about for you; Mistress Well-born must not be seen.

Quar. Do so, and find out a priest i' the meantime, I'll bring the licence. Lead, which way is't?

Edg. Here, sir, you are o' the backside o' the booth already, you may hear the noise. [*Exeunt.*

ACT IV. SCENE III

Another part of the Fair.

Ursula's *booth as before*: Knockem, Whit, Northern, Puppy, Cutting, Waspe *and* Mrs. Overdo, *all intoxicated.*

Kno. Whit, bid Val Cutting continue the vapours for a lift, Whit, for a lift.

Nor. I'll ne mare, I'll ne mare, the eale's too meeghty.

Kno. How now! my Galloway Nag, the staggers? ha! Whit, gi' him a slit i' the forehead. Cheer up, man, a needle and thread to stitch his ears. I'd cure him now an' I had it, with a little butter and garlic, long-pepper, and grains. Where's my horn? I'll gi' him a mash, presently, shall take away his dizziness.

Pup. Why, where are you, zurs? do you vlinch, and leave us i' the zuds, now?

Nor. I'll ne mare, I' is e'en as vull as a paiper's bag, by my troth, I.

Pup. Do my northern cloth zhrink i' the wetting? ha?

Kno. Why, well said, old flea-bitten, thou'lt never tire, I see. [*They fall to their vapours again.*

Cut. No, sir, but he may tire, if it please him.

Whi. Who told dee sho? that he vuld never teer, man?

Cut. No matter who told him so, so long as he knows.

Kno. Nay, I know nothing, sir, pardon me there.

Enter Edgworth *and* Quarlous.

Edg. They are at it still, sir, this they call vapours.

Whi. He shall not pardon dee, captain, dou shalt not be pardon'd. Pre' de shweet heart, do not pardon him.

Cut. 'Slight, I'll pardon him an' I list, whosoever says nay to't.

Quar. Where's Numps? I miss him.

Was. Why, I say nay to't.

Quar. O there he is!

Kno. To what do you say nay, sir? [*Here they continue their game of vapours, which is nonsense. Every man to oppose the last man that spoke: whether it concern'd him, or no.*]

Was. To anything, whatsoever it is, so long as I not like it.

Whi. Pardon me, little man, dou musht like it a little.

Cut. No, he must not like it at all, sir, there you are i' the wrong.

Whi. I tink I be, he musht not like it, indeed.

Cut. Nay, then he both must, and will like it, sir, for all you.

Kno. If he have reason, he may like it, sir.

Whi. By no meansh, captain, upon reason, he may like nothing upon reason.

Was. I have no reason, nor I will hear of no reason, nor I will look for no reason, and he is an ass that either knows any, or looks for't from me.

Cut. Yes, in some sense you may have reason, sir.

Was. Aye, in some sense, I care not if I grant you.

Whi. Pardon me, thou ougsht to grant him nothing, in no shensh, if dou do love dyshelf, angry man.

Was. Why then, I do grant him nothing; and I have no sense.

Cut. 'Tis true, thou hast no sense indeed.

Was. 'Slid, but I have sense, now I think on't better, and I will grant him anything, do you see?

Kno. He is i' the right, and does utter a sufficient vapour.

Cut. Nay, it is no sufficient vapour, neither, I deny that.

Kno. Then it is a sweet vapour.

Cut. It may be a sweet vapour.

Was. Nay, it is no sweet vapour, neither, sir, it stinks, and I'll stand to't.

Whi. Yes, I think it dosh shtink, Captain. All vapour dosh shtink.

Was. Nay, then it does not stink, sir, and it shall not stink.

Cut. By your leave, it may, sir.

Was. Aye, by my leave, it may stink, I know that.

Whi. Pardon me, thou knowesht nothing, it cannot by thy leave, angry man.

Was. How can it not?

Kno. Nay, never question him, for he is i' the right.

Whi. Yesh, I am i' de right, I confesh it, so ish de little man too.

Was. I'll have nothing confess'd that concerns me. I am not i' the right, nor never was i' the right, nor never will be i' the right, while I am in my right mind.

Cut. Mind? why, here's no man minds you, sir, nor anything else.   [*They drink again.*

Pup. Vriend, will you mind this that we do?

Quar. Call you this vapours? this is such belching of quarrel as I never heard. Will you mind your business, sir?

Edg. You shall see, sir.

Nor. I'll ne mair, my waimb warks too mickle with this auready.

Edg. Will you take that, Master Waspe, that nobody should mind you?

Was. Why? what ha' you to do? is't any matter to you?

Edg. No, but methinks you should not be unminded though.

Was. Nor I wu' not be, now I think on't, do you hear new acquaintance, does no man mind me, say you?

Cut. Yes, sir, every man here minds you, but how?

Was. Nay, I care as little how, as you do. That was not my question.

Whi. No, nothing was ty question, tou art a learned man, and I am a valiant man, i' faith la, tou shalt speak for me, and I vill fight for tee.

Kno. Fight for him, Whit? A gross vapour, he can fight for himself.

Was. It may be I can, but it may be I wu' not, how then?

531

Cut. Why, then you may choose.

Was. Why, and I'll choose whether I'll choose or no.

Kno. I think you may, and 'tis true; and I allow it for a resolute vapour.

Was. Nay, then, I do think you do not think, and it is no resolute vapour.

Cut. Yes, in some sort he may allow you.

Kno. In no sort, sir, pardon me, I can allow him nothing. You mistake the vapour.

Was. He mistakes nothing, sir, in no sort.

Whi. Yes, I pre dee now, let him mistake.

Was. A turd i' your teeth, never pre dee me, for I will have nothing mistaken.

Kno. Turd, ha turd? a noisome vapour, strike Whit.

[*They fall by the ears.* Edgworth *steals the licence out of the box, and exit.*]

Mrs. Over. Why, gentlemen, why gentlemen, I charge you upon my authority, conserve the peace. In the King's name, and my husband's, put up your weapons. I shall be driven to commit you myself, else.

Quar. Ha, ha, ha.

Was. Why do you laugh, sir?

Quar. Sir, you'll allow me my christian liberty. I may laugh, I hope.

Cut. In some sort you may, and in some sort you may not, sir.

Kno. Nay, in some sort, sir, he may neither laugh nor hope, in this company.

Was. Yes, then he may both laugh and hope in any sort, an't please him.

Quar. Faith, and I will then, for it doth please me exceedingly.

Was. No exceeding neither, sir.

Kno. No, that vapour is too lofty.

Quar. Gentlemen, I do not play well at your game of vapours, I am not very good at it, but——

Cut. Do you hear, sir? I would speak with you in circle?

[*He draws a circle on the ground.*]

Quar. In circle, sir? what would you with me in circle?

Cut. Can you lend me a piece, a jacobus? in circle?

Quar. 'Slid, your circle will prove more costly than your vapours, then. Sir, no, I lend you none.

Cut. Your beard's not well turn'd up, sir.

Quar. How, rascal? are you playing with my beard? I'll break circle with you.   [*They draw all, and fight.*

Pup. Nor. Gentlemen, gentlemen!

Kno. [*Aside to Whit.*] Gather up, Whit, gather up, Whit, good vapours.   [*Exit.*

Mrs. Over. What mean you? are you rebels, gentlemen? shall I send out a sergeant-at-arms, or a writ o' rebellion, against you? I'll commit you upon my womanhood, for a riot, upon my justice-hood, if you persist.

     [*Exeunt* Quarlous *and* Cutting.

Was. Upon your justice-hood? Marry shit o' your hood, you'll commit? Spoke like a true justice of peace's wife, indeed, and a fine female lawyer! turd i' your teeth for a fee, now.

Mrs. Over. Why, Numps, in Master Overdo's name, I charge you.

Was. Good Mistress Underdo, hold your tongue.

Mrs. Over. Alas! poor Numps.

Was. Alas! and why alas from you, I beseech you? or why poor Numps, goody rich? am I come to be pitied by your tuft-taffata now? why, mistress, I knew Adam, the clerk, your husband, when he was Adam scrivener, and writ for twopence a sheet, as high as he bears his head now, or you your hood, dame. What are you, sir?

The Watch *come in.*

Bri. We be men, and no infidels; what is the matter, here, and the noises? can you tell?

Was. Heart, what ha' you to do? cannot a man quarrel in quietness but he must be put out on 't by you? what are you?

Bri. Why, we be His Majesty's Watch, sir.

Was. Watch? 'Sblood, you are a sweet watch, indeed. A body would think and you watch'd well a nights, you should be contented to sleep at this time a day. Get you to your fleas and your clock-beds, you rogues, your kennels, and lie down close.

Bri. Down? yes, we will down I warrant you, down with him in His Majesty's name, down, down with him, and carry him away to the pigeon-holes.

[*Watch* seize Waspe *and carry him off.*

Mrs. Over. I thank you, honest friends, in the behalf o' the Crown, and the peace, and in Master Overdo's name, for suppressing enormities.

Whi. Stay, Bristle, here ish a noder brash o' drunkards, but very quiet, special drunkards, will pay dee five shillings very well. Take 'em to dee, in de graish o' God: one of 'em does change cloth for ale in the Fair here, te oder ish a strong man, a mighty man, my Lord Mayor's man, and a wrestler. He has wrestled so long with the bottle, here, that the man with the beard hash almosht streek up hish heelsh.

Bri. 'Slid, the clerk o' the market has been to cry him all the Fair over, here, for my Lord's service.

Whi. Tere he ish, pre de taik him hensh, and make ty best on him. How now, woman o' shilk, vat ailsh ty shweet faish? art tou melancholy?

Mrs. Over. A little distemper'd with these enormities; shall I entreat a courtesy of you, Captain?

Whi. Entreat a hundred, velvet voman, I vill do it, shpeak out.

Mrs. Over. I cannot with modesty speak it out, but——

Whi. I vill do it, and more, and more, for dee. What Ursula and't be bitch, and't be bawd, and't be!

Enter Ursula.

Urs. How now, rascal? what roar you for? old pimp.

Whi. Here, put up de cloaks, Ursh; de purchase; pre dee now, shweet Ursh, help dis good brave voman to a jordan, and't be.

Urs. 'Slid, call your Captain Jordan to her, can you not?

Whi. Nay, pre dee leave dy consheits, and bring the velvet woman to de——

Urs. I bring her, hang her: heart, must I find a common pot for every punk i' your purlieus?

Whi. O good voordsh, Ursh, it ish a guest o' velvet, i' fait la.

Urs. Let her sell her hood, and buy a sponge, with a pox to her, my vessel is employed, sir. I have but one and 'tis the bottom of an old bottle. An honest proctor and his wife are at it within, if she'll stay her time, so. [*Exit.*

Whi. As soon ash tou cansht, shweet Ursh. Of a valiant man I tink I am the patientsh man i' the world, or in all Smithfield.

Re-enter Knockem.

Kno. How now, Whit? close vapours, stealing your leaps? covering in corners, ha?

Whi. No fait, captain, dough tou beesht a vishe man, dy vit is a mile hence now. I vas procuring a shmall courtesy for a woman of fashion here.

Mrs. Over. Yes, captain, though I am justice of peace's wife, I do love men of war, and the sons of the sword, when they come before my husband.

Kno. Say'st thou so, filly? thou shalt have a leap presently, I'll horse thee myself, else.

Urs. Come, will you bring her in now? and let her take her turn?

Whi. Gramercy, good Ursh, I tank dee.

Mrs. Over. Master Overdo shall thank her. [*Exit.*

Re-enter Ursula, *followed by* Littlewit *and* Win.

Lit. Good Gammor Urs; Win and I are exceedingly beholden to you, and to Captain Jordan, and Captain Whit. Win, I'll be bold to leave you i' this good company, Win: for half an hour or so, Win, while I go and see how my matter goes forward, and if the puppets be perfect: and then I'll come and fetch you, Win.

Win. Will you leave me alone with two men, John?

Lit. Aye, they are honest gentlemen, Win, Captain Jordan, and Captain Whit, they'll use you very civilly, Win, God b' w' you, Win. [*Exit.*

Urs. What, 's her husband gone?

Kno. On his false gallop, Urs, away.

Urs. An' you be right Bartholomew-birds, now show yourselves so: we are undone for want of fowl i' the Fair, here. Here will be Zekiel Edgworth, and three or four gallants with him at night, and I ha' neither plover nor quail for 'em: persuade this between you two, to become a bird o' the game, while I work the velvet woman within, as you call her.

Kno. I conceive thee, Urs! go thy ways. [*Exit* Ursula.] Doest thou hear, Whit? is't not pity, my delicate dark chestnut here, with the fine lean head, large forehead, round eyes, even mouth, sharp ears, long neck, thin crest, close withers, plain back, deep sides, short fillets, and full flanks: with a round belly, a plump buttock, large thighs, knit knees, straight legs, short pasterns, smooth hoofs, and short heels; should lead a dull honest woman's life, that might live the life of a lady?

Whi. Yes, by my fait and trot it is, captain: de honesht woman's life is a scurvy dull life, indeed, la.

Win. How, sir, is an honest woman's life a scurvy life?

Whi. Yes fait, shweetheart, believe him, de leef of a bond-woman! but if dou vilt harken to me, I vill make tee a free-woman, and a lady: dou shalt live like a lady, as te captain saish.

Kno. Aye, and be honest too, sometimes: have her wires and her tires, her green gowns, and velvet petticoats.

Whi. Aye, and ride to Ware and Rumford i' dy coash, shee de players, be in love vit 'em; sup vit gallantsh, be drunk, and cost de noting.

Kno. Brave vapours!

Whi. And lie by twenty on 'em, if dou pleash, shweetheart.

Win. What, and be honest still; that were fine sport.

Whi. Tish common, shweet heart, tou may'st do it, by my hand: it shall be justified to ty husband's faish, now: tou shalt be as honesht as the skin between his hornsh, la!

Kno. Yes, and wear a dressing, top and top-gallant, to compare with e'er a husband on 'em all, for a fore-top: it is the vapour of spirit in the wife to cuckold, nowadays, as it is the vapour of fashion in the husband not to suspect. Your prying cat-eyed-citizen is an abominable vapour.

Win. Lord, what a fool have I been!

Whi. Mend then, and do everything like a lady, hereafter, never know ty husband from another man.

Kno. Nor any one man from another, but i' the dark.

Whi. Aye, and then it ish no dishgrash to know any man.

Urs. [*Within.*] Help, help here.

Kno. How now? what vapour's there?

Re-enter Ursula.

Urs. O, you are a sweet Ranger! and look well to your walks. Yonder is your Punk of Turnbull, Ramping Alice, has fallen upon the poor gentlewoman within, and pull'd her hood over her ears, and her hair through it.

Alice enters, beating the Justice's wife.

Mrs. Over. Help, help, i' the King's name.

Alice. A mischief on you, they are such as you are, that undo us, and take our trade from us, with your tuft-taffata haunches.

Kno. How now, Alice!

Alice. The poor common whores can ha' no traffic for the privy rich ones; your caps and hoods of velvet call away our customers and lick the fat from us.

Urs. Peace, you foul ramping jade, you——

Alice. Od'-foot, you bawd in grease, are you talking?

Kno. Why, Alice, I say.

Alice. Thou sow of Smithfield, thou.

Urs. Thou tripe of Turnbull.

Kno. Cat-a-mountain-vapours! ha!

Urs. You know where you were taw'd lately, both lash'd and slash'd you were in Bridewell.

Alice. Aye, by the same token, you rid that week, and break out the bottom o' the cart, night-tub.

Kno. Why, lion face! ha! do you know who I am? shall I tear ruff, slit waistcoat, make rags of petticoat? ha! go to, vanish, for fear of vapours. Whit, a kick, Whit, in the parting vapour. [*They kick* Alice *out.*] Come brave woman, take a good heart, thou shalt be a lady, too.

Whi. Yes fait, dey shall all both be ladies, and write Madam. I vill do 't myself for dem. Do, is the vord, and D is the middle letter of Madam, DD, put 'em together and make deeds, without which all words are alike, la.

Kno. 'Tis true, Ursula, take 'em in, open thy wardrobe, and fit 'em to their calling. Green gowns, crimson petticoats, green women! my lord mayor's green women! guests o' the game, true bred. I'll provide you a coach to take the air in.

Win. But do you think you can get one?

Kno. O, they are as common as wheelbarrows, where there are great dunghills. Every pettifogger's wife has 'em, for first he buys a coach, that he may marry, and then he marries that he may be made cuckold in 't: For if their wives ride not to their cuckolding, they do 'em no credit. [*Exeunt* Ursula, Mrs. Lit., *and* Mrs. Over.] Hide, and be hidden; ride, and be ridden, says the vapour of experience.

Enter Troubleall.

Tro. By what warrant does it say so?

Kno. Ha! mad child o' the Pie-pouldres, art thou there? fill us a fresh can, Urs, we may drink together.

Tro. I may not drink without a warrant, captain.

Kno. 'S'lood, thou'll not stale without a warrant, shortly. Whit, give me pen, ink and paper. I'll draw him a warrant presently.

Tro. It must be Justice Overdo's.

Kno. I know, man. Fetch the drink, Whit.

Whi. I pre dee now, be very brief, captain; for de new ladies stay for dee.   [*Exit, and re-enters with a can.*

Kno. O, as brief as can be, here 'tis already. [*Gives* Troubleall *a paper.*] Adam Overdo.

Tro. Why, now, I'll pledge you, captain.

Kno. Drink it off. I'll come to thee, anon, again. [*Exeunt.*

ACT IV. SCENE IV

The back of Ursula's *booth.* Justice Overdo *in the stocks.*

Enter Quarlous *with the licence, and* Edgworth.

Quar. Well, sir. You are now discharg'd: beware of being spied, hereafter. [*To the cutpurse.*]

Edg. Sir, will it please you, enter in here, at Ursula's, and take part of a silken gown, a velvet petticoat, or a wrought smock: I am promis'd such: and I can spare any gentleman a moiety.

Quar. Keep it for your companions in beastliness, I am none of 'em, sir. If I had not already forgiven you a greater trespass, or thought you yet worth my beating, I would instruct your manners to whom you made your offers. But go your ways, talk not to me, the hangman is only fit to discourse with you; the hand of beadle is too merciful a punishment for your trade of life. [*Exit* Edgworth.] I am sorry I employ'd this fellow; for he thinks me such: *Facinus quos inquinat, æquat.* But it was for sport. And would I make it serious, the getting of this licence is nothing to me, without other circumstances concur. I do think how impertinently I labour, if the word be not mine that the ragged fellow mark'd: And what advantage I have given Ned Winwife in this time now, of working her, though it be mine. He'll go near to form to her what a debauch'd rascal I am, and fright her out of all good conceit of me: I should do so by him, I am sure, if I had the opportunity. But my hope is in her temper, yet; and it must needs be next to despair, that is grounded on any part of a woman's discretion. I would give, by my troth, now, all I could spare (to my clothes, and my sword) to meet my tatter'd soothsayer again, who was my judge i' the question, to know certainly whose word he has damn'd or sav'd. For, till then, I live but under a reprieve. I must seek him. Who be these?

Enter Waspe *with the officers.*

Was. Sir, you are a Welsh cuckold, and a prating runt, and no constable.

Bri. You say very well. Come put in his leg in the middle roundel, and let him hole there.

[*They put him in the stocks.*

Was. You stink of leeks, metheglyn, and cheese, you rogue.

Bri. Why, what is that to you, if you sit sweetly in the stocks in the meantime? if you have a mind to stink too, your breeches sit close enough to your bum. Sit you merry, sir.

Quar. How now, Numps?

Was. It is no matter, how; pray you look off.

Quar. Nay, I'll not offend you, Numps. I thought you had sat there to be seen.

Was. And to be sold, did you not? pray you mind your business, an' you have any.

Quar. Cry you mercy, Numps. Do's your leg lie high enough?

Enter Haggis.

Bri. How now, neighbour Haggis, what says Justice Overdo's worship to the other offenders?

Hag. Why, he says just nothing, what should he say? Or where should he say? He is not to be found, man. He ha' not been seen i' the Fair, here, all this live-long day, never since seven o'clock i' the morning. His clerks know not what to think on't. There is no court of Pie-pouldres yet. Here they be return'd.

Enter others of the Watch *with* Busy.

Bri. What shall be done with 'em, then, in your discretion?

Hag. I think we were best put 'em in the stocks, in discretion (there they will be safe in discretion) for the valour of an hour, or such a thing, till his worship come.

Bri. It is but a hole matter if we do, neighbour Haggis, come, sir, here is company for you, heave up the stocks.

[*As they open the stocks,* Waspe *puts his shoe on his hand, and slips it in for his leg.*

Was. I shall put a trick upon your Welsh diligence, perhaps.   [*Aside.*

Bri. Put in your leg, sir.   [*To* Busy.

Quar. What, Rabbi Busy! is he come?

[*They bring* Busy, *and put him in.*

Busy. I do obey thee; the lion may roar, but he cannot bite. I am glad to be thus separated from the heathen of the land, and put apart in the stocks, for the holy cause.

Was. What are you, sir?

Busy. One that rejoiceth in his affliction, and sitteth here to prophesy the destruction of Fairs and May-games, Wakes, and Whitsun-ales, and doth sigh and groan for the reformation of these abuses.

Was. And do you sigh, and groan too, or rejoice in your affliction?

Jus. I do not feel it, I do not think of it, it is a thing without me. Adam, thou art above these batteries, these contumelies. *In te manca ruit fortuna*, as thy friend Horace says; thou art one, *Quem neque pauperies, neque mors, neque vincula terrent.* And therefore, as another friend of thine says (I think it be thy friend Persius), *Non te quæsiveris extra.*

Quar. What's here? a stoic i' the stocks? the fool is turn'd philosopher.

Busy. Friend, I will leave to communicate my spirit with you, if I hear any more of those superstitious relics, those lists of Latin, the very rags of Rome, and patches of Popery.

Was. Nay, an' you begin to quarrel, gentlemen, I'll leave you. I ha' paid for quarrelling too lately: look you, a device, but shifting in a hand for a foot. God b' w' you.

[*He gets out.*

Busy. Wilt thou then leave thy brethren in tribulation?

Was. For this once, sir.   [*Runs out.*

Busy. Thou art a halting neutral: stay him there, stop him: that will not endure the heat of persecution.

Bri. How now, what's the matter?

Busy. He is fled, he is fled, and dares not sit it out.

Bri. What, has he made an escape, which way? follow, neighbour Haggis.   [*Exeunt* Watch *and* Haggis.

Enter Dame Purecraft.

Pure. O me! in the stocks! have the wicked prevail'd?

Busy. Peace, religious sister, it is my calling, comfort yourself, an extraordinary calling, and done for my better standing, my surer standing, hereafter.

The madman enters.

Tro. By whose warrant, by whose warrant, this?

Quar. O, here's my man dropt in I look'd for.

Jus. Ha!

Pure. O good sir, they have set the faithful here to be wonder'd at; and provided holes for the holy of the land.

Tro. Had they warrant for it? show'd they Justice Overdo's hand? if they had no warrant they shall answer it.

Re-enter Haggis.

Bri. Sure you did not lock the stocks sufficiently, neighbour Toby!

Hag. No! see if you can lock 'em better.

Bri. They are very sufficiently lock'd, and truly, yet some thing is in the matter.

Tro. True, your warrant is the matter that is in question, by what warrant?

Bri. Madman, hold your peace, I will put you in his room else, in the very same hole, do you see?

Quar. How! is he a madman?

Tro. Show me Justice Overdo's warrant, I obey you.

Hag. You are a mad fool, hold your tongue.

[*Exeunt* Haggis *and* Bristle.

Tro. In Justice Overdo's name, I drink to you, and here's my warrant. [*Shows his can.*

Jus. Alas, poor wretch! how it yearns my heart for him!

Quar. If he be mad, it is in vain to question him. I'll try, though. Friend, there was a gentlewoman show'd you two names some hour since, Argalus and Palemon, to mark in a book; which of 'em was it you mark'd?

Tro. I mark no name, but Adam Overdo, that is the name of names, he only is the sufficient magistrate; and that name I reverence; show it me.

Quar. This fellow's mad indeed: I am further off, now, than afore.

Jus. I shall not breathe in peace, till I have made him some amends.

Quar. Well, I will make another use of him is come in my head: I have a nest of beards in my trunk, one something like this.

Re-enter Haggis *and* Bristle.

Bri. This mad fool has made me that I know not whether I have lock'd the stocks or no, I think I lock'd 'em.

Tro. Take Adam Overdo in your mind, and fear nothing.

Bri. 'Slid, madness itself! hold thy peace, and take that.

Tro. Strikest thou without a warrant? take thou that.

[*The madman fights with 'em and they leave open the stocks.*

Busy. We are delivered by miracle; fellow in fetters, let us not refuse the means; this madness was of the spirit: The malice of the enemy hath mock'd itself.

[*Exeunt* Busy *and* Overdo.

Pure. Mad, do they call him! the world is mad in error, but he is mad in truth: I love him o' the sudden (the cunning man said all true), and shall love him more and more. How well it becomes a man to be mad in truth! O, that I might be his yoke-fellow, and be mad with him, what a many should we draw to madness in truth, with us! [*Exit.*

[*The Watch missing them, are affrighted.*

Bri. How now! all scap'd? where's the woman? it is witchcraft! Her velvet hat is a witch, o' my conscience, or my key! t' one! The madman was a devil and I am an ass; so bless me, my place, and mine office. [*Exeunt.*

ACT V. SCENE I

The Fair, as before.

The puppet-show booth.

Lanthorn Leatherhead, *dressed as a puppet showman,*
Filcher *and* Sharkwell *with a flag.*

Lea. Well, luck and Saint Bartholomew; out with the
sign of our invention, in the name of Wit, and do you beat
the drum, the while; All the fowl i' the Fair, I mean all the
dirt in Smithfield (that's one of Master Littlewit's car-
whitchets now) will be thrown at our banner today, if the
matter does not please the people. O the motions that I,
Lanthorn Leatherhead, have given light to i' my time, since
my Master Pod died! Jerusalem was a stately thing; and
so was Nineveh and the city of Norwich, and Sodom and
Gomorrah; with the rising o' the prentices; and pulling
down the bawdy houses there, upon Shrove Tuesday; but
the Gunpowder Plot, there was a get-penny! I have pre-
sented that to an eighteen or twenty-pence audience, nine
times in an afternoon. Your home-born projects prove ever
the best, they are so easy and familiar, they put too much
learning i' their things now o' days: and that I fear will be
the spoil o' this. Littlewit? I say, Micklewit! if not too
mickle! look to your gathering there, good man Filcher.

Fil. I warrant you, sir.

Lea. And there come any gentlefolks, take twopence a
piece, Sharkwell.

Sha. I warrant you, Sir, threepence an' we can. [*Exeunt.*

ACT V. SCENE II

Another part of the Fair.

The Justice *comes in like a porter.*

Jus. This latter disguise I have borrow'd of a porter, shall
carry me out to all my great and good ends; which, how-
ever interrupted, were never destroyed in me: neither is

the hour of my severity yet come, to reveal myself, wherein cloud-like, I will break out in rain and hail, lightning and thunder, upon the head of enormity. Two main works I have to prosecute: first, one is to invent some satisfaction for the poor kind wretch who is out of his wits for my sake, and yonder I see him coming, I will walk aside, and project for it.

Enter Winwife *and* Grace.

Winw. I wonder where Tom Quarlous is, that he returns not; it may be he is struck in here to seek us.

Gra. See here's our madman again.

    [Quarlous *in the habit of the madman is mistaken by* Dame Purecraft, *who follows him in.*

Quar. I have made myself as like him as his gown and cap will give me leave.

Pure. Sir, I love you, and would be glad to be mad with you in truth.

Winw. How! my widow in love with a madman?

Pure. Verily, I can be as mad in spirit as you.

Quar. By whose warrant? leave your canting. Gentlewoman, have I found you? (save ye, quit ye, and multiply ye) where's your book? 'twas a sufficient name I mark'd, let me see 't, be not afraid to shew 't me.

    [*He desires to see the book of* Mistress Grace.

Gra. What would you with it, sir?

Quar. Mark it again, and again, at your service.

Gra. Here it is, sir, this was it you mark'd.

Quar. Palemon? fare you well, fare you well.

Winw. How, Palemon!

Gra. Yes, faith, he has discover'd it to you now, and therefore 'twere vain to disguise it longer, I am yours, sir, by the benefit of your fortune.

Winw. And you have him, mistress, believe it, that shall never give you cause to repent her benefit, but make you rather to think that in this choice she had both her eyes.

Gra. I desire to put it to no danger of protestation.

              [*Exeunt* Grace *and* Winwife.

Quar. Palemon, the word, and Winwife the man?

Pure. Good sir, vouchsafe a yokefellow in your madness, shun not one of the sanctified sisters, that would draw with you, in truth.

Quar. Away, you are a herd of hypocritical proud ignorants, rather wild than mad. Fitter for woods, and the society of beasts than houses and the congregation of men. You are the second part of the society of canters, outlaws to order and discipline, and the only privileg'd churchrobbers of Christendom. Let me alone. Palemon, the word, and Winwife the man?

Pure. I must uncover myself unto him, or I shall never enjoy him, for all the cunning men's promises. [*Aside.*] Good sir, hear me, I am worth six thousand pound, my love to you is become my rack, I'll tell you all, and the truth: since you hate the hypocrisy of the party-coloured brotherhood. These seven years, I have been a wilful holy widow, only to draw feasts and gifts from my entangled suitors: I am also by office an assisting sister of the deacons, and a devourer, instead of a distributor of the alms. I am a special maker of marriages for our decayed brethren with our rich widows; for a third part of their wealth, when they are married, for the relief of the poor elect; as also our poor handsome young virgins with our wealthy bachelors, or widowers; to make them steal from their husbands, when I have confirmed them in the faith, and got all put into their custodies. And if I ha' not my bargain, they may sooner turn a scolding drab into a silent minister than make me leave pronouncing reprobation, and damnation unto them. Our elder, Zeal-of-the-land, would have had me, but I know him to be the capital knave of the land, making himself rich, by being made feoffee in trust to deceased brethren and cozening their heirs by swearing the absolute gift of their inheritance. And thus having eas'd my conscience, and utter'd my heart with the tongue of my love: enjoy all my deceits together, I beseech you. I should not have revealed this to you, but that in time I think you are mad, and I hope you'll think me so too, sir?

Quar. Stand aside, I'll answer you presently. Why should not I marry this six thousand pound, now I think

on't? and a good trade too, that she has beside, ha? The
other wench, Winwife is sure of; there's no expectation
for me there! here I may make myself some saver, yet, if
she continue mad, there's the question. It is money that I
want, why should I not marry the money when 'tis offer'd
me? I have a licence and all, it is but razing out one name,
and putting in another. There's no playing with a man's
fortune! I am resolv'd! I were truly mad an' I would not!
well, come your ways, follow me, an' you will be mad, I'll
show you a warrant!   *[He takes her along with him.*

Pure. Most zealously, it is that I zealously desire.

Jus. [*Calls him.*] Sir, let me speak with you.

Quar. By whose warrant?

Jus. The warrant that you tender, and respect so; Justice
Overdo's! I am the man, friend Troubleall, though thus
disguis'd (as the careful magistrate ought) for the good of
the republic, in the Fair, and the weeding out of enormity.
Do you want a house or meat, or drink, or clothes? speak
whatsoever it is, it shall be supplied you, what want you?

Quar. Nothing but your warrant.

Jus. My warrant? for what?

Quar. To be gone, sir.

Jus. Nay, I pray thee stay, I am serious, and have not
many words, nor much time to exchange with thee; think
what may do thee good.

Quar. Your hand and seal will do me a great deal of
good; nothing else in the whole Fair that I know.

Jus. If it were to any end, thou should'st have it will-
ingly.

Quar. Why, it will satisfy me, that's end enough, to
look on; an' you will not gi' it me, let me go.

Jus. Alas! thou shalt ha' it presently: I'll but step into the
scrivener's, hereby, and bring it. Do not go away.

    [The Justice *goes out.*

Quar. Why, this madman's shape will prove a very
fortunate one, I think! can a ragged robe produce these
effects? if this be the wise Justice, and he bring me his hand,
I shall go near to make some use on't. [*He returns.*] He is
come already!

Jus. Look thee! here is my hand and seal, Adam Overdo,
if there be anything to be written, above in the paper, that
thou want'st now, or at any time hereafter; think on 't; it is
my deed, I deliver it so. Can your friend write?

Quar. Her hand for a witness, and all is well.

Jus. With all my heart.

                [*He urgeth* Mistress Purecraft *to sign it.*

Quar. Why should not I ha' the conscience to make this
a bond of a thousand pound, now? or what I would else?

                              [*Aside.*

Jus. Look you, there it is; and I deliver it as my deed
again.

Quar. Let us now proceed in madness.

                [*He takes her in with him.*

Jus. Well, my conscience is much eas'd; I ha' done my
part, though it doth him no good, yet Adam hath offer'd
satisfaction! The sting is removed from hence: poor man,
he is much alter'd with his affliction, it has brought him
low! Now, for my other work, reducing the young man
I have follow'd so long in love from the brink of his bane,
to the centre of safety. Here, or in some such like vain
place, I shall be sure to find him. I will wait the good time.

                              [*Exit.*

ACT V. SCENE III

Another part of the Fair.

The Puppet-show booth.

Enter Sharkwell *and* Filcher—*with bills, followed by*
Cokes.

Cok. How now? what's here to do? friend, art thou the
master of the monuments?

Sha. 'Tis a motion, an 't please your worship.

                Enter Overdo *behind.*

Jus. My fantastical brother-in-law, Master Bartholomew
Cokes!

Cok. A motion, what's that? [*He reads the bill.*] 'The

ancient modern history of Hero and Leander, otherwise
called the Touch-stone of true Love with as true a trial
of friendship between Damon and Pythias, two faithful
friends o' the Bankside.' Pretty, i' faith; what's the mean-
ing on 't? is 't an interlude? or what is 't?

Fil. Yes, sir, please you come near; we'll take your
money within.

Cok. Back with these children; they do so follow me up
and down. [*The boys o' the Fair follow him.*

Enter Littlewit.

Lit. By your leave, friend.

Fil. You must pay, sir, an' you go in.

Lit. Who, I? I perceive thou know'st not me: call the
master o' the motion.

Sha. What, do you not know the author, fellow Filcher?
you must take no money of him; he must come in *gratis*:
Master Littlewit is a voluntary; he is the author.

Lit. Peace, speak not too loud, I would not have any
notice taken that I am the author, till we see how it passes.

Cok. Master Littlewit, how dost thou?

Lit. Master Cokes! you are exceeding well met: what, in
your doublet and hose, without a cloak or a hat?

Cok. I would I might never stir, as I am an honest man,
and by that fire; I have lost all i' the Fair, and all my
acquaintance too; did'st thou meet anybody that I know,
Master Littlewit? my man Numps, or my sister Overdo,
or Mistress Grace? pray thee, Master Littlewit, lend me
some money to see the interlude here. I'll pay thee again as
I am a gentleman. If thou'lt but carry me home, I have
money enough there.

Lit. O, sir, you shall command it. What, will a crown
serve you?

Cok. I think it will. What do we pay for coming in,
fellows?

Fil. Twopence, sir.

Cok. Twopence? there's twelvepence, friend; Nay, I am
a gallant, as simple as I look now; if you see me with my
man about me, and my artillery again.

Lit. Your man was i' the stocks, e'en now, sir.

Cok. Who, Numps?

Lit. Yes, faith.

Cok. For what, i' faith? I am glad o' that; remember to tell me on't anon; I have enough, now! What manner of matter is this, Master Littlewit? What kind of actors ha' you? Are they good actors?

Lit. Pretty youths, sir, all children both old and young, here's the master of 'em——

Enter Leatherhead.

Lea. Call me not Leatherhead, but Lantern.

[*Whispers to* Littlewit.

Lit. Master Lantern, that gives light to the business.

Cok. In good time, sir, I would fain see 'em, I would be glad to drink with the young company; which is the tiring-house?

Lea. Troth, sir, our tiring-house is somewhat little; we are but beginners, yet, pray pardon us; you cannot go upright in 't.

Cok. No? not now my hat is off? what would you have done with me, if you had had me, feather and all, as I was once today? Ha' you none of your pretty impudent boys, now; to bring stools, fill tobacco, fetch ale, and beg money, as they have at other houses? let me see some o' your actors.

Lit. Show him 'em, show him 'em, Master Lantern; this is a gentleman, that is a favourer of the quality.

[*Exit* Leatherhead.

Jus. Aye, the favouring of this licentious quality, is the consumption of many a young gentleman; a pernicious enormity.   [*Aside.*

Cok. What, do they live in baskets?

Re-enter Leatherhead.

Lea. They do live in a basket, sir, they are o' the small players.   [*He brings them out in a basket.*

Cok. These be players minors indeed. Do you call these players?

Lea. They are actors, sir, and as good as any, none dis-
prais'd, for dumb shows: indeed, I am the mouth of 'em all!

Cok. Thy mouth will hold 'em all. I think one tailor
would go near to beat all this company, with a hand bound
behind him.

Lit. Aye, and eat 'em all, too, an' they were in cake-
bread.

Cok. I thank you for that, Master Littlewit, a good jest!
which is your Burbage now?

Lea. What mean you by that, sir?

Cok. Your best actor. Your Field?

Lit. Good i' faith! you are even with me, sir.

Lea. This is he that acts young Leander, sir. He is ex-
tremely belov'd of the womenkind, they do so affect his
action, the green gamesters that come here, and this is
lovely Hero; this with the beard, Damon; and this, pretty
Pythias: this is the ghost of King Dionysius in the habit of
a scrivener: as you shall see anon at large.

Cok. Well, they are a civil company, I like 'em for that;
they offer not to fleer, nor jeer, nor break jests, as the great
players do: And then there goes not so much charge to
the feasting of 'em, or making 'em drunk, as to the other,
by reason of their littleness. Do they use to play perfect?
Are they never fluster'd?

Lea. No, sir. I thank my industry and policy for it; they
are as well-govern'd a company, though I say it——And
here is young Leander, is as proper an actor of his inches;
and shakes his head like an hostler.

Cok. But do you play it according to the printed book?
I have read that.

Lea. By no means, sir.

Cok. No? How then?

Lea. A better way, sir; that is too learned and poetical
for our audiences; what do they know what Hellespont is?
Guilty of true love's blood? or what Abydos is? or the
other Sestos hight?

Cok. Th' art i' the right, I do not know myself.

Lea. No, I have entreated Master Littlewit to take a little
pains to reduce it to a more familiar strain for our people.

Cok. How, I pray thee, good Master Littlewit?

Lit. It pleases him to make a matter of it, sir. But there is no such matter, I assure you: I have only made it a little easy and modern for the times, sir, that's all. As for the Hellespont, I imagine our Thames here; and then Leander I make a dyer's son about Puddle-wharf: and Hero a wench o' the Bank-side, who going over one morning to old Fish-street, Leander spies her land at Trig-stairs and falls in love with her. Now do I introduce Cupid, having metamorphos'd himself into a drawer, and he strikes Hero in love with a pint of sherry, and other pretty passages there are o' the friendship, that will delight you, sir, and please you of judgement.

Cok. I'll be sworn they shall; I am in love with the actors already, and I'll be allied to them presently. (They respect gentlemen, these fellows.) Hero shall be my fairing: But, which of my fairings? (Le' me see) i' faith, my fiddle! and Leander my fiddle-stick: Then Damon, my drum; and Pythias, my pipe, and the ghost of Dionysius, my hobby-horse. All fitted.

Enter Winwife *and* Grace.

Winw. Look yonder's your Cokes gotten in among his play-fellows; I thought we could not miss him at such a spectacle.

Gra. Let him alone, he is so busy he will never spy us.

Lea. Nay, good sir.

Cokes is handling the puppets.

Cok. I warrant thee, I will not hurt her, fellow; what, dost think me uncivil? I pray thee be not jealous: I am toward a wife.

Lit. Well, good Master Lantern, make ready to begin, that I may fetch my wife, and look you be perfect, you undo me else, i' my reputation.

Lea. I warrant you, sir, do not you breed too great an expectation of it among your friends: that's the only hurter of these things.

Lit. No, no, no.

Cok. I'll stay here, and see; pray thee let me see.

Winw. How diligent and troublesome he is!

Gra. The place becomes him, methinks.

Jus. My ward, Mistress Grace, in the company of a stranger? I doubt I shall be compell'd to discover myself before my time. [*Aside.*

Enter Knockem, Edgworth *and* Mrs. Littlewit, *followed by* Whit, *supporting* Mrs. Overdo, *masked.*

Fil. Twopence apiece, gentlemen, an excellent motion.

Kno. Shall we have fine fireworks, and good vapours?

Sha. Yes, captain, and waterworks, too.

Whi. I pree dee, take a care o' dy shmall lady, there, Edgworth, I will look to dish tall lady myself.

Lea. Welcome, gentlemen; welcome, gentlemen.

Whi. Predee, mashter o' de monshtersh, help a very sick lady here to a chair to shit in.

Lea. Presently, sir.

They bring Mistress Overdo *a chair.*

Whi. Good fait now, Ursula's ale, and aquavitae ish to blame for't; shit down, shweetheart, shit down, and shleep a little.

Edg. Madam, you are very welcome hither.

Kno. Yes, and you shall see very good vapours.

Jus. Here is my care come! I like to see him in so good company; and yet I wonder that persons of such fashion should resort hither! [*Aside.*

Edg. This is a very private house, madam.

Lea. Will it please your ladyship to sit, madam?

[*The* Cutpurse *courts* Mistress Littlewit.

Win. Yes, good-man. They do so all-to-be-madam me, I think they think me a very lady!

Edg. What else, madam?

Win. Must I put off my mask to him?

Edg. O, by no means.

Win. How should my husband know me, then?

Kno. Husband? an idle vapour; he must not know you, nor you him; there's the true vapour.

553

Jus. Yea. I will observe more of this. [*Aside.*] Is this a lady, friend?

Whi. Aye, and dat is anoder lady, shweetheart; if dou hasht a mind to 'em give me twelvepence from tee, and dou shalt have eder-oder on 'em!

Jus. I? This will prove my chiefest enormity: I will follow this. [*Aside.*

Edg. Is not this a finer life, lady, than to be clogg'd with a husband?

Win. Yes, a great deal. When will they begin, trow, in the name o' the motion?

Edg. By and by, madam; they stay but for company.

Kno. Do you hear, puppet-master, these are tedious vapours; when begin you?

Lea. We stay but for Master Littlewit, the author, who is gone for his wife; and we begin presently.

Win. That's I, that's I.

Edg. That was you, lady; but now you are no such poor thing.

Kno. Hang the author's wife, a running vapour! here be ladies will stay for ne'er a Delia of 'em all.

Whi. But hear me now, here ish one o' de ladish ashleep, stay till she but vake, man.

Enter Waspe.

Was. How now, friends? what's here to do?

Fil. Twopence a piece, sir, the best motion in the Fair.

Was. I believe you lie; if you do, I'll have my money again, and beat you.

Winw. Numps is come!

Was. Did you see a master of mine come in here, a tall young squire of Harrow o' the Hill, Master Bartholomew Cokes?

Fil. I think there be such a one within.

Was. Look he be, you were best: but it is very likely: I wonder I found him not at all the rest. I ha' been at the Eagle and the Black Wolf, and the Bull with the Five Legs and Two Pizzles; (he was a calf at Uxbridge Fair, two years ago). And at the dogs that dance the morrice, and the Hare o' the Tabor; and miss'd him at all these! Sure this must needs be some fine sight, that holds him so, if it have him.

Cok. Come, come, are you ready now?

Lea. Presently, sir.

Was. Hoyday, he's at work in his doublet and hose; do you hear, sir? are you employ'd, that you are bare-headed, and so busy?

Cok. Hold your peace, Numps; you ha' been i' the stocks, I hear.

Was. Do's he know that? nay, then the date of my authority is out; I must think no longer to reign, my government is at an end. He that will correct another, must want fault in himself.

Winw. Sententious Numps! I never heard so much from him, before.

Lea. Sure, Master Littlewit will not come; please you take your place, sir; we'll begin.

Cok. I pray thee do, mine ears long to be at it; and my eyes too. O Numps, i' the stocks, Numps? where's your sword, Numps?

Was. I pray you intend your game, sir; let me alone.

Cok. Well then, we are quit for all. Come, sit down, Numps: I'll interpret to thee: did you see Mistress Grace? it's no matter, neither, now I think on't, tell me anon.

Winw. A great deal of love and care, he expresses.

Gra. Alas! would you have him to express more than he has? That were tyranny.

Cok. Peace, ho! now, now.

Lea. Gentles, that no longer your expectations may wander,
Behold our chief actor, amorous Leander,
With a great deal of cloth, lap'd about him like a scarf,
For he yet serves his father, a dyer at Puddle-wharf,
Which place we'll make bold with, to call it our Abydus,
As the Bankside is our Sestos, and let it not be denied us.
Now, as he is beating, to make the dye take the fuller,
Who chances to come by, but fair Hero, in a sculler;

And seeing Leander's naked leg and goodly calf,
Cast at him, from the boat, a sheep's eye and a half.
Now she is landed, and the sculler come back;
By and by you shall see what Leander doth lack.

Lean. *Cole, Cole, old Cole.*

Lea.   *That is the sculler's name without control.*

Lean. *Cole, Cole, I say, Cole.*

Lea.   *We do hear you.*

Lean.   *Old Cole.*

Lea. *Old Cole? Is the dyer turn'd collier? how do you sell?*

Lean. *A pox o' your manners, kiss my hole here, and smell.*

Lea. *Kiss your hole, and smell? there's manners indeed.*

Lean. *Why, Cole, I say, Cole.*

Lea.   *It's the sculler you need!*

Lean. *Aye, and be hang'd.*

Lea.   *Be hang'd; look you yonder,*
Old Cole, you must go hang with master Leander.

Cole. *Where is he?*

Lean.   *Here, Cole, what fairest of fairs,*
Was that fare, that thou landedst but now at Trig-stairs?

Cok. *What was that, fellow? Pray thee tell me, I scarce*
understand 'em.

Lea. *Leander does ask, sir, what fairest of fairs*
Was the fare that he landed, but now, at Trig-stairs?

Cole. *It is lovely Hero.*

Lean.   *Nero?*

Cole.   *No, Hero.*

Lea.   *It is Hero,*
Of the Bankside, he saith, to tell you truth without erring,
Is come over into Fish-street to eat some fresh herring.
Leander says no more, but as fast as he can,
Gets on all his best clothes; and will after to the Swan.

Cok. *Most admirable good, is't not?*

Lea. *Stay, sculler.*

Cole.   *What say you?*

Lea.   *You must stay for Leander,*
And carry him to the wench.

Cole. *You rogue, I am no pander.*

Cok. He says he is no pander. 'Tis a fine language; I understand it now.

Lea. Are you no pander, goodman Cole? here's no man says you are,

You'll grow a hot Cole, it seems, pray you stay for your fare.

Cole. *Will he come away?*

Lea. *What do you say?*

Cole. *I'd ha' him come away.*

Lea. *Would you ha' Leander come away? why, pray sir, stay.*

You are angry, goodman Cole; I believe the fair maid
Come over wi' you a' trust: tell us, sculler, are you paid?

Cole. *Yes, goodman Hogrubber o' Pickthatch.*

Lea. *How, Hogrubber o' Pickthatch?*

Cole. *Aye, Hogrubber o' Pickthatch. Take you that.*

The Puppet *strikes him over the pate.*

Lea. *O, my head!*

Cole. *Harm watch, harm catch.*

Cok. Harm watch, harm catch, he says: very good i' faith, the Sculler had like to ha' knock'd you, sirrah.

Lea. Yes, but that his fare call'd him away.

Lean. *Row apace, row apace, row, row, row, row, row.*

Lea. *You are knavishly loaden, sculler, take heed where you go.*

Cole. *Knave i' your face, goodman rogue.*

Lean. *Row, row, row, row, row, row.*

Cok. He said knave i' your face, friend.

Lea. Aye, sir, I heard him. But there's no talking to these watermen, they will ha' the last word.

Cok. God's my life! I am not allied to the sculler, yet; he shall be Dauphin my boy. But my Fiddle-stick does fiddle in and out too much; I pray thee speak to him on't: tell him I would have him tarry in my sight, more.

Lea. I pray you be content; you'll have enough on him sir.

Now, gentles, I take it, here is none of you so stupid,

*but that you have heard of a little god of love, call'd
Cupid.*
*Who out of kindness to Leander, hearing he but saw her,
    this present day and hour, doth turn himself to a drawer.*
*And because he would have their first meeting to be merry,
    he strikes Hero in love to him, with a pint of sherry.*
*Which he tells her, from amorous Leander is sent her,
    who after him, into the room of Hero, doth venture.*

    Jonas. A pint of sack, score a pint of sack i' the Coney.
        [*Leander goes into* Mistress Hero's *room.*
    Cok. Sack? you said but e'en now it should be sherry.
    Jonas. Why so it is; sherry, sherry, sherry.
    Cok. Sherry, sherry, sherry. By my troth he makes me
merry. I must have a name for Cupid too. Let me see, thou
mightst help me now, an' thou would'st, Numps, at a dead
lift, but thou art dreaming o' the stocks, still! Do not think
on't, I have forgot it: 'tis but a nine days wonder, man; let
it not trouble thee.
    Was. I would the stocks were about your neck, sir; con-
dition I hung by the heels in them till the wonder were off
from you, with all my heart.
    Cok. Well said, resolute Numps: but hark you, friend,
where is the friendship all this while between my drum,
Damon, and my pipe, Pythias?
    Lea. You shall see by and by, sir.
    Cok. You think my hobby-horse is forgotten too; no,
I'll see 'em all enact before I go; I shall not know which to
love best, else.
    Kno. This gallant has interrupting vapours, troublesome
vapours, Whit, puff with him.
    Whi. No, I pre dee, captain, let him alone. He is a child
i' faith, la'.
    *Lea. Now, gentles, to the friends, who in number are
two,
    and lodg'd in that ale-house, in which fair Hero does do.
Damon (for some kindness done him the last week)
    is come fair Hero, in Fish-street, this morning to seek:
Pythias does smell the knavery of the meeting,
    and now you shall see their true friendly greeting.*

Pyth. *You whore-masterly slave, you.*

Cok. Whore-masterly slave, you? very friendly and familiar, that.

Damon.   *Whore-master i' thy face,*
Thou hast lain with her thyself, I'll prove i' this place.

Cok. Damon says Pythias has lain with her himself, he'll prove 't in this place.

Lea. They are whore-masters both, sir, that's a plain case.

Pyth. *You lie, like a rogue.*

Lea. *Do I lie like a rogue?*

Pyth. *A pimp, and a scab.*

Lea.   *A pimp, and a scab?*
I say between you, you have both but one drab.

Damon. *You lie again.*

Lea. *Do I lie again?*

Damon. *Like a rogue again.*

Lea. *Like a rogue again?*

Pyth. *And you are a pimp, again.*

Cok. And you are a pimp again, he says.

Damon. *And a scab, again.*

Cok. And a scab again, he says.

Lea. *And I say again you are both whore-masters again,*
And you have both but one drab again.   [*They fight.*

Damon & Pyth. *Dost thou, dost thou, dost thou?*

Lea. *What, both at once?*

Pyth. *Down with him, Damon.*

Damon. *Pink his guts, Pythias.*

Lea. *What, so malicious?*
Will ye murder me, masters both, i' mine own house?

Cok. Ho! well acted my drum, well acted my pipe, well acted still.

Was. Well acted, with all my heart.

Lea. *Hold, hold your hands.*

Cok. Aye, both your hands, for my sake! for you ha' both done well.

Damon. *Gramercy, pure Pythias.*

Pyth. *Gramercy, dear Damon.*

Cok. Gramercy to you both, my pipe, and my drum.

Damon & Pyth. Come now, we'll together to breakfast
  to Hero.
  Lea. *'Tis well, you can now go to breakfast to Hero,*
You have given me my breakfast with a hone and honere.
  Cok. How is't, friend, ha' they hurt thee?
  Lea. O no!
Between you and I, sir, we do but make show.
Thus gentles you perceive, without any denial,
  'twixt Damon and Pythias here, friendship's true trial.
Though hourly they quarrel thus, and roar each with other,
  they fight you no more than does brother with brother.
But friendly together, at the next man they meet,
  they let fly their anger, as here you might see't.
  Cok. Well, we have seen't, and thou hast felt it, what-
soever thou sayest, what's next? what's next?
  Lea. *This while young Leander with fair Hero is drink-*
    ing,
  and Hero grown drunk to any man's thinking!
Yet was it not three pints of sherry could flaw her,
  till Cupid distinguish'd like Jonas the drawer,
From under his apron, where his lechery lurks,
  put love in her sack. Now mark how it works.
  Hero. *O Leander, Leander, my dear, my dear Leander,*
I'll for ever be thy goose, so thou'lt be my gander.
  Cok. Excellently well said, Fiddle, she'll ever be his
goose, so he'll be her gander: was't not so?
  Lea. Yes, sir, but mark his answer now.
  Lean. *And sweetest of geese, before I go to bed,*
I'll swim o'er the Thames, my goose, thee to tread.
  Cok. Brave! he will swim o'er the Thames, and tread his
goose, to-night, he says.
  Lea. Aye, peace, sir, they'll be angry, if they hear you
eaves-dropping, now they are setting their match.
  Lean. *But lest the Thames should be dark, my goose, my*
    dear friend,
let thy window be provided of a candle's end.
  Hero. *Fear not, my gander, I protest I should handle*
my matters very ill if I had not a whole candle.
  Lean. *Well then, look to't, and kiss me to boot.*

*Lea. Now, here come the friends again, Pythias and
Damon,
and under their cloaks they have of bacon a gammon.*

Damon *and* Pythias *enter.*

*Pyth. Drawer, fill some wine here.
Lea. How, some wine there?
There's company already, sir, pray forbear!
Damon. 'Tis Hero.
Lea.   Yes, but she will not be taken,
after sack and fresh herring, with your Dunmow-bacon.
Pyth. You lie, it's Westfabian.
Lea.   Westphalian, you should say.
Damon. If you hold not your peace, you are a coxcomb,
I would say.*

[Leander *and* Hero *are kissing.*

*Pyth. What's here? what's here? kiss, kiss, upon kiss.
Lea. Aye, wherefore should they not? what harm is in
this? 'tis mistress Hero.
Damon. Mistress Hero's a whore.
Lea. Is she a whore? keep you quiet, or, sir knave, out
of door.
Damon. Knave out of door?
Hero. Yes, knave, out of door.
Damon. Whore out of door.*

[Here the Puppets *quarrel and fall together by the ears.*

*Hero. I say, knave, out of door.
Damon. I say, whore, out of door.
Pyth.   Yea, so say I too.
Hero. Kiss the whore o' the arse.
Lea. Now you ha' something to do:
you must kiss her o' the arse she says.
Damon & Pyth. So we will, so we will.* [They kick her.
*Hero. O my haunches, O my haunches, hold, hold.
Lea.   Stand'st thou still?
Leander, where art thou? stand'st thou still like a sot,
and not offer'st to break both their heads with a pot?
See who's at thine elbow! Puppet Jonas and Cupid.
Jonas. Upon 'em, Leander, be not so stupid.*

561

Lean. You goat-bearded slave!

Damon. You whore-master knave. [*They fight.*

Lean. Thou art a whore-master.

Jonas.   *Whore-masters all.*

Lea. See, Cupid with a word has ta'en up the brawl.

Kno. These be fine vapours!

Cok. By this good day they fight bravely! do they not, Numps?

Was. Yes, they lack'd but you to be their second, all this while.

Lea. This tragical encounter, falling out thus to busy us,
It raises up the ghost of their friend Dionysius:
Not like a monarch, but the master of a school,
In a scrivener's furr'd gown, which shows he is no fool.
For therein he hath wit enough to keep himself warm.
O Damon, he cries, and Pythias; what harm
Hath poor Dionysius done you in his grave,
That after his death, you should fall out thus, and rave,
And call amorous Leander whore-master knave?

Damon. I cannot, I will not, I promise you, endure it.

Busy *rushes in.*

Busy. Down with Dagon, down with Dagon, 'tis I will no longer endure your profanations.

Lea. What mean you, sir?

Busy. I will remove Dagon there, I say, that idol, that heathenish idol, that remains (as I may say) a beam, a very beam, not a beam of the sun nor a beam of the moon, nor a beam of a balance, neither a house-beam, nor a weaver's beam, but a beam in the eye, in the eye of the brethren; a very great beam, an exceeding great beam; such as are your stage-players, rhymers, and morrice-dancers, who have walked hand in hand, in contempt of the brethren and the cause; and been borne out by instruments of no mean countenance.

Lea. Sir, I present nothing but what is licens'd by authority.

Busy. Thou art all license. even licentiousness itself, Shimei!

Lea. I have the Master of the Revel's hand for't, sir.

Busy. The master of the rebel's hand, thou hast; Satan's! hold thy peace, thy scurrility, shut up thy mouth, thy profession is damnable, and in pleading for it thou dost plead for Baal. I have long opened my mouth wide and gaped, I have gaped as the oyster for the tide, after thy destruction: but cannot compass it by suit or dispute; so that I look for a bickering, ere long, and then a battle.

Kno. Good Banbury-vapours.

Cok. Friend, you'd have an ill match on't, if you bicker with him here; though he be no man o' the fist, he has friends that will go to cuffs for him. Numps, will not you take our side?

Edg. Sir, it shall not need; in my mind he offers him a fairer course, to end it by disputation! hast thou nothing to say for thyself, in defence of thy quality?

Lea. Faith, sir, I am not well studied in these controversies, between the hypocrites and us. But here's one of my motion, puppet Dionysius, shall undertake him, and I'll venture the cause on't.

Cok. Who? my hobby-horse? will he dispute with him?

Lea. Yes, sir, and make a hobby-ass of him, I hope.

Cok. That's excellent! indeed he looks like the best scholar of 'em all. Come, sir, you must be as good as your word now.

Busy. I will not fear to make my spirit and gifts known! assist me, zeal, fill me, fill me, that is, make me full.

Winw. What a desperate, profane wretch is this! is there any ignorance or impudence like his? to call his zeal to fill him against a puppet?

Quar. I know no fitter match than a puppet to commit with an hypocrite!

Busy. First, I say unto thee, idol, thou hast no calling.

Dion. *You lie, I am call'd Dionysius.*

Lea. The motion says you lie, he is call'd Dionysius i' the matter, and to that calling he answers.

Busy. I mean no vocation, idol, no present lawful calling.

Dion. *Is yours a lawful calling?*

Lea. The motion asketh if yours be a lawful calling?

Busy. Yes, mine is of the spirit.

Dion. Then idol is a lawful calling.

Lea. He says, then, idol is a lawful calling! for you call'd him idol, and your calling is of the spirit.

Cok. Well disputed, hobby-horse!

Busy. Take not part with the wicked, young gallant. He neigheth and hinneyeth, all is but hinnying sophistry. I call him idol again. Yes, I say, his calling, his profession is profane, it is profane, idol.

Dion. It is not profane!

Lea. It is not profane, he says.

Busy. It is profane.

Dion. It is not profane.

Busy. It is profane.

Dion. It is not profane.

Lea. Well said, confute him with *not*, still. You cannot bear him down with your base noise, sir.

Busy. Nor he me, with his treble creaking, though he creak like the chariot wheels of Satan: I am zealous for the cause——

Lea. As a dog for a bone.

Busy. And I say, it is profane, as being the page of Pride, and the waiting-woman of Vanity.

Dion. Yea? what say you to your tire-women, then?

Lea. Good.

Dion. Or feather-makers i' the Friers, that are o' your faction of faith? Are not they with their perukes, and their puffs, their fans, and their huffs, as much pages of Pride, and waiters upon Vanity? what say you? what say you? what say you?

Busy. I will not answer for them.

Dion. Because you cannot, because you cannot. Is a bugle-maker a lawful calling? or the confect-makers? such you have there: or your French fashioner? you'd have all the sin within yourselves, would you not? would you not?

Busy. No, Dagon.

Dion. What then, Dagonet? is a puppet worse than these?

Busy. Yes, and my main argument against you is that

you are an abomination: for the male among you putteth
on the apparel of the female, and the female of the male.

Dion. *You lie, you lie, you lie abominably.*

Cok. Good, by my troth, he has given him the lie thrice.

Dion. *It is your old stale argument against the players,
but it will not hold against the puppets; for we have neither
male nor female amongst us. And that thou may'st see, if
thou wilt, like a malicious purblind zeal as thou art.*

> [*The puppet takes up his garment.*

Edg. By my faith, there he has answer'd you, friend; by
plain demonstration.

Dion. *Nay, I'll prove, against e'er a Rabbin of 'em all,
that my standing is as lawful as his; that I speak by inspira-
tion, as well as he; that I have as little to do with learning
as he; and do scorn her helps as much as he.*

Busy. I am confuted, the cause hath failed me.

Dion. *Then be converted, be converted.*

Lea. Be converted, I pray you, and let the play go on!

Busy. Let it go on. For I am changed, and will become a
beholder with you!

Cok. That's brave, i' faith, thou hast carried it away,
hobby-horse, on with the play!

The Justice *discovers himself.*

Jus. Stay, now do I forbid; I, Adam Overdo! sit still, I
charge you.

Cok. What, my brother-i'-law!

Gra. My wise guardian!

Edg. Justice Overdo!

Jus. It is time to take enormity by the forehead, and
brand it; for I have discover'd enough.

Enter Quarlous *in* Troubleall's *clothes, as before, and* Dame Purecraft.

Quar. Nay, come, mistress bride. You must do as I do
now. You must be mad with me, in truth. I have here
Justice Overdo for it.

Jus. Peace, good Troubleall; come hither, and you shall
trouble none. I will take the charge of you and your

friend too; you also, young man, shall be my care, stand there.

Edg. Now, mercy upon me.

Kno. Would we were away, Whit, these are dangerous vapours, best fall off with our birds, for fear o' the cage.

[*They try to steal away.*

Jus. Stay, is not my name your terror?

Whi. Yesh, faith, man, and it ish for tat we would be gone, man.

Enter Littlewit.

Lit. O gentlemen! did you not see a wife of mine? I ha' lost my little wife, as I shall be trusted: my little pretty Win, I left her at the great woman's house in trust yonder, the pig-woman's, with Captain Jordan and Captain Whit, very good men, and I cannot hear of her. Poor fool, I fear she's stepp'd aside. Mother, did you not see Win?

Jus. If this grave matron be your mother, sir, stand by her, *et digito compesce labellum*, I may perhaps spring a wife for you, anon. Brother Bartholomew, I am sadly sorry to see you so lightly given, and such a disciple of enormity: with your grave governor Humphrey: but stand you both there, in the middle place; I will reprehend you in your course. Mistress Grace, let me rescue you out of the hands of the stranger.

Winw. Pardon me, sir, I am a kinsman of hers.

Jus. Are you so? of what name, sir?

Winw. Winwife, sir.

Jus. Master Winwife? I hope you have won no wife of her, sir. If you have, I will examine the possibility of it, at fit leisure. Now, to my enormities: look upon me, O London! and see me, O Smithfield! the example of justice, and Mirror of Magistrates: the true top of formality, and scourge of enormity. Hearken unto my labours, and but observe my discoveries; and compare Hercules with me, if thou dar'st, of old; or Columbus; Magellan; or our country man Drake of later times: stand forth, you weeds of enormity, and spread. First, Rabbi Busy, thou super-lunatical hypocrite. [*To* Leatherhead.] Next, thou other extremity,

thou profane professor of puppetry little better than
poetry: [*To* Whit.] Then thou strong debaucher, and
seducer of youth; witness this easy and honest young man:
[*Pointing to* Edgworth.] [*To* Knockem]. Now thou es-
quire of dames, madams, and twelvepenny ladies: now my
green madam herself, of the price. Let me unmask your
ladyship.

Lit. O my wife, my wife, my wife!
[*Discovers* Mrs. Littlewit.

Jus. Is she your wife? *Redde te Harpocratem!*

Enter Troubleall *with a dripping-pan, followed by* Ursula
and Nightingale.

Tro. By your leave, stand by, my masters, be uncover'd.

Urs. O stay him, stay him, help to cry, Nightingale; my
pan, my pan.

Jus. What's the matter?

Nig. He has stolen gammar Ursula's pan.

Tro. Yes, and I fear no man but Justice Overdo.

Jus. Ursula? where is she? O the sow of enormity, this!
welcome, stand you there; you, songster, there.

Urs. An' please your worship, I am in no fault: A gentle-
man stripp'd him in my booth, and borrow'd his gown and
hat; and he ran away with my goods, here, for it.

Jus. [*To* Quarlous.] Then this is the true madman, and
you are the enormity.

Quar. You are i' the right, I am mad, but from the gown
outward.

Jus. Stand you there.

Quar. Where you please, sir.

Mistress Overdo *is sick: and her husband is silenc'd.*

Mrs. Over. O lend me a basin, I am sick, I am sick;
where's Master Overdo? Bridget, call hither my Adam.

Jus. How?

Whi. Dy very own wife, i' fait, worshipful Adam.

Mrs. Over. Will not my Adam come at me? Shall I see
him no more, then?

567

Quar. Sir, why do you not go on with the enormity? are you oppress'd with it? I'll help you: hark you, sir, i' your ear—your innocent young man you have ta'en such care of all this day, is a cutpurse; that hath got all your brother Cokes his things, and help'd you to your beating and the stocks; if you have a mind to hang him now, and show him your magistrate's wit, you may: but I should think it were better recovering the goods, and to save your estimation in him. I thank you, sir, for the gift of your ward, Mistress Grace: look you, here is your hand and seal, by the way. Master Winwife, give you joy, you are Palemon, you are possess'd o' the gentlewoman, but she must pay me value, here's warrant for it. And honest madman, there's thy gown and cap again; I thank thee for my wife. Nay I can be mad, sweetheart [*To the widow*] when I please, still; never fear me: And careful Numps, where's he? I thank him for my licence.

Was. How!   [*Waspe misseth the licence.*

Quar. 'Tis true, Numps.

Was. I'll be hang'd then.

Quar. Look i' your box, Numps. Nay, sir [*To Overdo*], stand not you fix'd here, like a stake in Finsbury to be shot at, or the whipping post i' the Fair, but get your wife out o' the air, it will make her worse else; and remember you are but Adam, flesh and blood! you have your frailty, forget your other name of Overdo, and invite us all to supper. There you and I will compare our discoveries: and drown the memory of all enormity in your biggest bowl at home.

Cok. How now, Numps, ha' you lost it? I warrant 'twas when thou wert i' the stocks: why dost not speak?

Was. I will never speak while I live, again, for ought I know.

Jus. Nay, Humphrey, if I be patient, you must be so too; this pleasant conceited gentleman hath wrought upon my judgement, and prevail'd: I pray you take care of your sick friend, Mistress Alice, and my good friends all——

Quar. And no enormities.

Jus. I invite you home with me to my house, to supper: I will have none fear to go along, for my intents are *ad*

*correctionem, non ad destructionem; Ad ædificandum, non
ad diruendum*: so lead on.

Cok. Yes, and bring the actors along, we'll ha' the rest o'
the play at home.   [*Exeunt.*

THE END

The Epilogue

Your Majesty hath seen the play, and you
    Can best allow it from your ear and view.
You know the scope of writers, and what store
    Of leave is given them, if they take not more,
And turn it into licence: you can tell
    If we have us'd that leave you gave us well:
Or whether we to rage or licence break,
    Or be profane, or make profane men speak?
This is your power to judge, great sir, and not
    The envy of a few. Which if we have got,
We value less what their dislike can bring,
    If it so happy be, t' have pleas'd the King.

PRINTED IN GREAT BRITAIN
AT THE UNIVERSITY PRESS, OXFORD
BY VIVIAN RIDLER
PRINTER TO THE UNIVERSITY